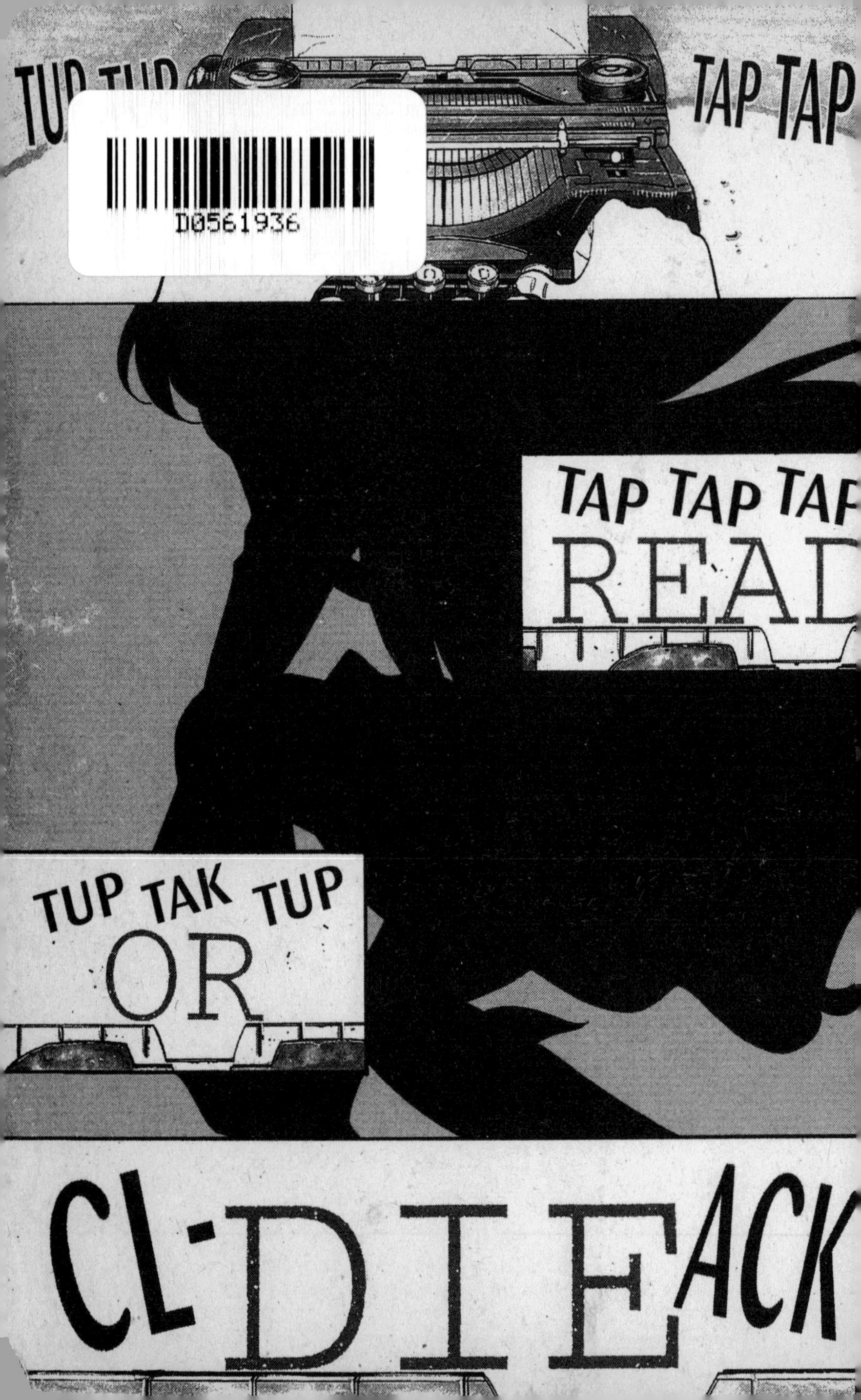
TAP TAP
TUP TUP
TAP TAP TAP
READ
TUP TAK TUP
OR
CL-ACK
DIE

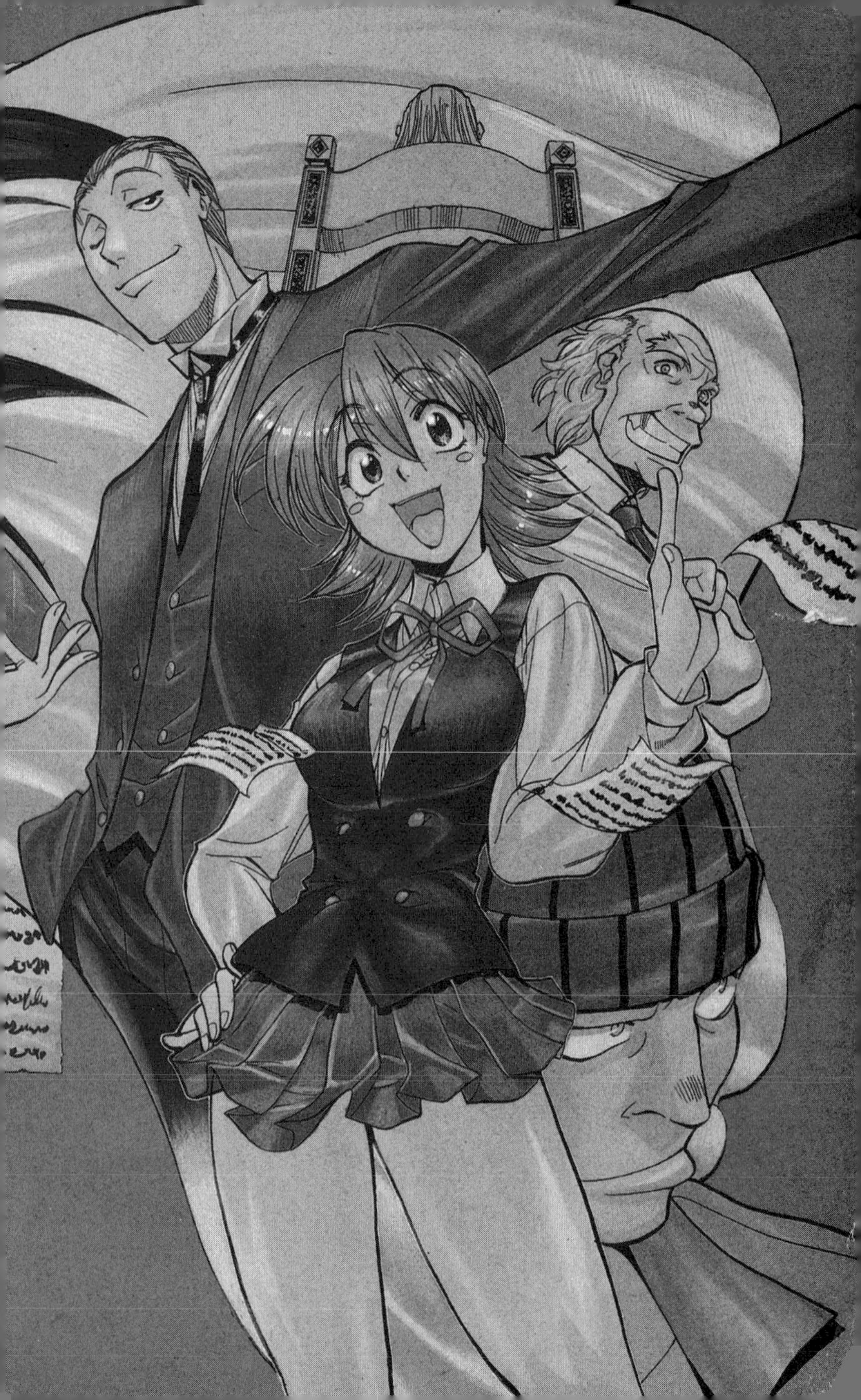

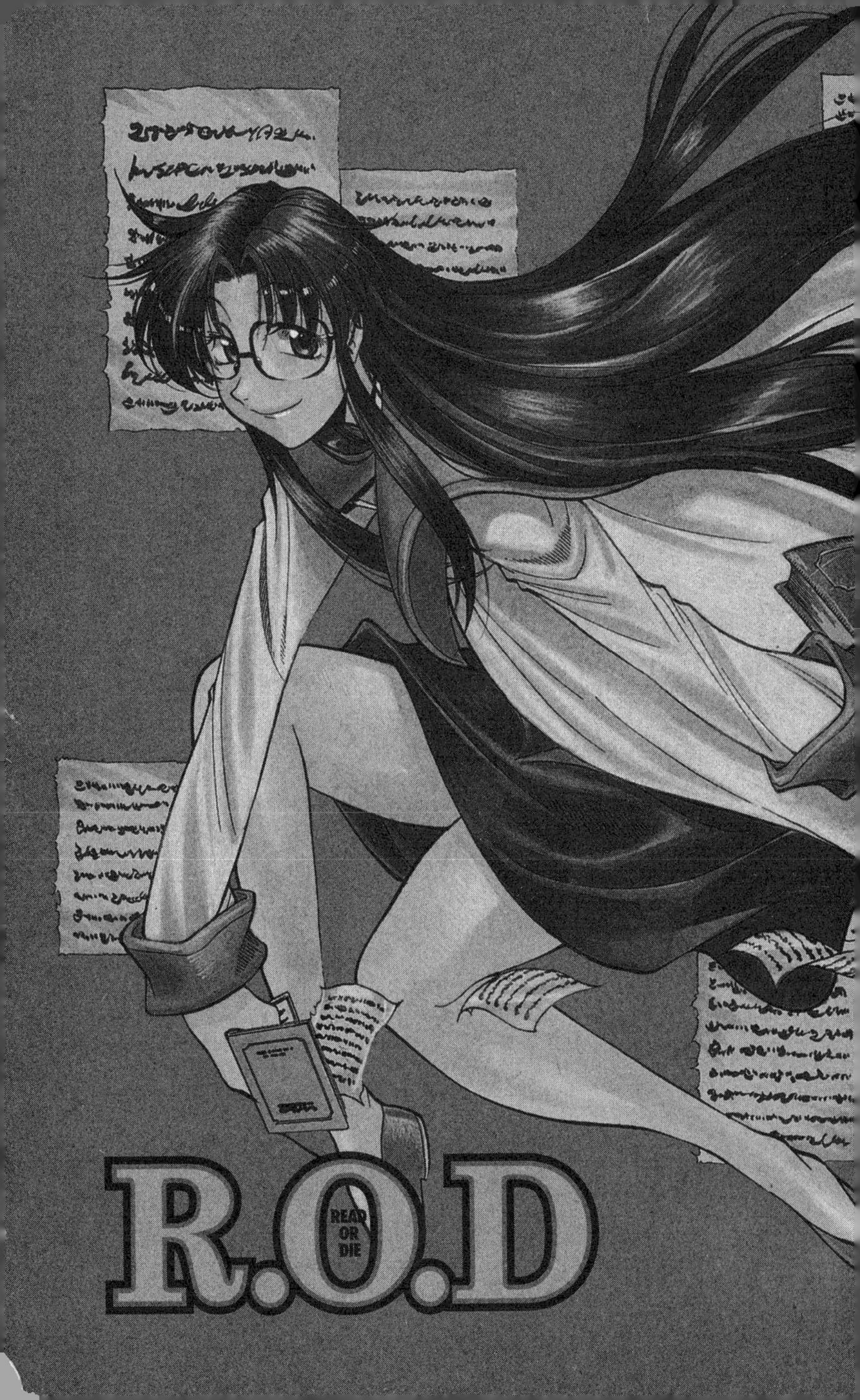
R.O.D
READ OR DIE

CONTENTS

THE LAST LITERATURE D-LINE OF U.K. AGENT YOMIKO READMAN "THE PAPER"

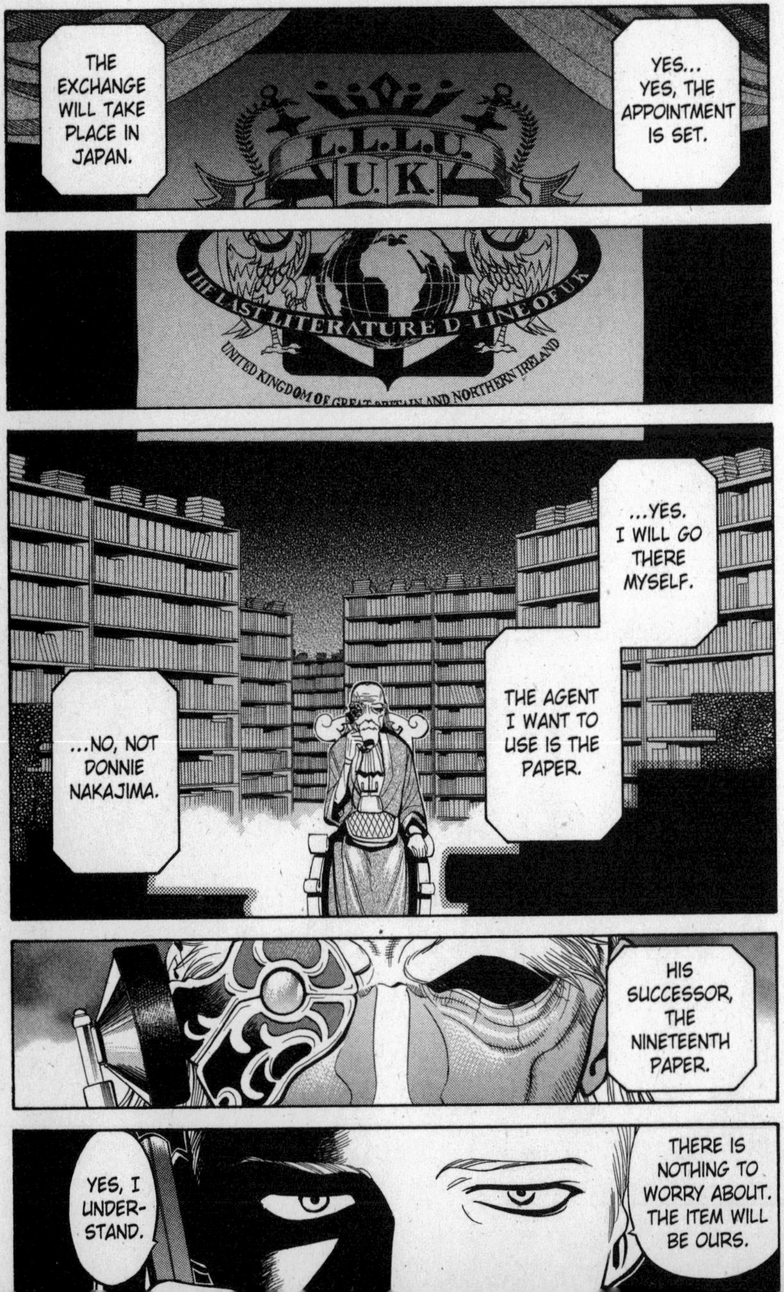
YES... YES, THE APPOINTMENT IS SET.
THE EXCHANGE WILL TAKE PLACE IN JAPAN.
L.L.L.U.
U.K.
THE LAST LITERATURE D-LINE OF UK
UNITED KINGDOM OF GREAT BRITAIN AND NORTHERN IRELAND
...YES. I WILL GO THERE MYSELF.
THE AGENT I WANT TO USE IS THE PAPER.
...NO, NOT DONNIE NAKAJIMA.
HIS SUCCESSOR, THE NINETEENTH PAPER.
THERE IS NOTHING TO WORRY ABOUT. THE ITEM WILL BE OURS.
YES, I UNDERSTAND.

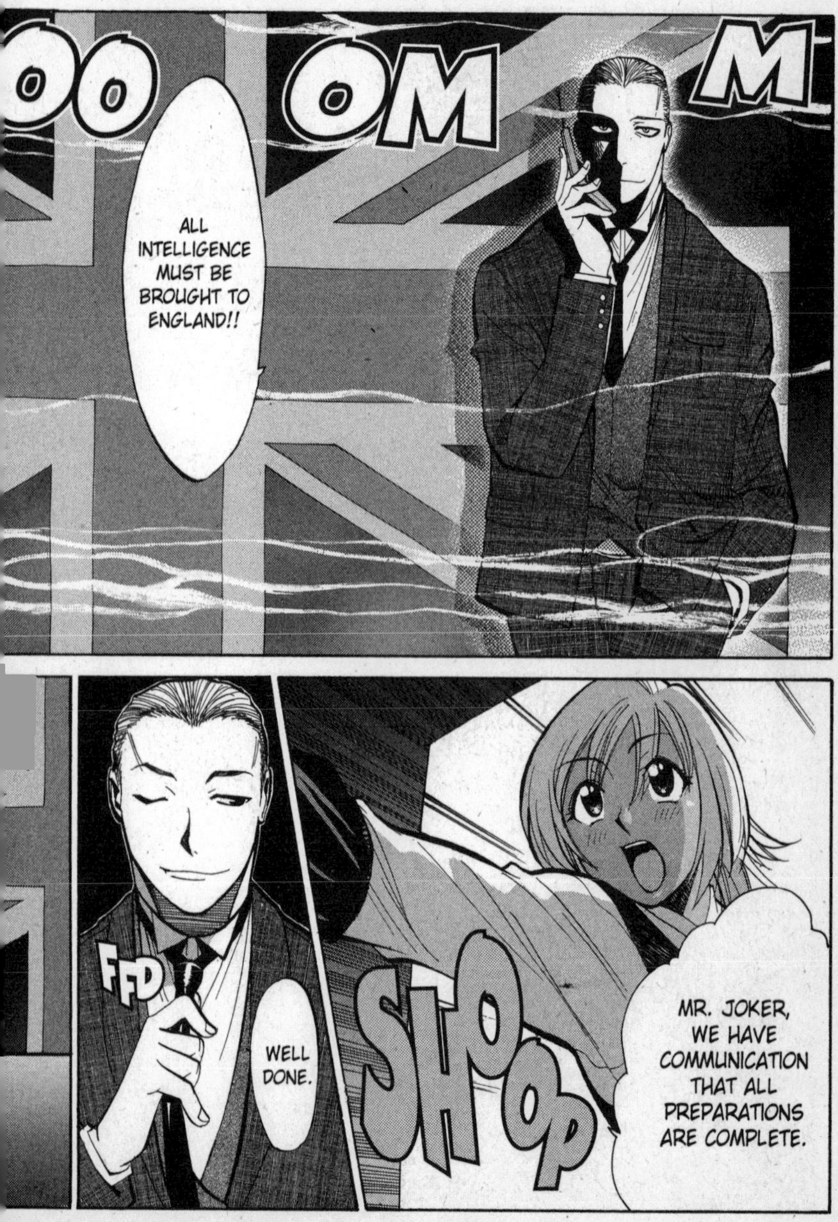
OO OM M
ALL INTELLIGENCE MUST BE BROUGHT TO ENGLAND!!
MR. JOKER, WE HAVE COMMUNICATION THAT ALL PREPARATIONS ARE COMPLETE.
SHOOP
FFD
WELL DONE.

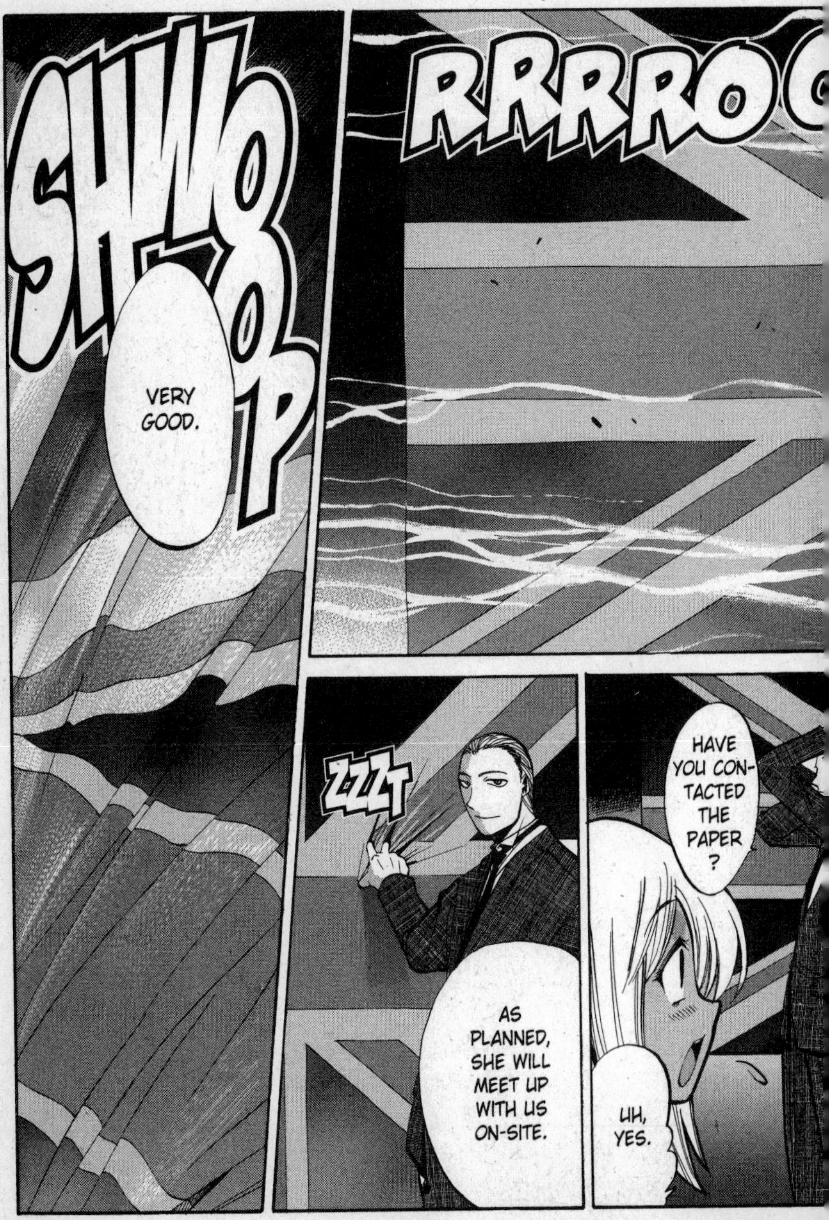
RRRROO
HAVE YOU CONTACTED THE PAPER?
UH, YES.
ZZZT
AS PLANNED, SHE WILL MEET UP WITH US ON-SITE.
SHWOOOP
VERY GOOD.

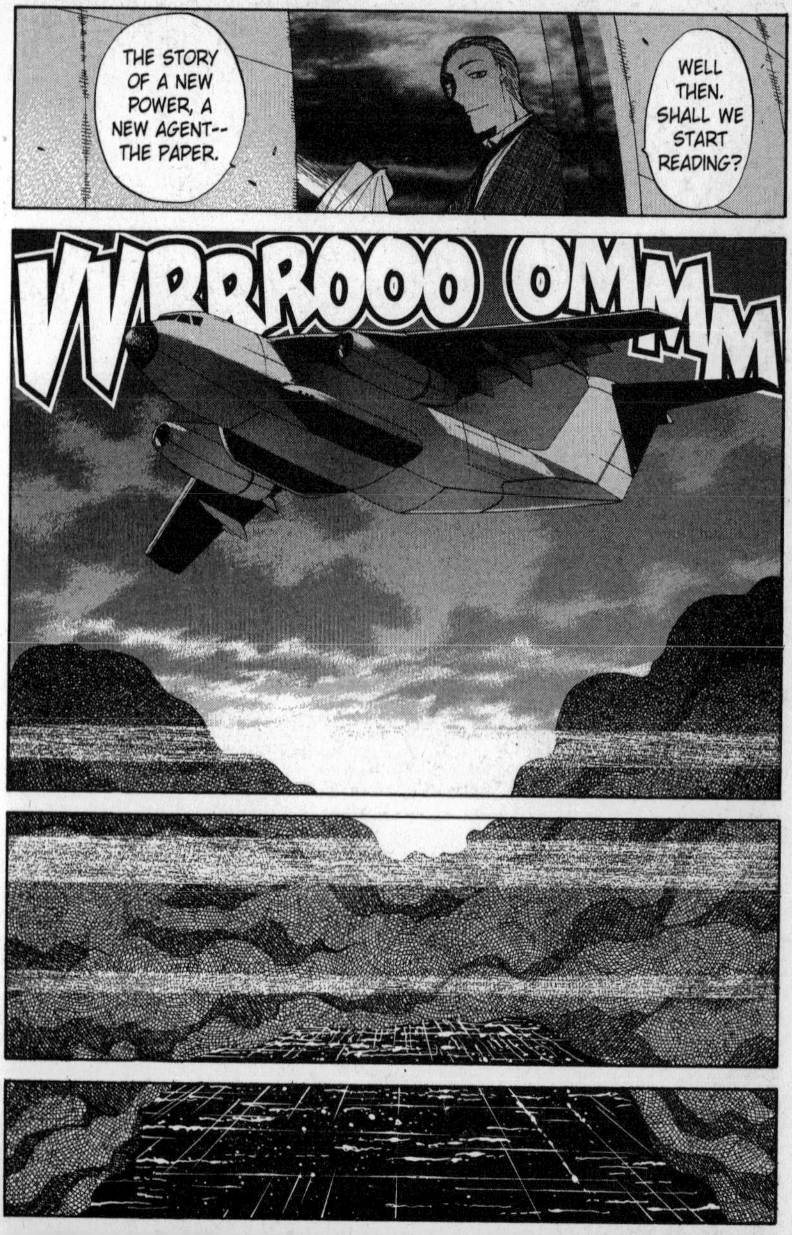
WELL THEN. SHALL WE START READING?
THE STORY OF A NEW POWER, A NEW AGENT-- THE PAPER.
VVRRROOO OMMMM

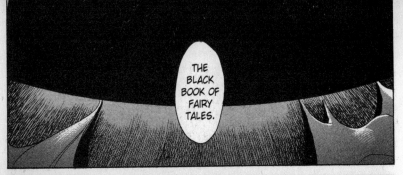

THE BLACK BOOK OF FAIRY TALES.
SHWOONT
THE COMPLETE COLLECTION OF EROTIC AND GROTESQUE STORIES PENNED BY ANGELICA LARSTON IN 1643 FOR THE EXCLUSIVE ENJOYMENT OF THE ARISTOCRACY.
THIS IS THE SOLE EXTANT AUTHENTIC COPY.
FAIRY TALE COLLECTORS THE WORLD OVER ARE DROOLING FOR THIS RARE BOOK.
A BOOK LIKE THIS NEVER SURFACES TWICE.
TCHK
TCHK
IT'S VERY EXPENSIVE.
RROOOO MMM M
I'VE EVEN COME TO MEET YOU AT THE SITE YOU REQUESTED.

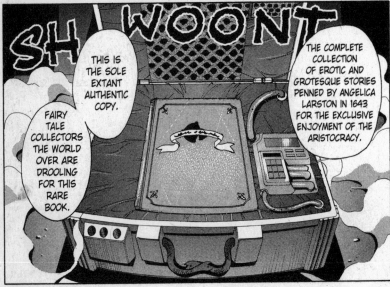

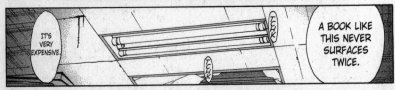

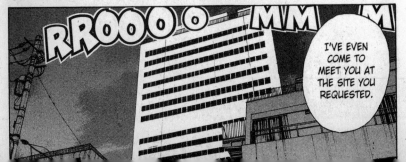

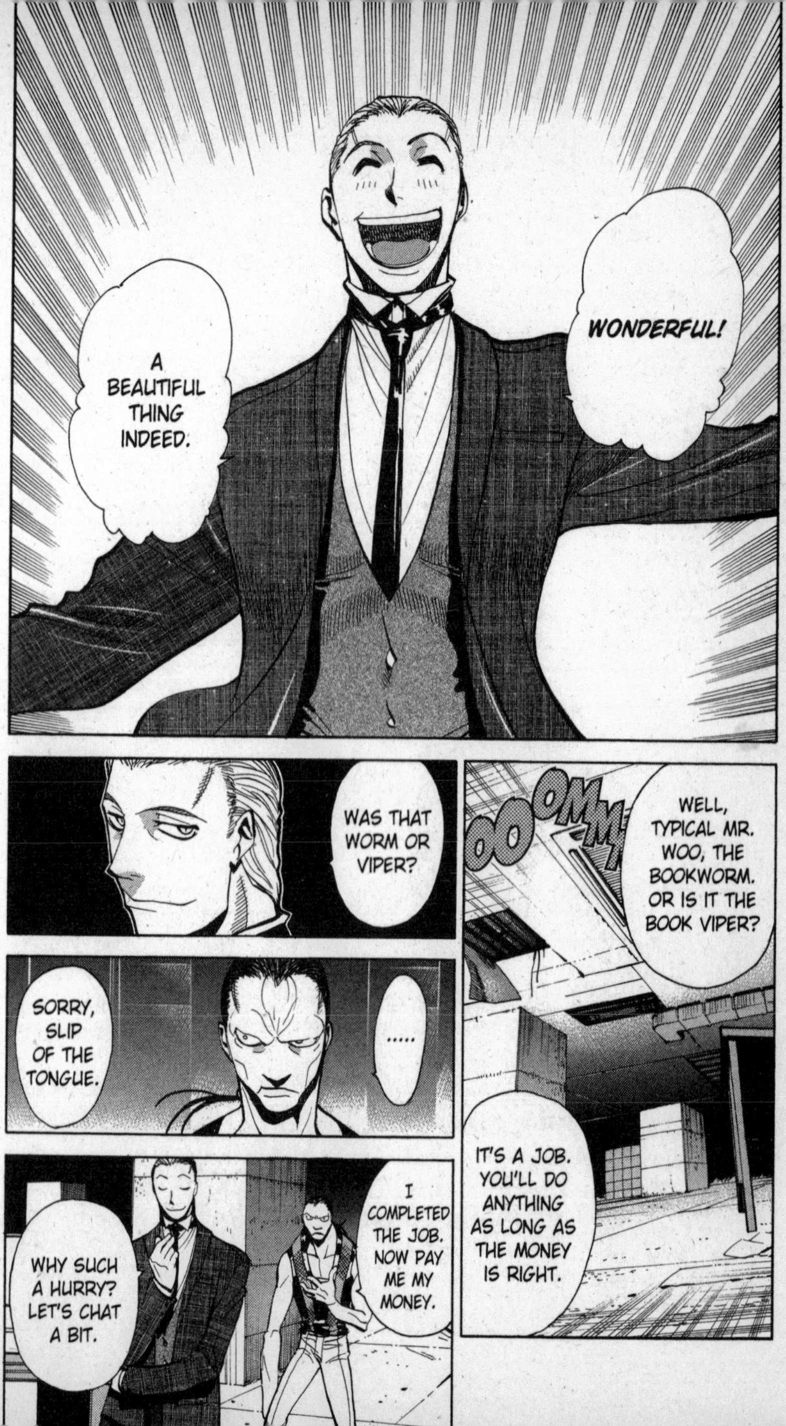
WONDERFUL!
A BEAUTIFUL THING INDEED.
OOOMM
WELL, TYPICAL MR. WOO, THE BOOKWORM. OR IS IT THE BOOK VIPER?
IT'S A JOB. YOU'LL DO ANYTHING AS LONG AS THE MONEY IS RIGHT.
WAS THAT WORM OR VIPER?
.....
SORRY, SLIP OF THE TONGUE.
I COMPLETED THE JOB. NOW PAY ME MY MONEY.
WHY SUCH A HURRY? LET'S CHAT A BIT.

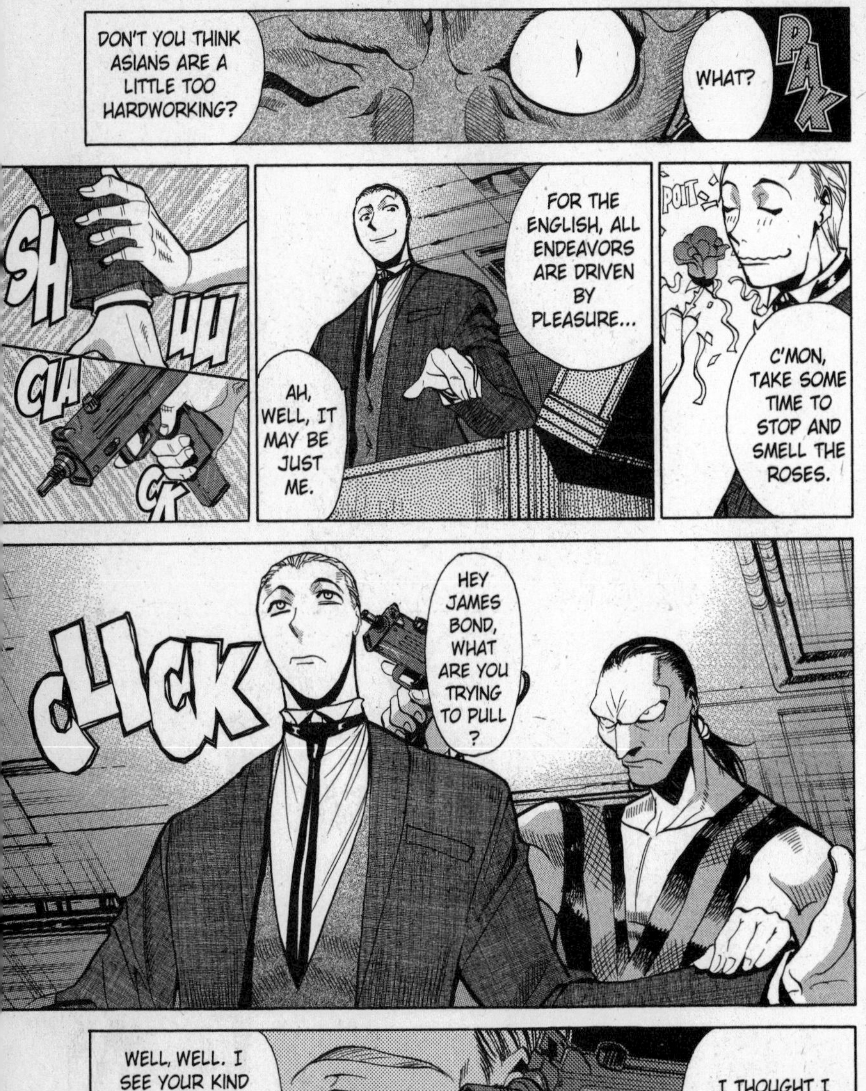
PAK
WHAT?
DON'T YOU THINK ASIANS ARE A LITTLE TOO HARDWORKING?
POIT
C'MON, TAKE SOME TIME TO STOP AND SMELL THE ROSES.
FOR THE ENGLISH, ALL ENDEAVORS ARE DRIVEN BY PLEASURE...
AH, WELL, IT MAY BE JUST ME.
SHUU
CLACK
HEY JAMES BOND, WHAT ARE YOU TRYING TO PULL?
CLICK
I THOUGHT I TOLD YOU TO COME ALONE.
Ohh, Sensei, this is scary.
WELL, WELL. I SEE YOUR KIND STILL USES ONE OF THOSE WHEN JUST HAVING A CONVERSATION.

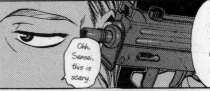

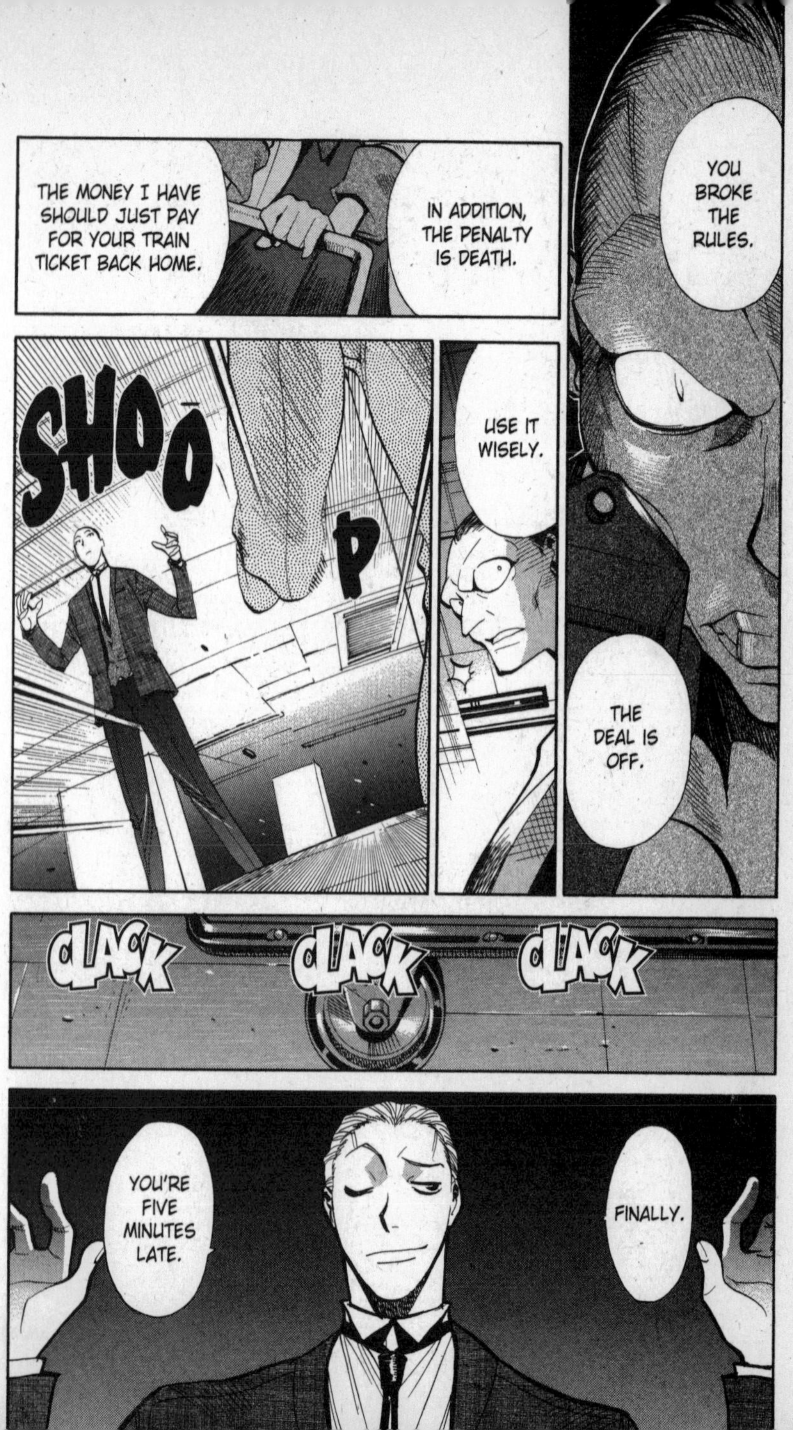
YOU BROKE THE RULES.
THE DEAL IS OFF.
IN ADDITION, THE PENALTY IS DEATH.
THE MONEY I HAVE SHOULD JUST PAY FOR YOUR TRAIN TICKET BACK HOME.
USE IT WISELY.
SHOOP
CLACK
CLACK
CLACK
FINALLY.
YOU'RE FIVE MINUTES LATE.

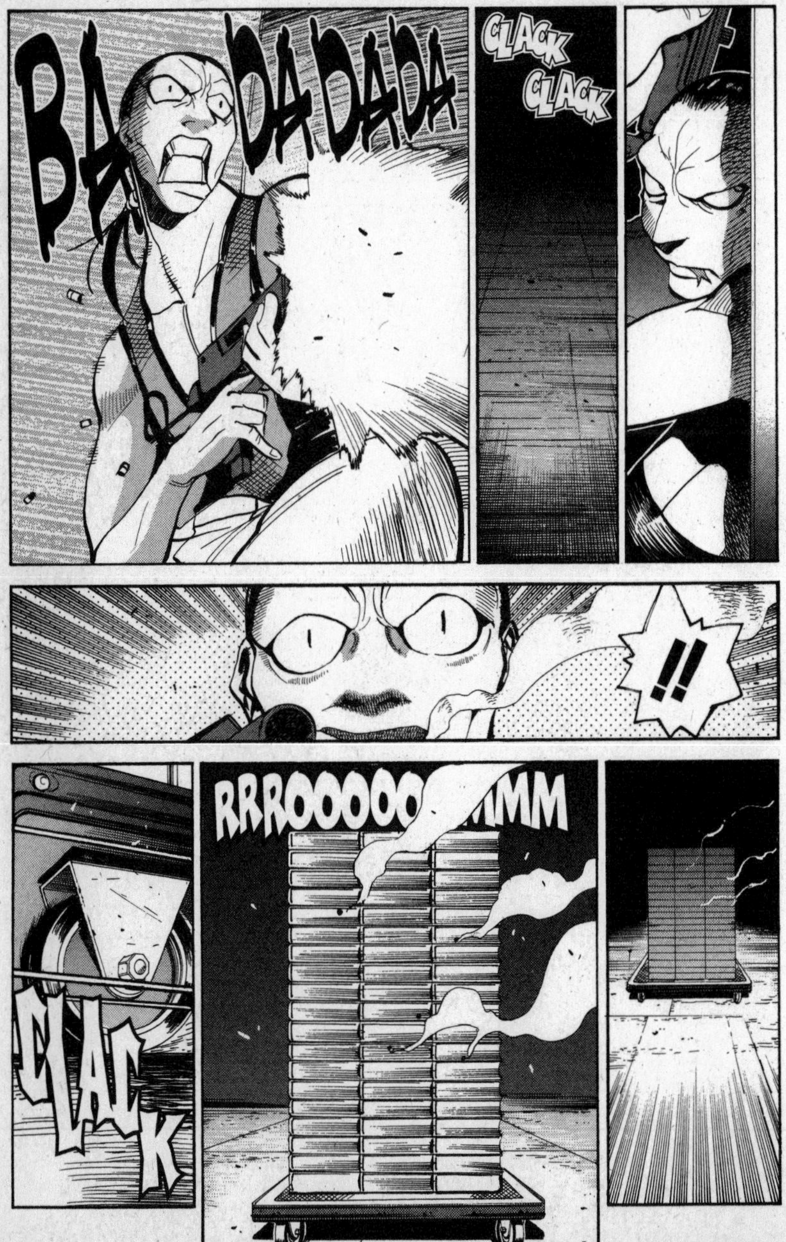
CLACK
CLACK
BA DA DADA
!!
RRROOOOOMMM
CLACK

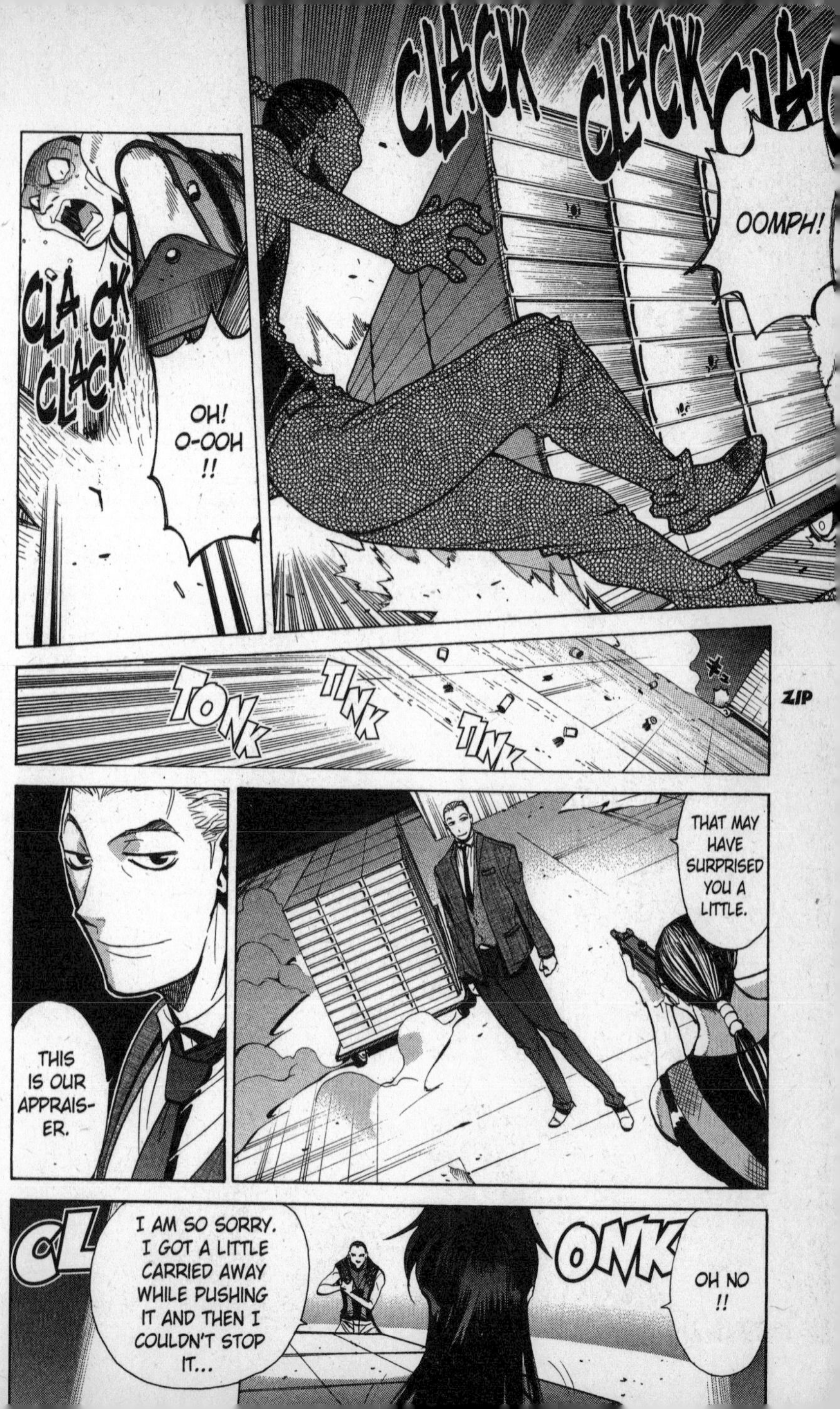
CLACK CLACK CLAC
OOMPH!
CLACK CLACK
OH! O-OOH !!
ZIP
TINK
TONK
TINK
THAT MAY HAVE SURPRISED YOU A LITTLE.
THIS IS OUR APPRAISER.
OH NO !!
ONK
I AM SO SORRY. I GOT A LITTLE CARRIED AWAY WHILE PUSHING IT AND THEN I COULDN'T STOP IT...
CL

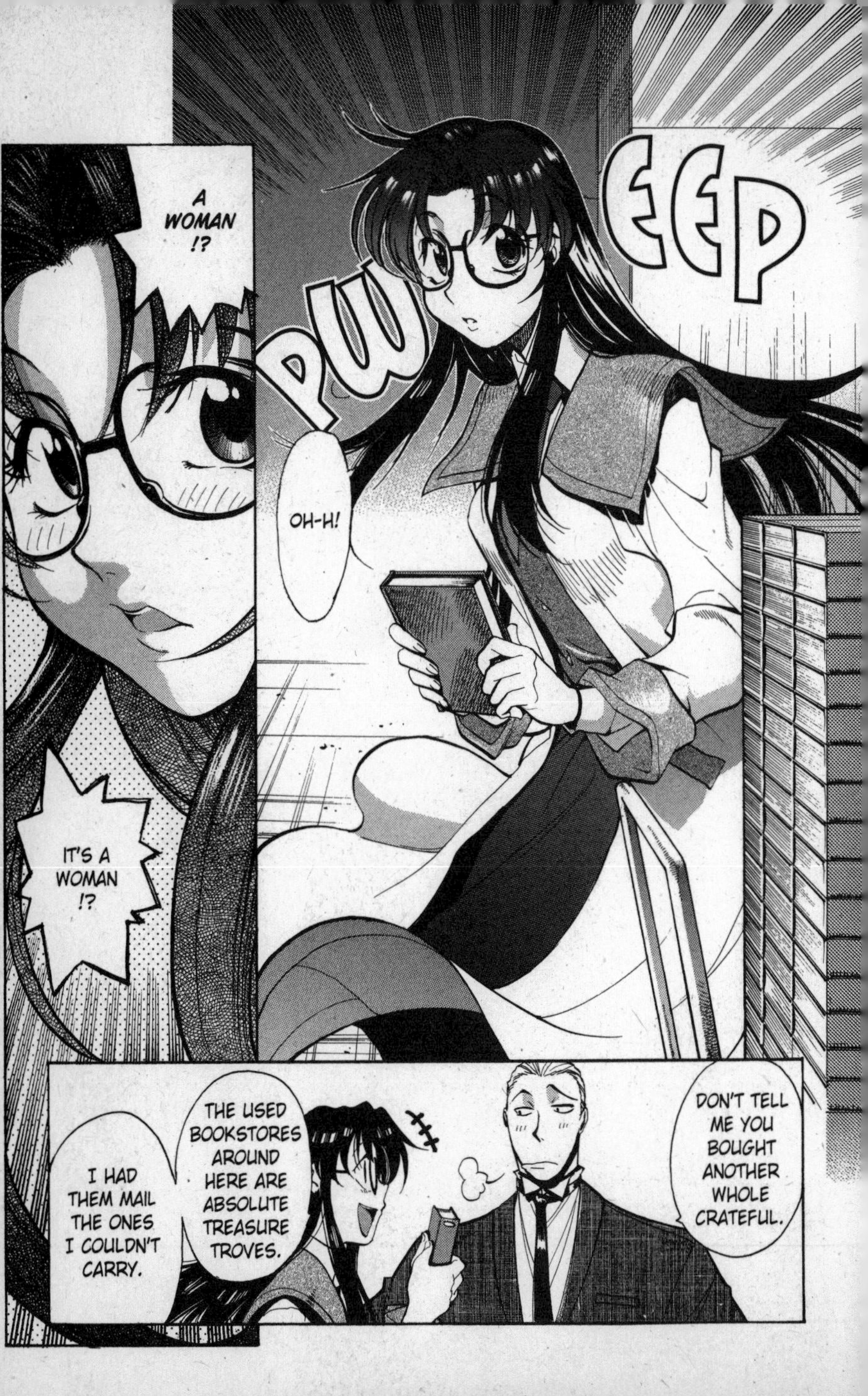
PUW EEP
OH-H!
A WOMAN !?
IT'S A WOMAN !?
DON'T TELL ME YOU BOUGHT ANOTHER WHOLE CRATEFUL.
THE USED BOOKSTORES AROUND HERE ARE ABSOLUTE TREASURE TROVES.
I HAD THEM MAIL THE ONES I COULDN'T CARRY.

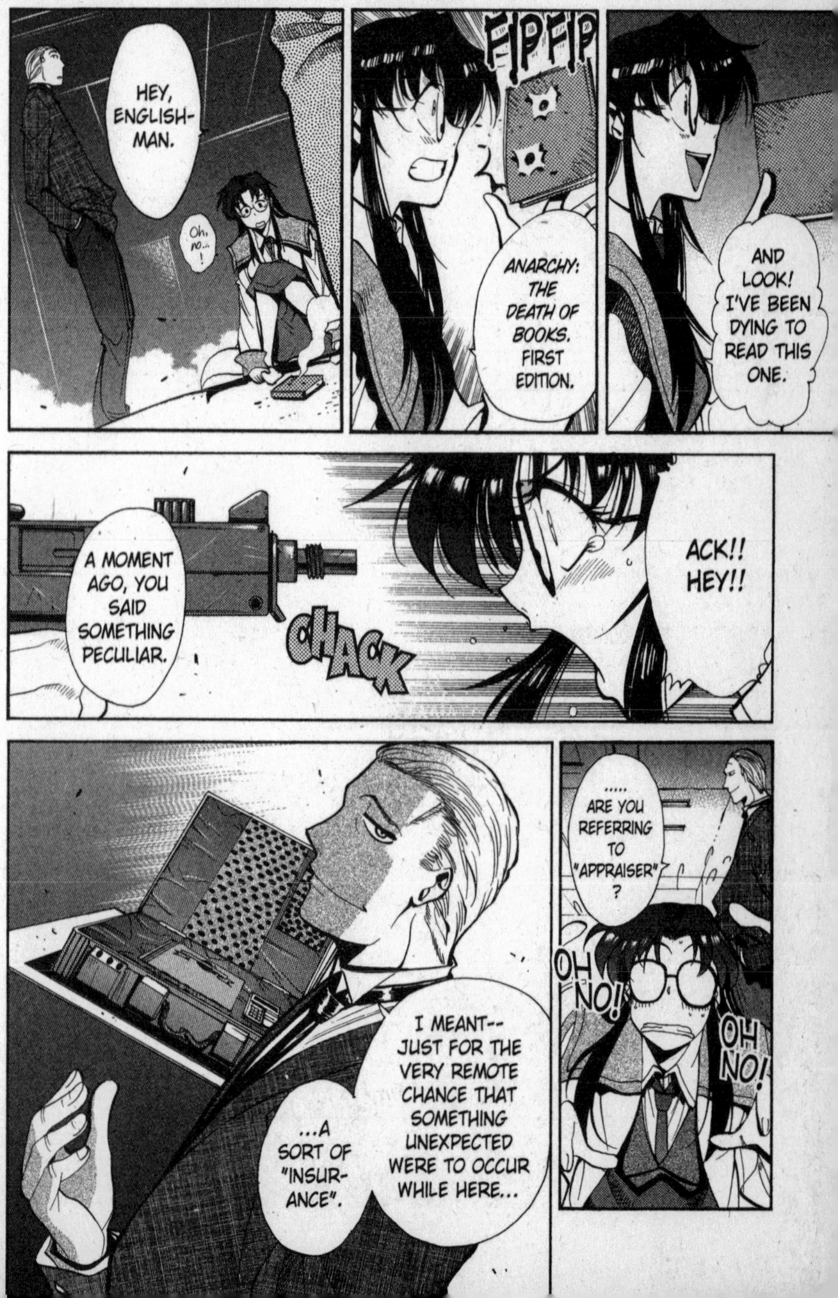
AND LOOK! I'VE BEEN DYING TO READ THIS ONE.
FIPFIP
ANARCHY: THE DEATH OF BOOKS. FIRST EDITION.
HEY, ENGLISH-MAN.
Oh, no...!
ACK!! HEY!!
CHACK
A MOMENT AGO, YOU SAID SOMETHING PECULIAR.
..... ARE YOU REFERRING TO "APPRAISER"?
OH NO!
OH NO!
I MEANT-- JUST FOR THE VERY REMOTE CHANCE THAT SOMETHING UNEXPECTED WERE TO OCCUR WHILE HERE...
...A SORT OF "INSUR-ANCE".

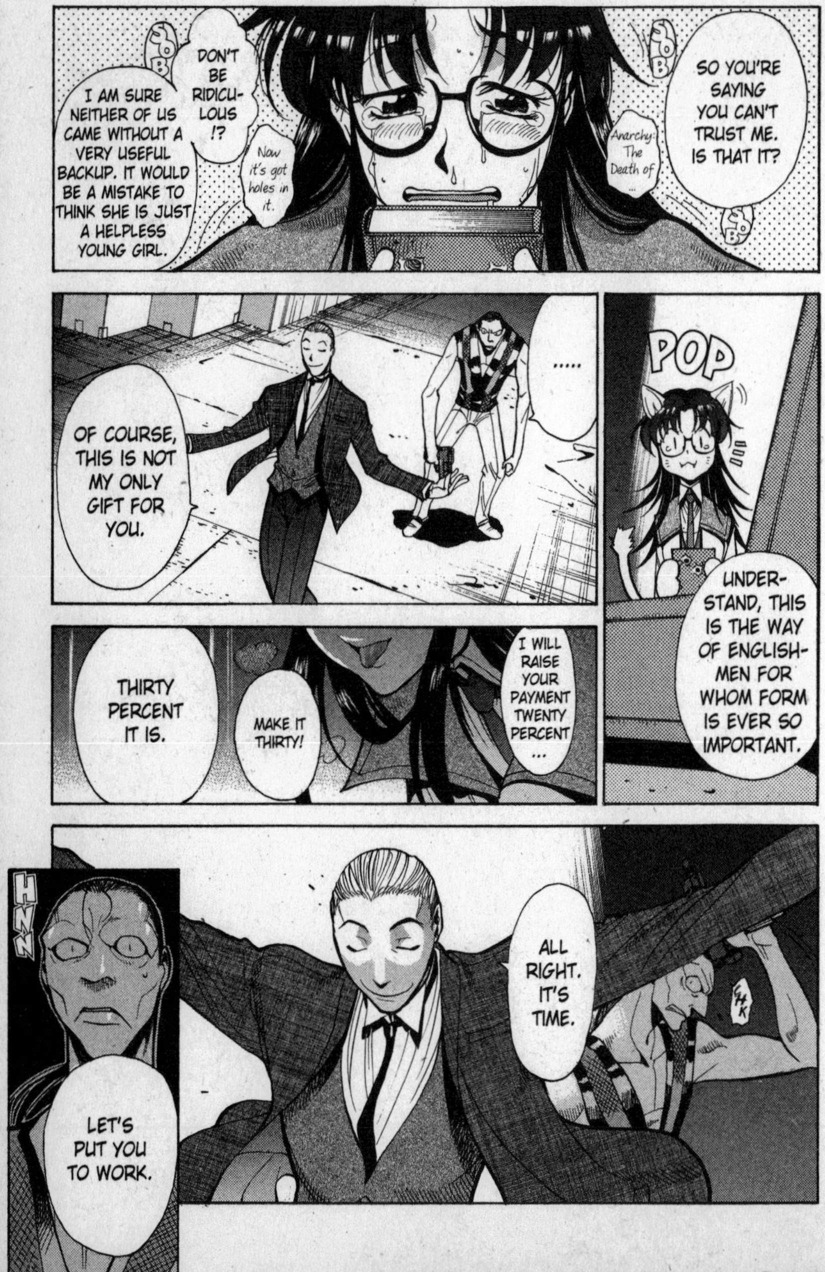
SOB
SO YOU'RE SAYING YOU CAN'T TRUST ME. IS THAT IT?
Anarchy: The Death of ...
SOB
Now it's got holes in it.
DON'T BE RIDICULOUS !?
SOB
I AM SURE NEITHER OF US CAME WITHOUT A VERY USEFUL BACKUP. IT WOULD BE A MISTAKE TO THINK SHE IS JUST A HELPLESS YOUNG GIRL.
POP
UNDER-STAND, THIS IS THE WAY OF ENGLISH-MEN FOR WHOM FORM IS EVER SO IMPORTANT.
.....
OF COURSE, THIS IS NOT MY ONLY GIFT FOR YOU.
I WILL RAISE YOUR PAYMENT TWENTY PERCENT ...
MAKE IT THIRTY!
THIRTY PERCENT IT IS.
CHK
ALL RIGHT. IT'S TIME.
HNN
LET'S PUT YOU TO WORK.

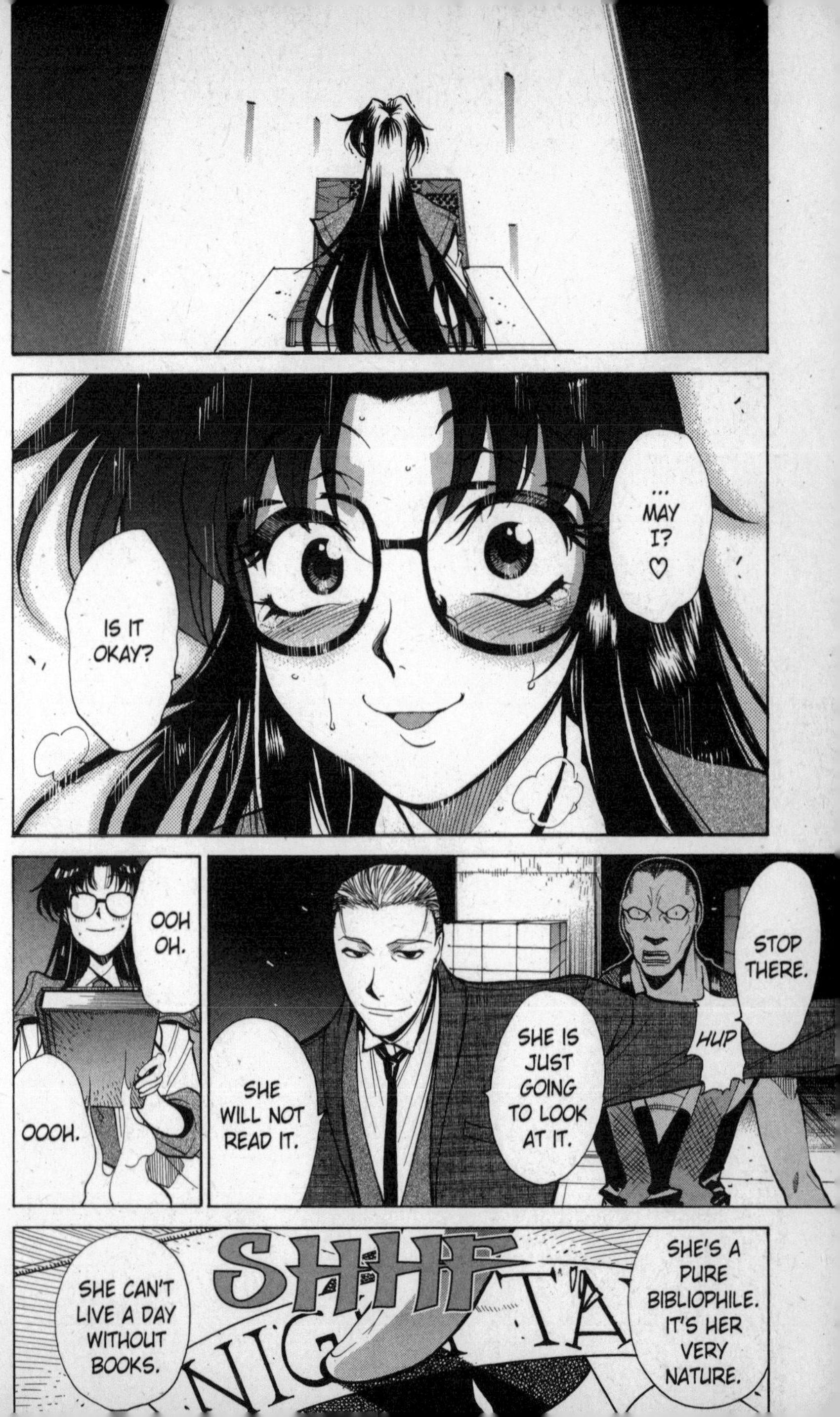
...MAY I? ♡
IS IT OKAY?
STOP THERE.
HUP
SHE IS JUST GOING TO LOOK AT IT.
SHE WILL NOT READ IT.
OOH OH.
OOOH.
SHE'S A PURE BIBLIOPHILE. IT'S HER VERY NATURE.
SHHF
SHE CAN'T LIVE A DAY WITHOUT BOOKS.

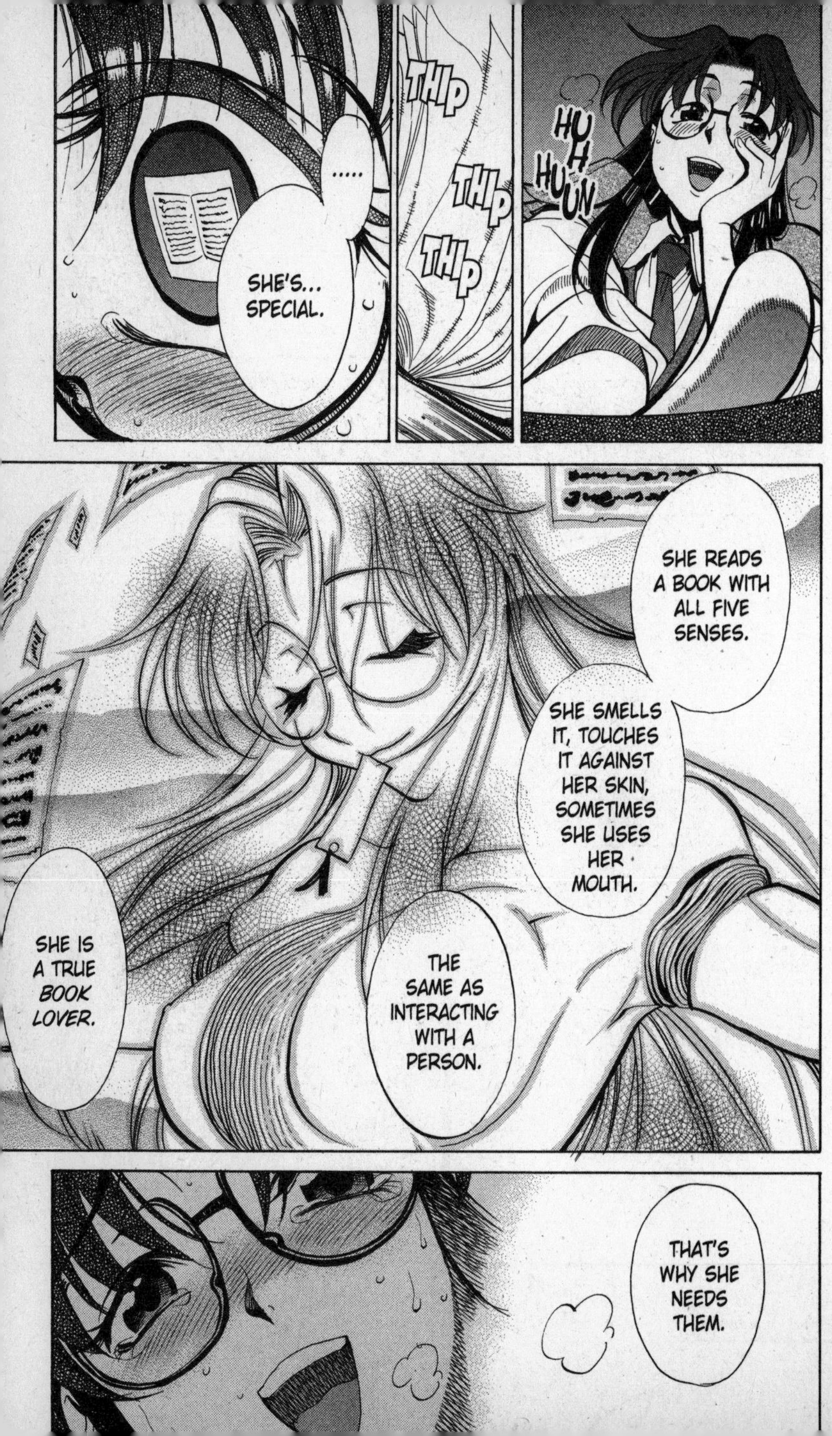
HUH HUUN
THIP
THIP
THIP
.....
SHE'S... SPECIAL.
SHE READS A BOOK WITH ALL FIVE SENSES.
SHE SMELLS IT, TOUCHES IT AGAINST HER SKIN, SOMETIMES SHE USES HER MOUTH.
THE SAME AS INTERACTING WITH A PERSON.
SHE IS A TRUE BOOK LOVER.
THAT'S WHY SHE NEEDS THEM.

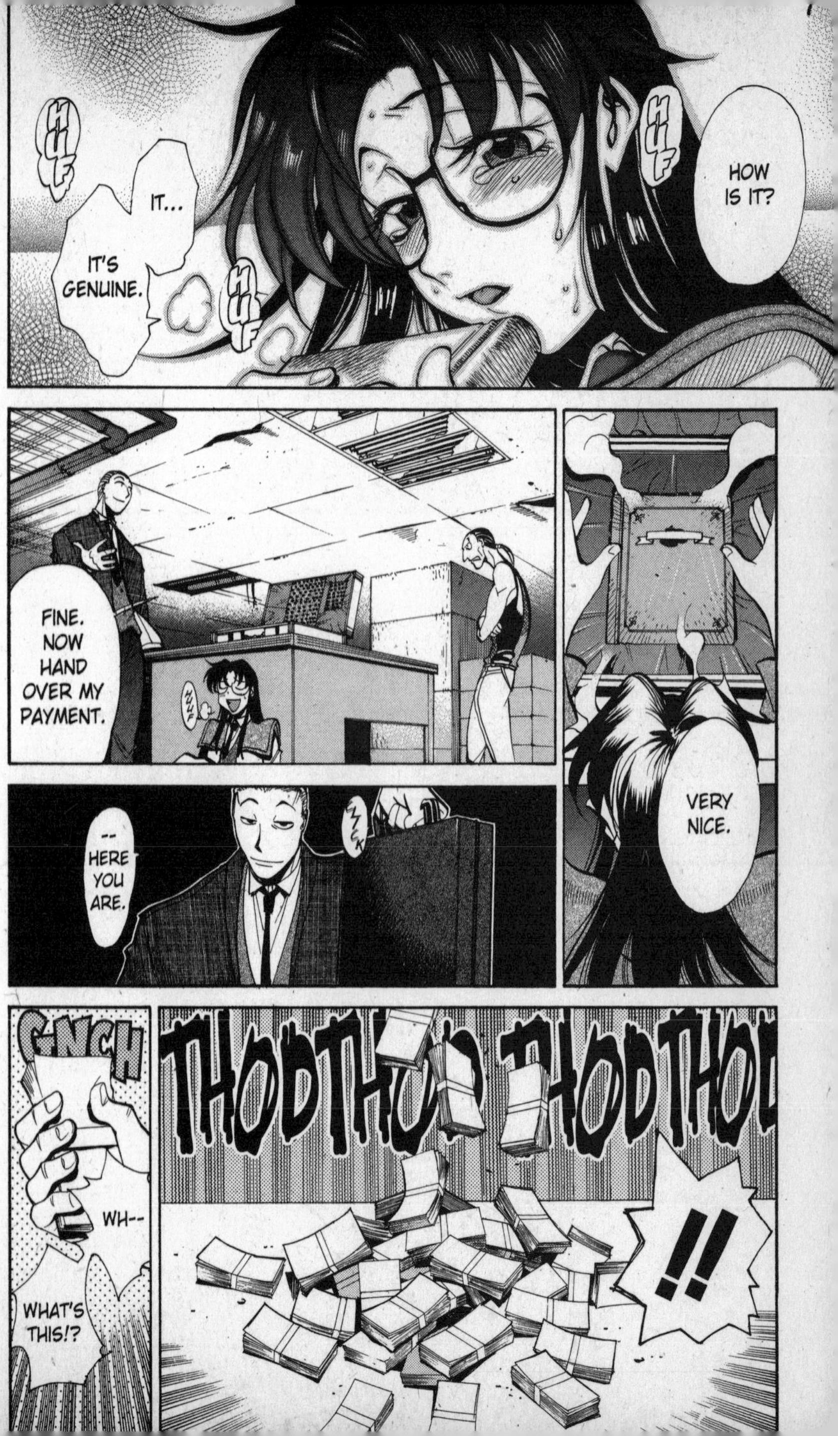
HOW IS IT?
HUF
HUF
IT...
IT'S GENUINE.
HUF
VERY NICE.
FINE. NOW HAND OVER MY PAYMENT.
HUF
-- HERE YOU ARE.
THODTHOD THODTHOD
!!
GNCH
WH--
WHAT'S THIS!?

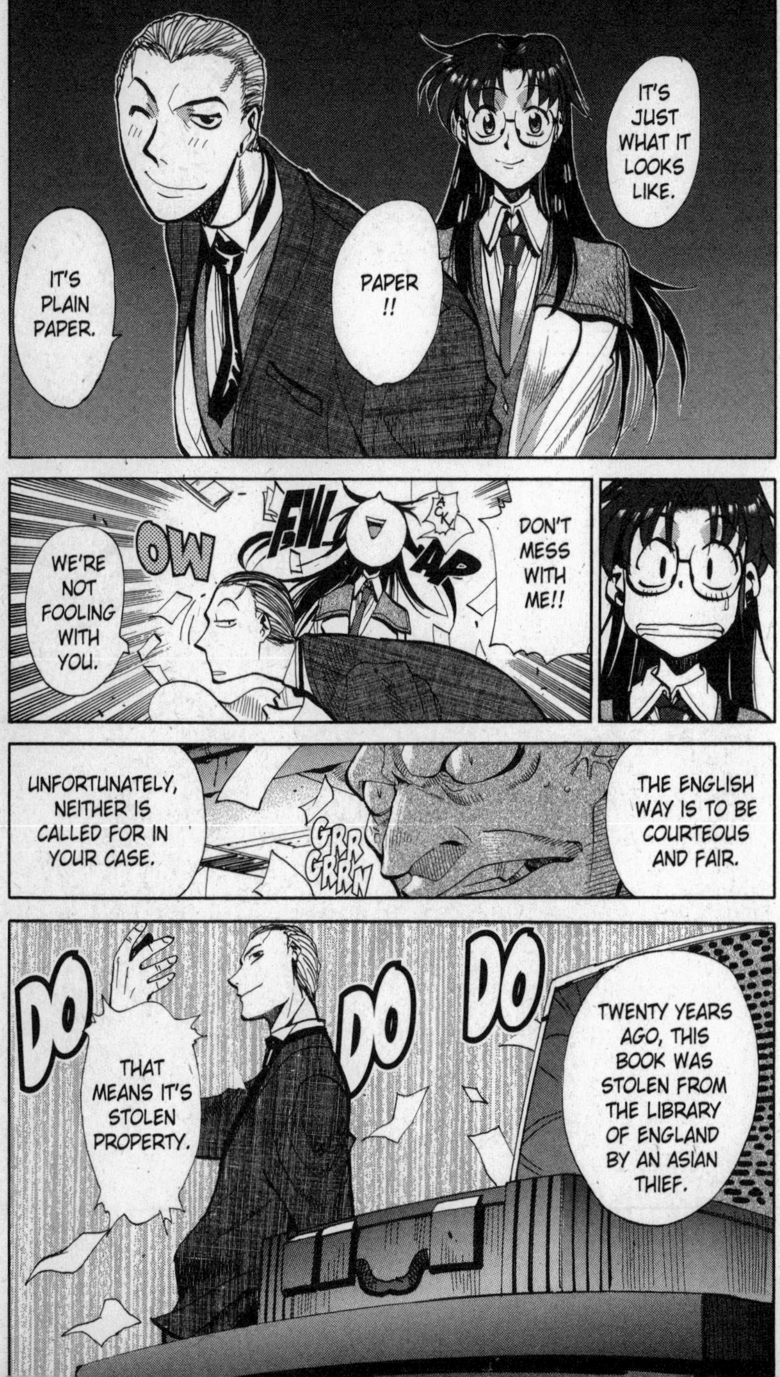
IT'S JUST WHAT IT LOOKS LIKE.
PAPER!!
IT'S PLAIN PAPER.
DON'T MESS WITH ME!!
ACK
FWAP
OW
WE'RE NOT FOOLING WITH YOU.
THE ENGLISH WAY IS TO BE COURTEOUS AND FAIR.
GRRR GRRRN
UNFORTUNATELY, NEITHER IS CALLED FOR IN YOUR CASE.
TWENTY YEARS AGO, THIS BOOK WAS STOLEN FROM THE LIBRARY OF ENGLAND BY AN ASIAN THIEF.
DO DO DO
THAT MEANS IT'S STOLEN PROPERTY.

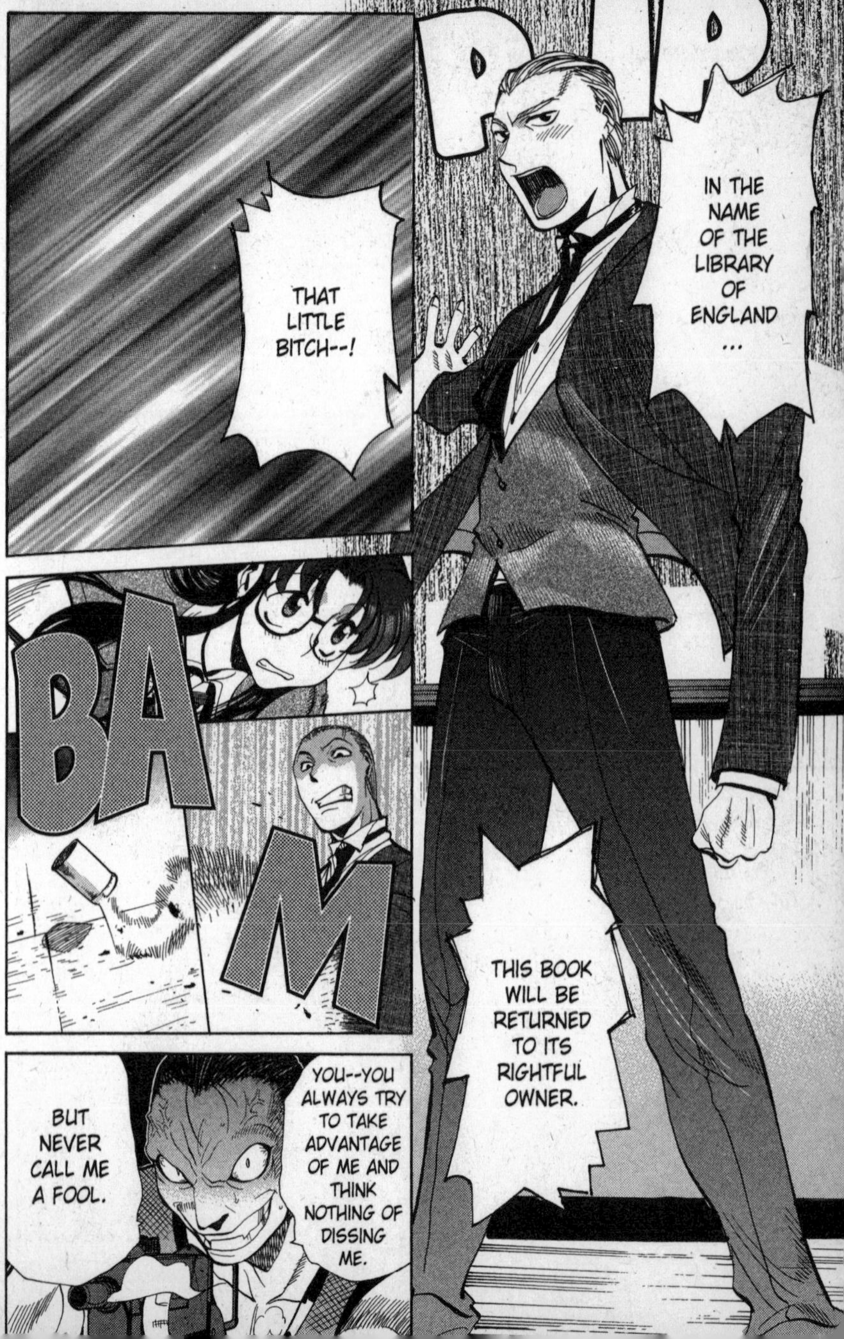
IN THE NAME OF THE LIBRARY OF ENGLAND ...
THIS BOOK WILL BE RETURNED TO ITS RIGHTFUL OWNER.
THAT LITTLE BITCH--!
BAM
YOU--YOU ALWAYS TRY TO TAKE ADVANTAGE OF ME AND THINK NOTHING OF DISSING ME.
BUT NEVER CALL ME A FOOL.

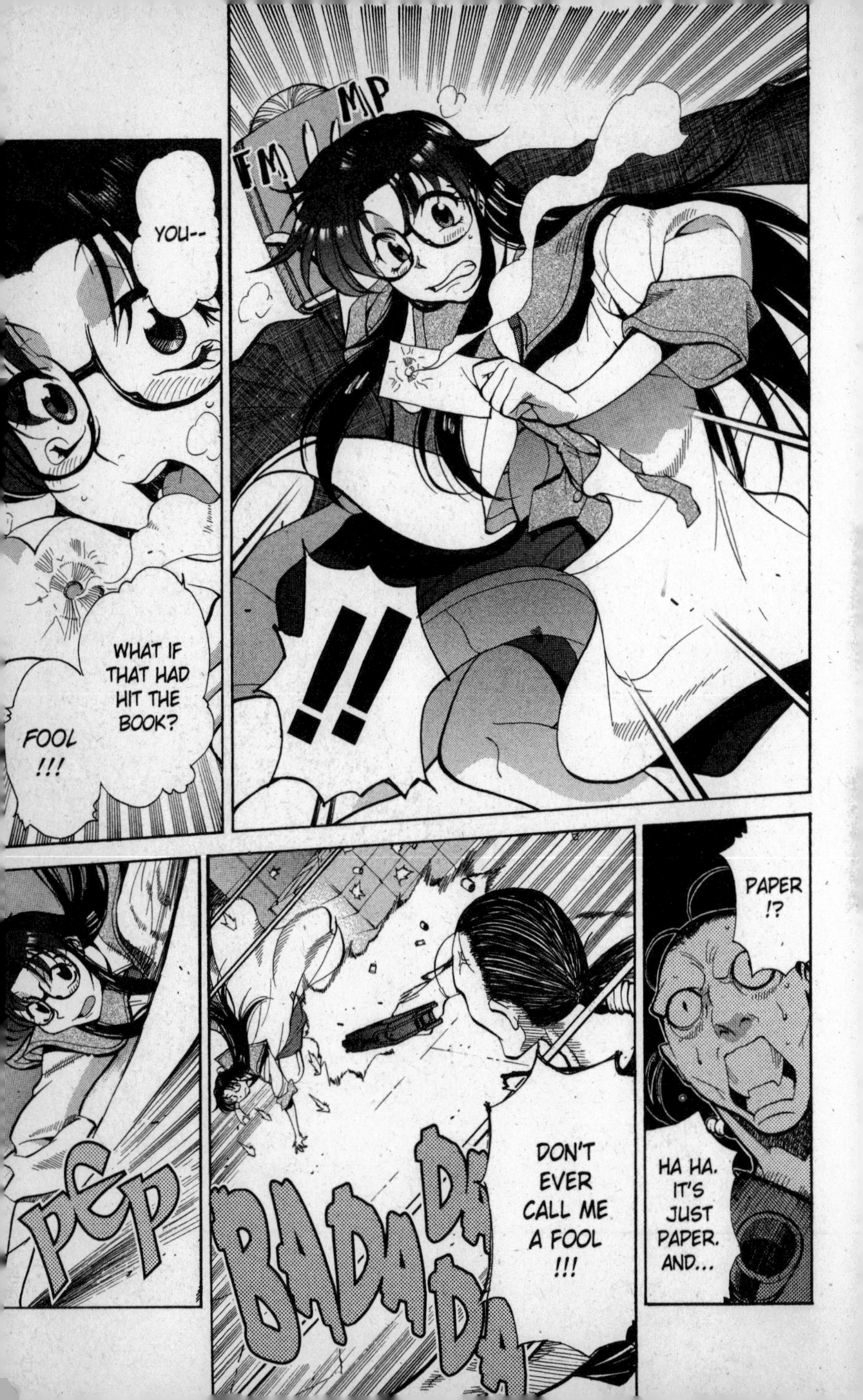
FMMP
!!
YOU--
WHAT IF THAT HAD HIT THE BOOK?
FOOL !!!
PAPER !?
HA HA. IT'S JUST PAPER. AND...
DON'T EVER CALL ME A FOOL !!!
BADADADA
PEP

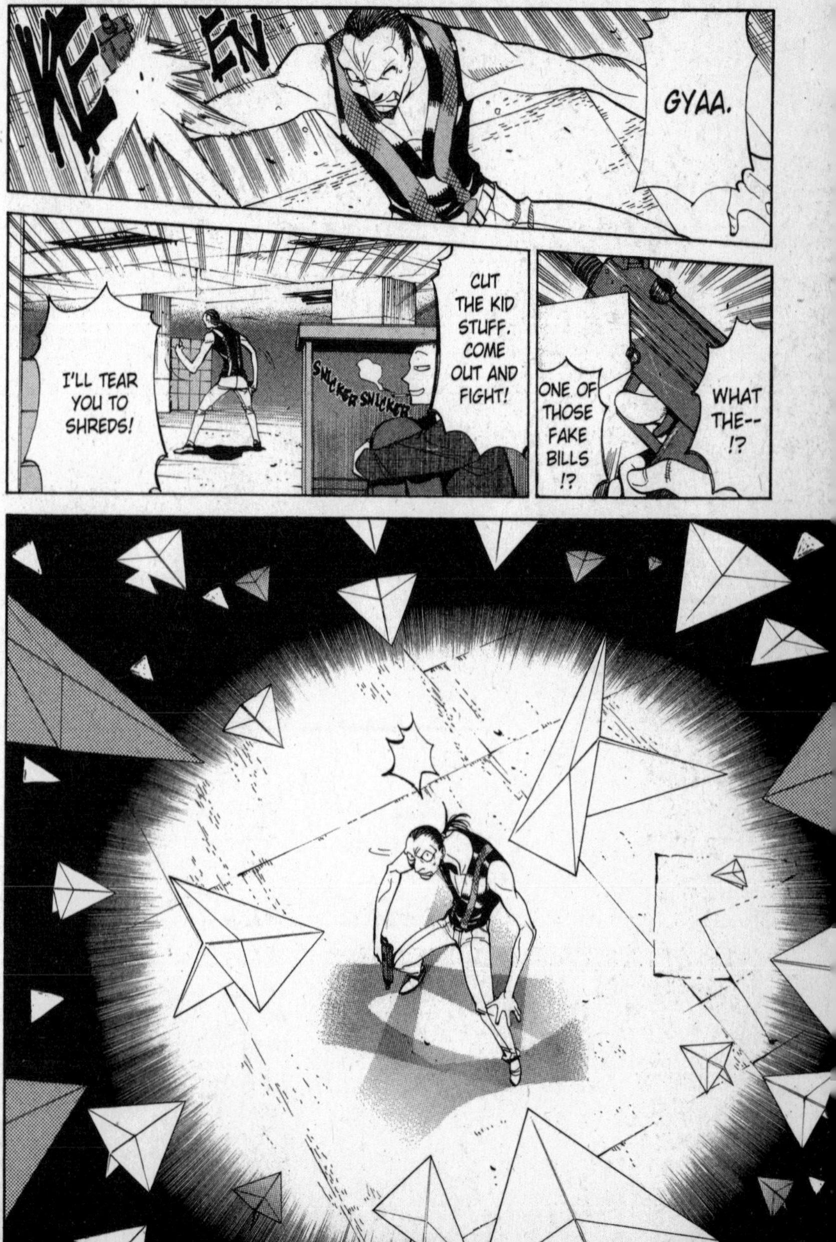
GYAA.
KEEN
WHAT THE--!?
ONE OF THOSE FAKE BILLS!?
CUT THE KID STUFF. COME OUT AND FIGHT!
SNICKER SNICKER
I'LL TEAR YOU TO SHREDS!

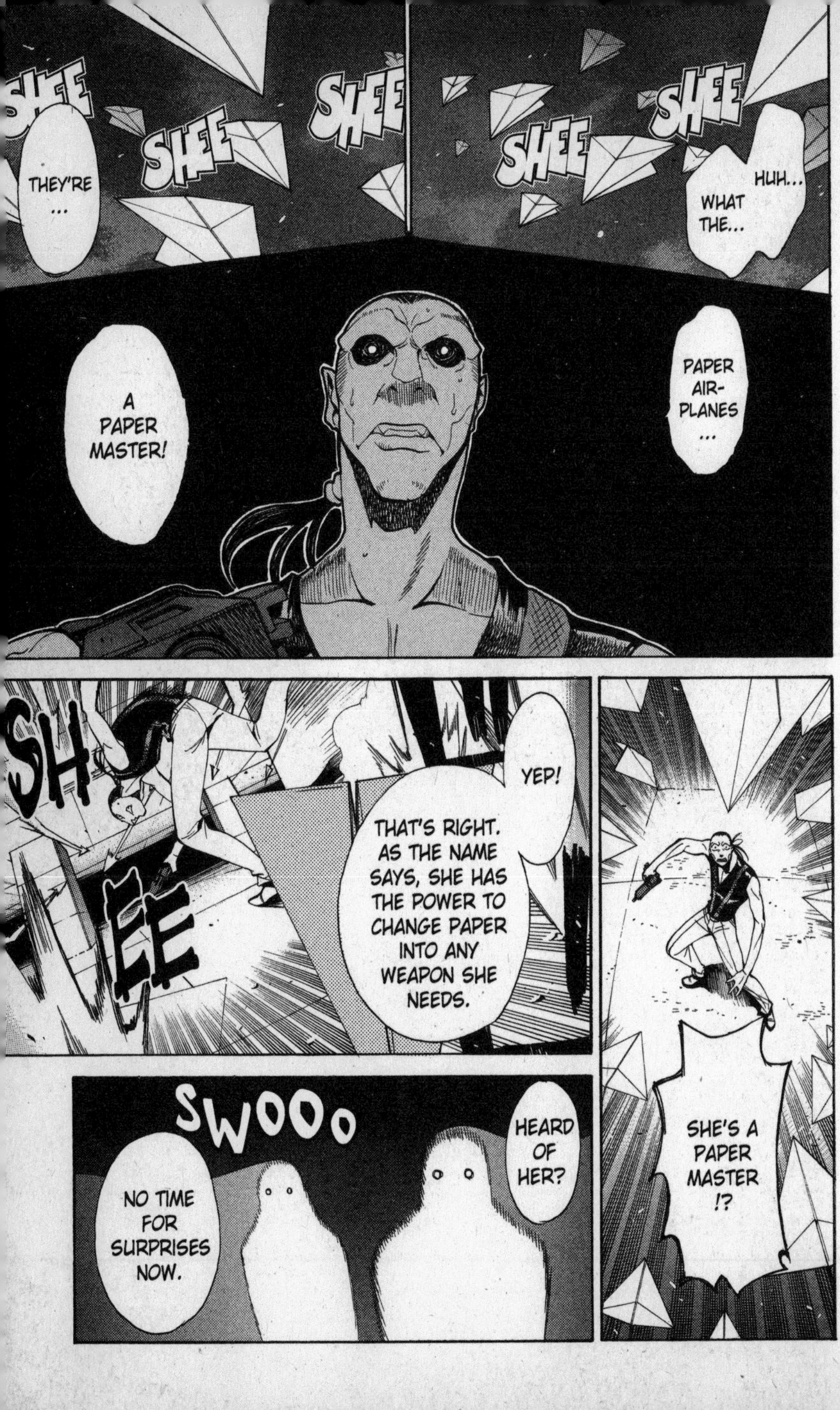
SHEE
SHEE
HUH... WHAT THE...
SHEE
SHEE
SHEE
THEY'RE ...
PAPER AIR-PLANES ...
A PAPER MASTER!
SHE'S A PAPER MASTER !?
YEP!
THAT'S RIGHT. AS THE NAME SAYS, SHE HAS THE POWER TO CHANGE PAPER INTO ANY WEAPON SHE NEEDS.
SHEE
HEARD OF HER?
SWOOO
NO TIME FOR SURPRISES NOW.

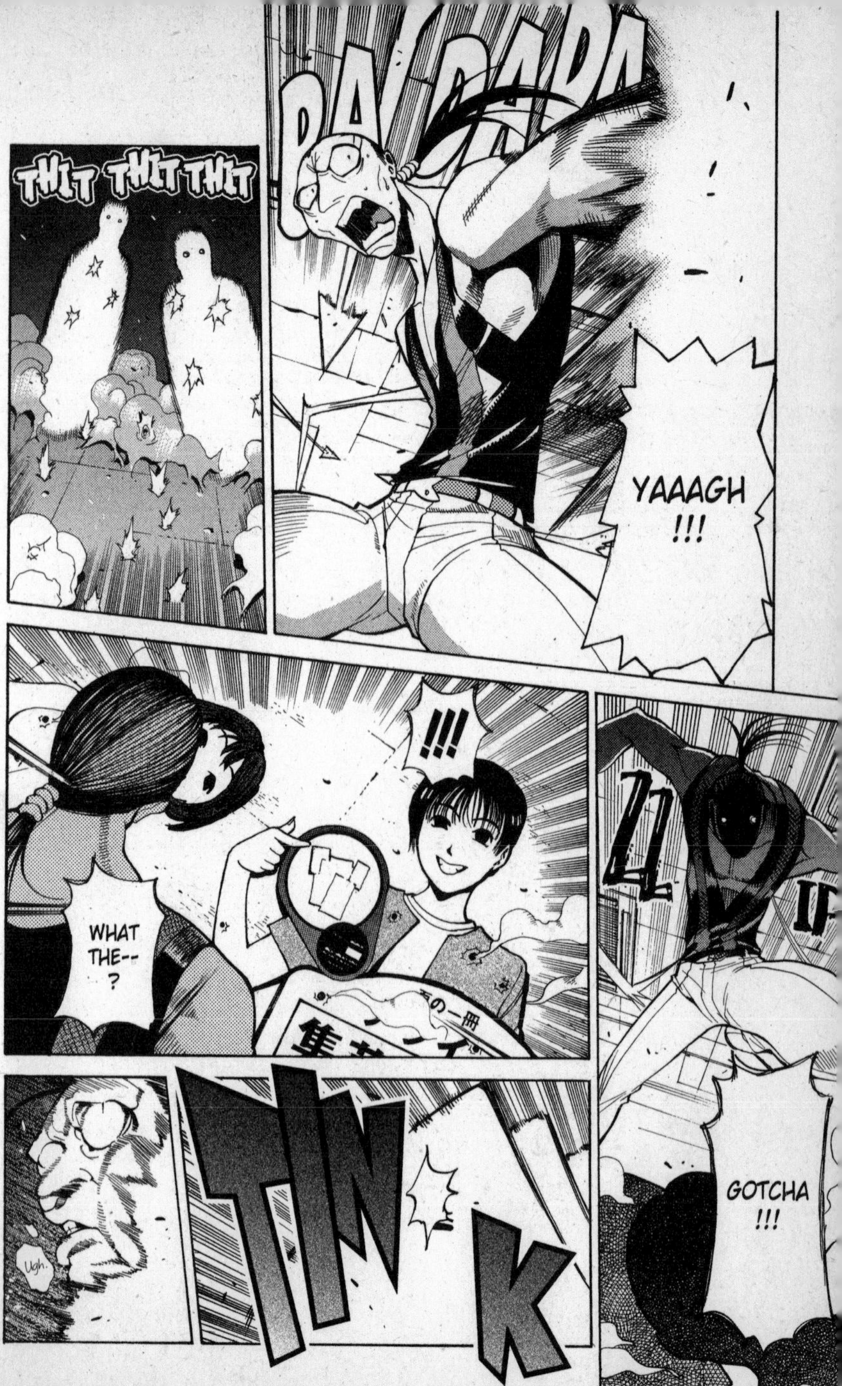
PA DADA
YAAAGH !!!
THIT THIT THIT
GOTCHA !!!
!!!
WHAT THE-- ?
TINK
Ugh.

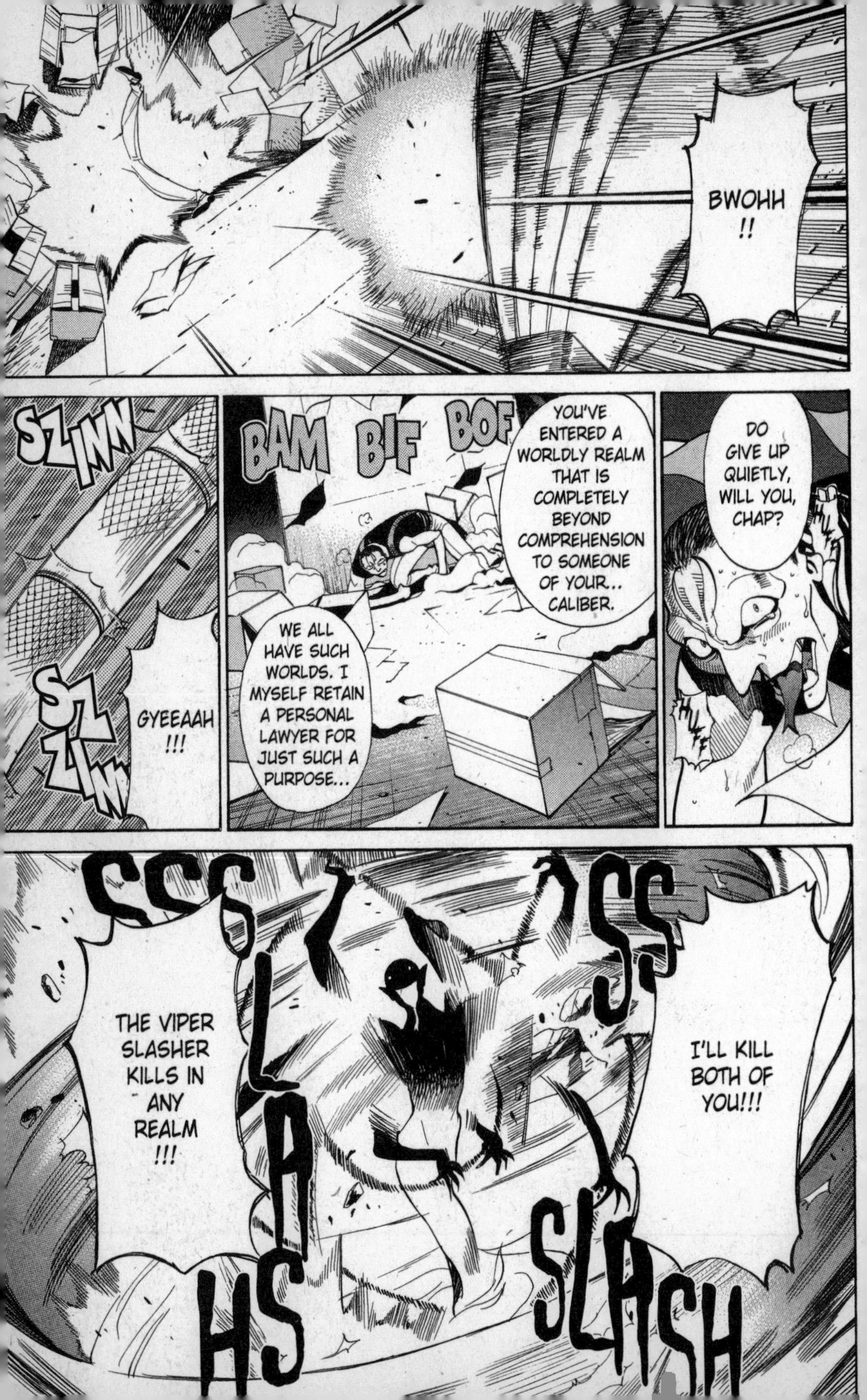
BWOHH!!
DO GIVE UP QUIETLY, WILL YOU, CHAP?
BAM BIF BOF
YOU'VE ENTERED A WORLDLY REALM THAT IS COMPLETELY BEYOND COMPREHENSION TO SOMEONE OF YOUR.. CALIBER.
WE ALL HAVE SUCH WORLDS. I MYSELF RETAIN A PERSONAL LAWYER FOR JUST SUCH A PURPOSE...
SZINN
GYEEAAH!!!
I'LL KILL BOTH OF YOU!!!
SLASH
THE VIPER SLASHER KILLS IN ANY REALM!!!

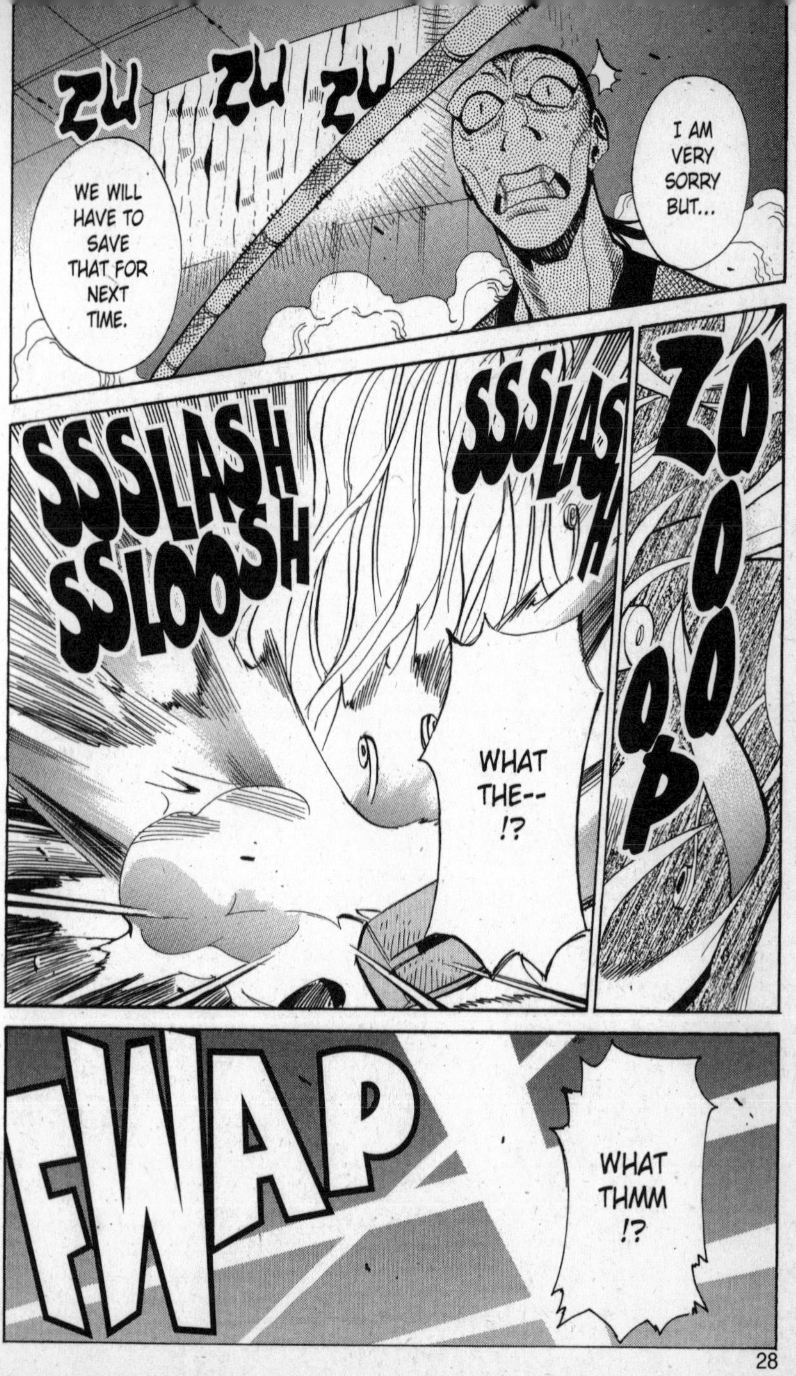
I AM VERY SORRY BUT...
ZU ZU ZU
WE WILL HAVE TO SAVE THAT FOR NEXT TIME.
ZOOOOOP
SSSLASH
WHAT THE-- !?
SSSLASH SSLOOSH
WHAT THMM !?
FWAP

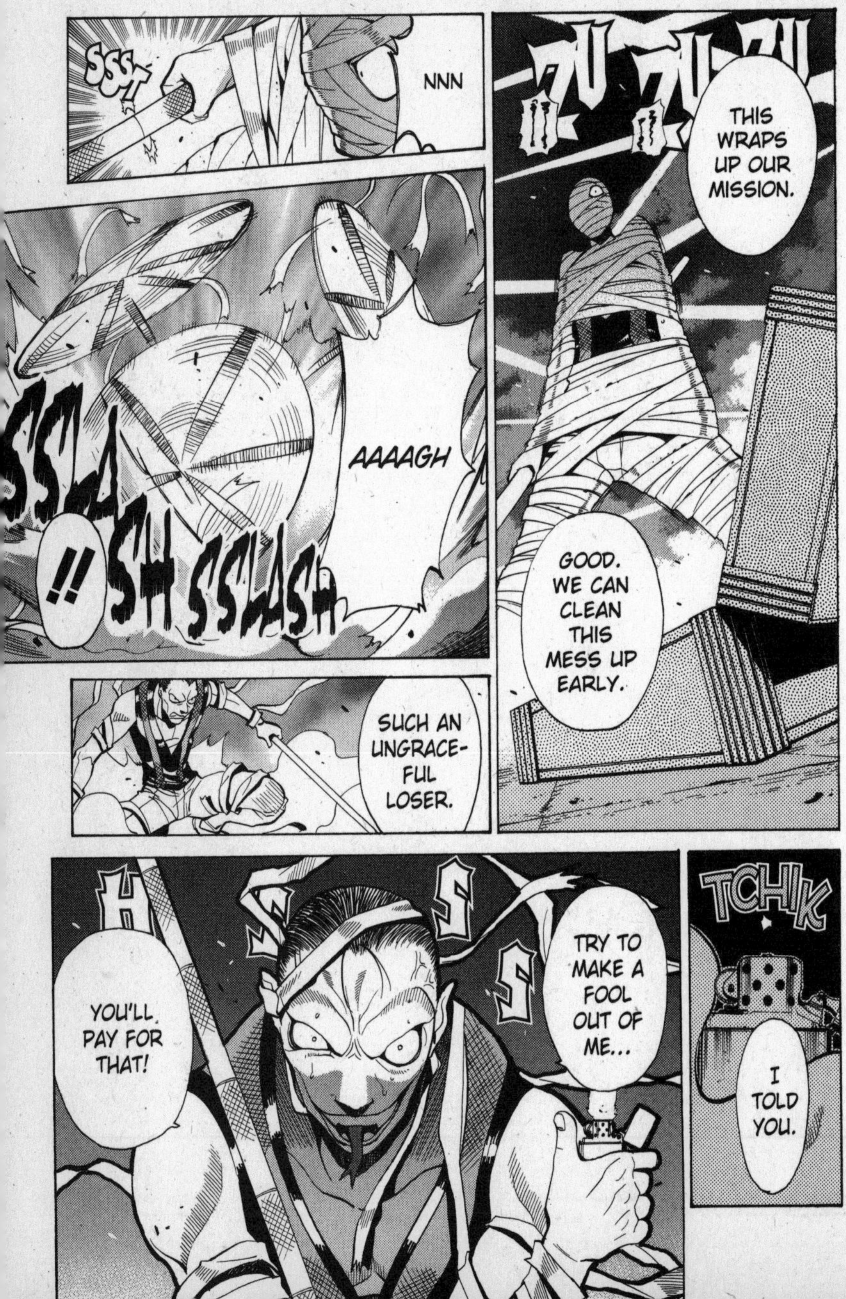
THIS WRAPS UP OUR MISSION.
GOOD. WE CAN CLEAN THIS MESS UP EARLY.
NNN
SSST
!!
AAAAGH
SSLASH SSLASH
SUCH AN UNGRACEFUL LOSER.
TCHIK
I TOLD YOU.
TRY TO MAKE A FOOL OUT OF ME...
HSSS
YOU'LL PAY FOR THAT!

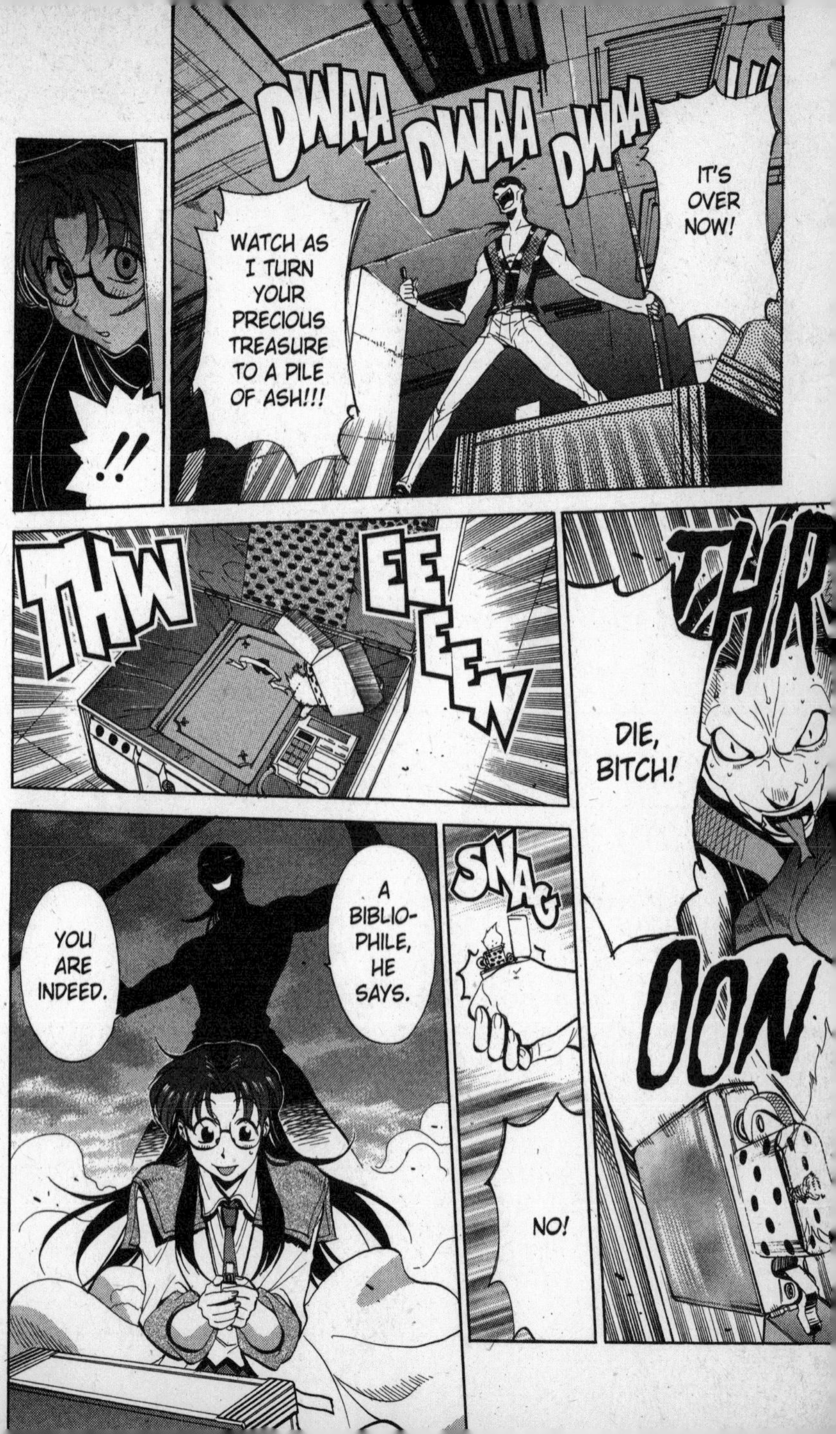

DWAA DWAA DWAA
IT'S OVER NOW!
WATCH AS I TURN YOUR PRECIOUS TREASURE TO A PILE OF ASH!!!
!!
THR
DIE, BITCH!
OON
THW
EE
EEEN
SNAG
NO!
A BIBLIO-PHILE, HE SAYS.
YOU ARE INDEED.

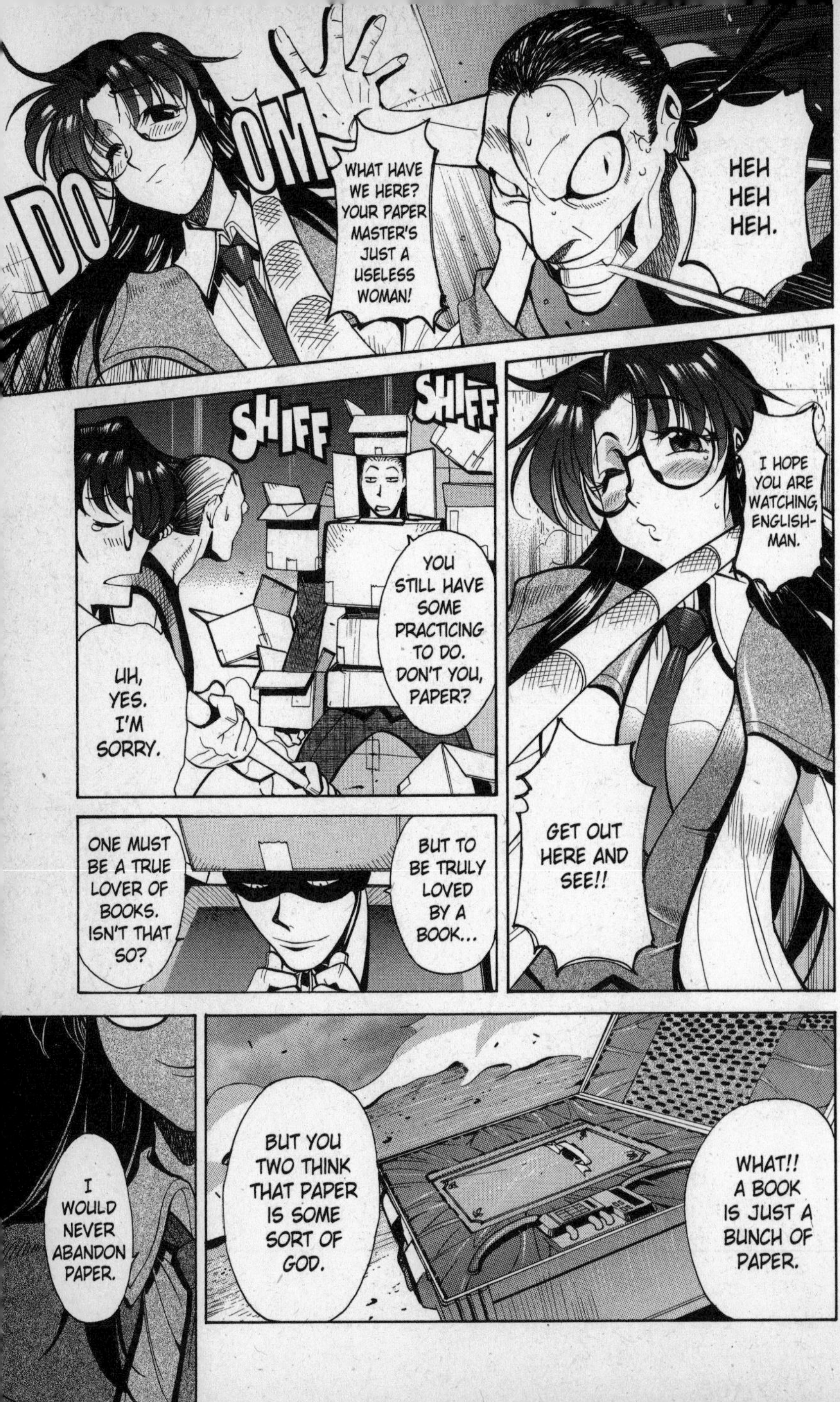
HEH HEH HEH.
WHAT HAVE WE HERE? YOUR PAPER MASTER'S JUST A USELESS WOMAN!
DOOM
I HOPE YOU ARE WATCHING, ENGLISH-MAN.
GET OUT HERE AND SEE!!
SHIFF
SHIFF
YOU STILL HAVE SOME PRACTICING TO DO. DON'T YOU, PAPER?
UH, YES. I'M SORRY.
BUT TO BE TRULY LOVED BY A BOOK...
ONE MUST BE A TRUE LOVER OF BOOKS. ISN'T THAT SO?
WHAT!! A BOOK IS JUST A BUNCH OF PAPER.
BUT YOU TWO THINK THAT PAPER IS SOME SORT OF GOD.
I WOULD NEVER ABANDON PAPER.

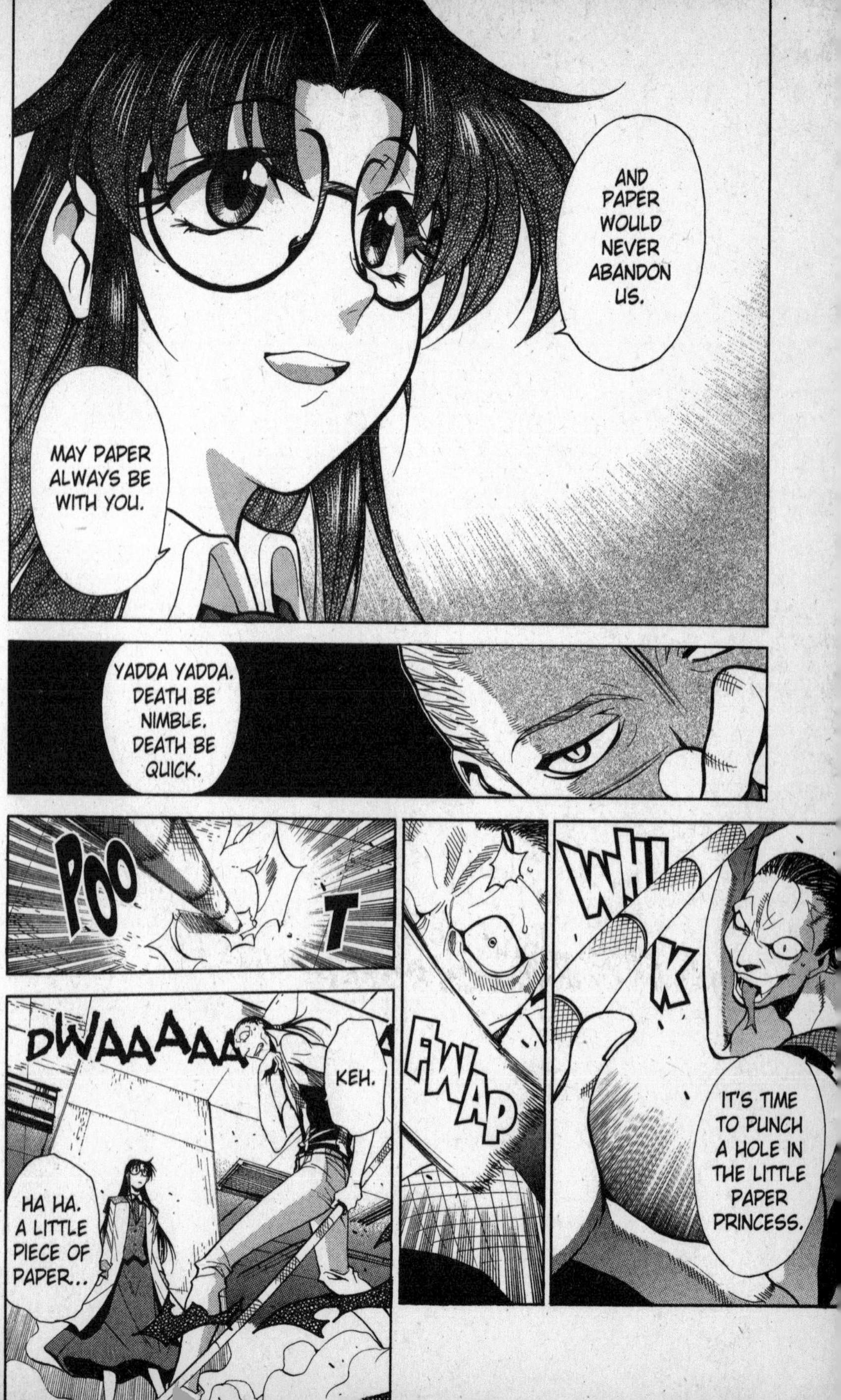
AND PAPER WOULD NEVER ABANDON US.
MAY PAPER ALWAYS BE WITH YOU.
YADDA YADDA. DEATH BE NIMBLE. DEATH BE QUICK.
WHIK
IT'S TIME TO PUNCH A HOLE IN THE LITTLE PAPER PRINCESS.
FWAP
POO T
DWAAAAAA
KEH.
HA HA. A LITTLE PIECE OF PAPER...

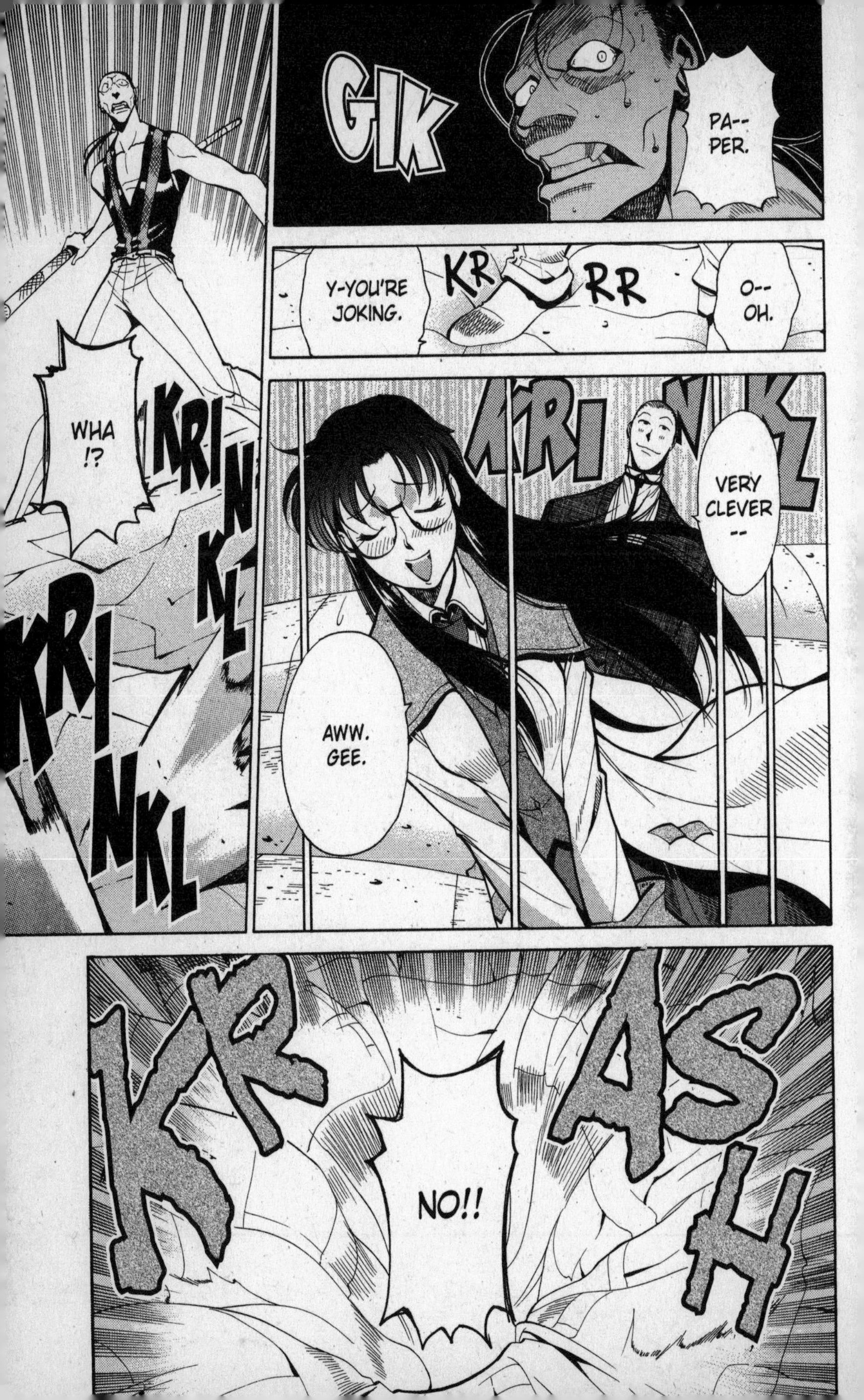
GIK
PA-- PER.
O-- OH.
KR RR
Y-YOU'RE JOKING.
KRINKL
VERY CLEVER --
AWW. GEE.
WHA !?
KRINKL
KRINKL
KRASH
NO!!

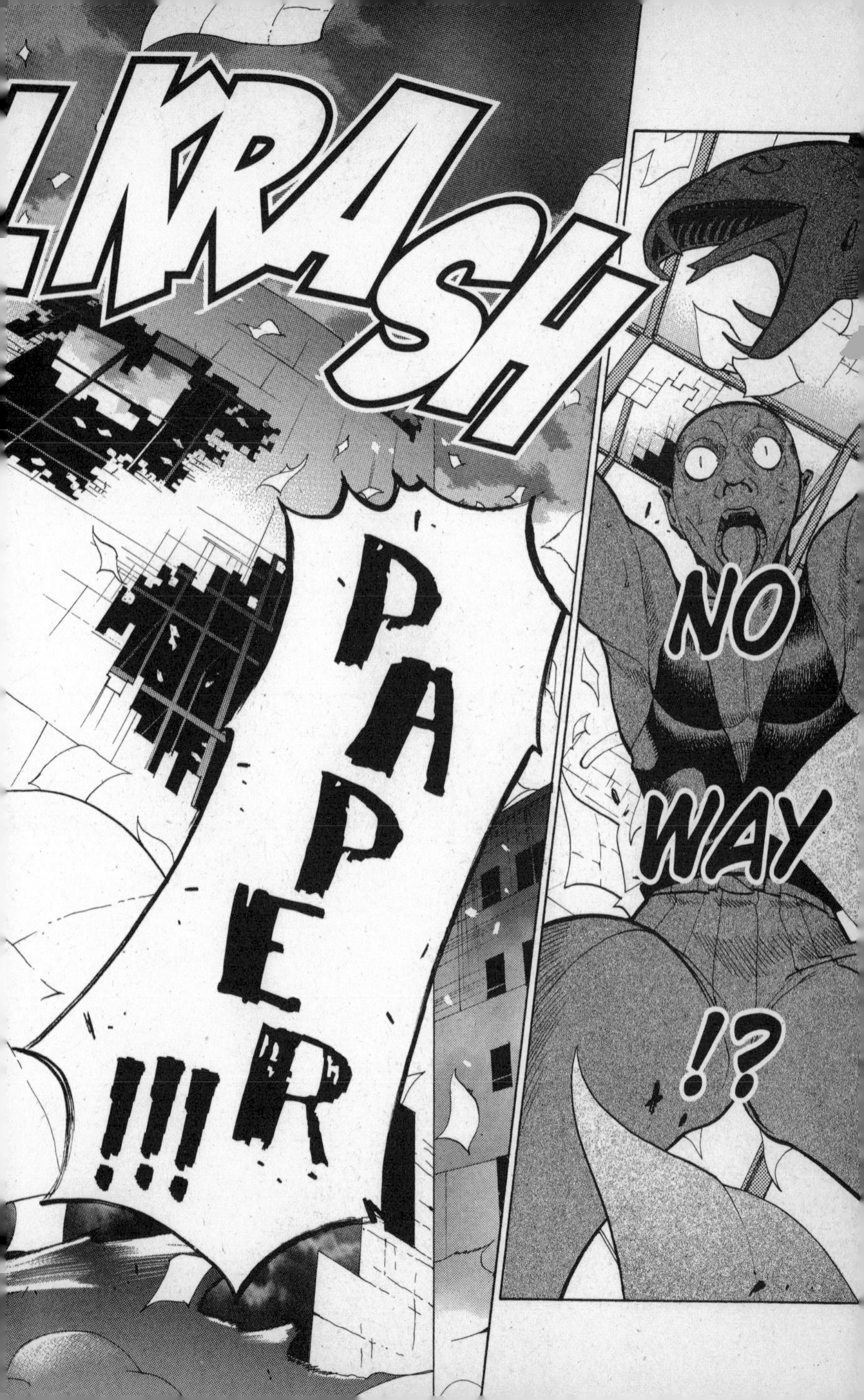
NO WAY!?
KRASH
PAPER!!!

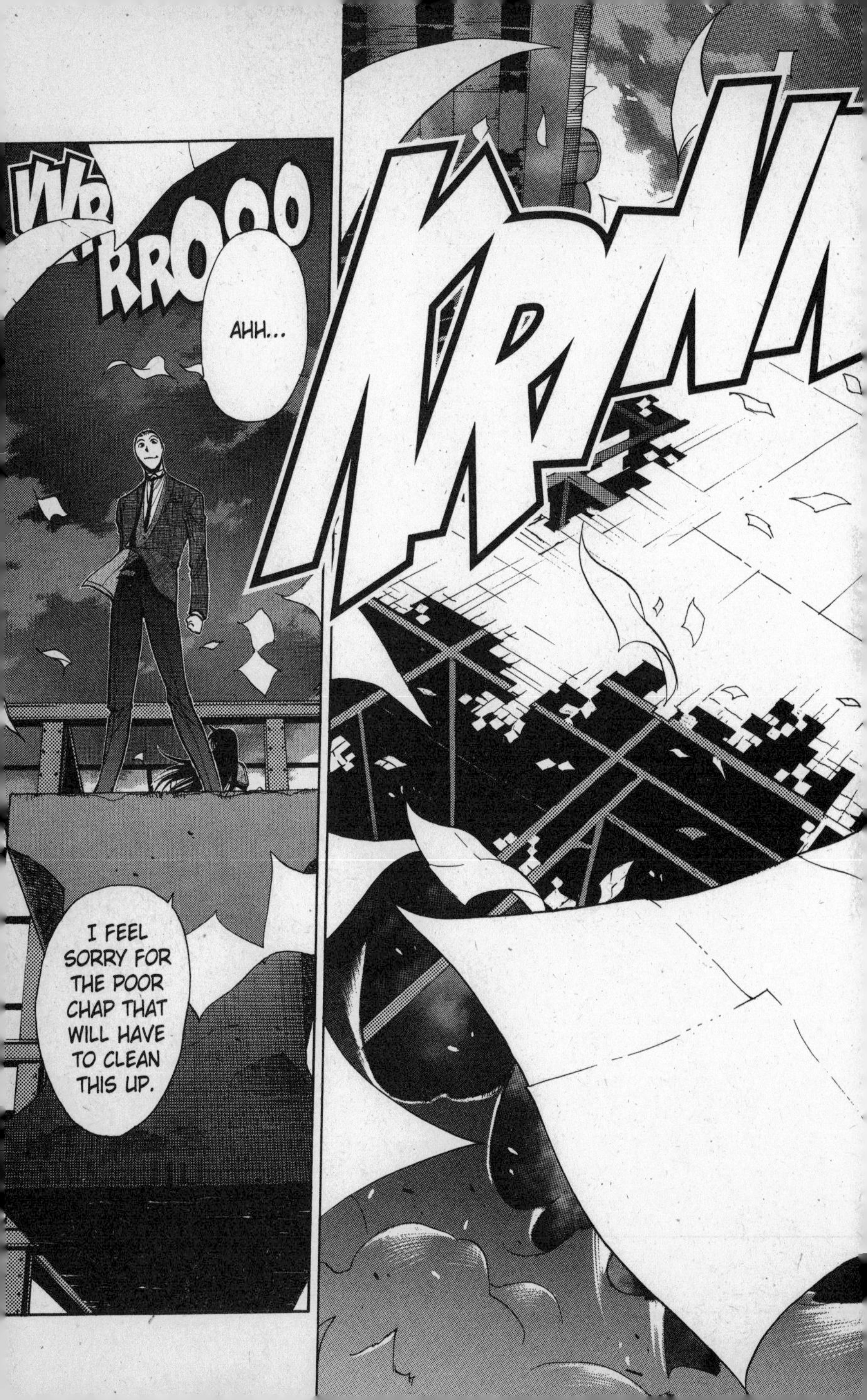
AHH...
I FEEL SORRY FOR THE POOR CHAP THAT WILL HAVE TO CLEAN THIS UP.

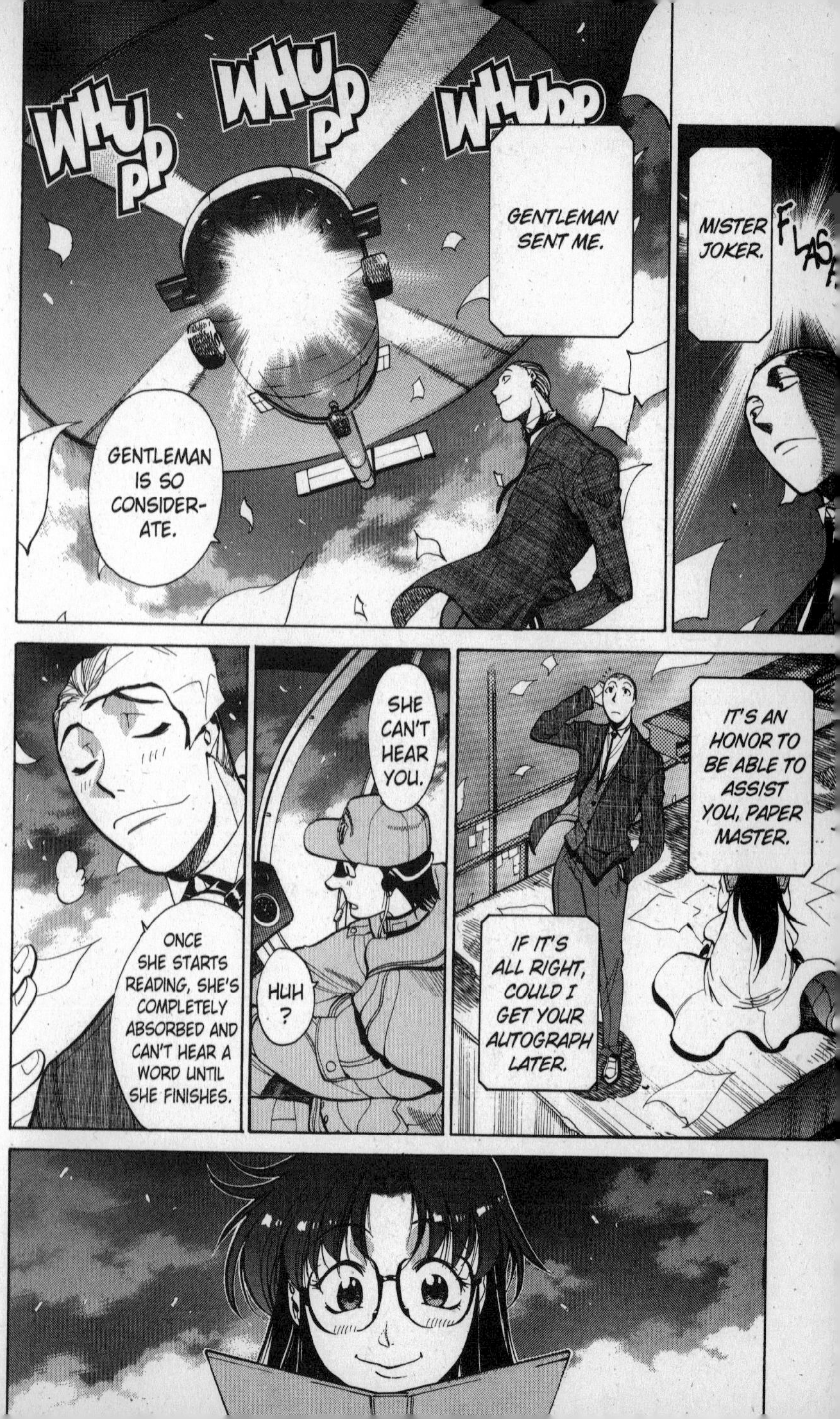
MISTER JOKER.
FLAS
WHUPP
GENTLEMAN SENT ME.
WHUPP
WHUPP
GENTLEMAN IS SO CONSIDER-ATE.
IT'S AN HONOR TO BE ABLE TO ASSIST YOU, PAPER MASTER.
IF IT'S ALL RIGHT, COULD I GET YOUR AUTOGRAPH LATER.
SHE CAN'T HEAR YOU.
HUH?
ONCE SHE STARTS READING, SHE'S COMPLETELY ABSORBED AND CAN'T HEAR A WORD UNTIL SHE FINISHES.

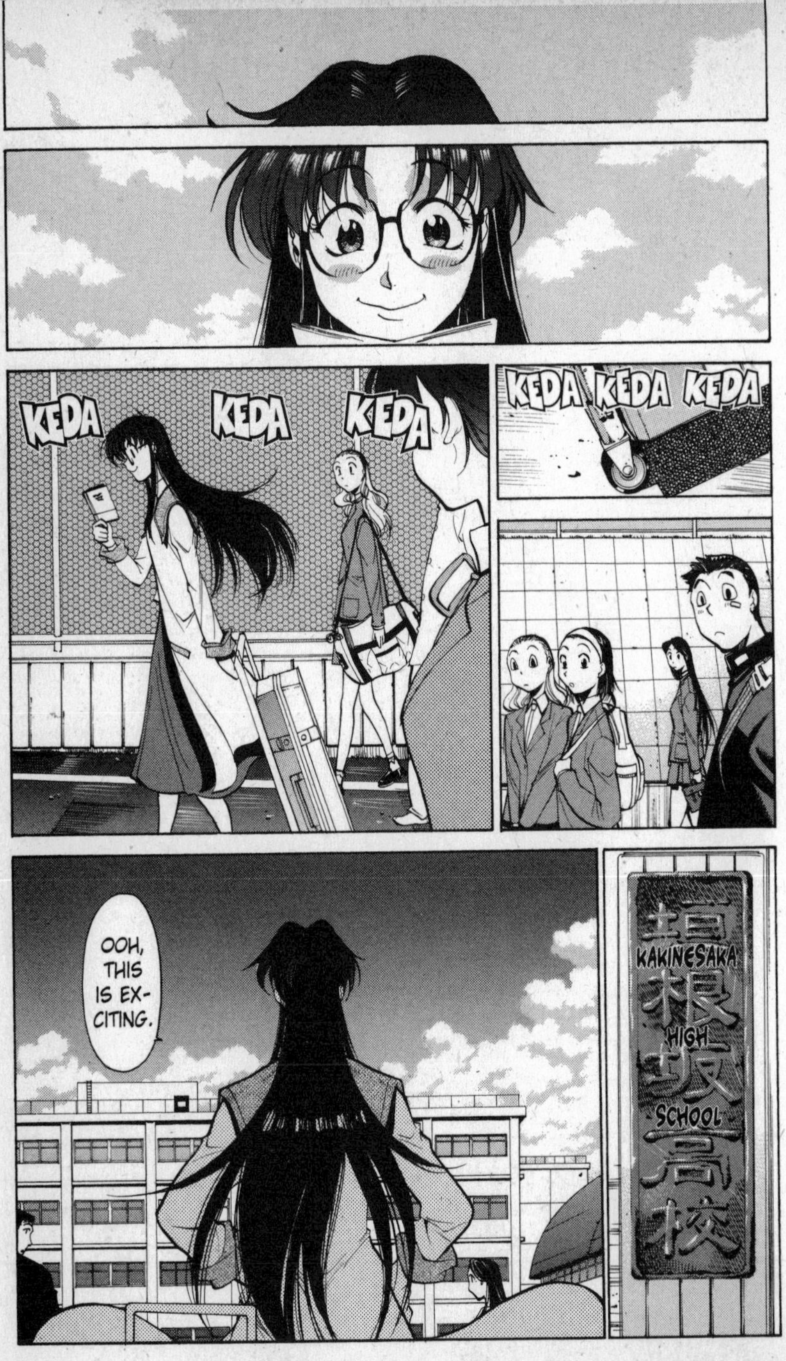
KEDA KEDA KEDA
KEDA
KEDA
KEDA
垣根坂高校
KAKINESAKA HIGH SCHOOL
OOH, THIS IS EX-CITING.

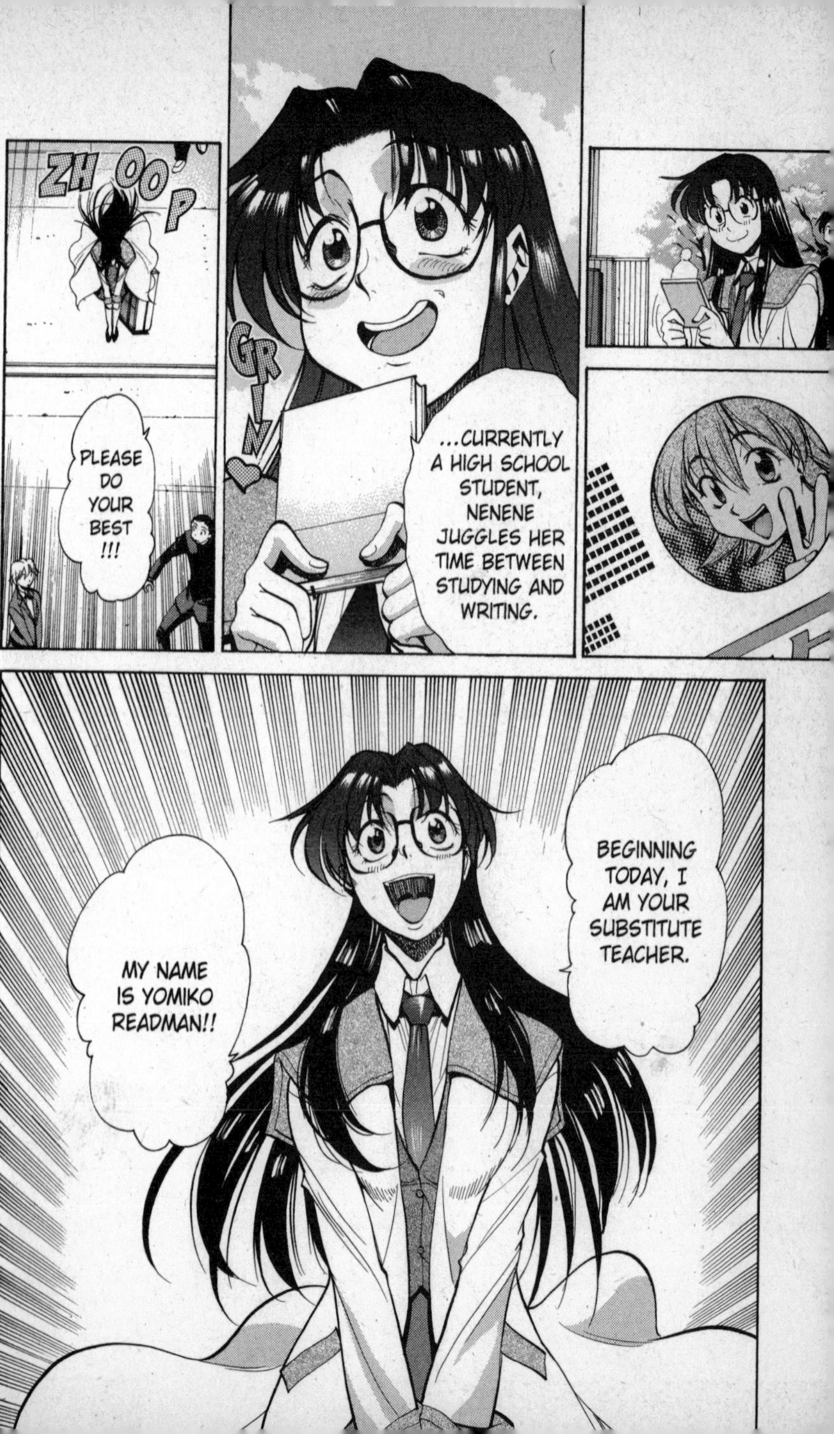
GRIN
...CURRENTLY A HIGH SCHOOL STUDENT, NENENE JUGGLES HER TIME BETWEEN STUDYING AND WRITING.
ZHOOP
PLEASE DO YOUR BEST!!!
BEGINNING TODAY, I AM YOUR SUBSTITUTE TEACHER.
MY NAME IS YOMIKO READMAN!!

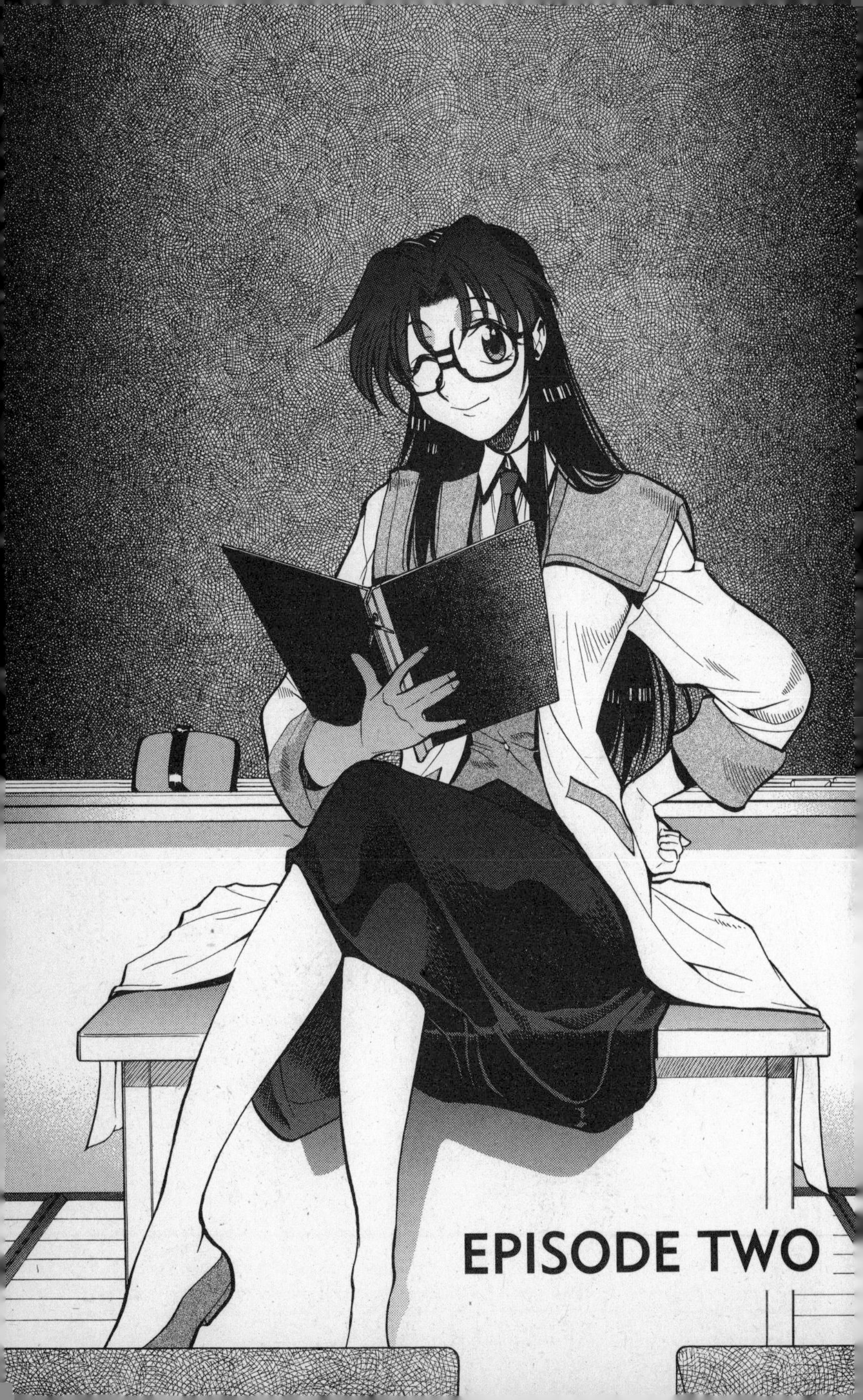

EPISODE TWO

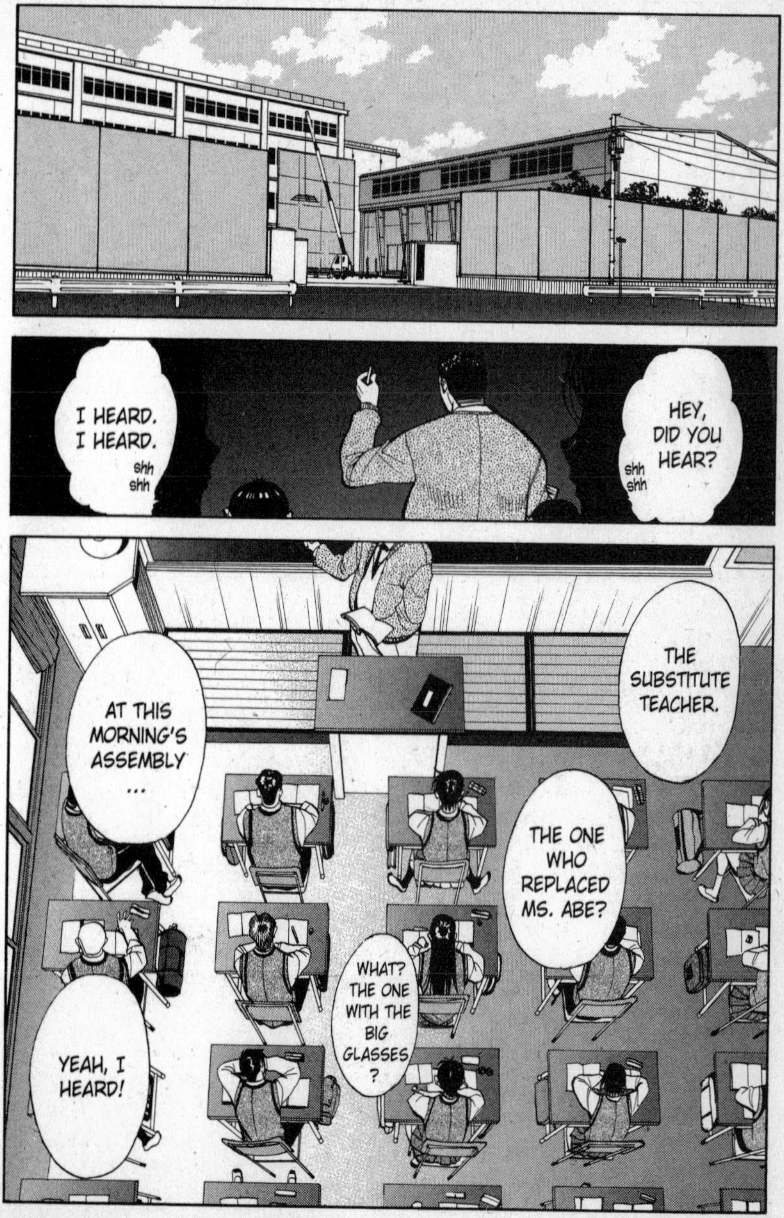
HEY, DID YOU HEAR?
shh shh
I HEARD. I HEARD.
shh shh
THE SUBSTITUTE TEACHER.
AT THIS MORNING'S ASSEMBLY ...
THE ONE WHO REPLACED MS. ABE?
WHAT? THE ONE WITH THE BIG GLASSES ?
YEAH, I HEARD!

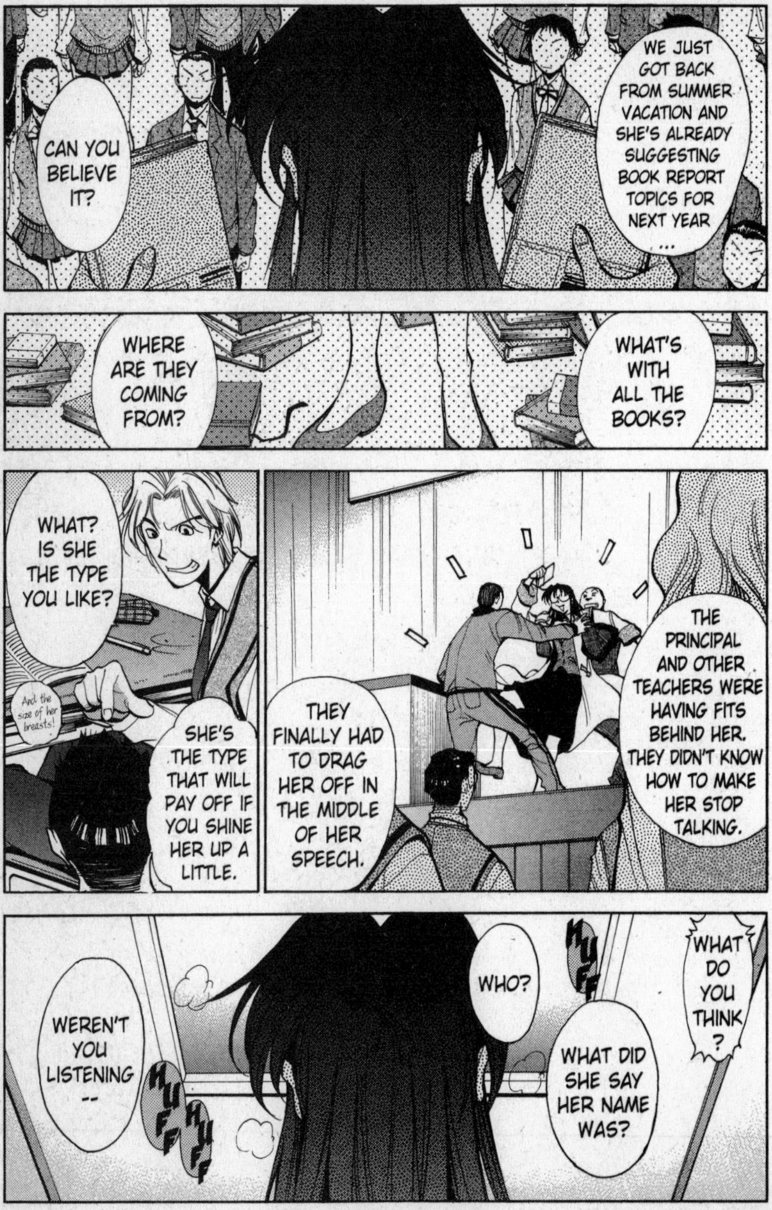
WE JUST GOT BACK FROM SUMMER VACATION AND SHE'S ALREADY SUGGESTING BOOK REPORT TOPICS FOR NEXT YEAR ...
CAN YOU BELIEVE IT?
WHAT'S WITH ALL THE BOOKS?
WHERE ARE THEY COMING FROM?
THE PRINCIPAL AND OTHER TEACHERS WERE HAVING FITS BEHIND HER. THEY DIDN'T KNOW HOW TO MAKE HER STOP TALKING.
THEY FINALLY HAD TO DRAG HER OFF IN THE MIDDLE OF HER SPEECH.
WHAT? IS SHE THE TYPE YOU LIKE?
And the size of her breasts!
SHE'S THE TYPE THAT WILL PAY OFF IF YOU SHINE HER UP A LITTLE.
WHAT DO YOU THINK?
HUFF
WHO?
WHAT DID SHE SAY HER NAME WAS?
WEREN'T YOU LISTENING --
HUFF
HUFF

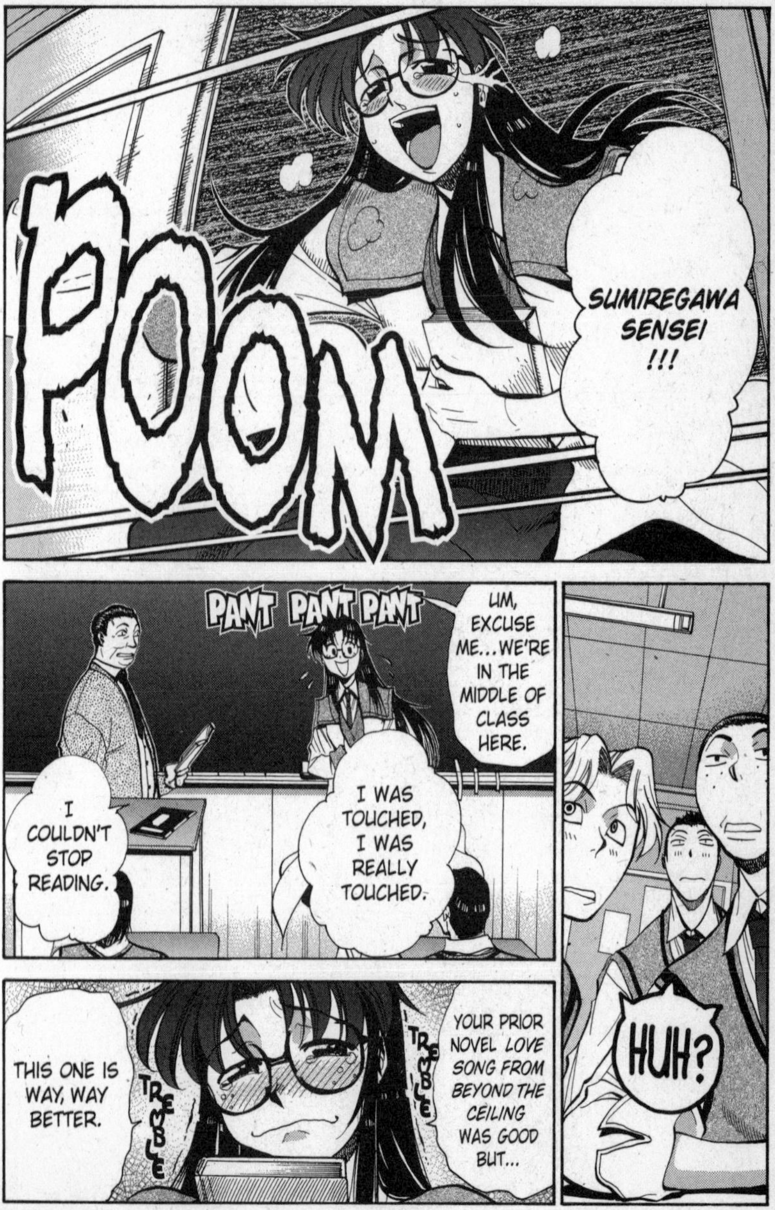
SUMIREGAWA SENSEI !!!
POOM
HUH?
UM, EXCUSE ME...WE'RE IN THE MIDDLE OF CLASS HERE.
PANT PANT PANT
I WAS TOUCHED, I WAS REALLY TOUCHED.
I COULDN'T STOP READING.
YOUR PRIOR NOVEL *LOVE SONG FROM BEYOND THE CEILING* WAS GOOD BUT...
TREMBLE
THIS ONE IS WAY, WAY BETTER.
TREMBLE

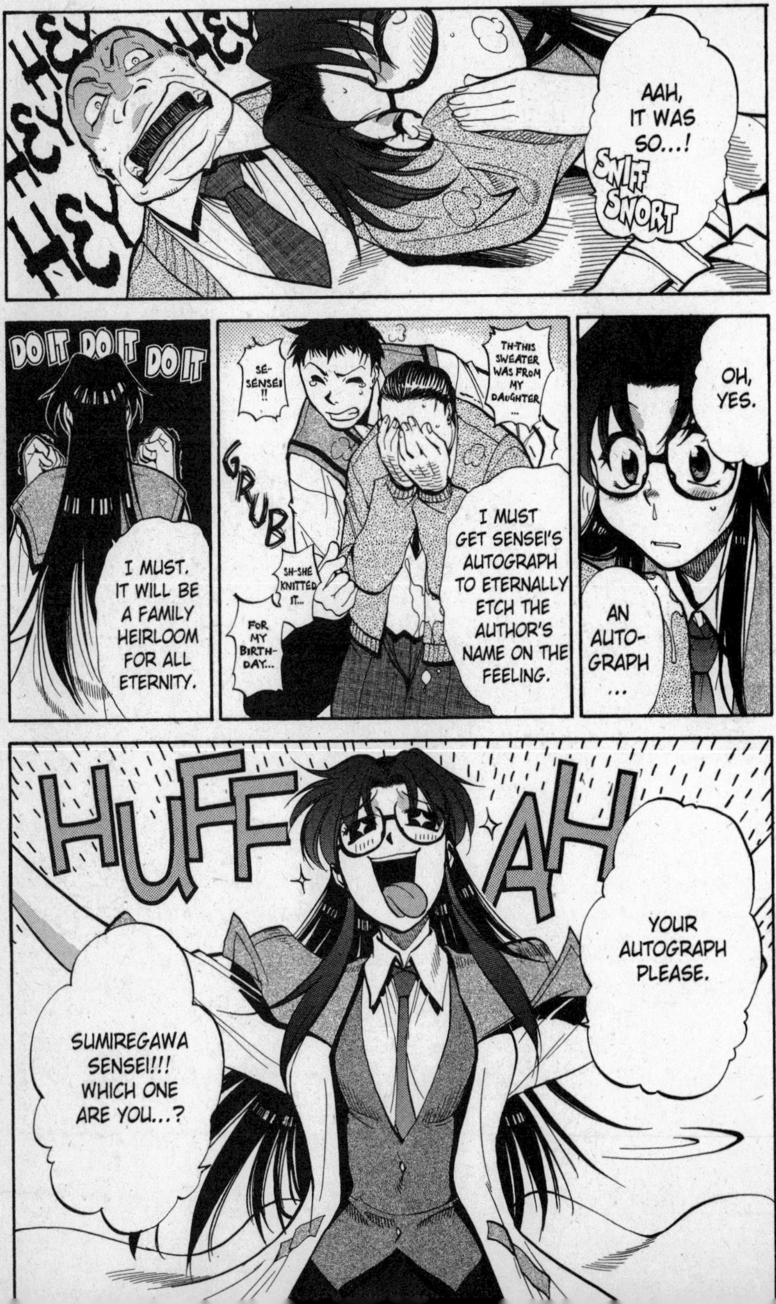
AAH, IT WAS SO...!
SNIFF SNORT
HEY HEY HEY HEY HEY HEY
OH, YES.
AN AUTO-GRAPH ...
TH-THIS SWEATER WAS FROM MY DAUGHTER ...
SE-SENSEI !!
I MUST GET SENSEI'S AUTOGRAPH TO ETERNALLY ETCH THE AUTHOR'S NAME ON THE FEELING.
GRUB
SH-SHE KNITTED IT...
FOR MY BIRTH-DAY...
DO IT DO IT DO IT
I MUST. IT WILL BE A FAMILY HEIRLOOM FOR ALL ETERNITY.
HUFF
AH
YOUR AUTOGRAPH PLEASE.
SUMIREGAWA SENSEI!!! WHICH ONE ARE YOU...?

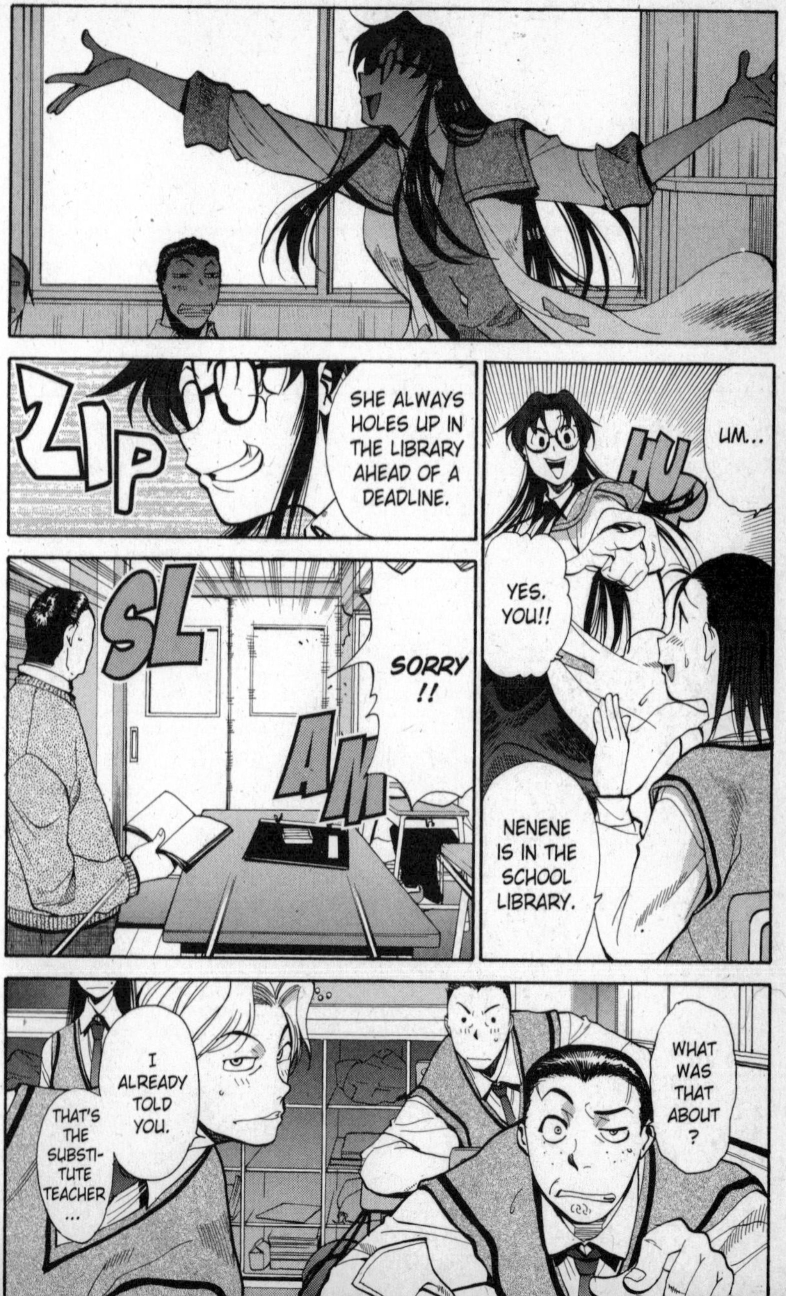
UM...
HU
YES. YOU!!
NENENE IS IN THE SCHOOL LIBRARY.
ZIP
SHE ALWAYS HOLES UP IN THE LIBRARY AHEAD OF A DEADLINE.
SL
AM
SORRY !!
WHAT WAS THAT ABOUT ?
I ALREADY TOLD YOU.
THAT'S THE SUBSTI- TUTE TEACHER ...

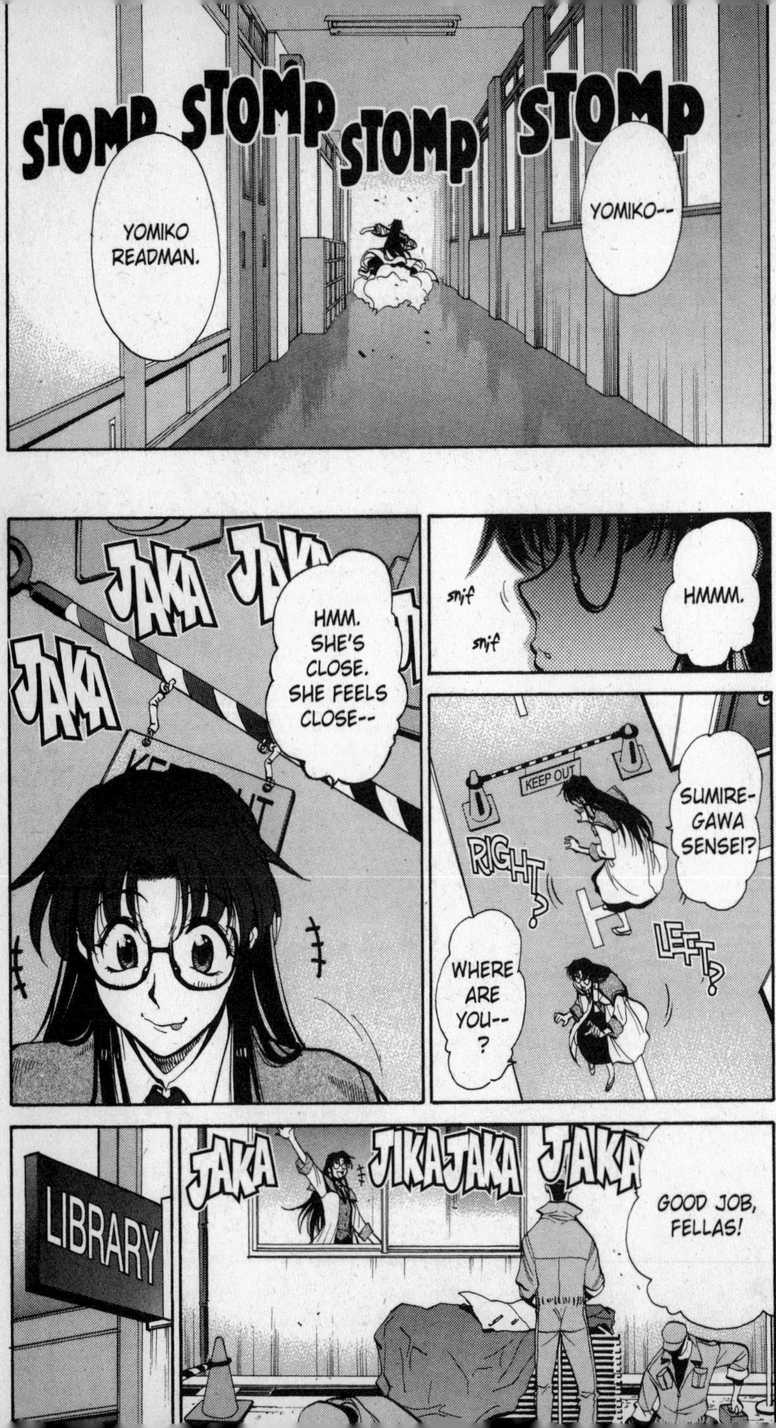
STOMP
STOMP
STOMP
STOMP
YOMIKO--
YOMIKO READMAN.
HMMM.
snif
snif
SUMIRE-GAWA SENSEI?
RIGHT?
LEFT?
WHERE ARE YOU--?
HMM. SHE'S CLOSE. SHE FEELS CLOSE--
JAKA
JAKA
JAKA
GOOD JOB, FELLAS!
JAKA
JAKA
JIKA
JAKA
LIBRARY

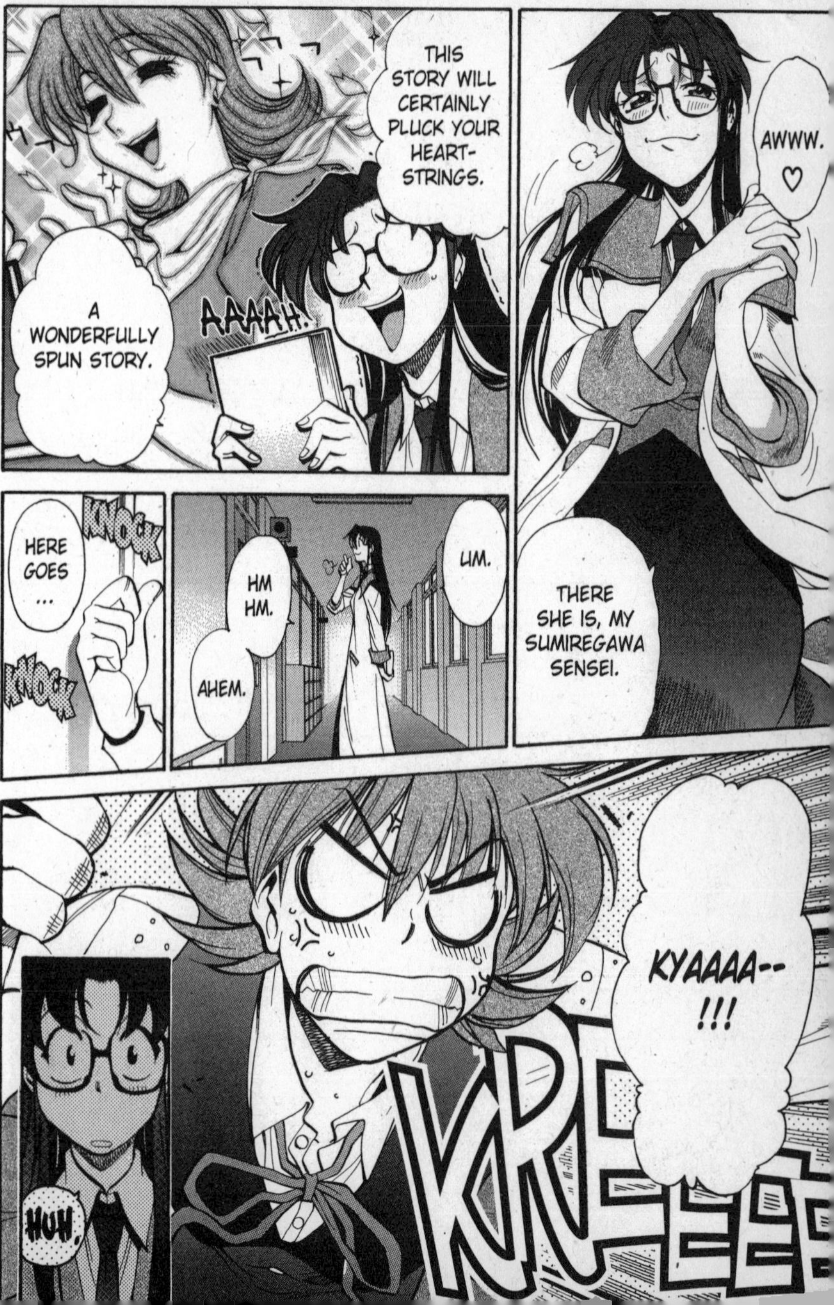
AWWW. ♡
THERE SHE IS, MY SUMIREGAWA SENSEI.
THIS STORY WILL CERTAINLY PLUCK YOUR HEART-STRINGS.
A WONDERFULLY SPUN STORY.
AAAAH.
UM.
HM HM.
AHEM.
KNOCK
HERE GOES ...
KNOCK
KYAAAA-- !!!
KREEE
HUH.

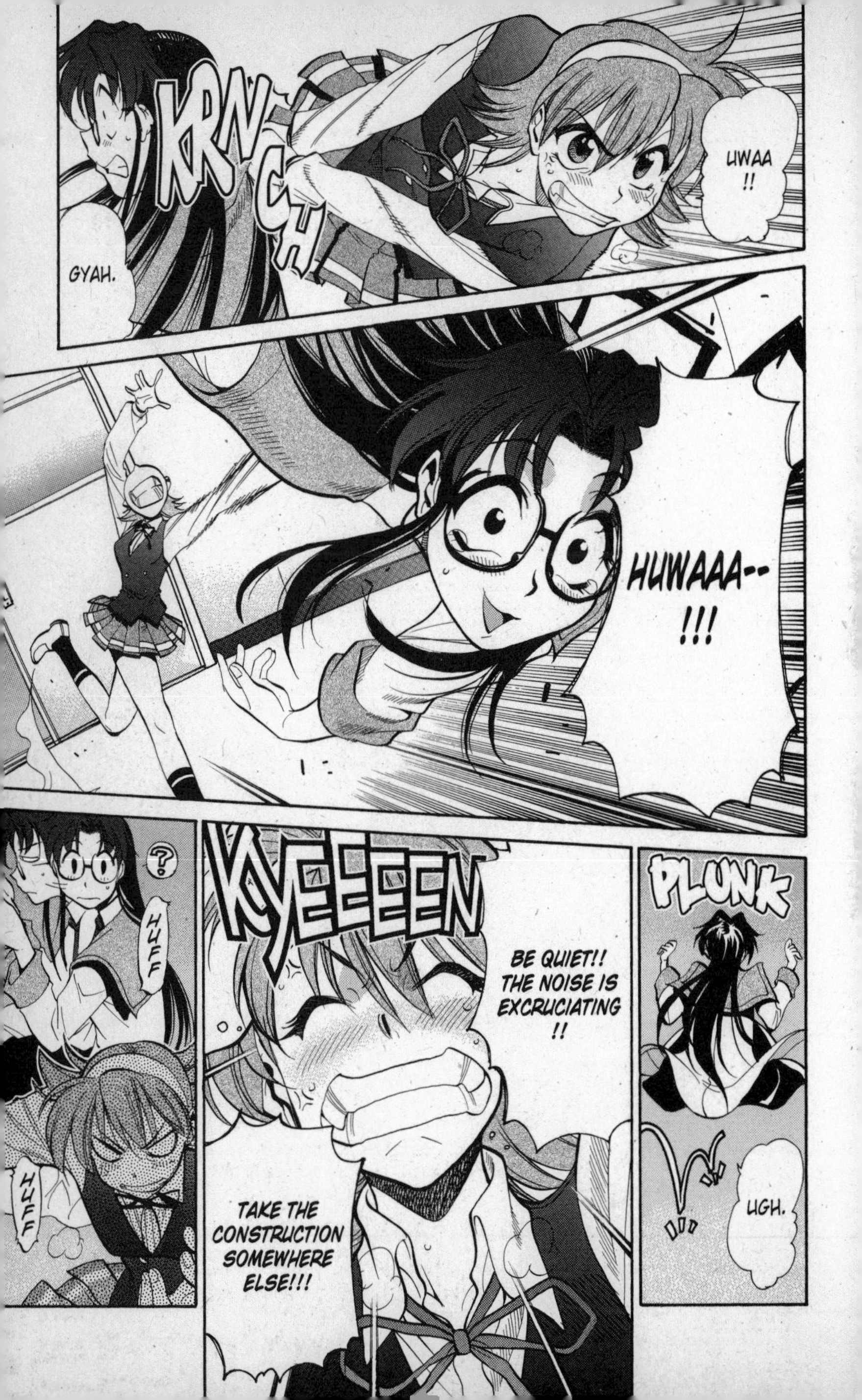
UWAA !!
KRNCH
GYAH.
HUWAAA-- !!!
PLUNK
UGH.
KYEEEEN
BE QUIET!! THE NOISE IS EXCRUCIATING !!
TAKE THE CONSTRUCTION SOMEWHERE ELSE!!!
?
HUFF
HUFF

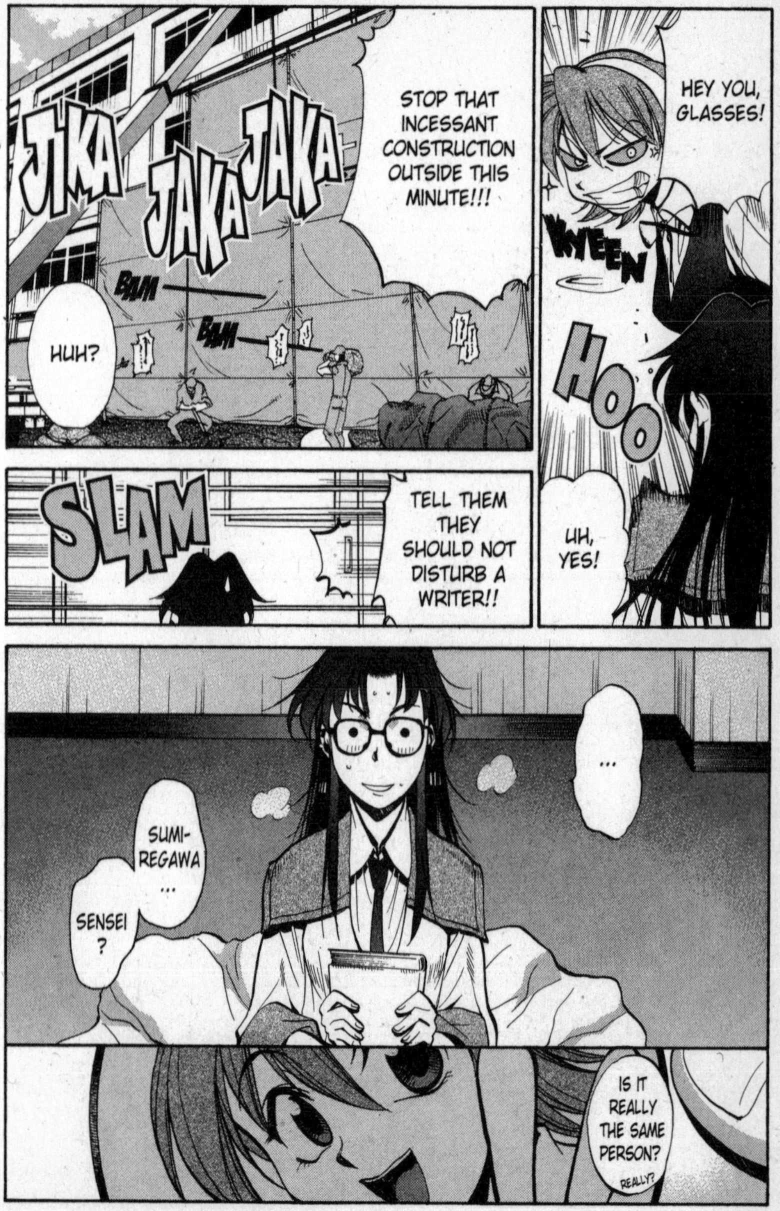
HEY YOU, GLASSES!
WYEEN
HOO
UH, YES!
STOP THAT INCESSANT CONSTRUCTION OUTSIDE THIS MINUTE!!!
JAKA
JAKA
JIKA
BAM
BAM
HUH?
TELL THEM THEY SHOULD NOT DISTURB A WRITER!!
SLAM
...
SUMI-REGAWA ...
SENSEI ?
IS IT REALLY THE SAME PERSON?
REALLY?

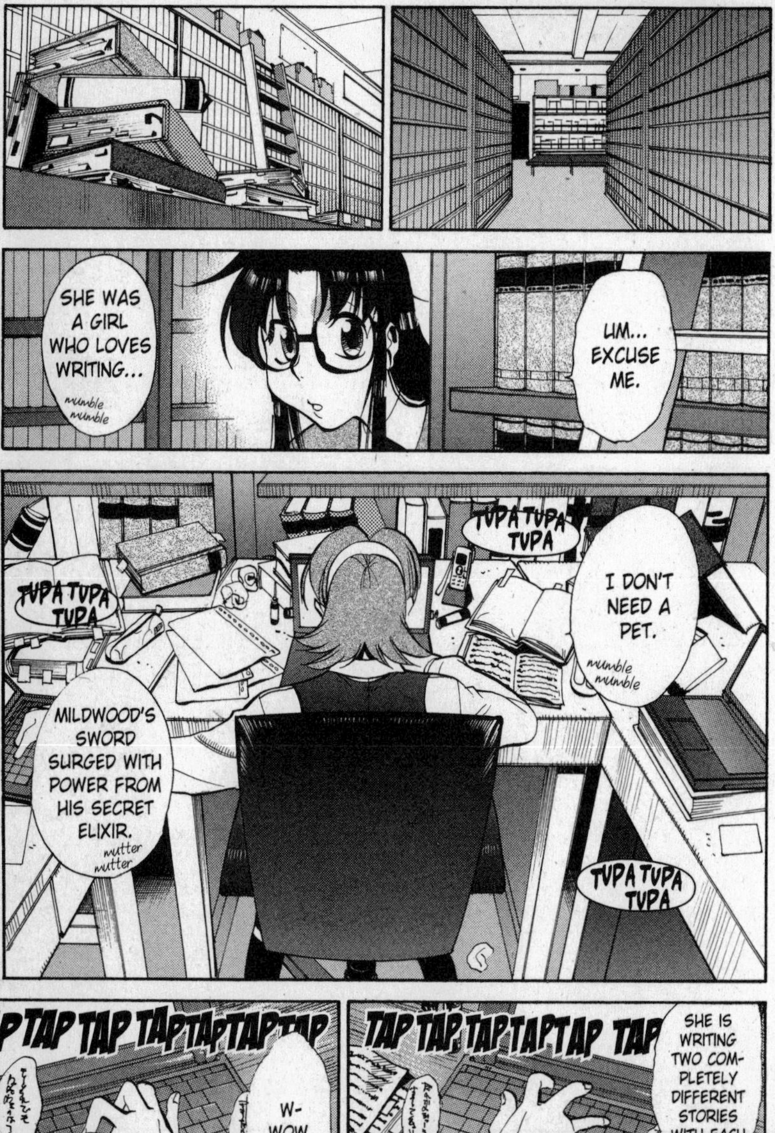
UM... EXCUSE ME.
SHE WAS A GIRL WHO LOVES WRITING...
mumble mumble
TUPA TUPA TUPA
I DON'T NEED A PET.
mumble mumble
TUPA TUPA TUPA
MILDWOOD'S SWORD SURGED WITH POWER FROM HIS SECRET ELIXIR.
mutter mutter
TUPA TUPA TUPA
TAP TAP TAP TAPTAP TAP
SHE IS WRITING TWO COMPLETELY DIFFERENT STORIES WITH EACH HAND...
TAP TAP TAP TAPTAPTAPTAP
W-WOW.

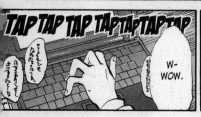

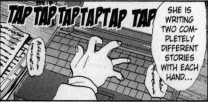

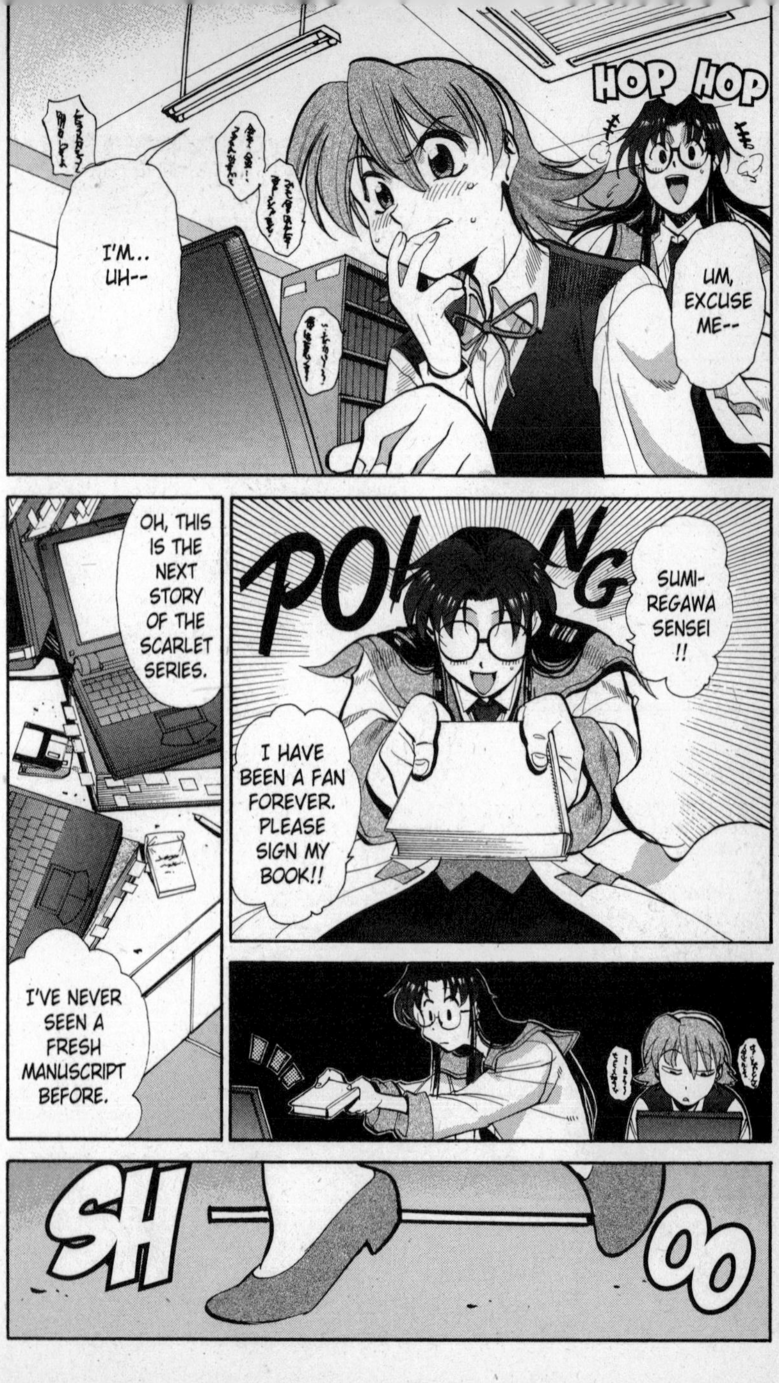
HOP HOP
UM, EXCUSE ME--
I'M.. UH--
POING
SUMI-REGAWA SENSEI !!
I HAVE BEEN A FAN FOREVER. PLEASE SIGN MY BOOK!!
OH, THIS IS THE NEXT STORY OF THE SCARLET SERIES.
I'VE NEVER SEEN A FRESH MANUSCRIPT BEFORE.
SH--OO

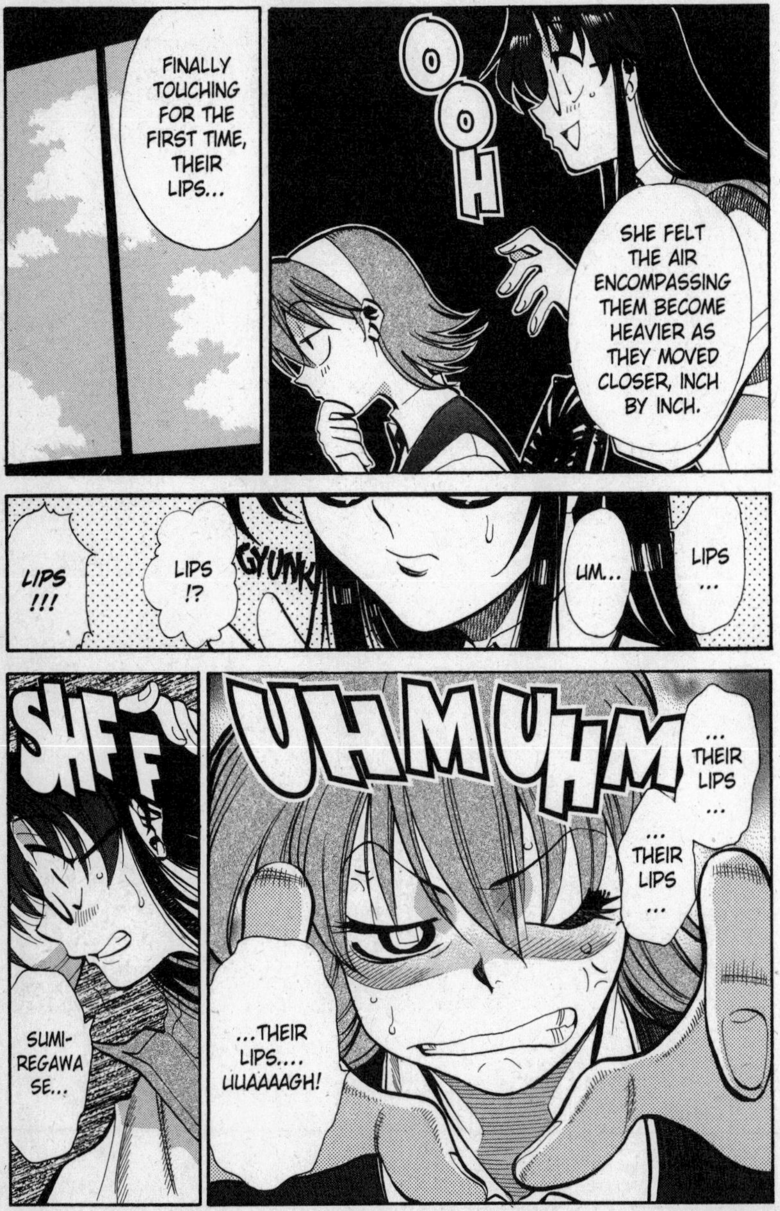
OOOH
SHE FELT THE AIR ENCOMPASSING THEM BECOME HEAVIER AS THEY MOVED CLOSER, INCH BY INCH.
FINALLY TOUCHING FOR THE FIRST TIME, THEIR LIPS...
LIPS ...
UM...
GYUNK
LIPS !?
LIPS !!!
UHM UHM
... THEIR LIPS ...
... THEIR LIPS ...
...THEIR LIPS.... UUAAAAGH!
SHFF
SUMI-REGAWA SE...

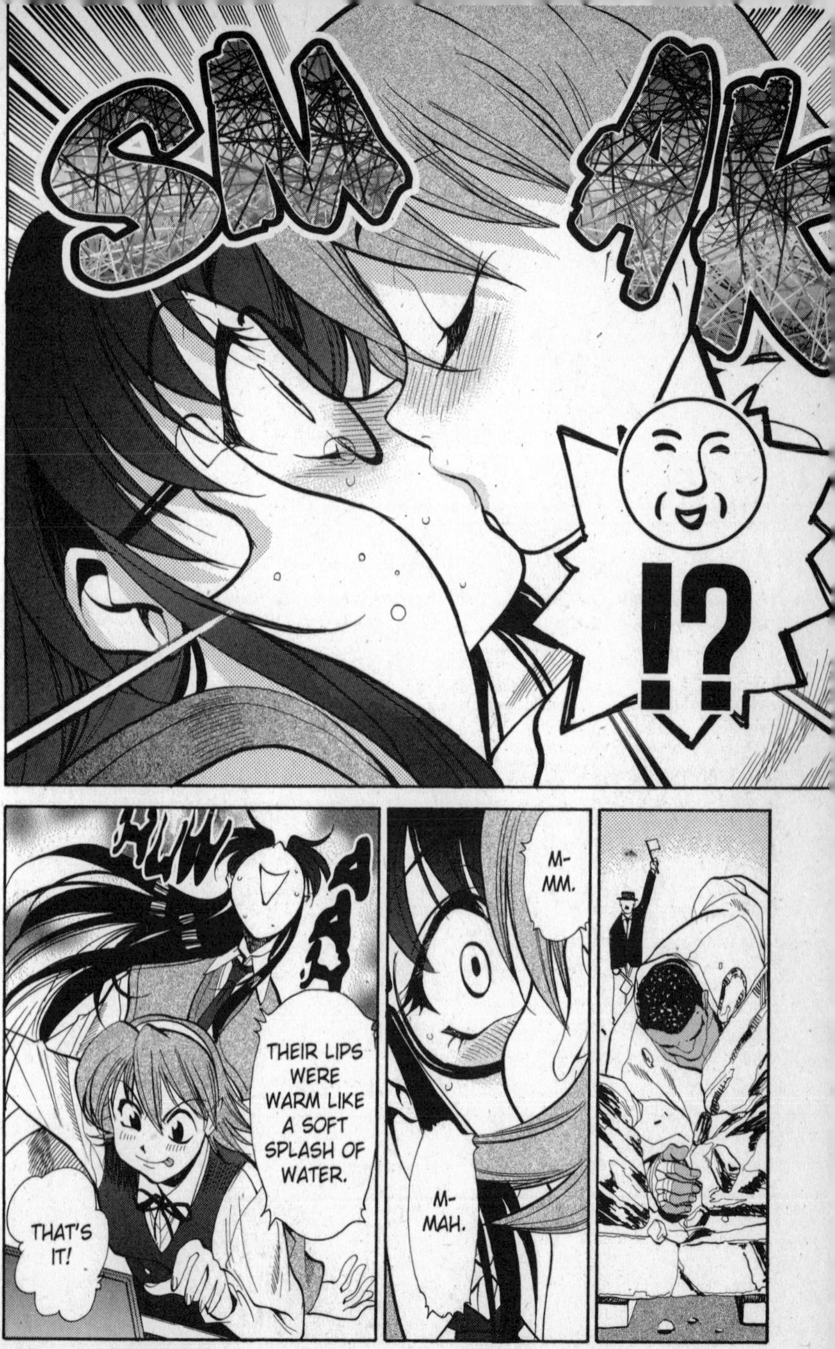
!?
M-MM.
M-MAH.
THEIR LIPS WERE WARM LIKE A SOFT SPLASH OF WATER.
THAT'S IT!

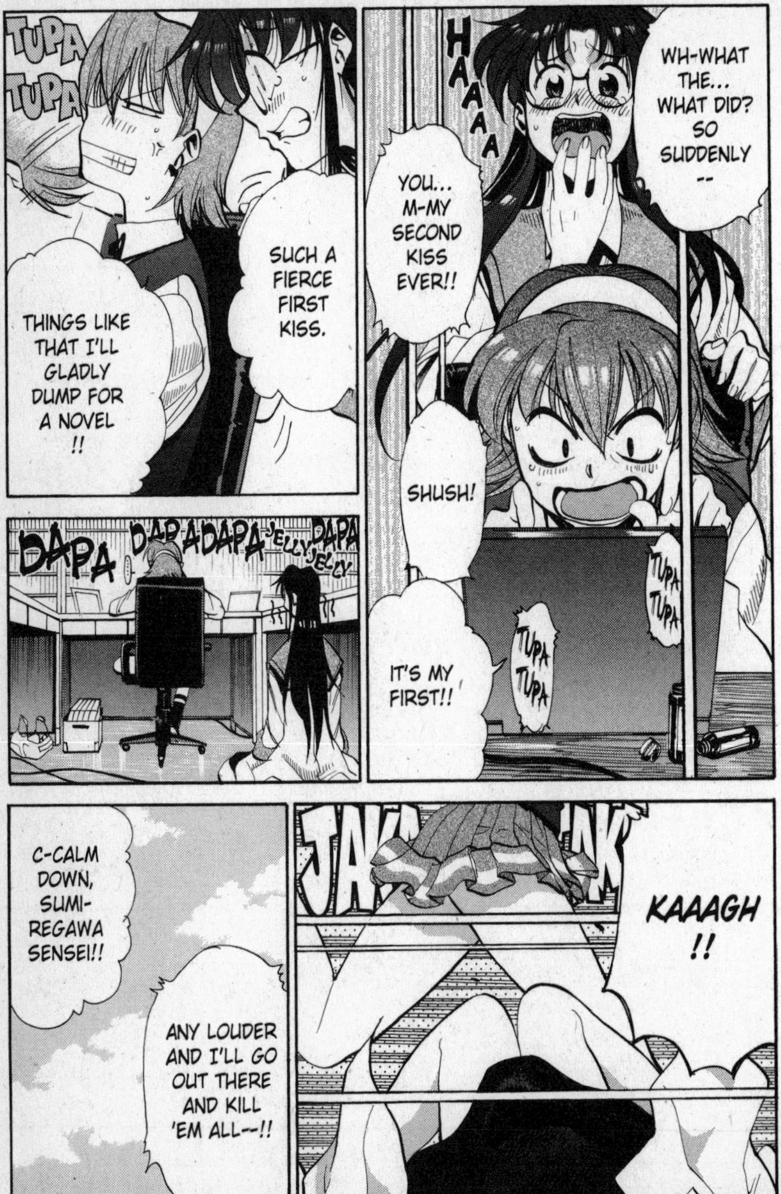
HAAAA
WH-WHAT THE... WHAT DID? SO SUDDENLY --
YOU... M-MY SECOND KISS EVER!!
SHUSH!
TUPA TUPA
TUPA TUPA
IT'S MY FIRST!!
TUPA TUPA
SUCH A FIERCE FIRST KISS.
THINGS LIKE THAT I'LL GLADLY DUMP FOR A NOVEL !!
DAPA DADADAPA JELLY JELLY DAPA
KAAAGH !!
C-CALM DOWN, SUMI-REGAWA SENSEI!!
ANY LOUDER AND I'LL GO OUT THERE AND KILL 'EM ALL--!!

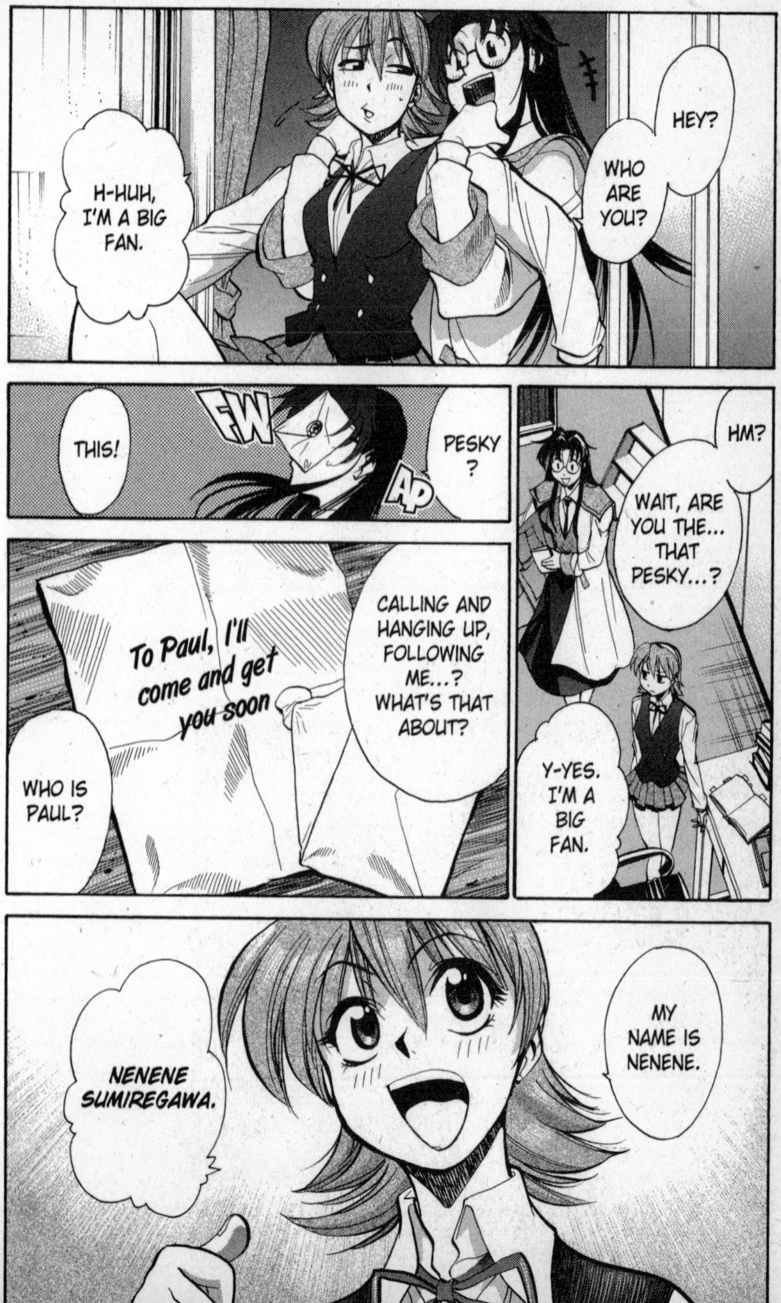
HEY?
WHO ARE YOU?
H-HUH, I'M A BIG FAN.
HM?
WAIT, ARE YOU THE... THAT PESKY...?
Y-YES. I'M A BIG FAN.
PESKY ?
FWAP
THIS!
CALLING AND HANGING UP, FOLLOWING ME...? WHAT'S THAT ABOUT?
To Paul, I'll come and get you soon
WHO IS PAUL?
MY NAME IS NENENE.
NENENE SUMIREGAWA.

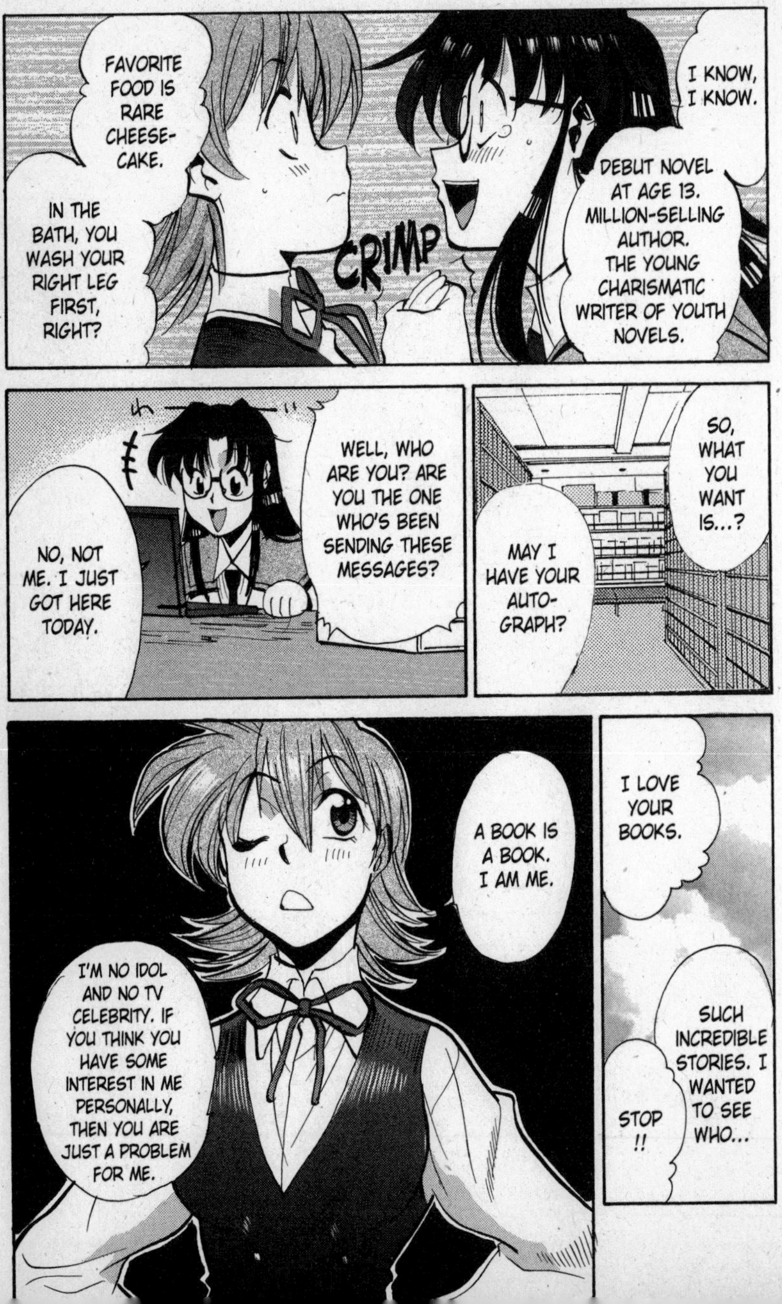
I KNOW, I KNOW.
DEBUT NOVEL AT AGE 13. MILLION-SELLING AUTHOR. THE YOUNG CHARISMATIC WRITER OF YOUTH NOVELS.
FAVORITE FOOD IS RARE CHEESE-CAKE.
CRIMP
IN THE BATH, YOU WASH YOUR RIGHT LEG FIRST, RIGHT?
SO, WHAT YOU WANT IS...?
MAY I HAVE YOUR AUTO-GRAPH?
WELL, WHO ARE YOU? ARE YOU THE ONE WHO'S BEEN SENDING THESE MESSAGES?
NO, NOT ME. I JUST GOT HERE TODAY.
I LOVE YOUR BOOKS.
SUCH INCREDIBLE STORIES. I WANTED TO SEE WHO...
STOP !!
A BOOK IS A BOOK. I AM ME.
I'M NO IDOL AND NO TV CELEBRITY. IF YOU THINK YOU HAVE SOME INTEREST IN ME PERSONALLY, THEN YOU ARE JUST A PROBLEM FOR ME.

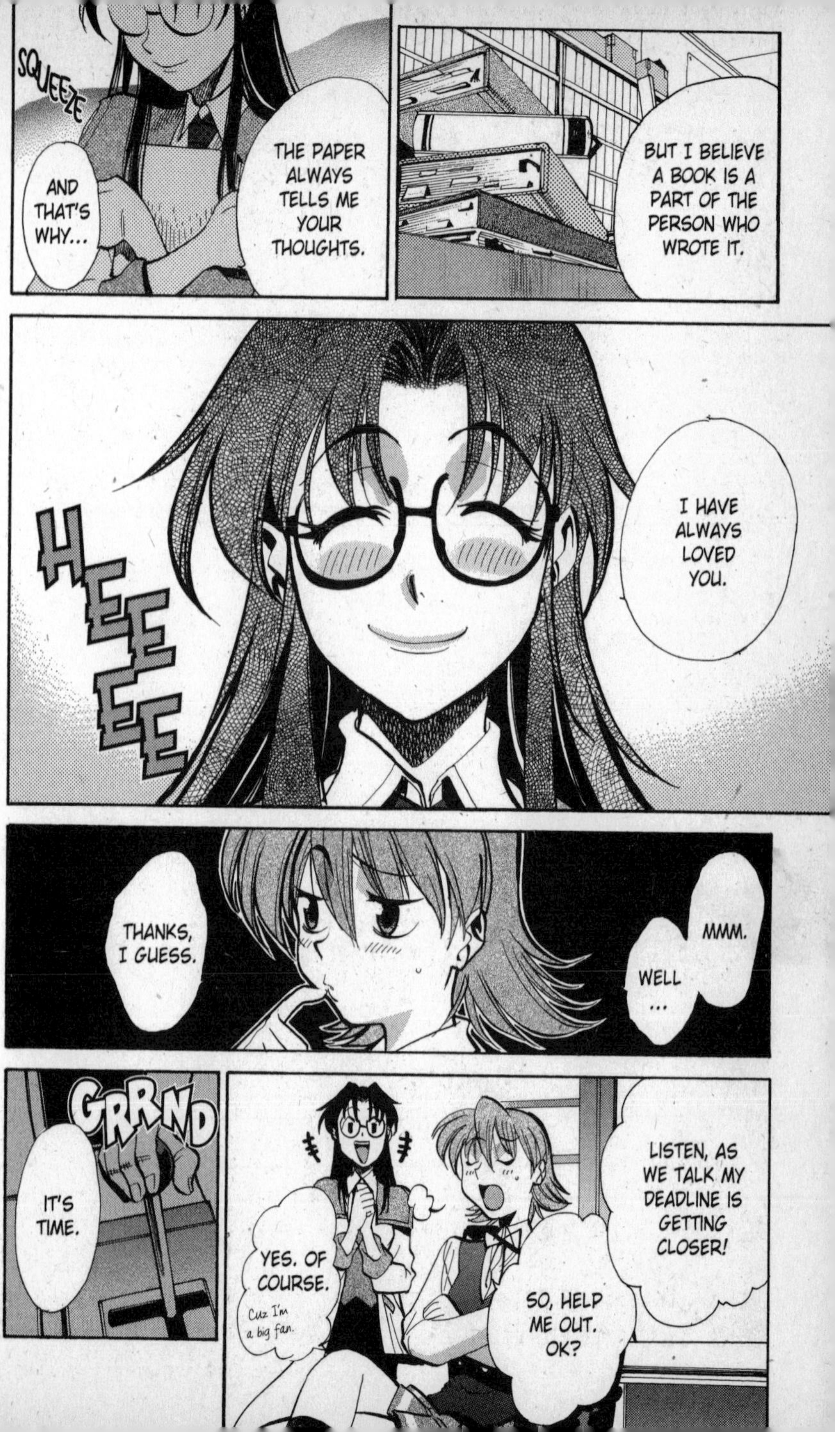
BUT I BELIEVE A BOOK IS A PART OF THE PERSON WHO WROTE IT.
THE PAPER ALWAYS TELLS ME YOUR THOUGHTS.
SQUEEZE
AND THAT'S WHY...
I HAVE ALWAYS LOVED YOU.
HEEEEE
MMM.
WELL ...
THANKS, I GUESS.
LISTEN, AS WE TALK MY DEADLINE IS GETTING CLOSER!
SO, HELP ME OUT. OK?
YES. OF COURSE.
Cuz I'm a big fan.
GRRND
IT'S TIME.

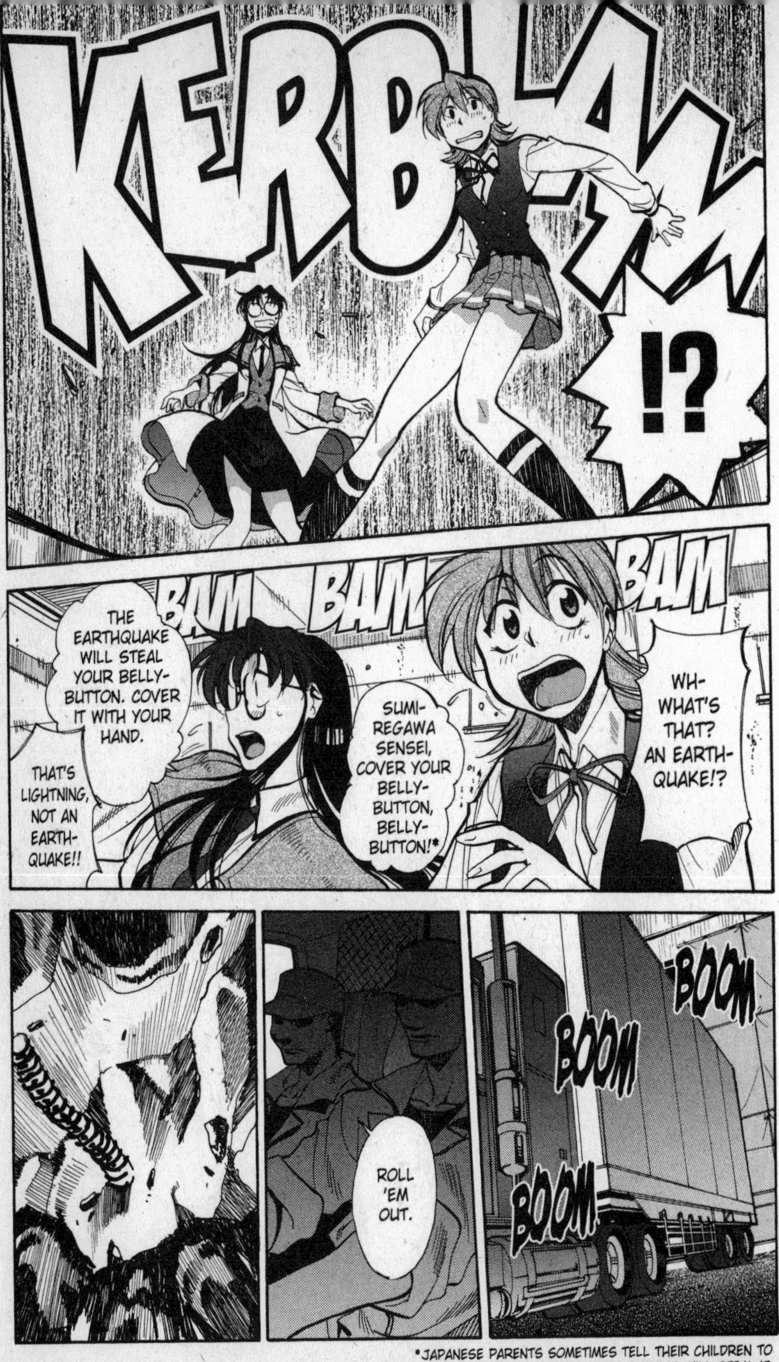
KERBLAM
!?
BAM BAM BAM
WH-WHAT'S THAT? AN EARTHQUAKE!?
SUMIREGAWA SENSEI, COVER YOUR BELLYBUTTON, BELLYBUTTON!*
THE EARTHQUAKE WILL STEAL YOUR BELLYBUTTON. COVER IT WITH YOUR HAND.
THAT'S LIGHTNING, NOT AN EARTHQUAKE!!
BOOM
BOOM
BOOM
ROLL 'EM OUT.

*JAPANESE PARENTS SOMETIMES TELL THEIR CHILDREN TO COVER THEIR BELLYBUTTONS OR LIGHTNING WILL STEAL IT.

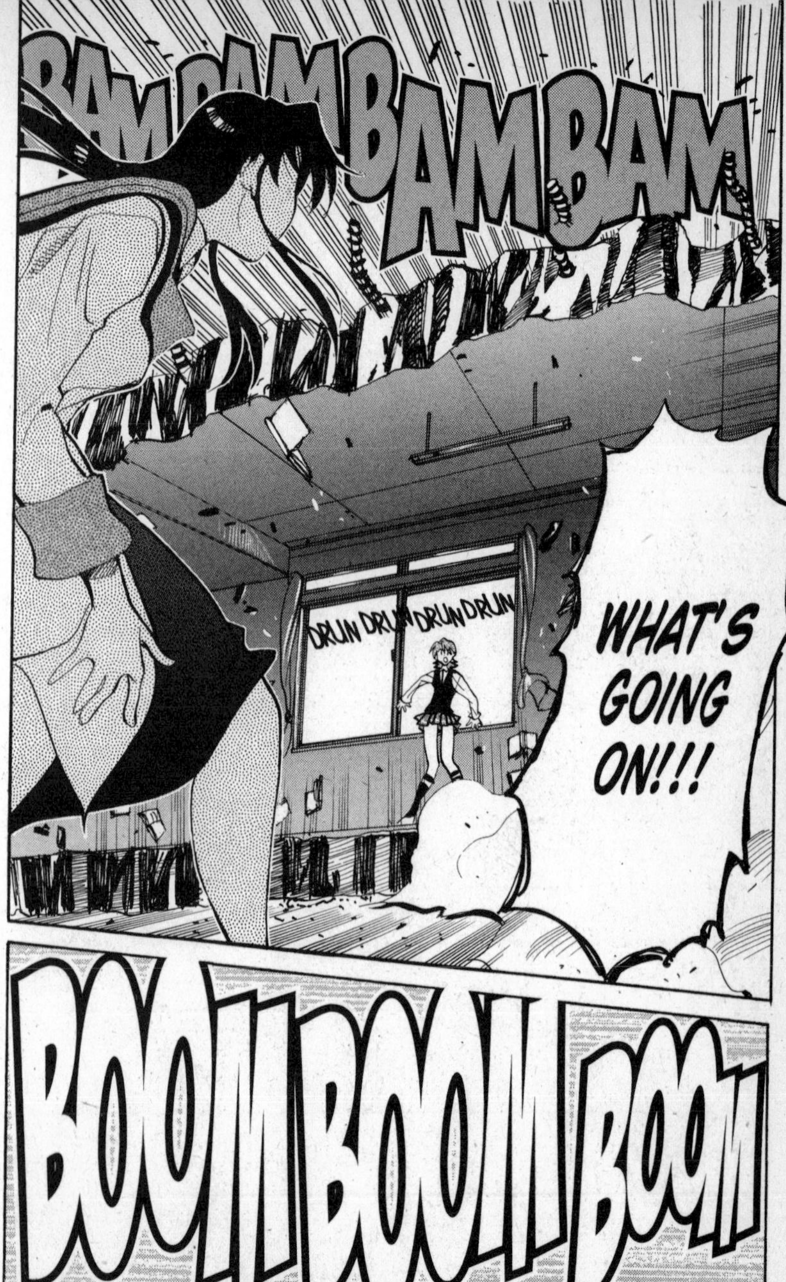
BAM BAM BAM BAM
WHAT'S GOING ON!!!
DRUN DRUN DRUN DRUN
BOOM BOOM BOOM

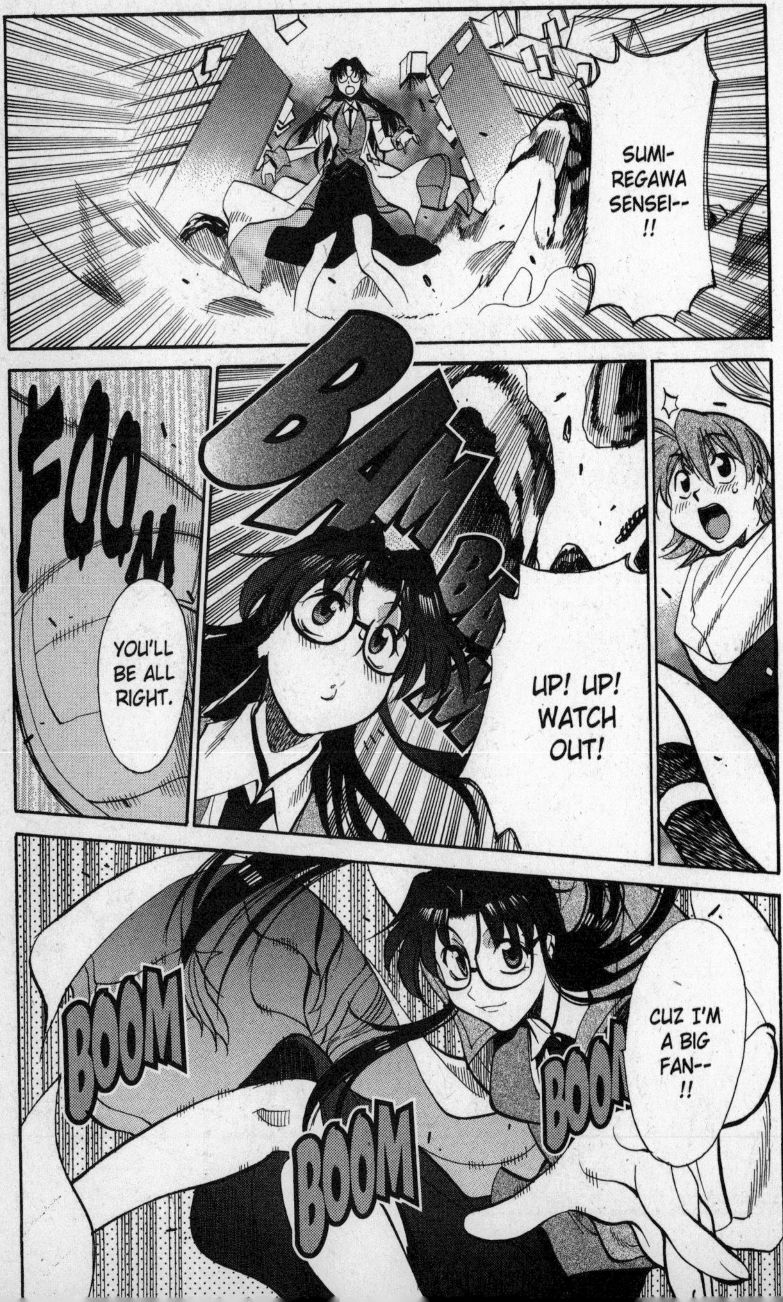
SUMI-REGAWA SENSEI--!!
BAM
UP! UP! WATCH OUT!
FOOM
YOU'LL BE ALL RIGHT.
CUZ I'M A BIG FAN--!!
BOOM
BOOM

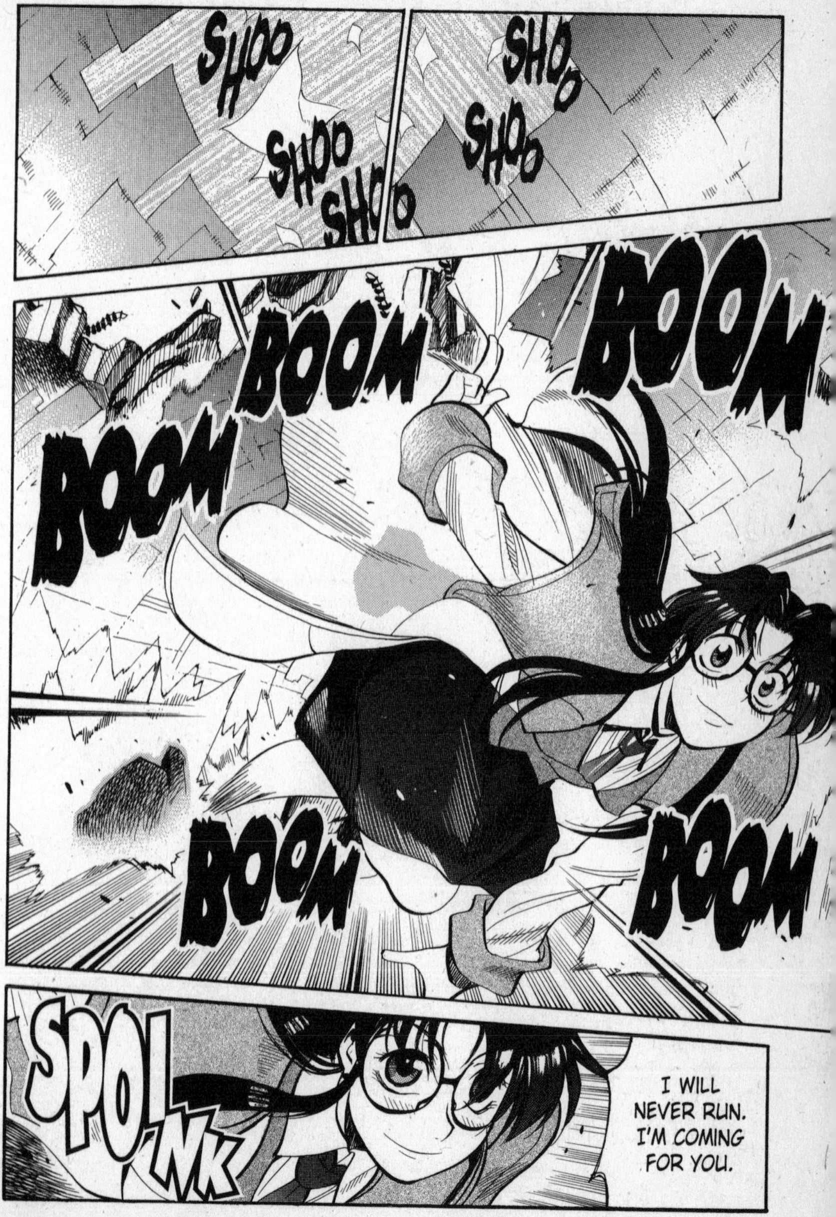
SHOO
SHOO
SHOO
SHOO
SHOO
BOOM
BOOM
BOOM
BOOM
BOOM
I WILL NEVER RUN. I'M COMING FOR YOU.
SPOINK

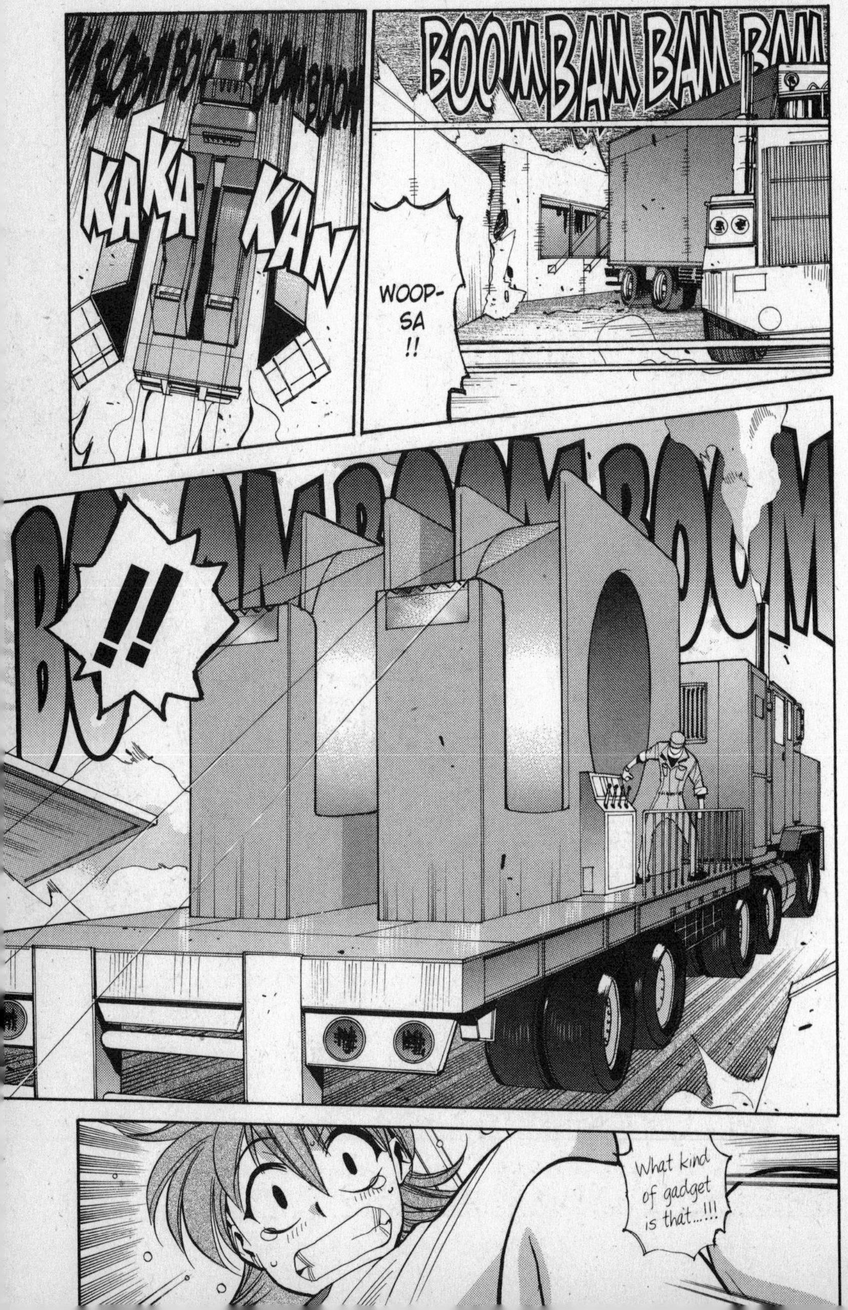
BOOM BAM BAM BAM
WOOP-SA !!
BOOM BOOM BOOM BOOM
KAKA KAN
BOOM
!!
What kind of gadget is that...!!!

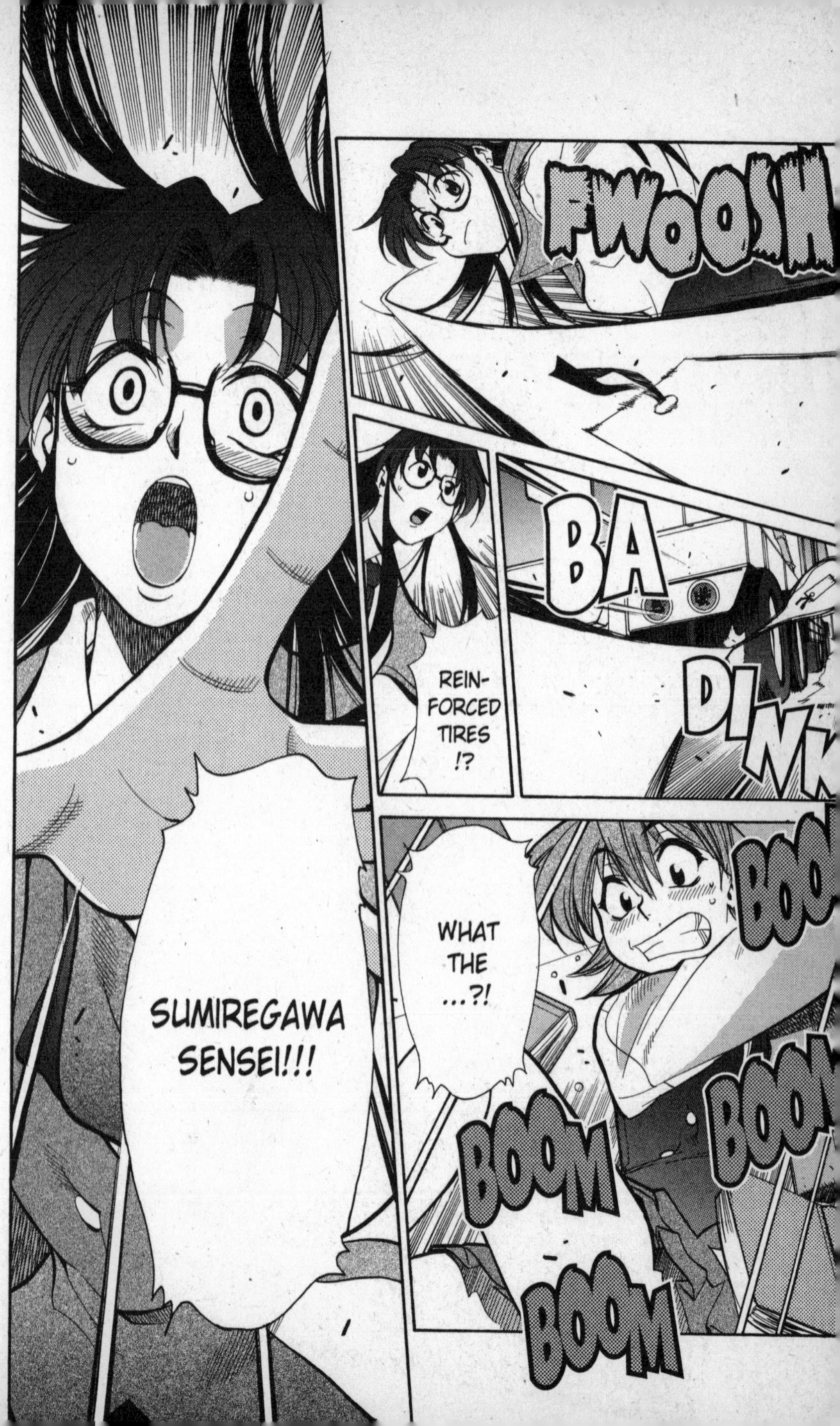
FWOOSH
BA
DINK
REIN-FORCED TIRES !?
WHAT THE ...?!
BOOM
BOOM
SUMIREGAWA SENSEI!!!

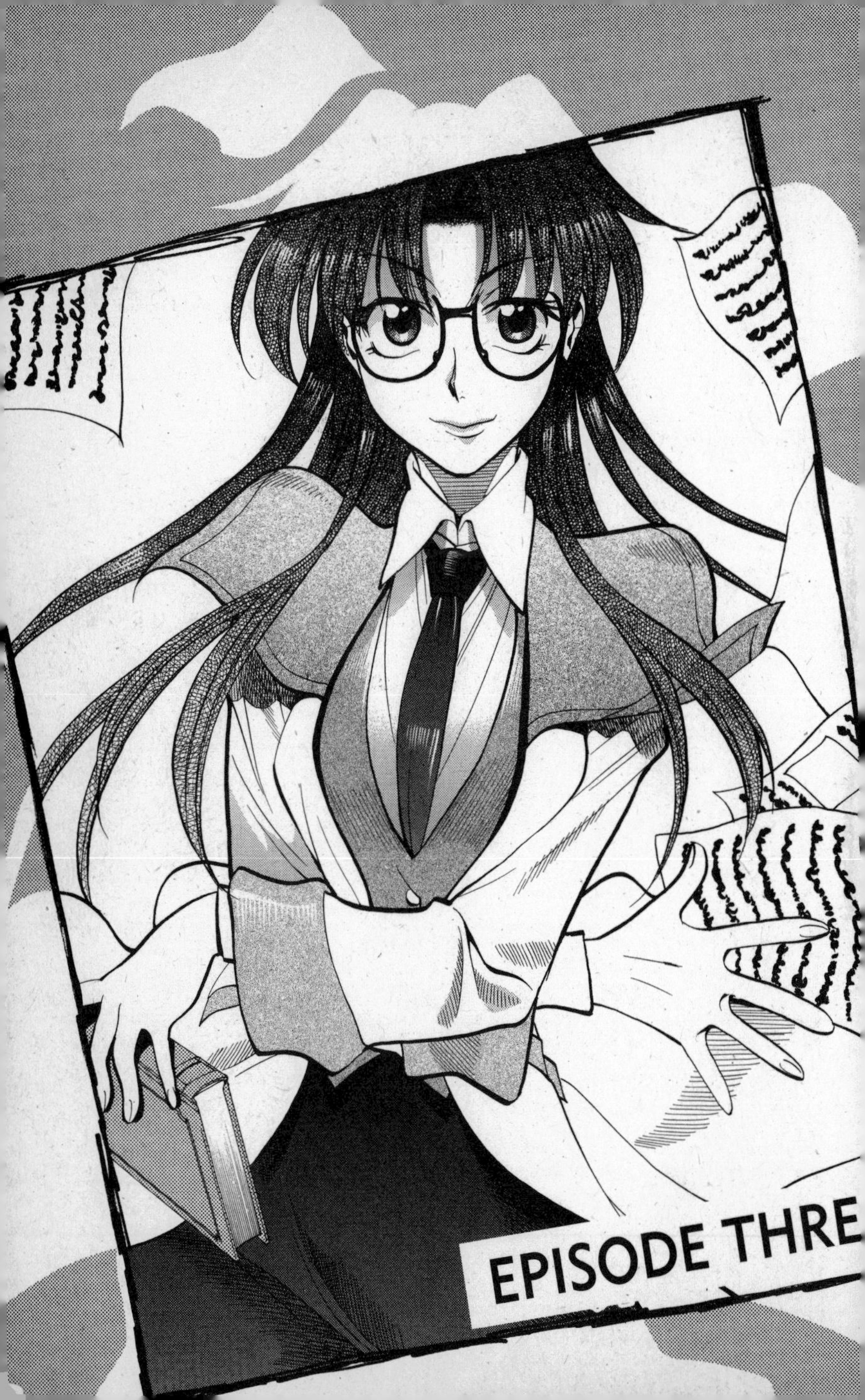
EPISODE THRE

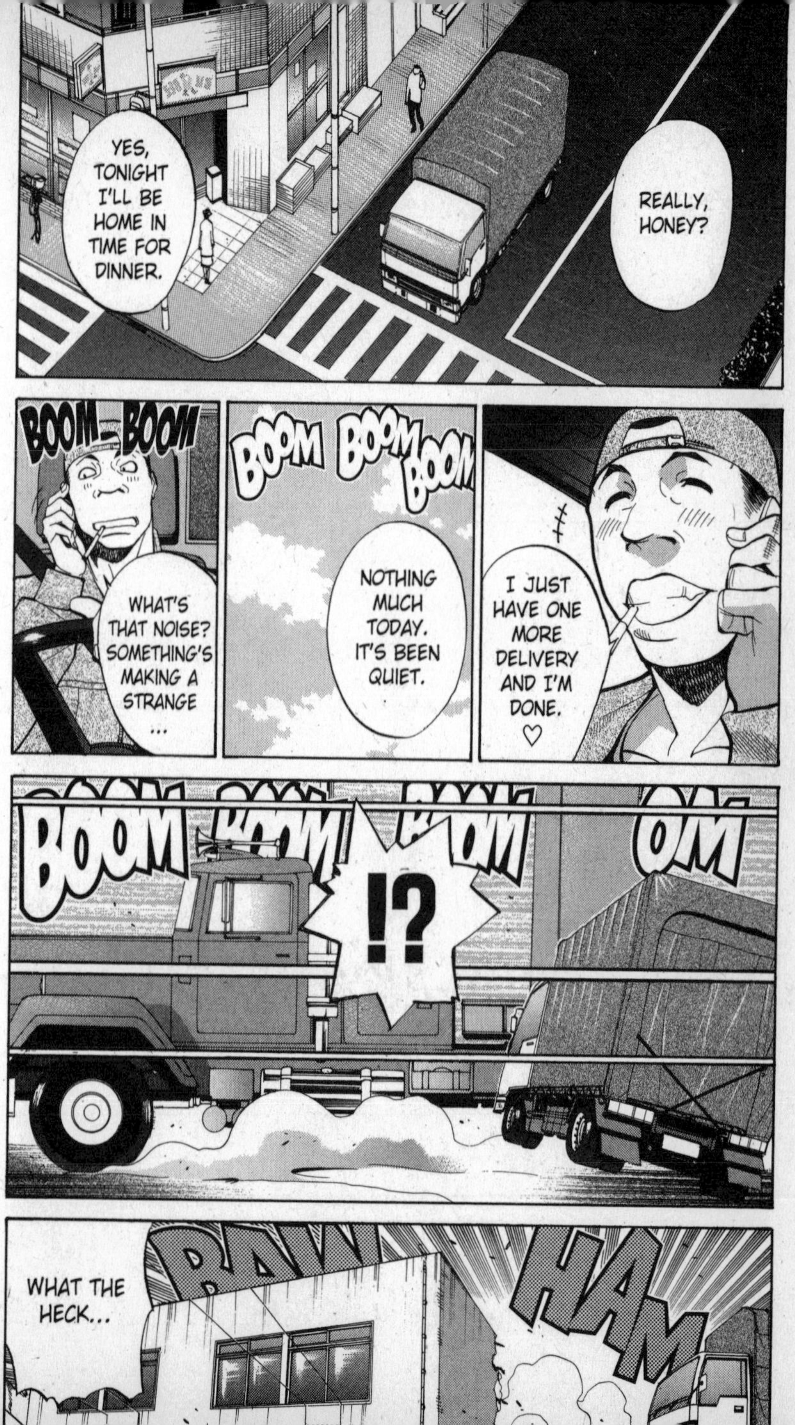
REALLY, HONEY?
YES, TONIGHT I'LL BE HOME IN TIME FOR DINNER.
I JUST HAVE ONE MORE DELIVERY AND I'M DONE. ♡
BOOM BOOM BOOM
NOTHING MUCH TODAY. IT'S BEEN QUIET.
BOOM BOOM
WHAT'S THAT NOISE? SOMETHING'S MAKING A STRANGE ...
BOOM
!?
WHAT THE HECK...

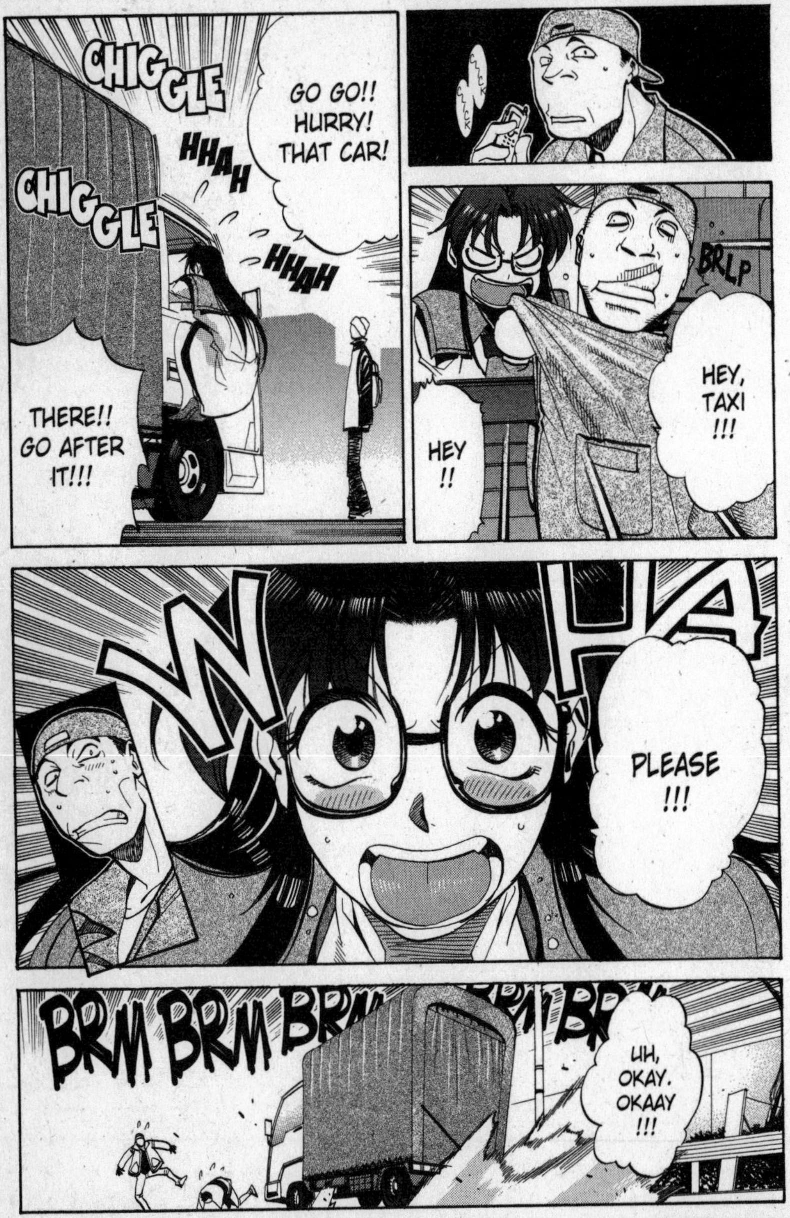
CLICK
CLICK
BRLP
HEY, TAXI !!!
HEY !!
GO GO!! HURRY! THAT CAR!
CHIGGLE
HHAH
CHIGGLE
HHAH
THERE!! GO AFTER IT!!!
WHA
PLEASE !!!
UH, OKAY. OKAAY !!!
BRM BRM

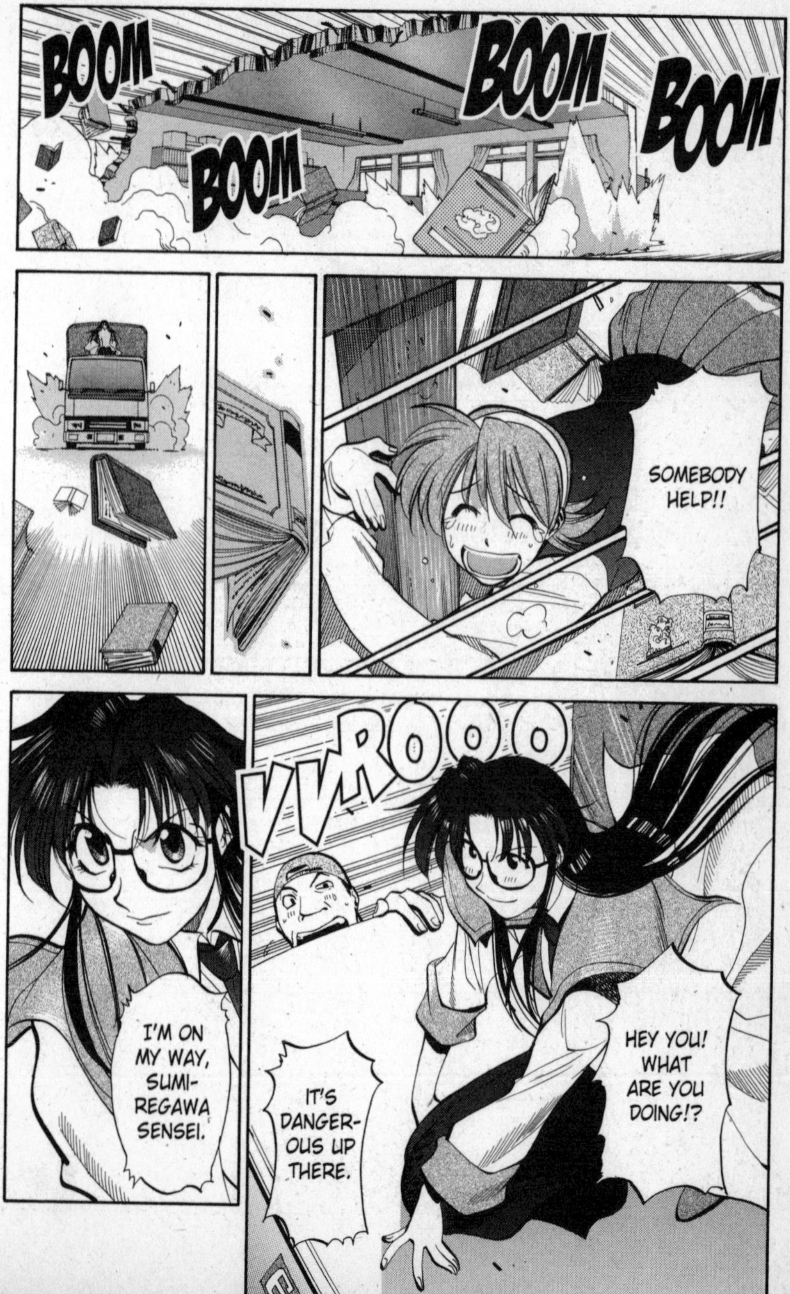
BOOM
BOOM
BOOM
BOOM
SOMEBODY HELP!!
VVROOO
HEY YOU! WHAT ARE YOU DOING!?
IT'S DANGER-OUS UP THERE.
I'M ON MY WAY, SUMI-REGAWA SENSEI.

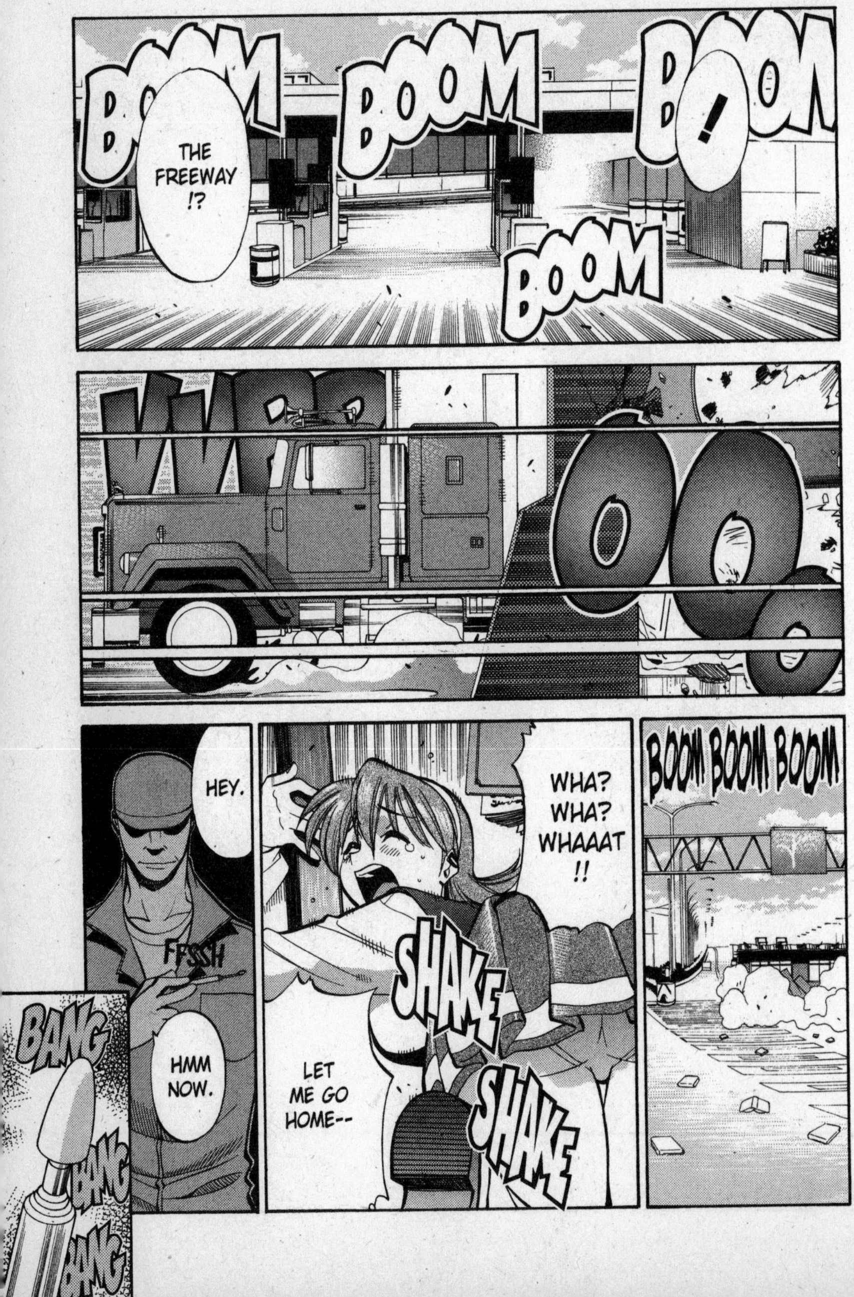
BOOM
!
BOOM
BOOM
THE FREEWAY !?
BOOM
BOOM BOOM BOOM
WHA? WHA? WHAAAT !!
SHAKE
LET ME GO HOME--
SHAKE
HEY.
FFSSH
HMM NOW.
BANG
BANG
BANG

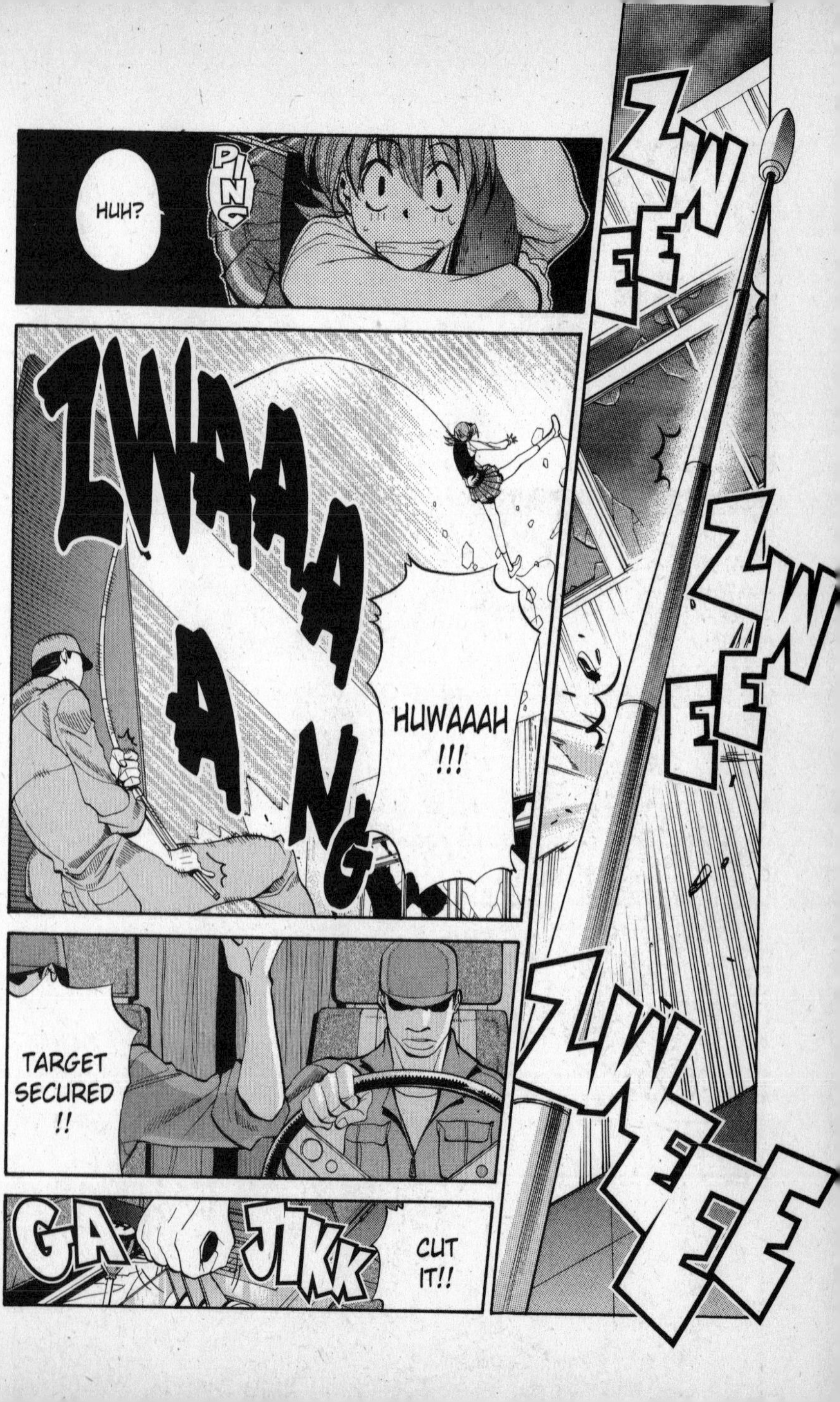
ZWEEE
ZWEEE
ZWEEEE
PING
HUH?
ZWAAAAANG
HUWAAAH !!!
TARGET SECURED !!
CUT IT!!
GAJIKK

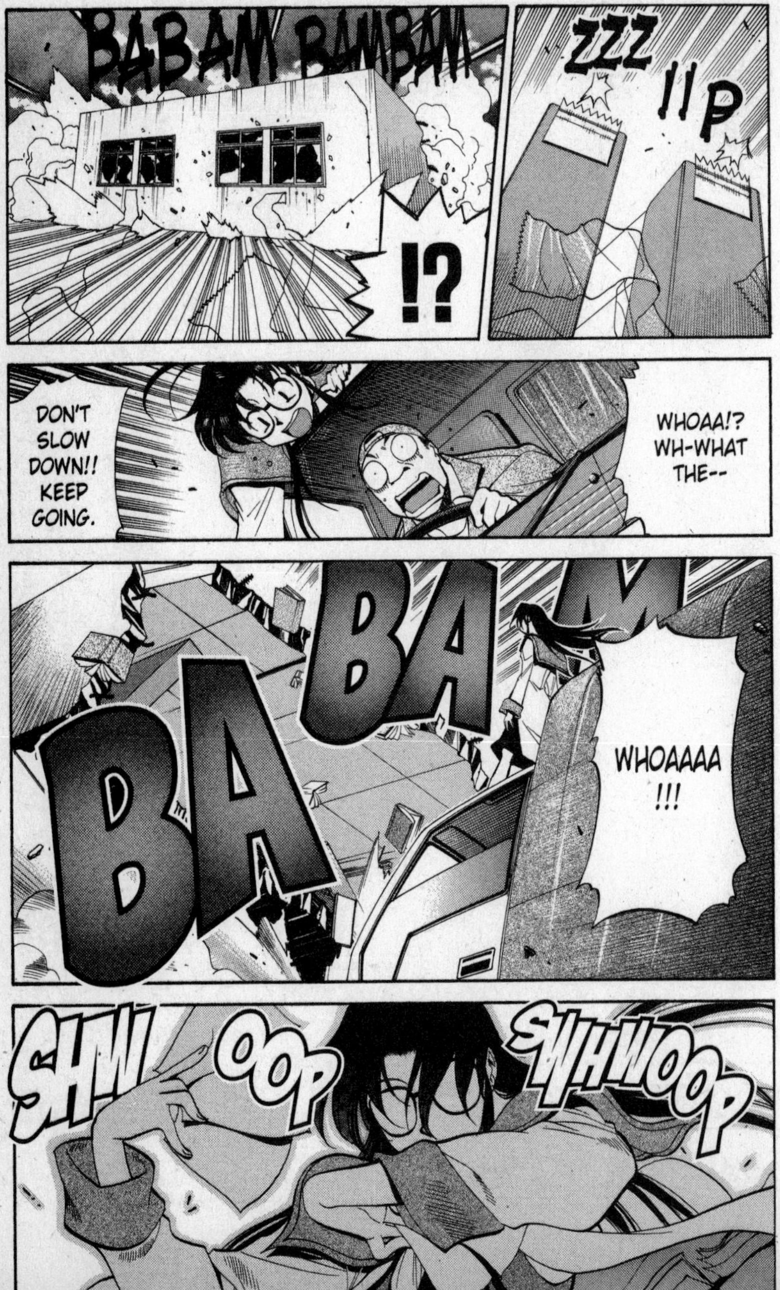
ZZZ
!!P
BABAM BAMBAM
!?
WHOAA!? WH-WHAT THE--
DON'T SLOW DOWN!! KEEP GOING.
BABABAM
WHOAAAA !!!
SWHWOOP
SHWOOP

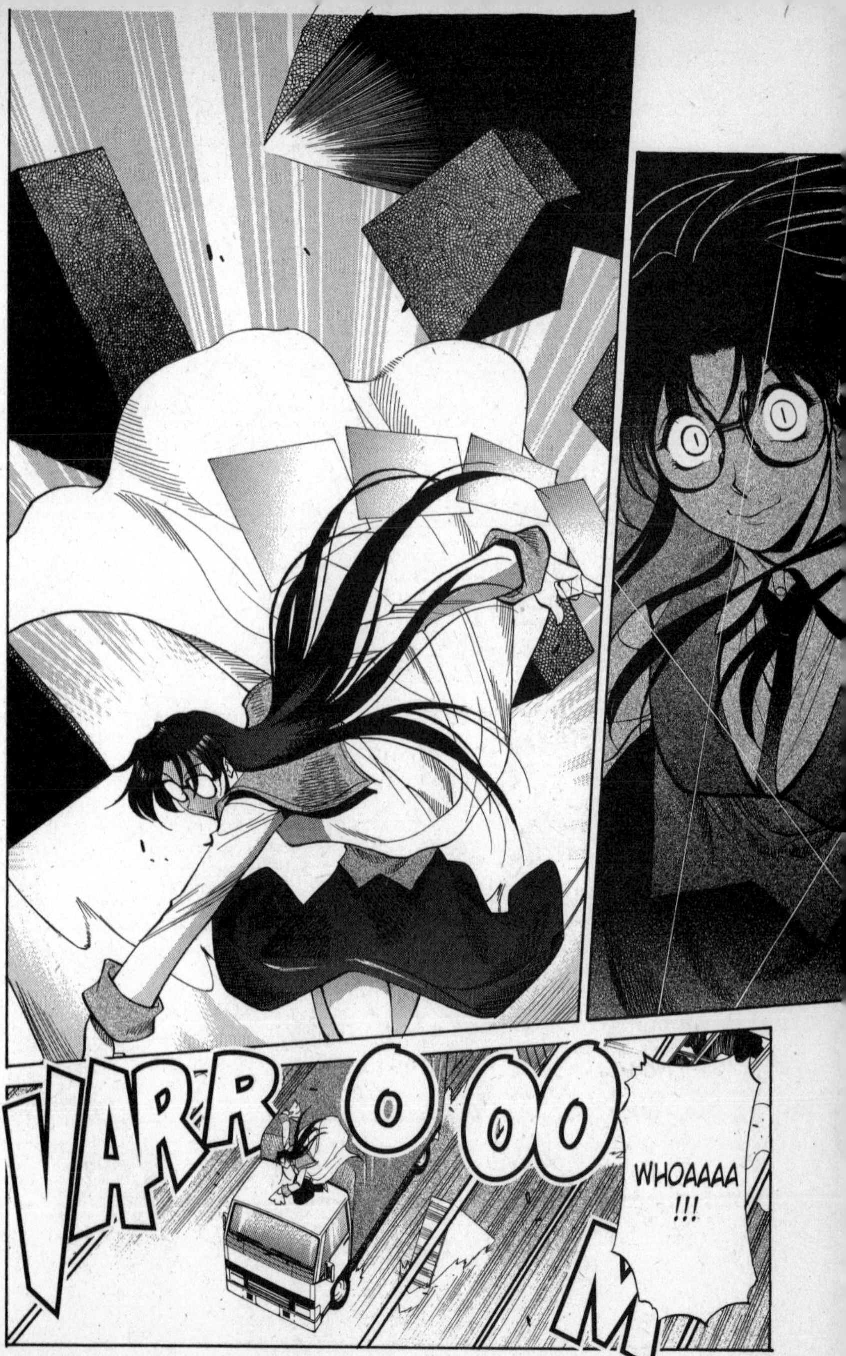
VARROOOOM
WHOAAAA !!!

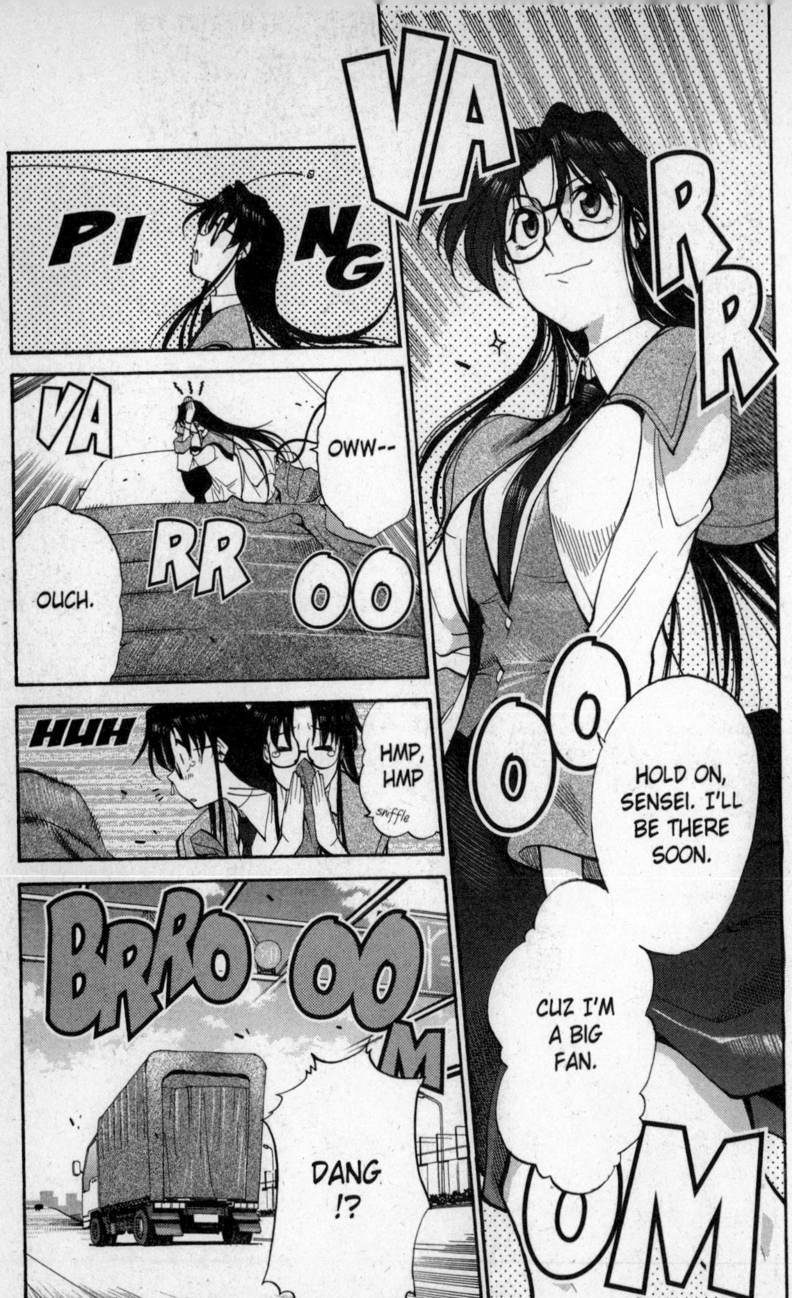
VA
RR
HOLD ON, SENSEI. I'LL BE THERE SOON.
CUZ I'M A BIG FAN.
OOO
OM
PI NG
VA
OWW--
RR
OO
OUCH.
HUH
HMP, HMP
sniffle
BRRO OO M
DANG !?

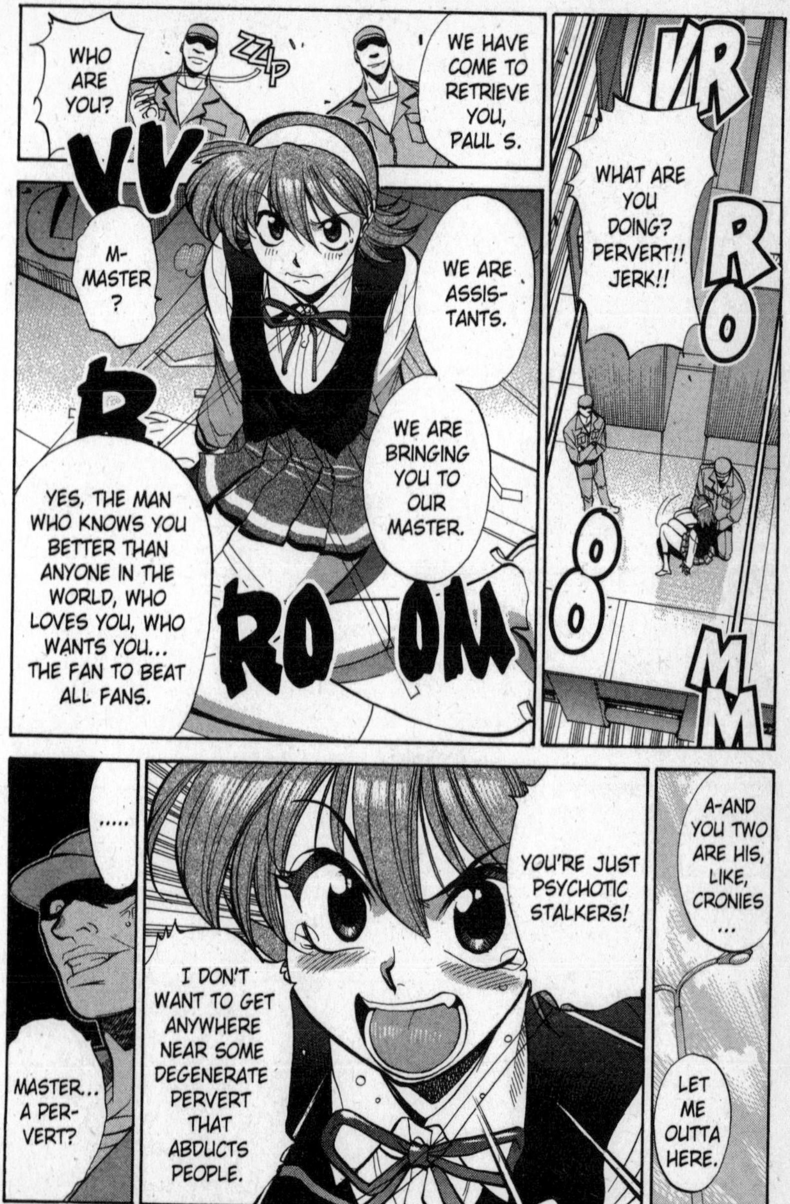
VRROOOMM
WHAT ARE YOU DOING? PERVERT!! JERK!!
WE HAVE COME TO RETRIEVE YOU, PAUL S.
ZZAP
WHO ARE YOU?
WE ARE ASSISTANTS.
WE ARE BRINGING YOU TO OUR MASTER.
M-MASTER?
YES, THE MAN WHO KNOWS YOU BETTER THAN ANYONE IN THE WORLD, WHO LOVES YOU, WHO WANTS YOU... THE FAN TO BEAT ALL FANS.
VVRROOM
A-AND YOU TWO ARE HIS, LIKE, CRONIES...
LET ME OUTTA HERE.
YOU'RE JUST PSYCHOTIC STALKERS!
I DON'T WANT TO GET ANYWHERE NEAR SOME DEGENERATE PERVERT THAT ABDUCTS PEOPLE.
.....
MASTER... A PERVERT?

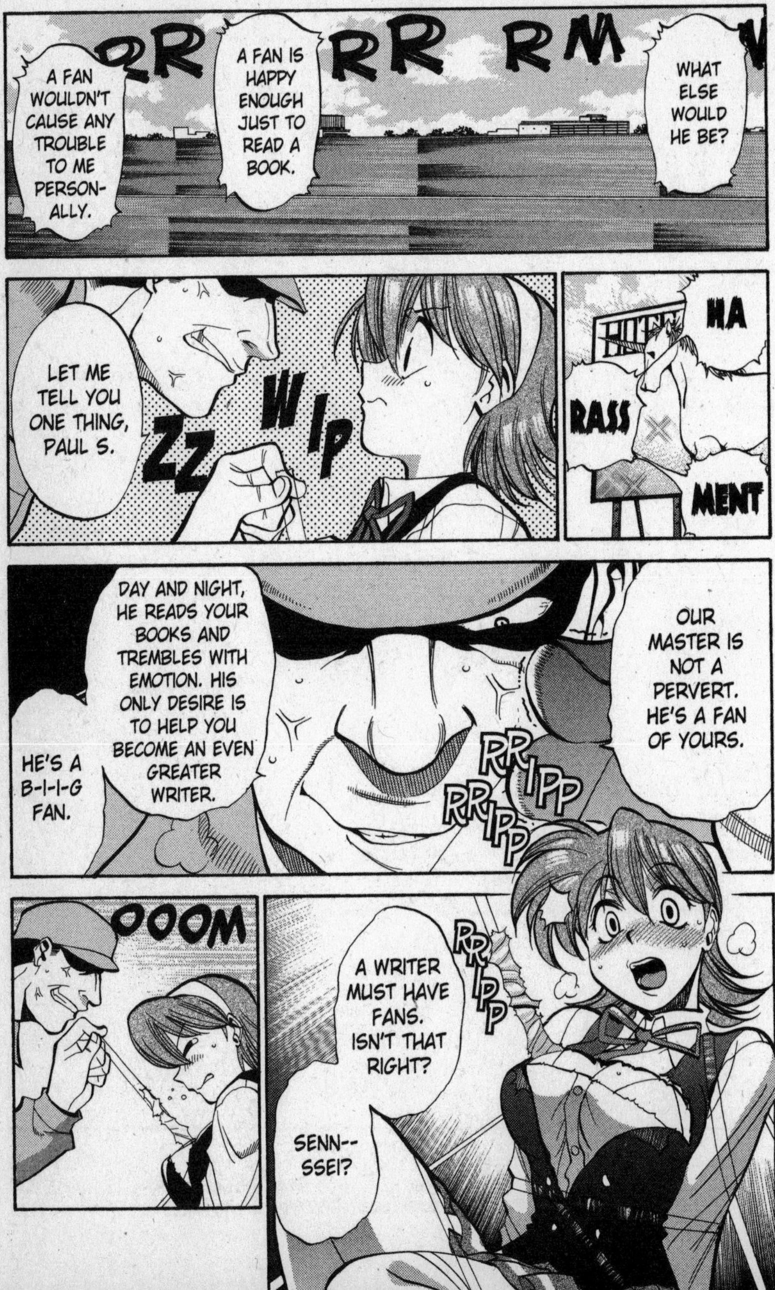
RR RR RM
WHAT ELSE WOULD HE BE?
A FAN IS HAPPY ENOUGH JUST TO READ A BOOK.
A FAN WOULDN'T CAUSE ANY TROUBLE TO ME PERSON-ALLY.
HA
RASS
MENT
LET ME TELL YOU ONE THING, PAUL S.
WIP
ZZ
OUR MASTER IS NOT A PERVERT. HE'S A FAN OF YOURS.
RRIPP
RRIPP
DAY AND NIGHT, HE READS YOUR BOOKS AND TREMBLES WITH EMOTION. HIS ONLY DESIRE IS TO HELP YOU BECOME AN EVEN GREATER WRITER.
HE'S A B-I-I-G FAN.
RRIPP
A WRITER MUST HAVE FANS. ISN'T THAT RIGHT?
SENN-- SSEI?
OOOM

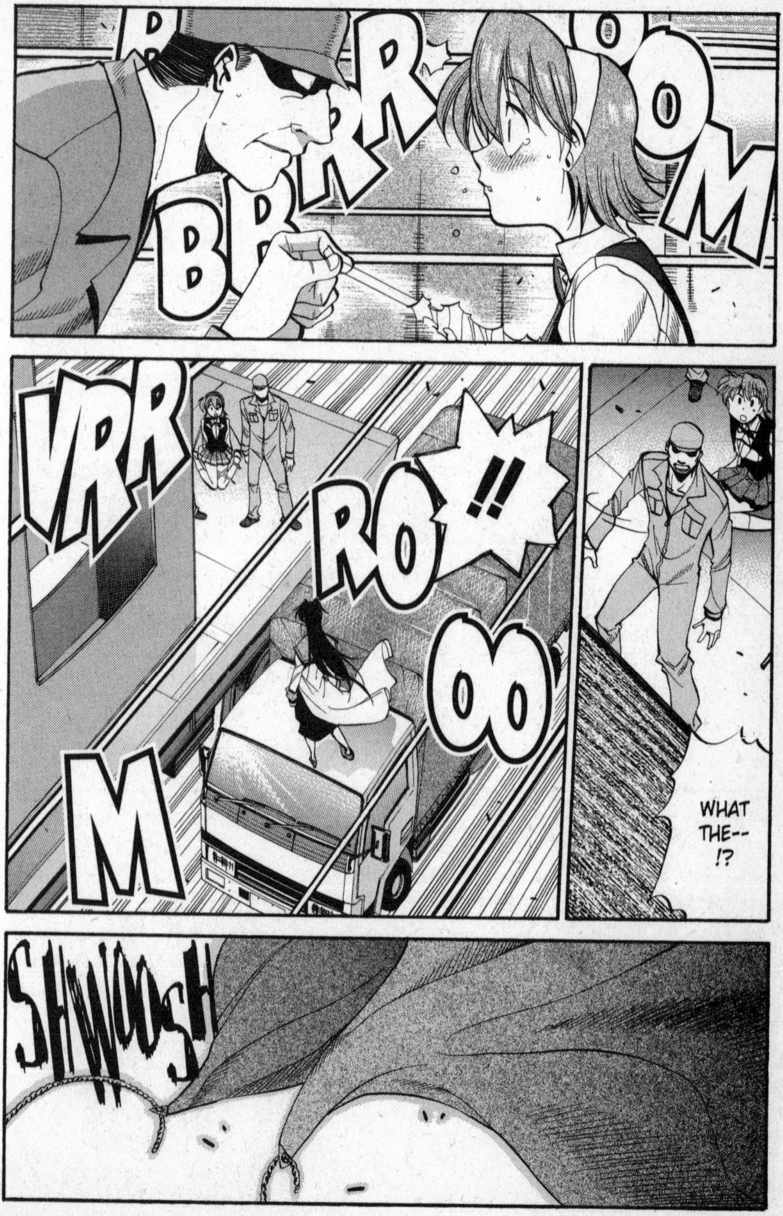
BRRROOOM
WHAT THE--!?
VRRROOOM
!!
SHWOOSH

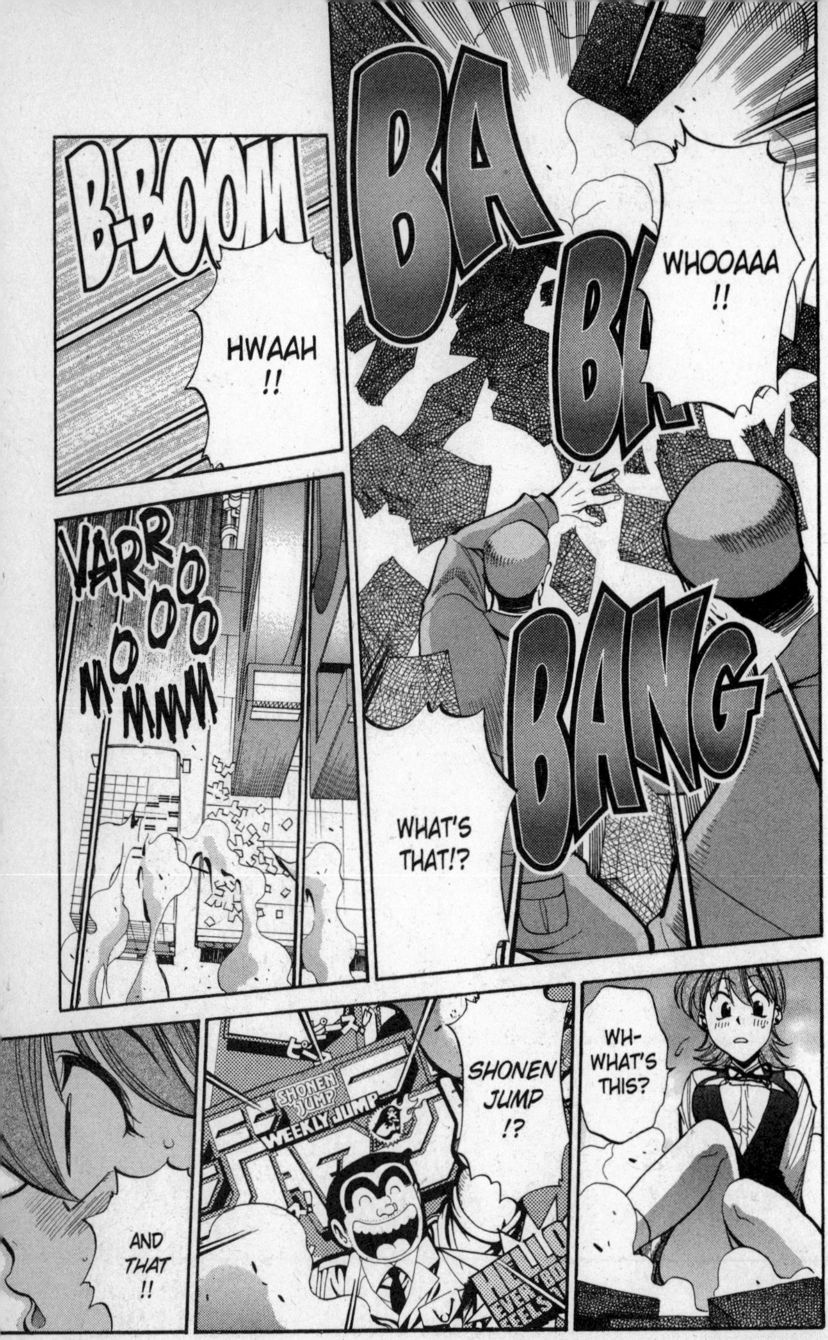
WHOOAAA !!
BA
BA
BANG
WHAT'S THAT!?
B-BOOM
HWAAH !!
VARROOOOMNNNN
WH- WHAT'S THIS?
SHONEN JUMP !?
SHONEN JUMP
WEEKLY JUMP
AND THAT !!

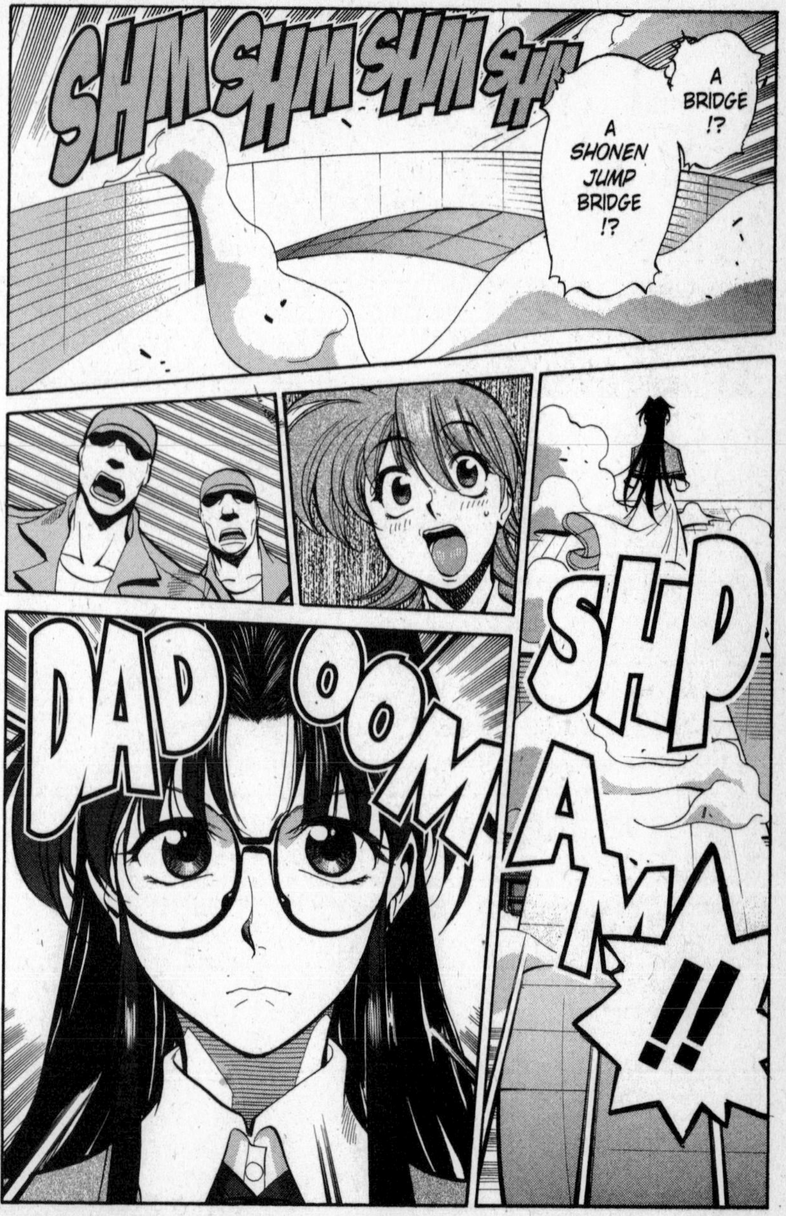
A BRIDGE !?
A SHONEN JUMP BRIDGE !?
SHM SHM SHM SH
SHPAM!!
DADOOM

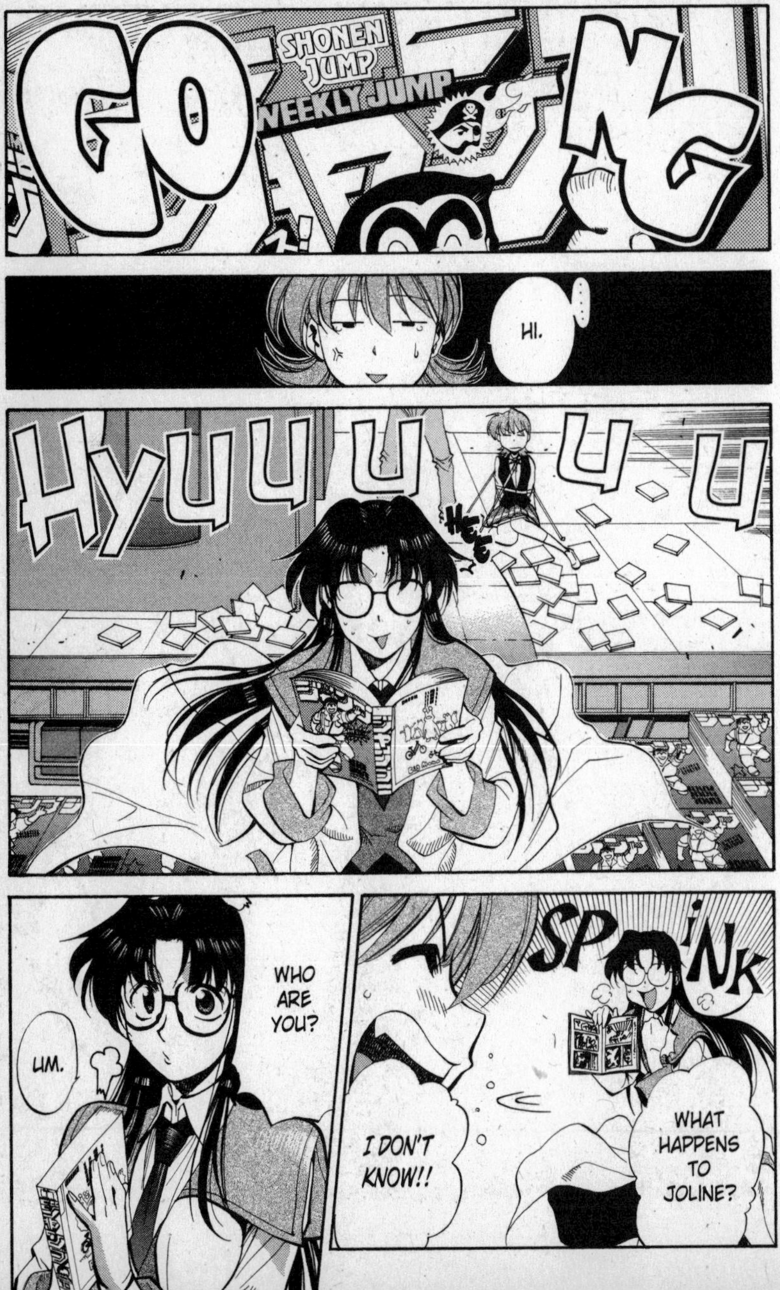

SHONEN JUMP
WEEKLY JUMP
...
HI.
HYUUUU U U
SPiNK
WHAT HAPPENS TO JOLINE?
I DON'T KNOW!!
WHO ARE YOU?
UM.

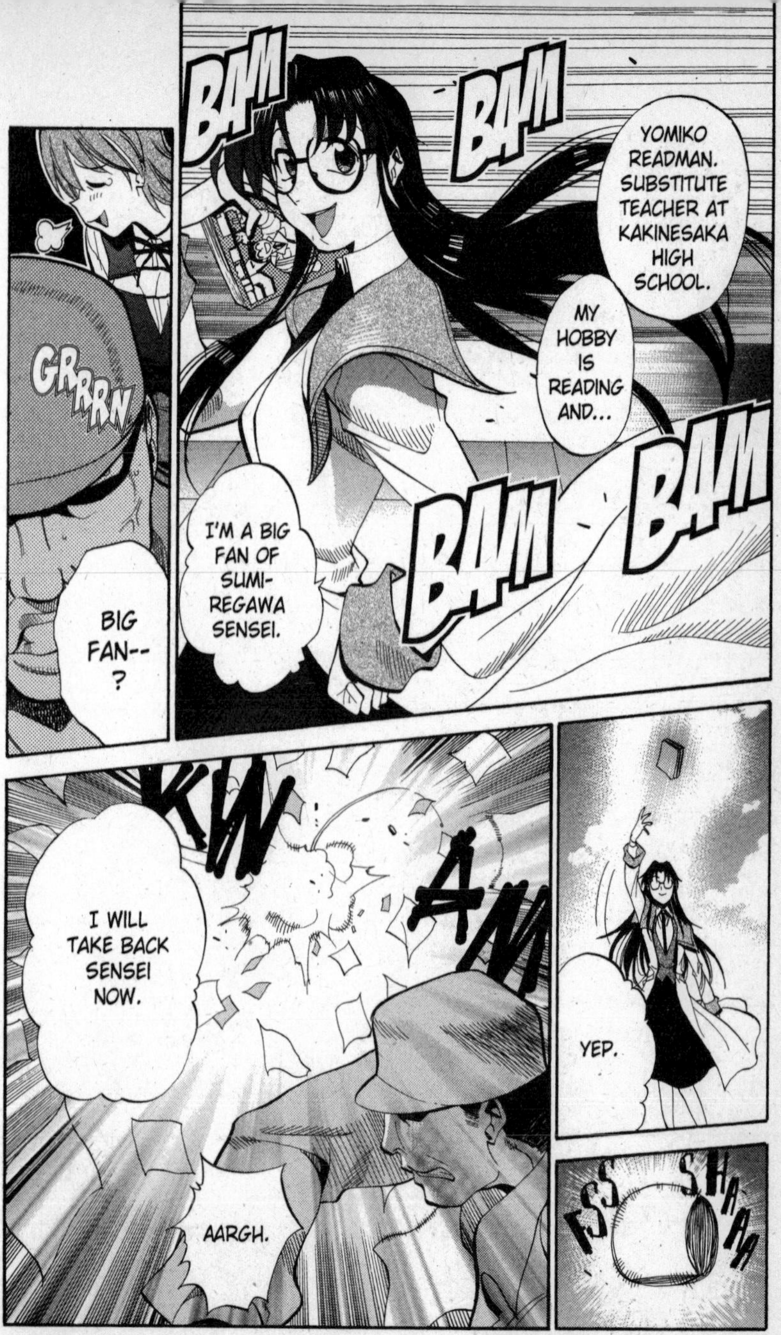
BAM
BAM
YOMIKO READMAN. SUBSTITUTE TEACHER AT KAKINESAKA HIGH SCHOOL.
MY HOBBY IS READING AND...
BAM
BAM
I'M A BIG FAN OF SUMI-REGAWA SENSEI.
GRRRRN
BIG FAN-- ?
YEP.
TSS
SHAAA
KWAAM
I WILL TAKE BACK SENSEI NOW.
AARGH.

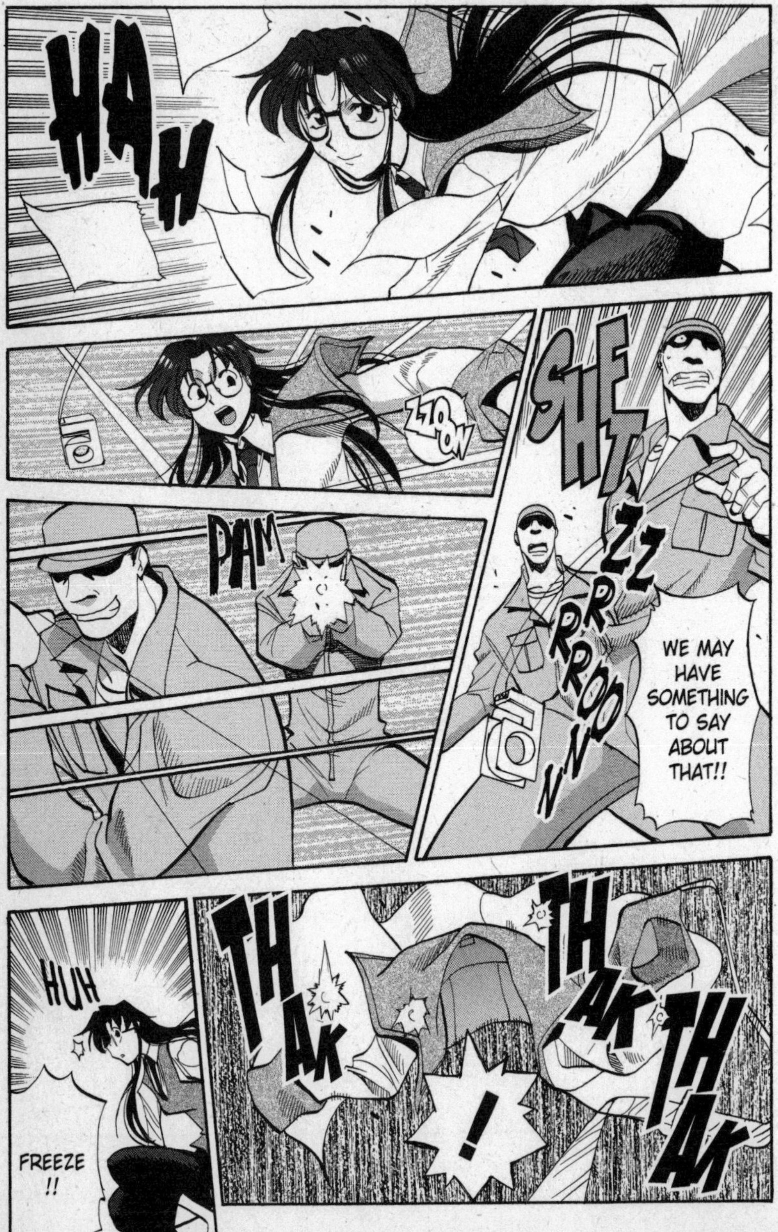
HAH
SHFT
ZZRRRROONN
WE MAY HAVE SOMETHING TO SAY ABOUT THAT!!
ZZOOM
PAM
THAK
THAK
THAK
!
HUH
FREEZE !!

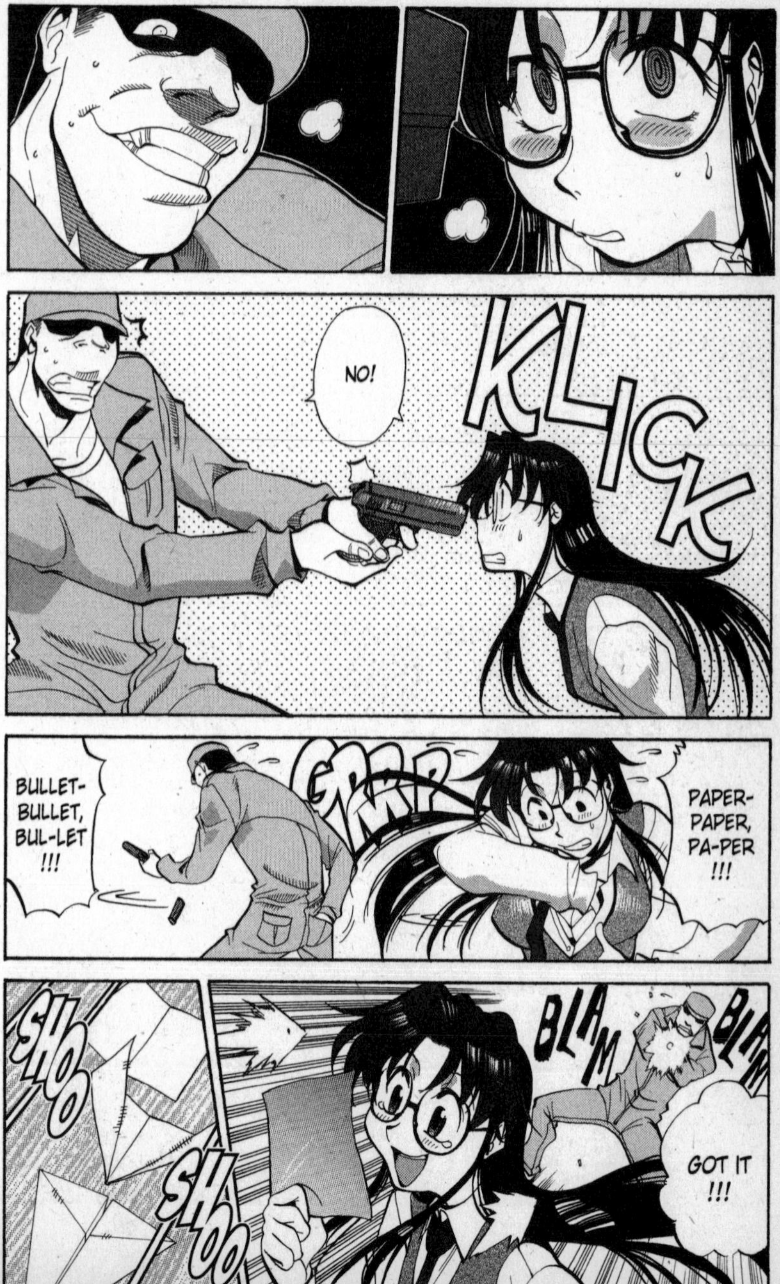
KLICK
NO!
PAPER-PAPER, PA-PER !!!
BULLET-BULLET, BUL-LET !!!
BLAM
BLAM
GOT IT !!!
SHOO
SHOO

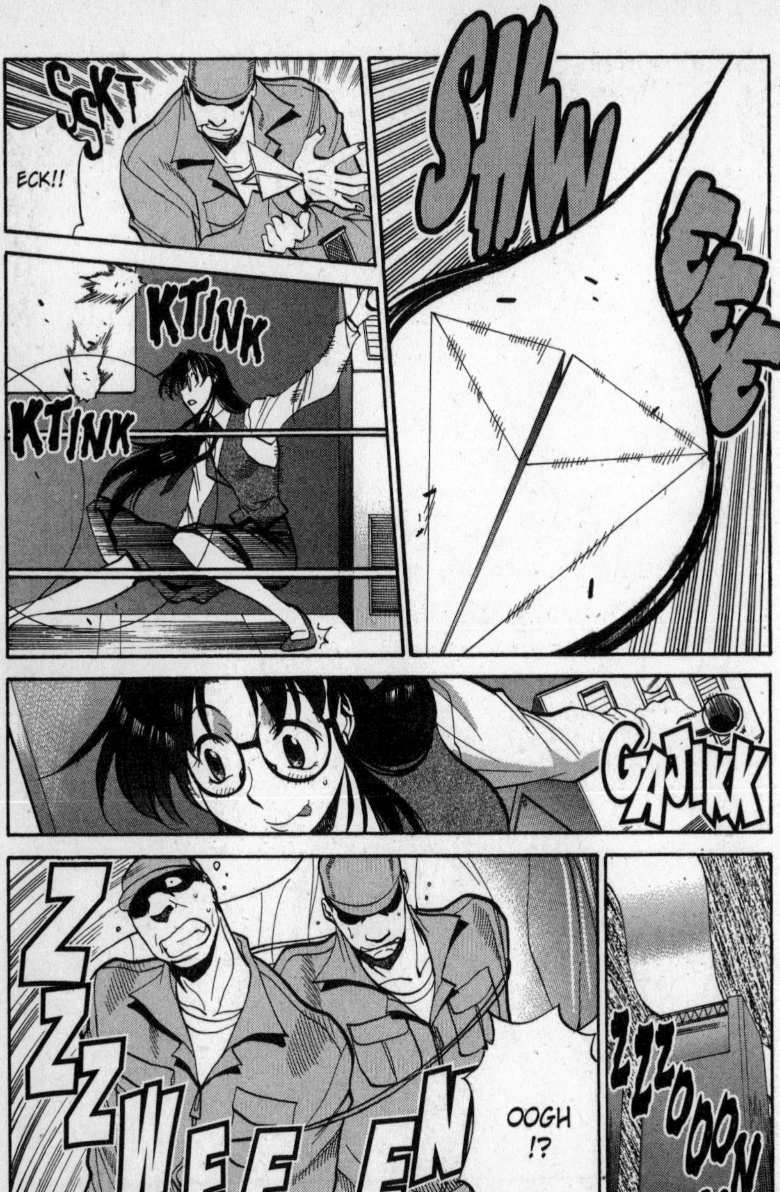
SHWEEEE
SCKT
ECK!!
KTINK
KTINK
GAJIKK
ZZZOOONN
ZZWEEEN
OOGH !?

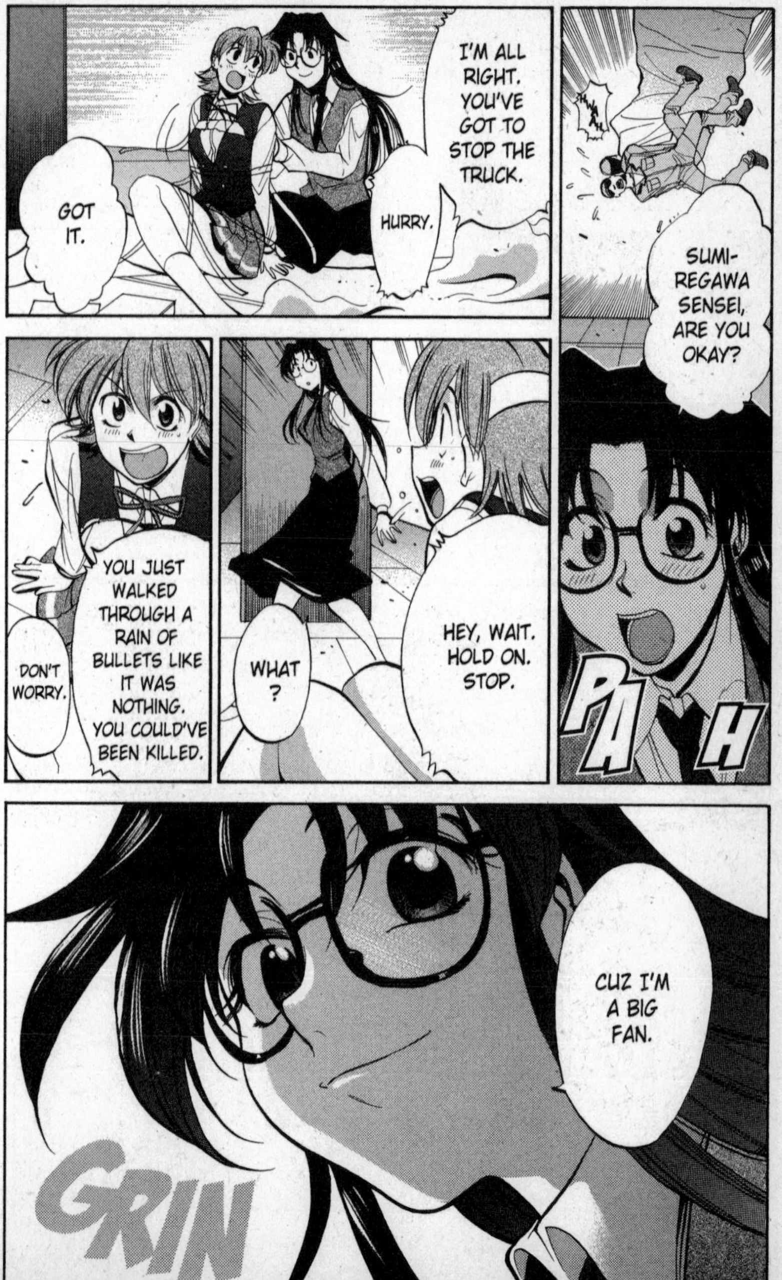
HWAAH
SUMI-REGAWA SENSEI, ARE YOU OKAY?
PAH
I'M ALL RIGHT. YOU'VE GOT TO STOP THE TRUCK.
HURRY.
GOT IT.
HEY, WAIT. HOLD ON. STOP.
WHAT?
YOU JUST WALKED THROUGH A RAIN OF BULLETS LIKE IT WAS NOTHING. YOU COULD'VE BEEN KILLED.
DON'T WORRY.
CUZ I'M A BIG FAN.
GRIN

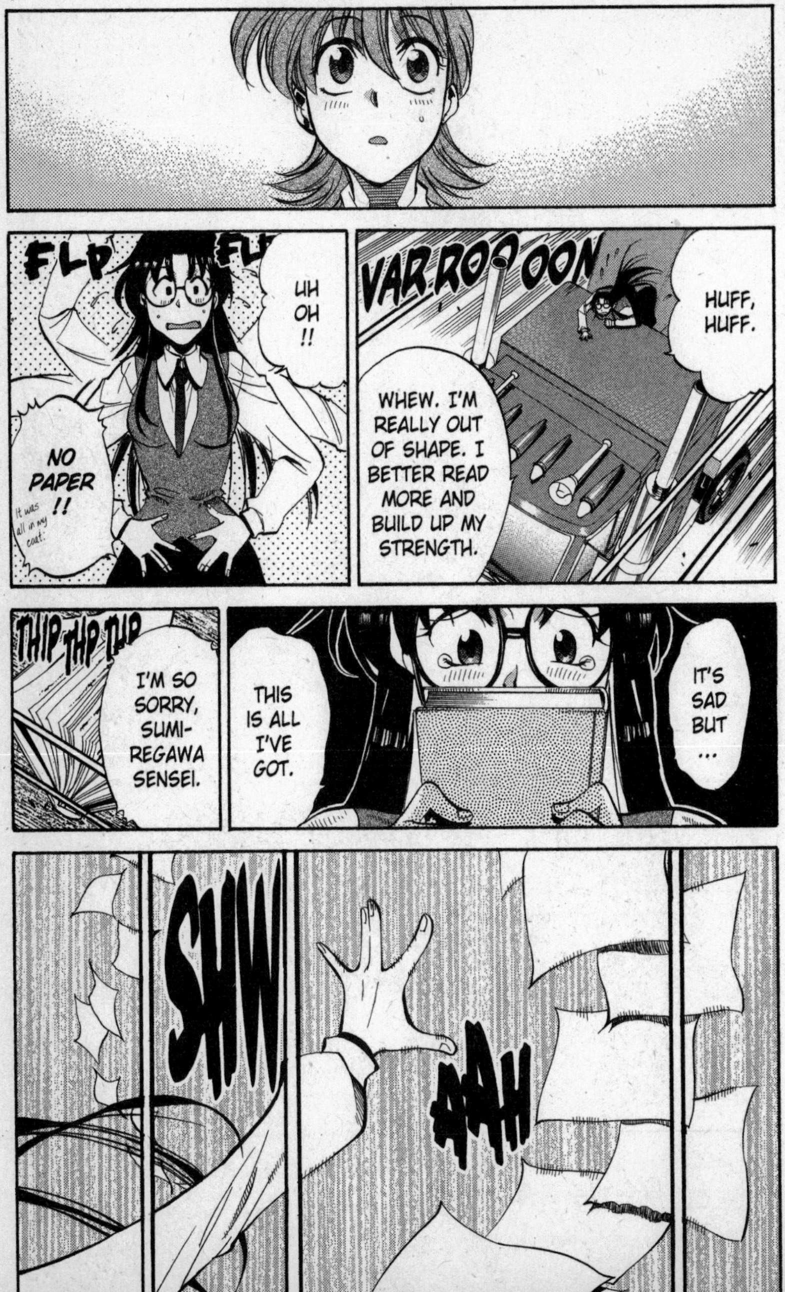
VAR ROOOON
HUFF, HUFF.
WHEW. I'M REALLY OUT OF SHAPE. I BETTER READ MORE AND BUILD UP MY STRENGTH.
FLP
UH OH !!
NO PAPER !!
It was all in my coat.
IT'S SAD BUT ...
THIS IS ALL I'VE GOT.
THIP THP
I'M SO SORRY, SUMI-REGAWA SENSEI.
SHW
AAH

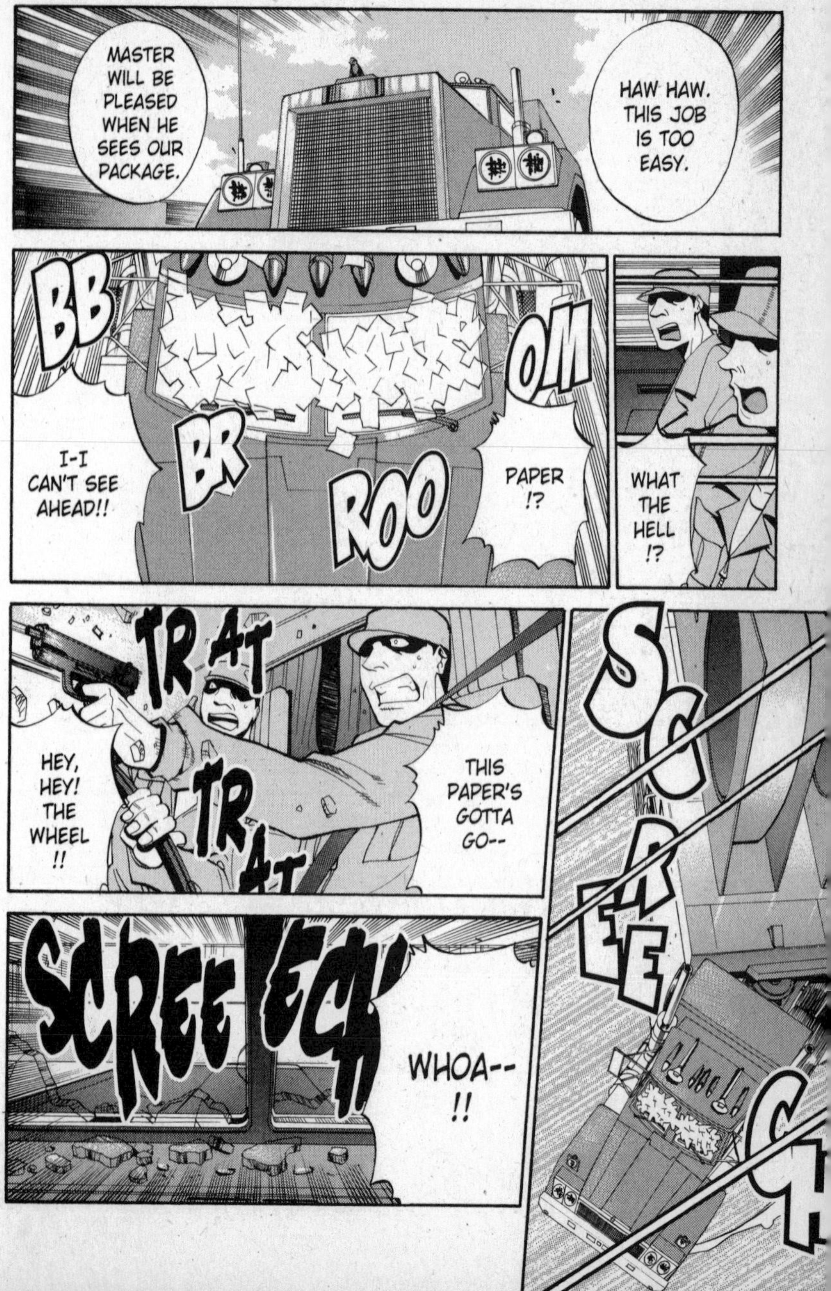
HAW HAW. THIS JOB IS TOO EASY.
MASTER WILL BE PLEASED WHEN HE SEES OUR PACKAGE.
WHAT THE HELL !?
BB OOM
PAPER !?
BR ROO
I-I CAN'T SEE AHEAD!!
SCREE CH
TR AT
THIS PAPER'S GOTTA GO--
TR AT
HEY, HEY! THE WHEEL !!
SCREEECH
WHOA-- !!

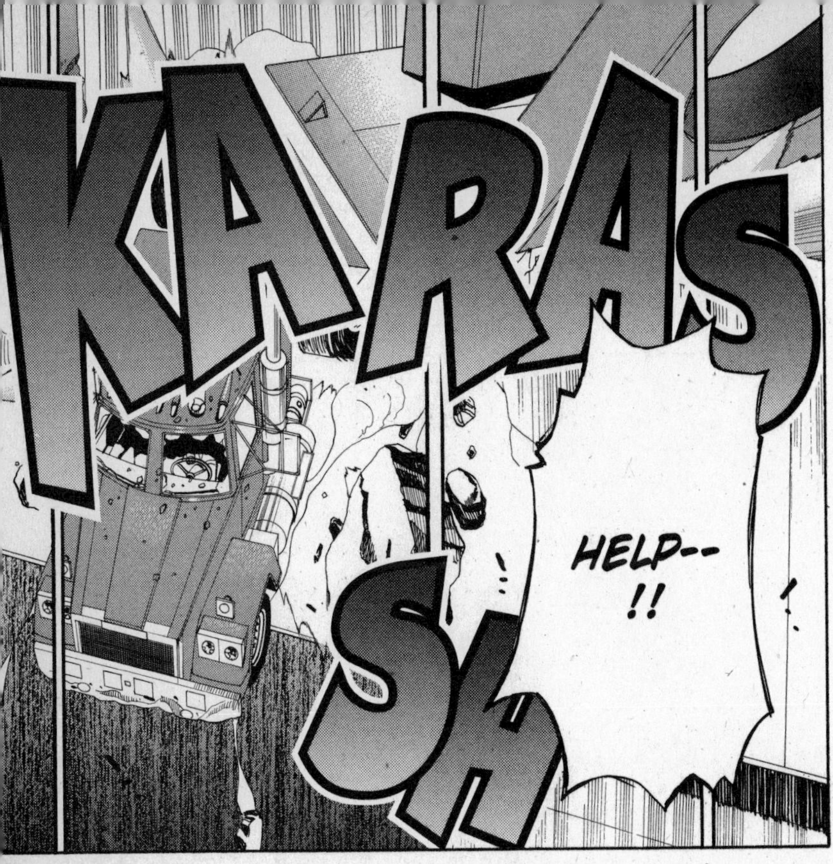
KARASSH
HELP-- !!

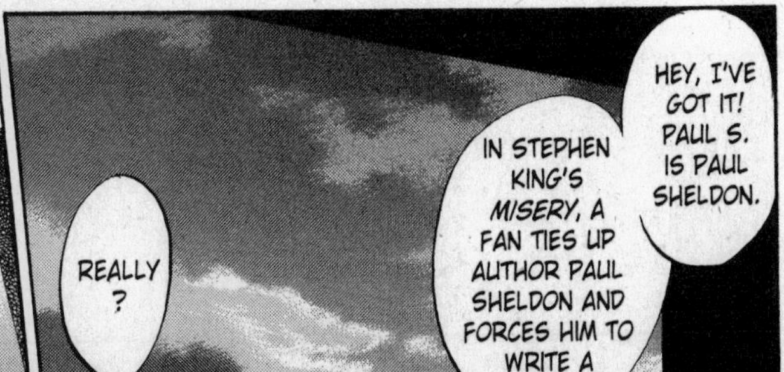
HEY, I'VE GOT IT! PAUL S. IS PAUL SHELDON.
IN STEPHEN KING'S *MISERY*, A FAN TIES UP AUTHOR PAUL SHELDON AND FORCES HIM TO WRITE A SEQUEL.
REALLY ?

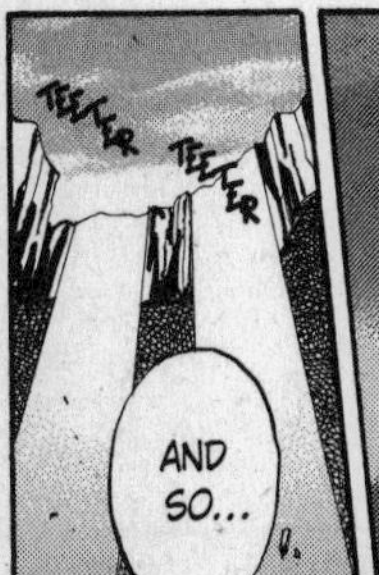
TEETER TEETER
AND SO...

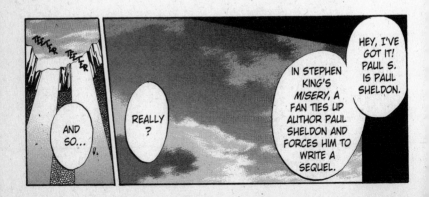

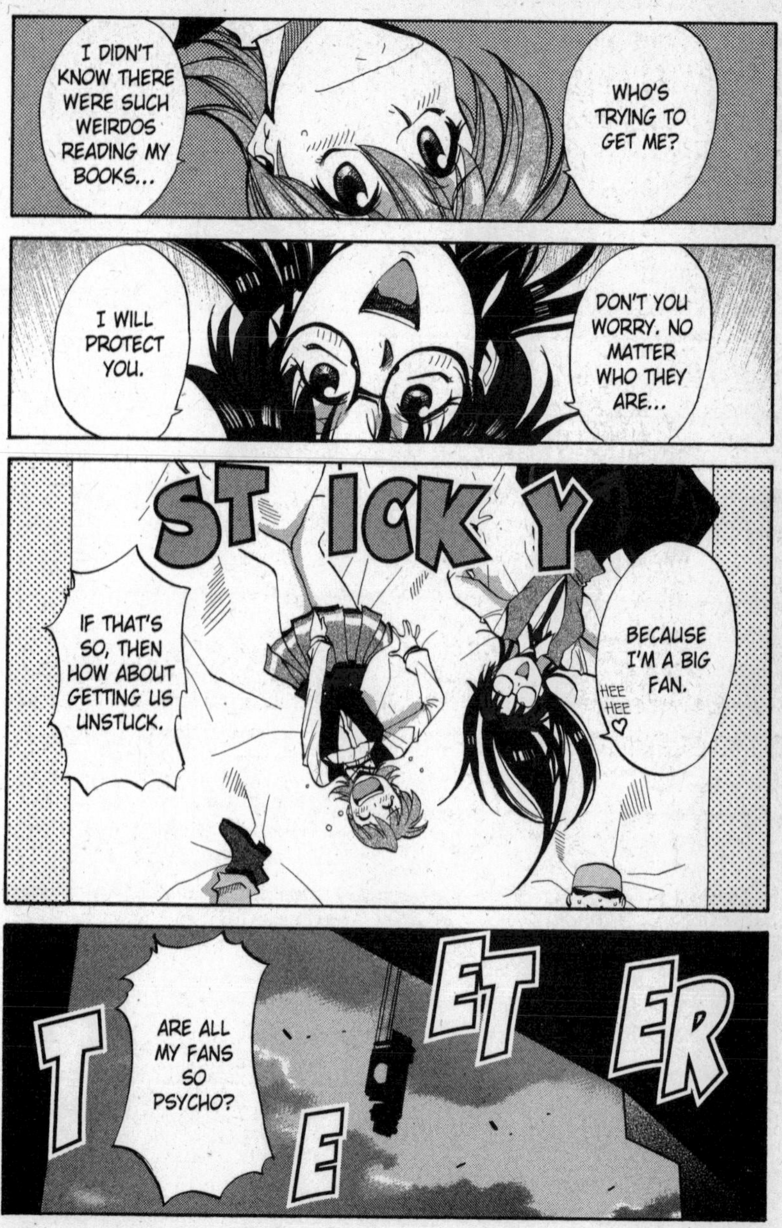
WHO'S TRYING TO GET ME?
I DIDN'T KNOW THERE WERE SUCH WEIRDOS READING MY BOOKS...
DON'T YOU WORRY. NO MATTER WHO THEY ARE...
I WILL PROTECT YOU.
STICKY
BECAUSE I'M A BIG FAN.
HEE HEE ♡
IF THAT'S SO, THEN HOW ABOUT GETTING US UNSTUCK.
TEETER
ARE ALL MY FANS SO PSYCHO?

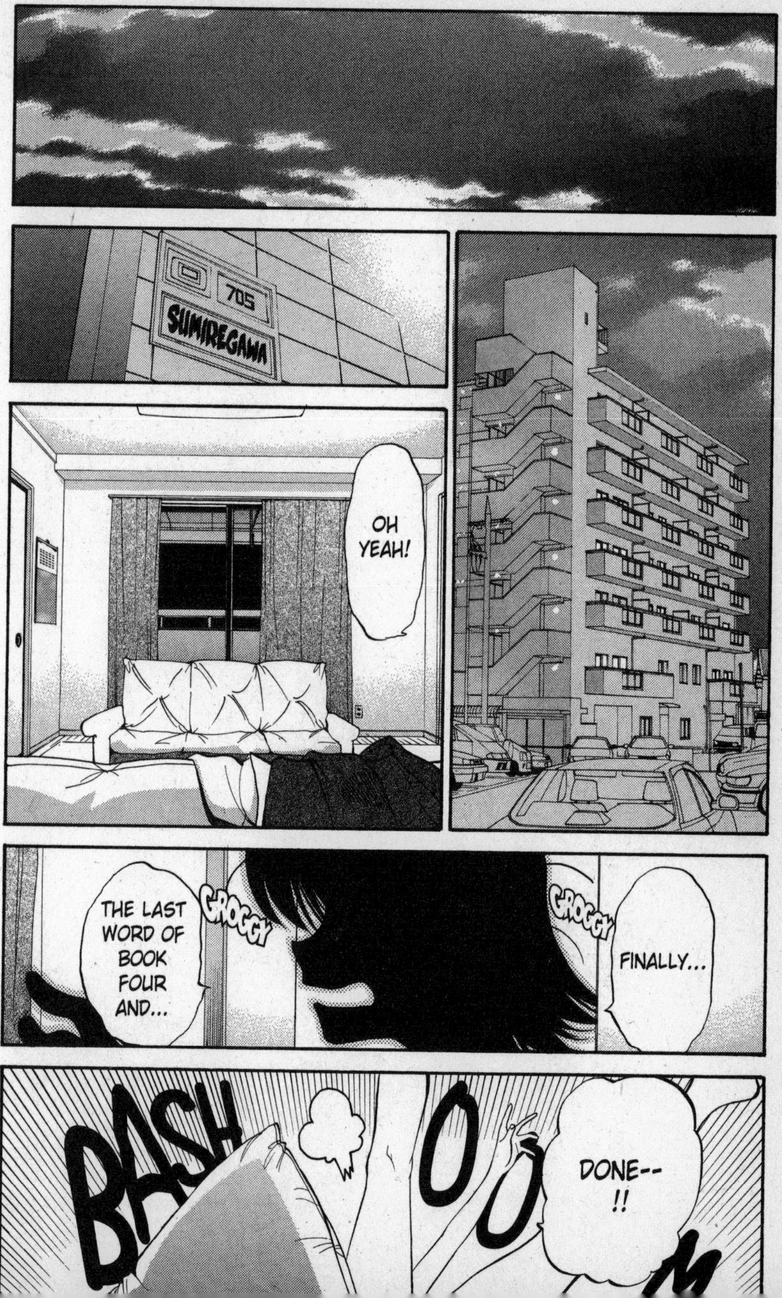
SUMIREGAWA
705
OH YEAH!
GROGGY
FINALLY...
GROGGY
THE LAST WORD OF BOOK FOUR AND...
DONE-- !!
OOM
BASH

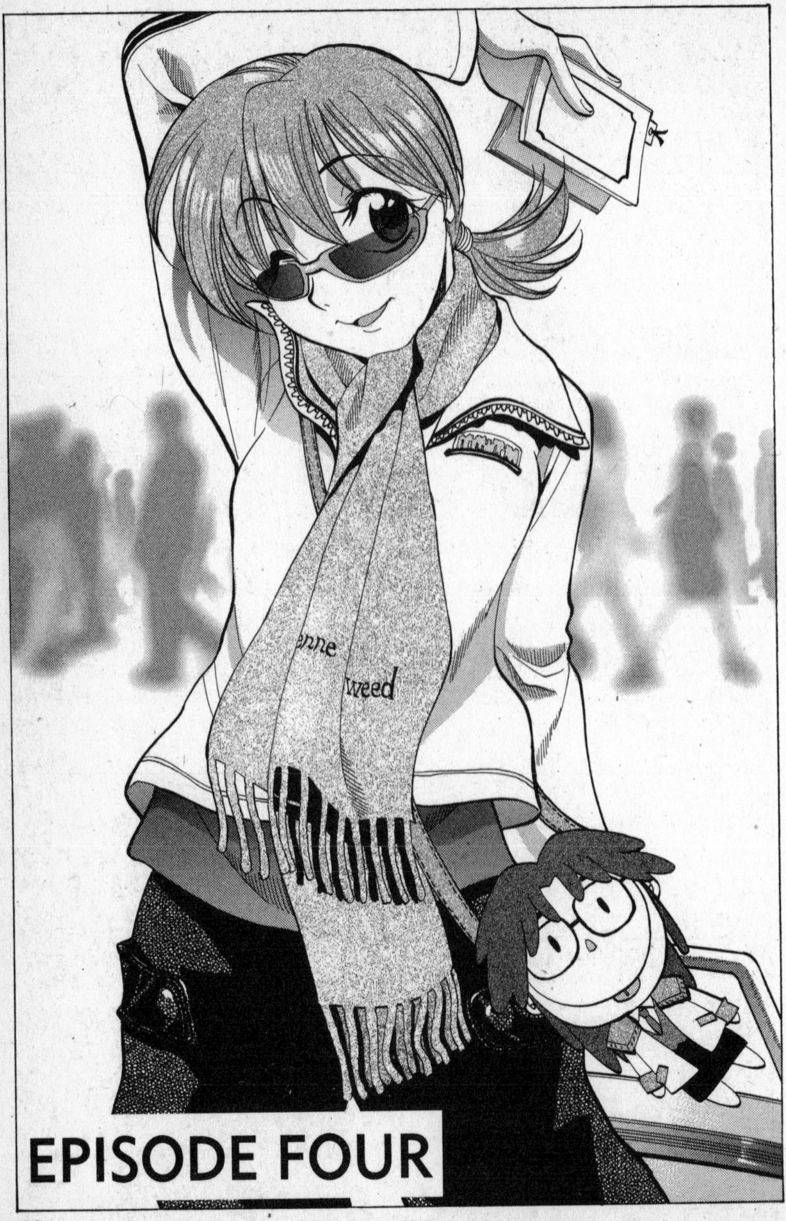
EPISODE FOUR
enne
weed

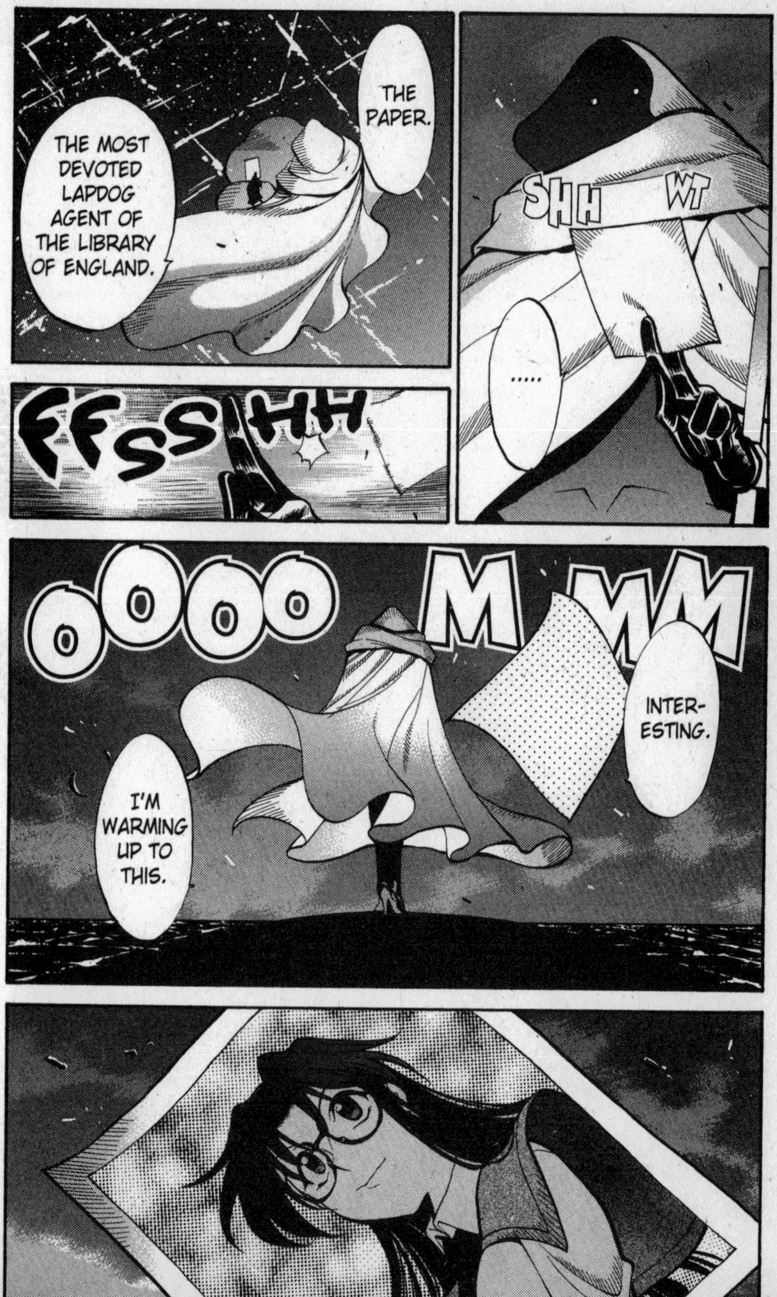
SHH
WT
.....
THE PAPER.
THE MOST DEVOTED LAPDOG AGENT OF THE LIBRARY OF ENGLAND.
FFSSHH
OOOOO MMM
INTER-ESTING.
I'M WARMING UP TO THIS.

EPISODE FOUR

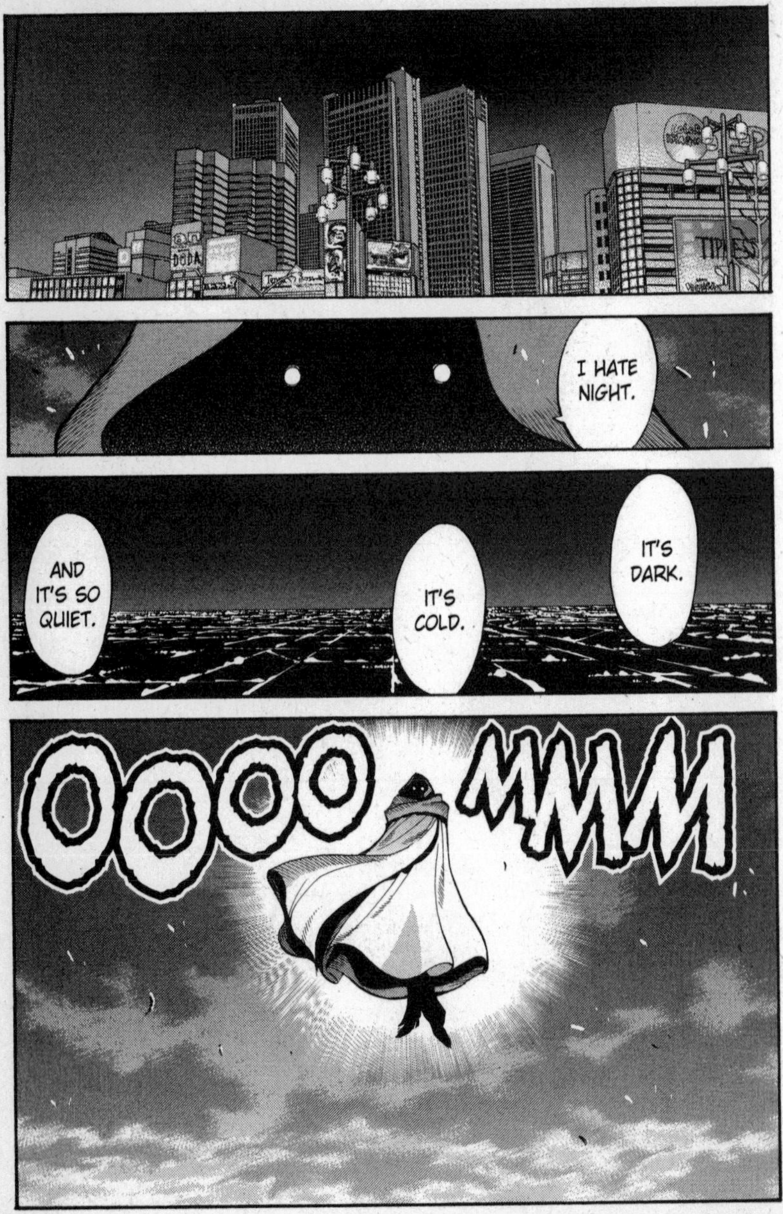
DODA
TIPNESS
I HATE NIGHT.
IT'S DARK.
IT'S COLD.
AND IT'S SO QUIET.
OOOOMMM

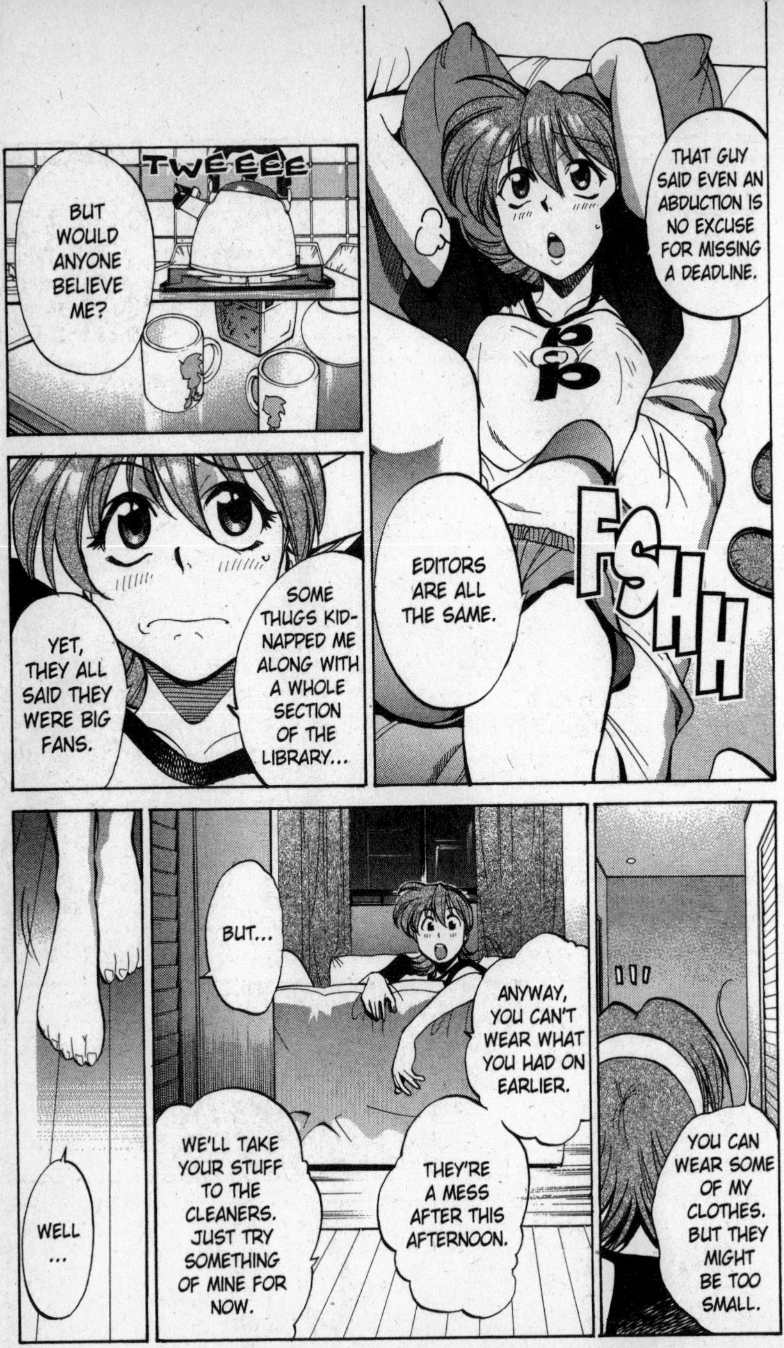
THAT GUY SAID EVEN AN ABDUCTION IS NO EXCUSE FOR MISSING A DEADLINE.
EDITORS ARE ALL THE SAME.
FSHH
TWEEEE
BUT WOULD ANYONE BELIEVE ME?
SOME THUGS KID-NAPPED ME ALONG WITH A WHOLE SECTION OF THE LIBRARY...
YET, THEY ALL SAID THEY WERE BIG FANS.
YOU CAN WEAR SOME OF MY CLOTHES. BUT THEY MIGHT BE TOO SMALL.
ANYWAY, YOU CAN'T WEAR WHAT YOU HAD ON EARLIER.
THEY'RE A MESS AFTER THIS AFTERNOON.
WE'LL TAKE YOUR STUFF TO THE CLEANERS. JUST TRY SOMETHING OF MINE FOR NOW.
BUT...
WELL ...

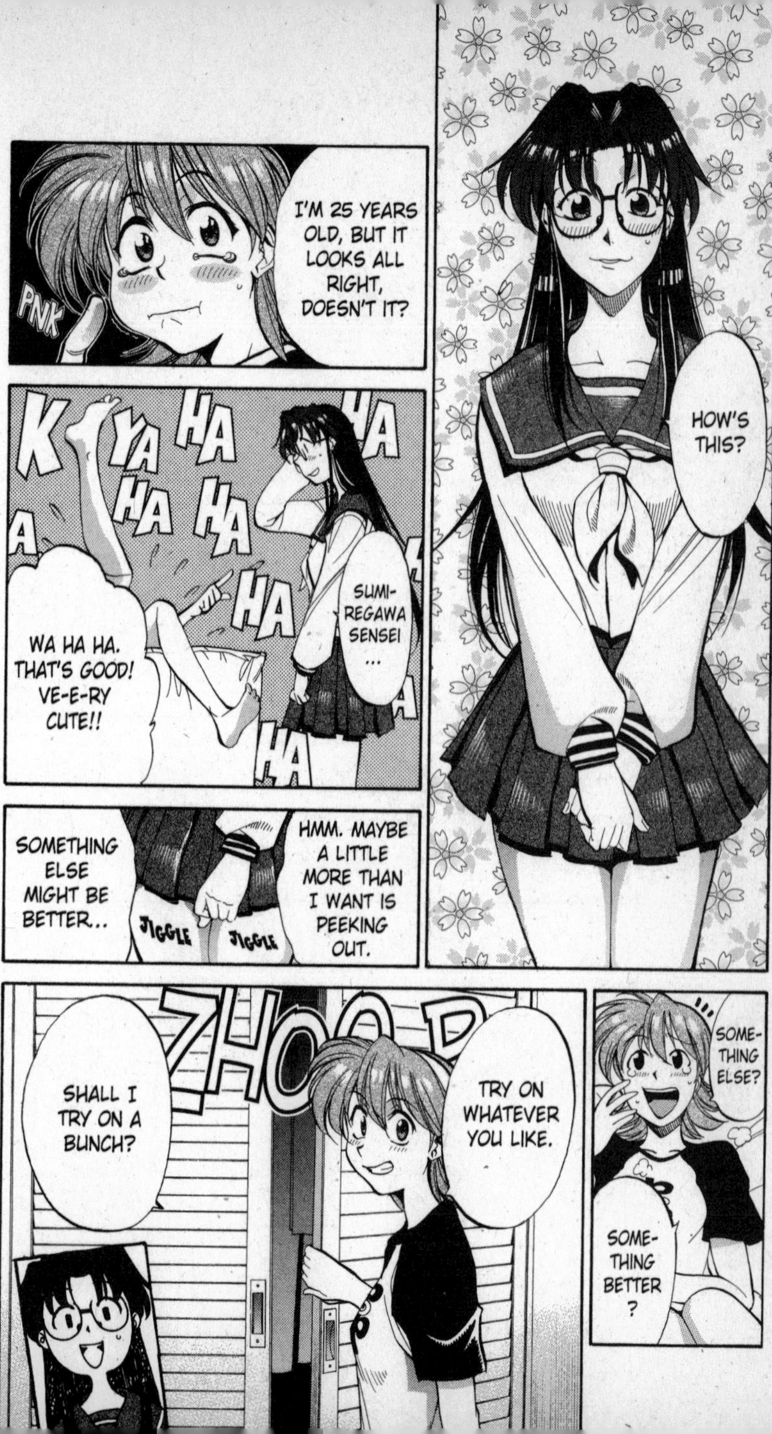
HOW'S THIS?
I'M 25 YEARS OLD, BUT IT LOOKS ALL RIGHT, DOESN'T IT?
PNK
KYA HA HA HA HA HA HA HA HA
SUMI-REGAWA SENSEI ...
WA HA HA. THAT'S GOOD! VE-E-RY CUTE!!
HMM. MAYBE A LITTLE MORE THAN I WANT IS PEEKING OUT.
JIGGLE
JIGGLE
SOMETHING ELSE MIGHT BE BETTER..
SOME-THING ELSE?
SOME-THING BETTER ?
TRY ON WHATEVER YOU LIKE.
ZHOOD
SHALL I TRY ON A BUNCH?

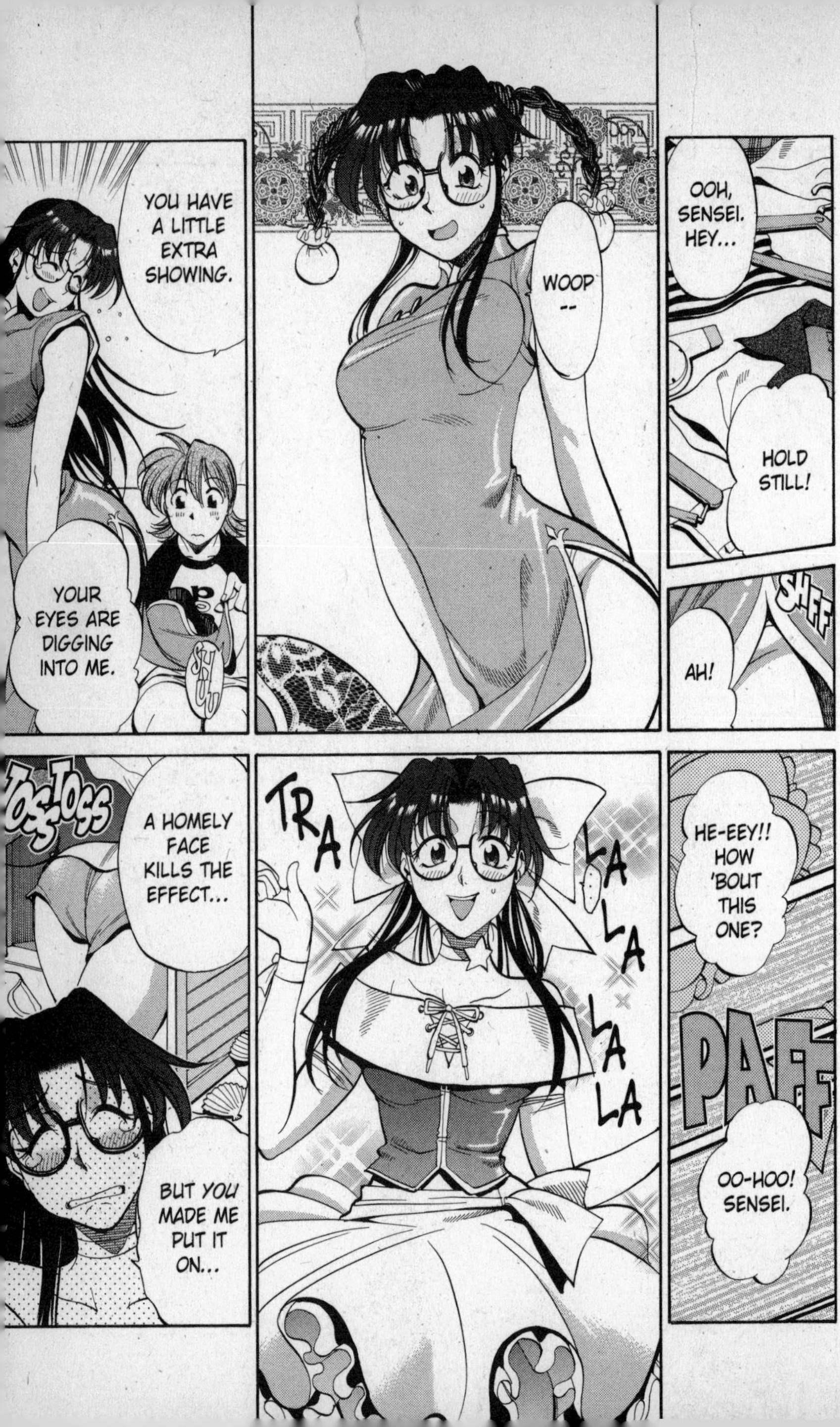
OOH, SENSEI. HEY...
HOLD STILL!
SHEFF
AH!
WOOP --
YOU HAVE A LITTLE EXTRA SHOWING.
YOUR EYES ARE DIGGING INTO ME.
SHUU
HE-EEY!! HOW 'BOUT THIS ONE?
PAFF
OO-HOO! SENSEI.
TRA LA LA LA LA LA
TOSS TOSS
A HOMELY FACE KILLS THE EFFECT...
BUT YOU MADE ME PUT IT ON...

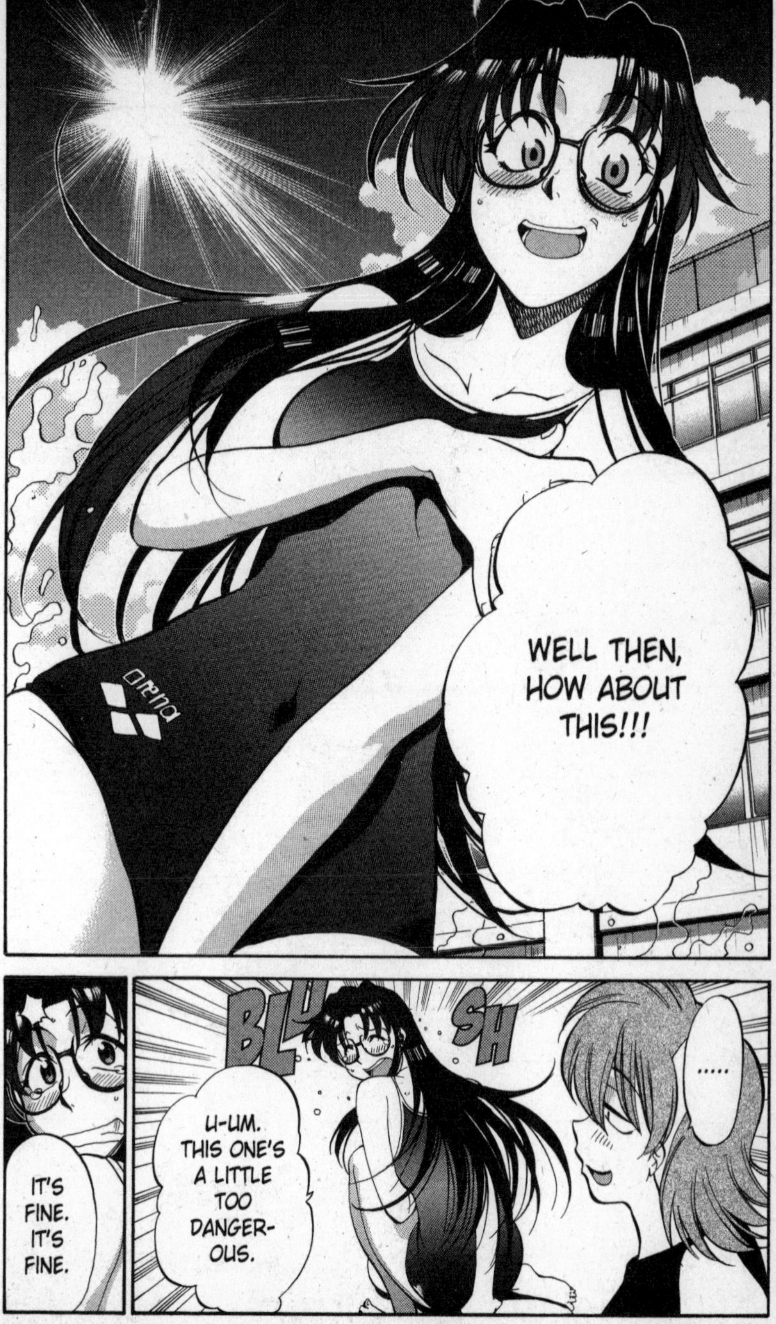
WELL THEN, HOW ABOUT THIS!!!
.....
BLUSH
U-UM. THIS ONE'S A LITTLE TOO DANGER-OUS.
IT'S FINE. IT'S FINE.

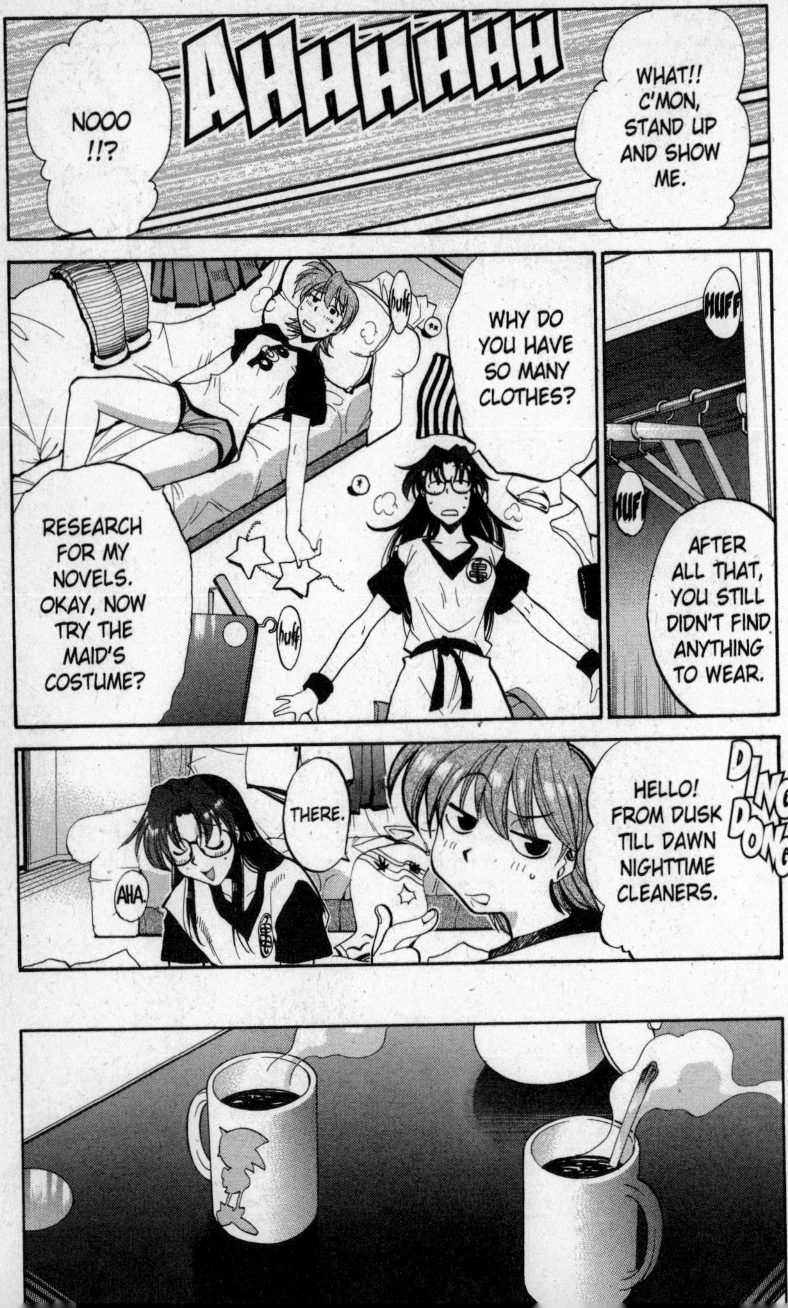
WHAT!! C'MON, STAND UP AND SHOW ME.
AHHHHHHH
NOOO !!?
HUFF
AFTER ALL THAT, YOU STILL DIDN'T FIND ANYTHING TO WEAR.
HUFF
WHY DO YOU HAVE SO MANY CLOTHES?
huff
RESEARCH FOR MY NOVELS. OKAY, NOW TRY THE MAID'S COSTUME?
huff
DING DONG
HELLO! FROM DUSK TILL DAWN NIGHTTIME CLEANERS.
THERE.
AHA.

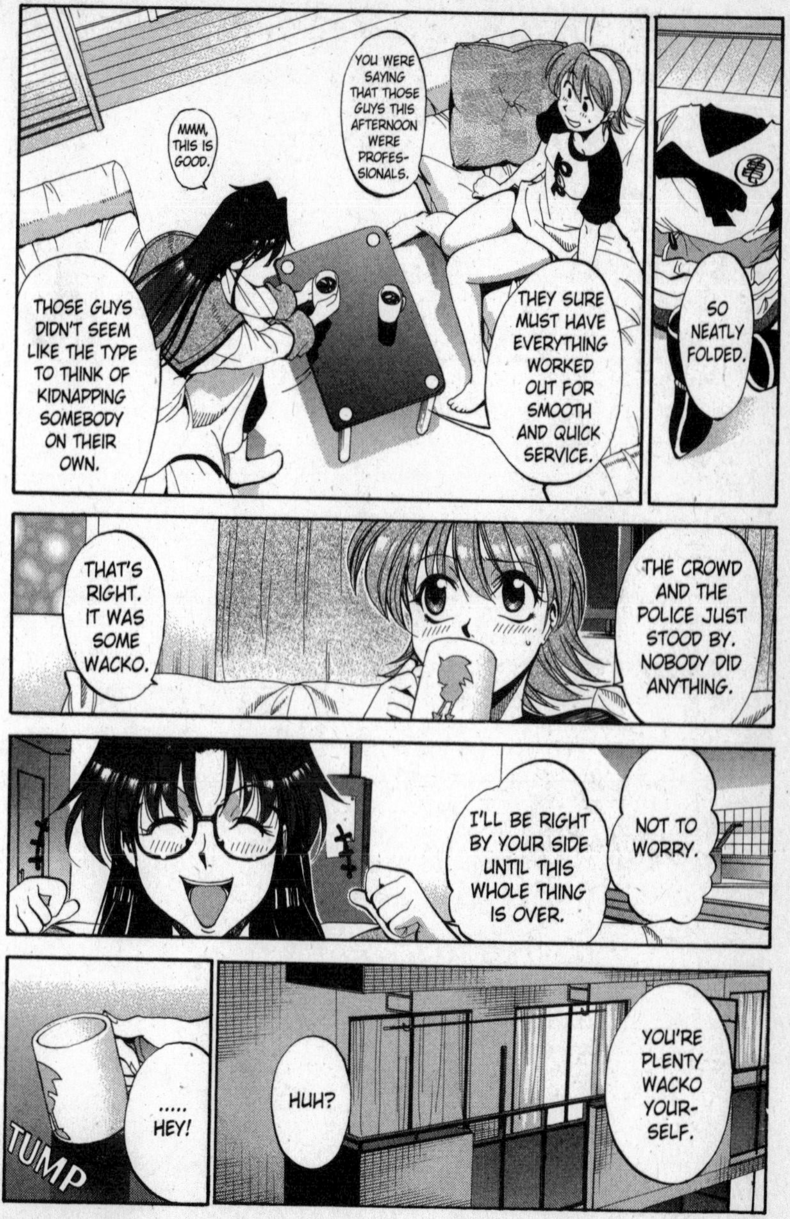
SO NEATLY FOLDED.
YOU WERE SAYING THAT THOSE GUYS THIS AFTERNOON WERE PROFES-SIONALS.
MMM, THIS IS GOOD.
THEY SURE MUST HAVE EVERYTHING WORKED OUT FOR SMOOTH AND QUICK SERVICE.
THOSE GUYS DIDN'T SEEM LIKE THE TYPE TO THINK OF KIDNAPPING SOMEBODY ON THEIR OWN.
THE CROWD AND THE POLICE JUST STOOD BY. NOBODY DID ANYTHING.
THAT'S RIGHT. IT WAS SOME WACKO.
NOT TO WORRY.
I'LL BE RIGHT BY YOUR SIDE UNTIL THIS WHOLE THING IS OVER.
YOU'RE PLENTY WACKO YOUR-SELF.
HUH?
..... HEY!
TUMP

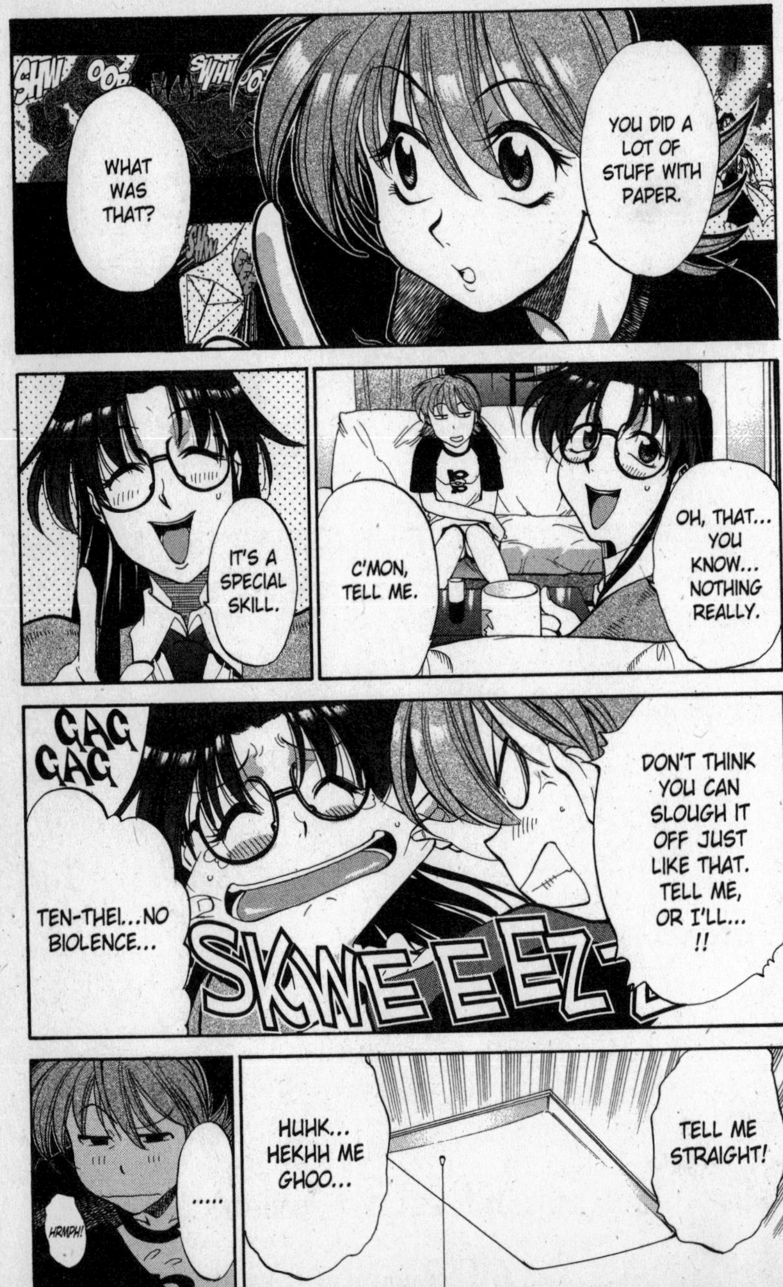
YOU DID A LOT OF STUFF WITH PAPER.
SHWOOP SHWOOP
WHAT WAS THAT?
OH, THAT... YOU KNOW... NOTHING REALLY.
C'MON, TELL ME.
IT'S A SPECIAL SKILL.
DON'T THINK YOU CAN SLOUGH IT OFF JUST LIKE THAT. TELL ME, OR I'LL... !!
SKWE EEZ
GAG GAG
TEN-THEI...NO BIOLENCE...
TELL ME STRAIGHT!
HUHK... HEKHH ME GHOO...
.....
HRMPH!

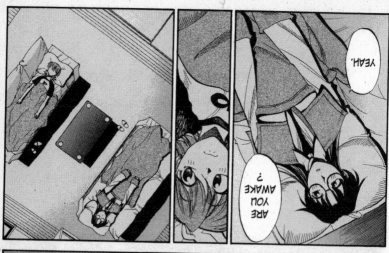

ARE YOU AWAKE?

YEAH.

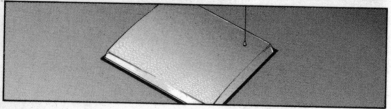

FINE, DON'T TELL ME. A LOT HAPPENED TODAY AND I'M WORN OUT, ANYWAY.

AHHUH.

PUFF

BUT YOU WILL TELL ME EVERYTHING TOMORROW.

OKAY.

HRN HRN

GOT IT?

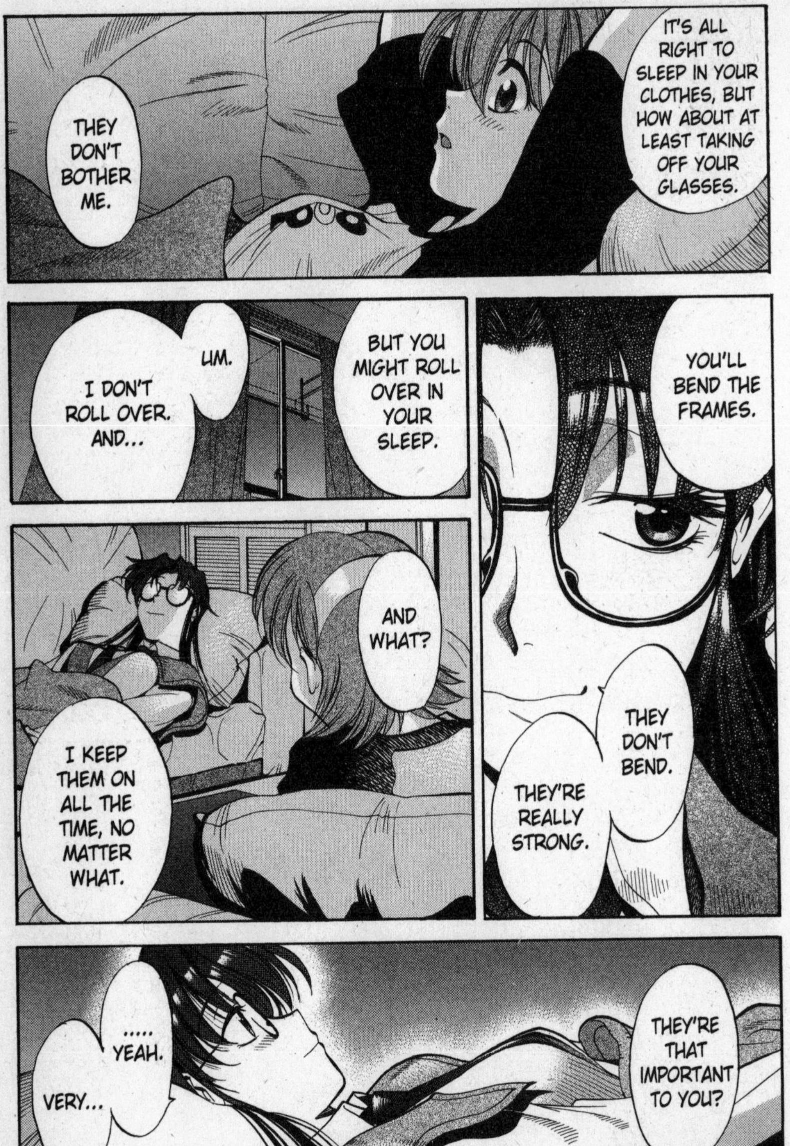
IT'S ALL RIGHT TO SLEEP IN YOUR CLOTHES, BUT HOW ABOUT AT LEAST TAKING OFF YOUR GLASSES.
THEY DON'T BOTHER ME.
YOU'LL BEND THE FRAMES.
THEY DON'T BEND.
THEY'RE REALLY STRONG.
BUT YOU MIGHT ROLL OVER IN YOUR SLEEP.
UM.
I DON'T ROLL OVER. AND...
AND WHAT?
I KEEP THEM ON ALL THE TIME, NO MATTER WHAT.
THEY'RE THAT IMPORTANT TO YOU?
..... YEAH.
VERY...

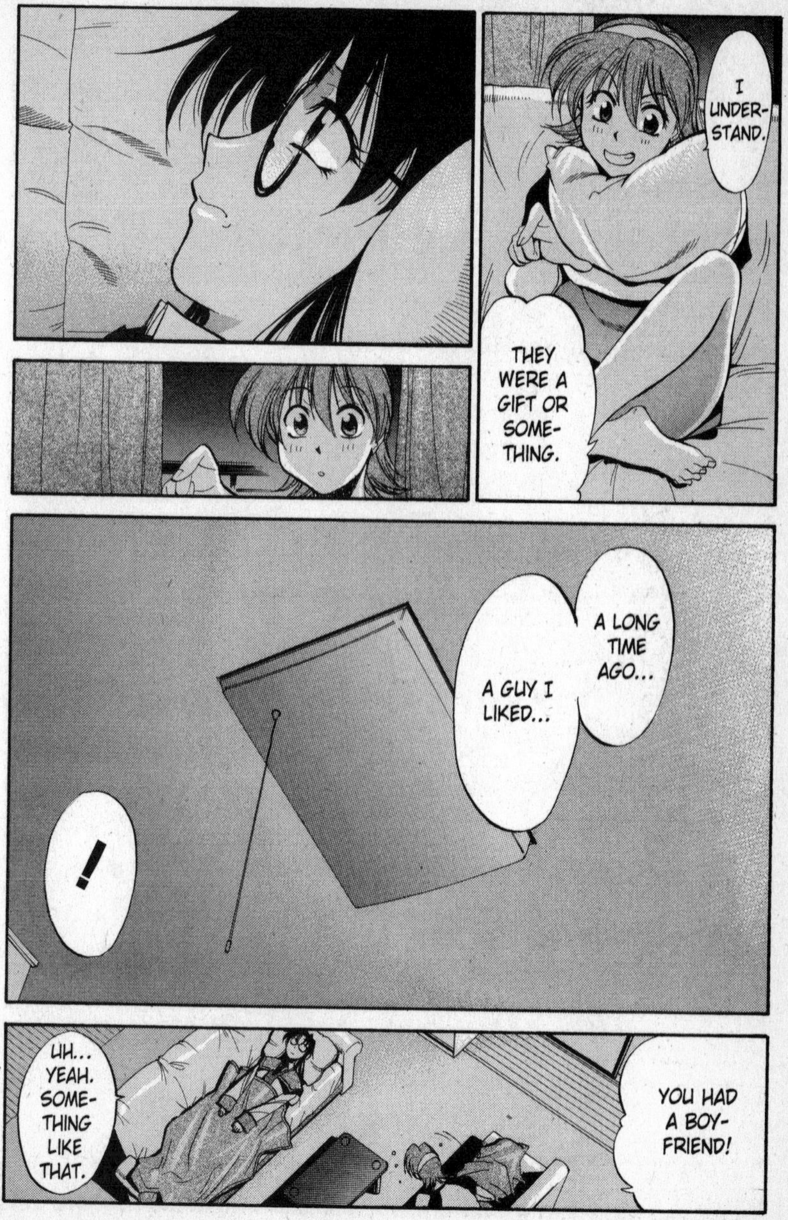
I UNDER-STAND.
THEY WERE A GIFT OR SOME-THING.
A LONG TIME AGO...
A GUY I LIKED...
!
YOU HAD A BOY-FRIEND!
UH... YEAH. SOME-THING LIKE THAT.

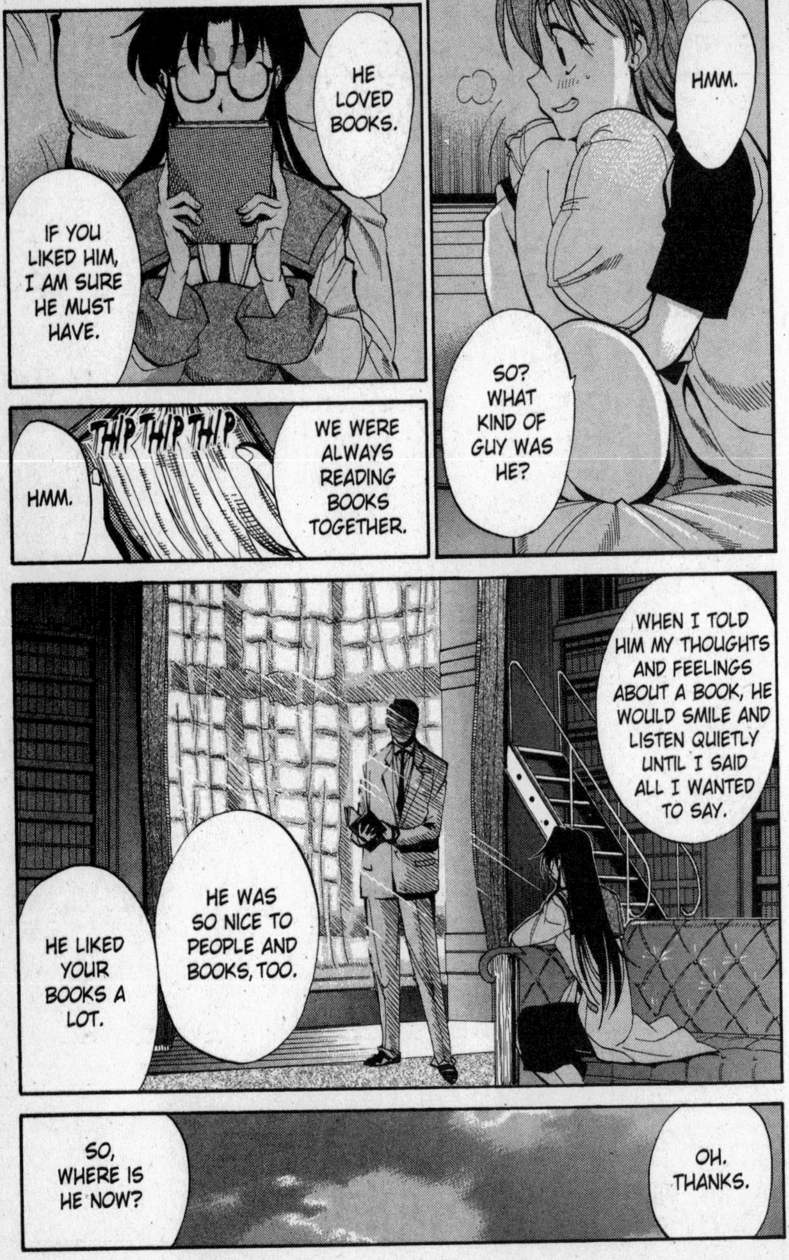
HMM.
SO? WHAT KIND OF GUY WAS HE?
HE LOVED BOOKS.
IF YOU LIKED HIM, I AM SURE HE MUST HAVE.
WE WERE ALWAYS READING BOOKS TOGETHER.
THIP THIP THIP
HMM.
WHEN I TOLD HIM MY THOUGHTS AND FEELINGS ABOUT A BOOK, HE WOULD SMILE AND LISTEN QUIETLY UNTIL I SAID ALL I WANTED TO SAY.
HE WAS SO NICE TO PEOPLE AND BOOKS, TOO.
HE LIKED YOUR BOOKS A LOT.
OH. THANKS.
SO, WHERE IS HE NOW?

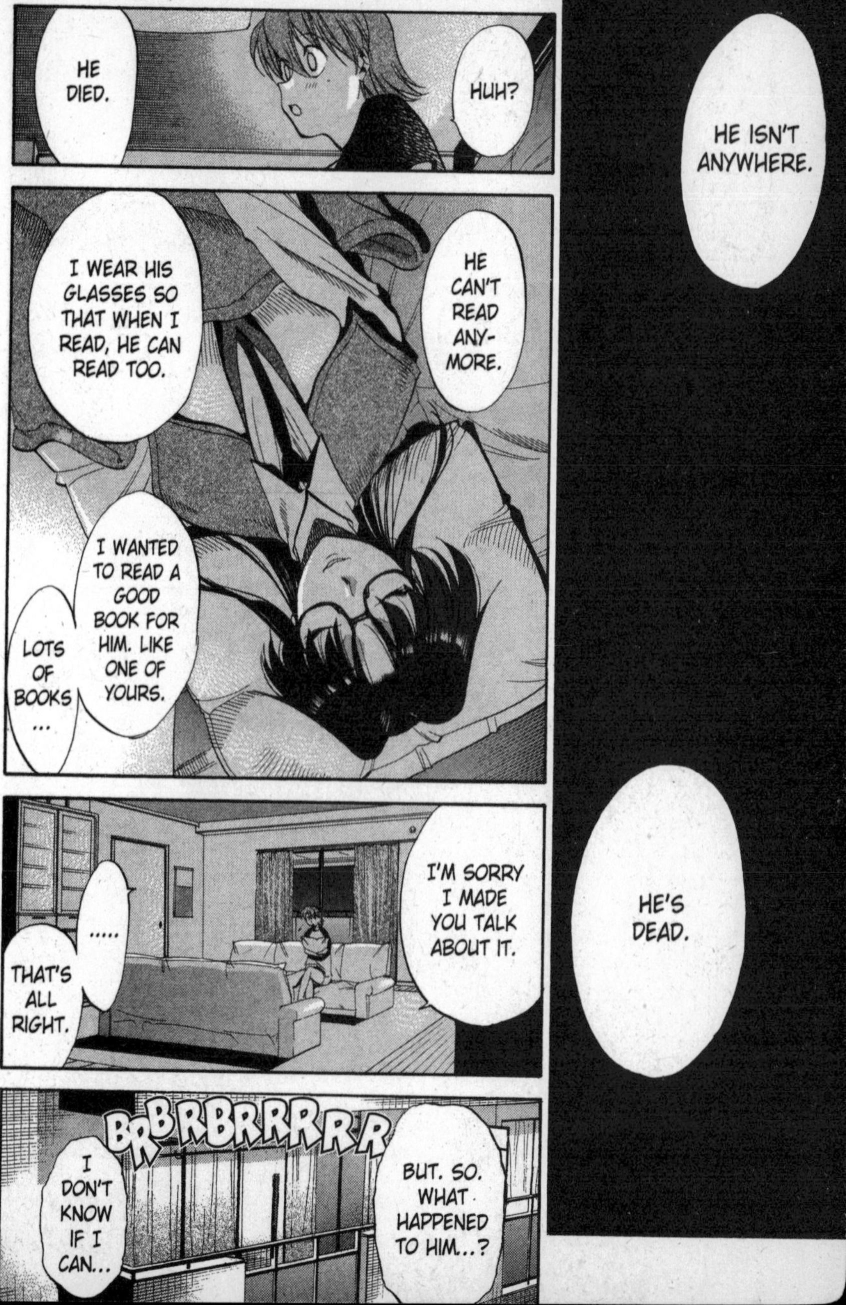
HE ISN'T ANYWHERE.
HE'S DEAD.
HUH?
HE DIED.
HE CAN'T READ ANY-MORE.
I WEAR HIS GLASSES SO THAT WHEN I READ, HE CAN READ TOO.
I WANTED TO READ A GOOD BOOK FOR HIM. LIKE ONE OF YOURS.
LOTS OF BOOKS ...
I'M SORRY I MADE YOU TALK ABOUT IT.
.....
THAT'S ALL RIGHT.
BRBRBRRRRRR
BUT. SO. WHAT HAPPENED TO HIM...?
I DON'T KNOW IF I CAN...

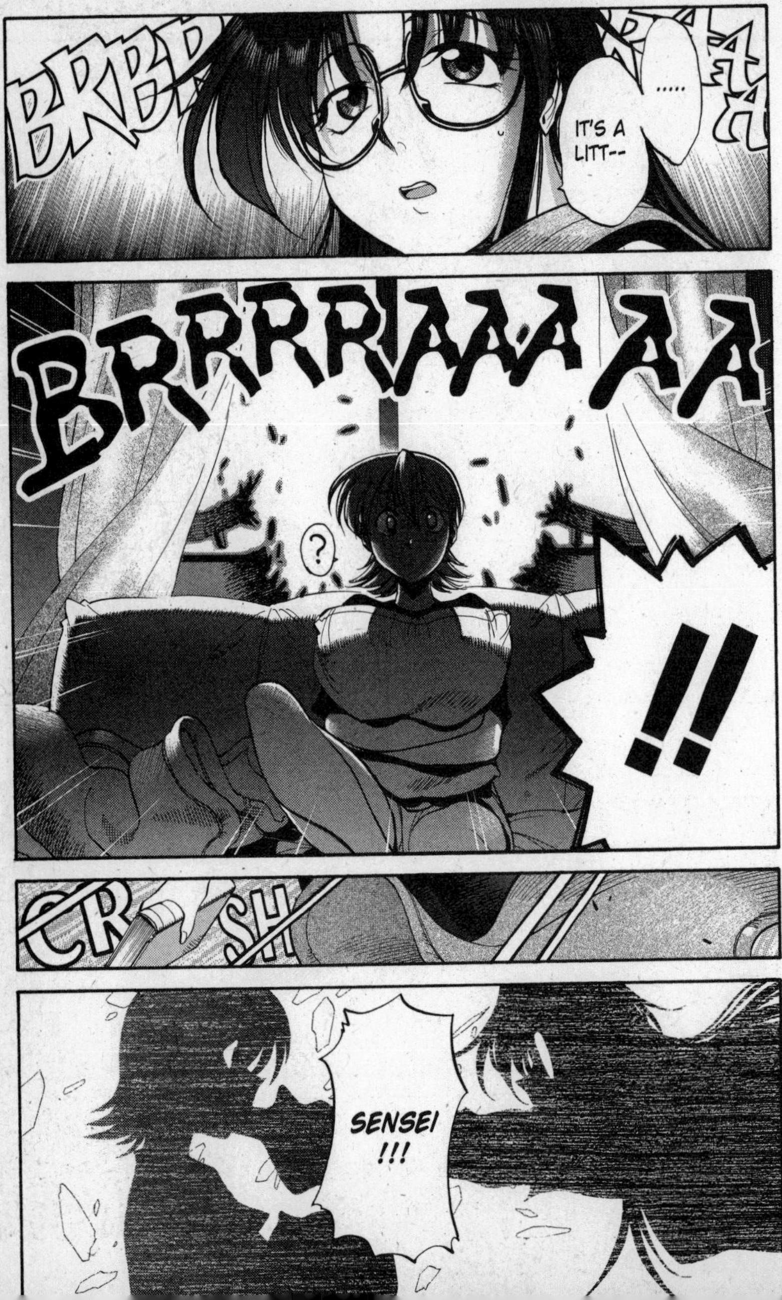
.....
IT'S A LITT--
BRBB
BRRRRIAAAAAA
?
!!
CRSH
SENSEI !!!

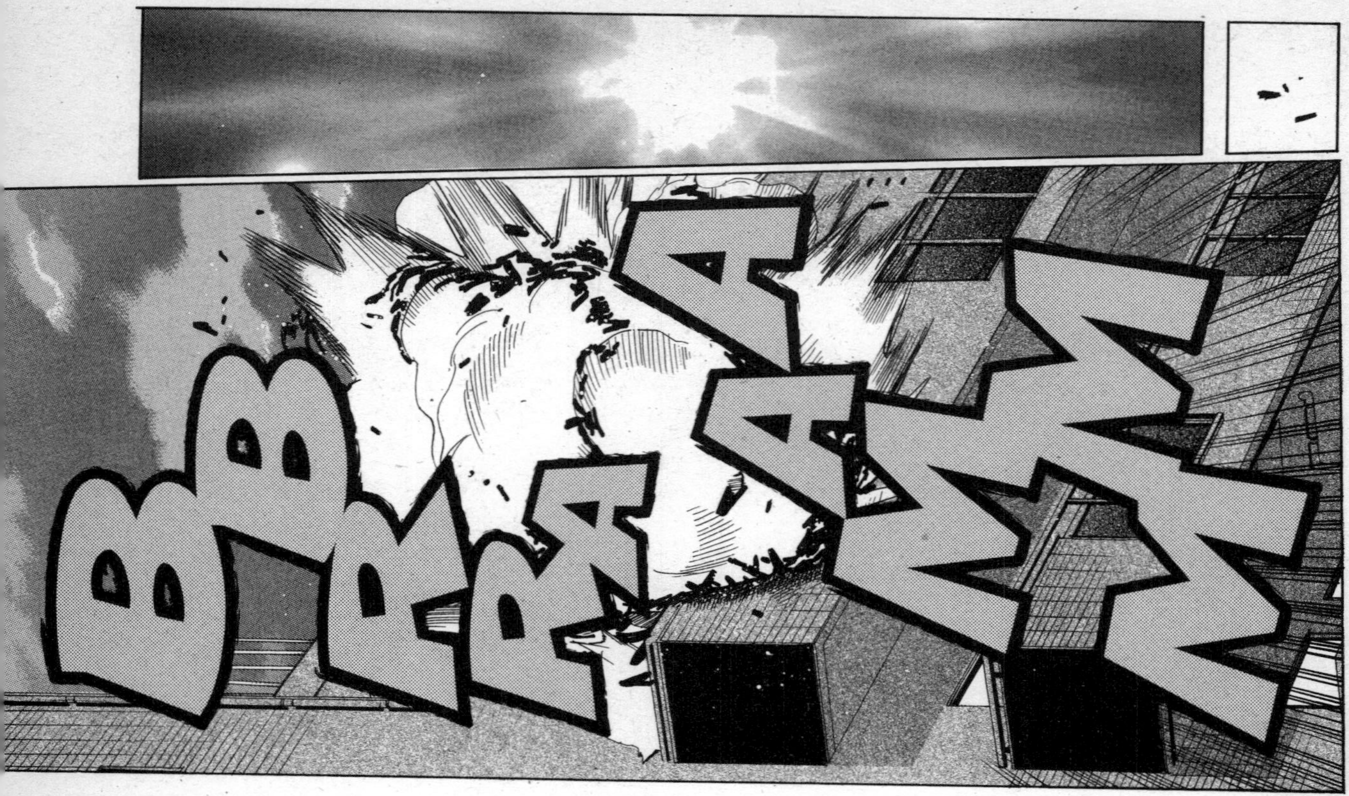
BBRAAAMM

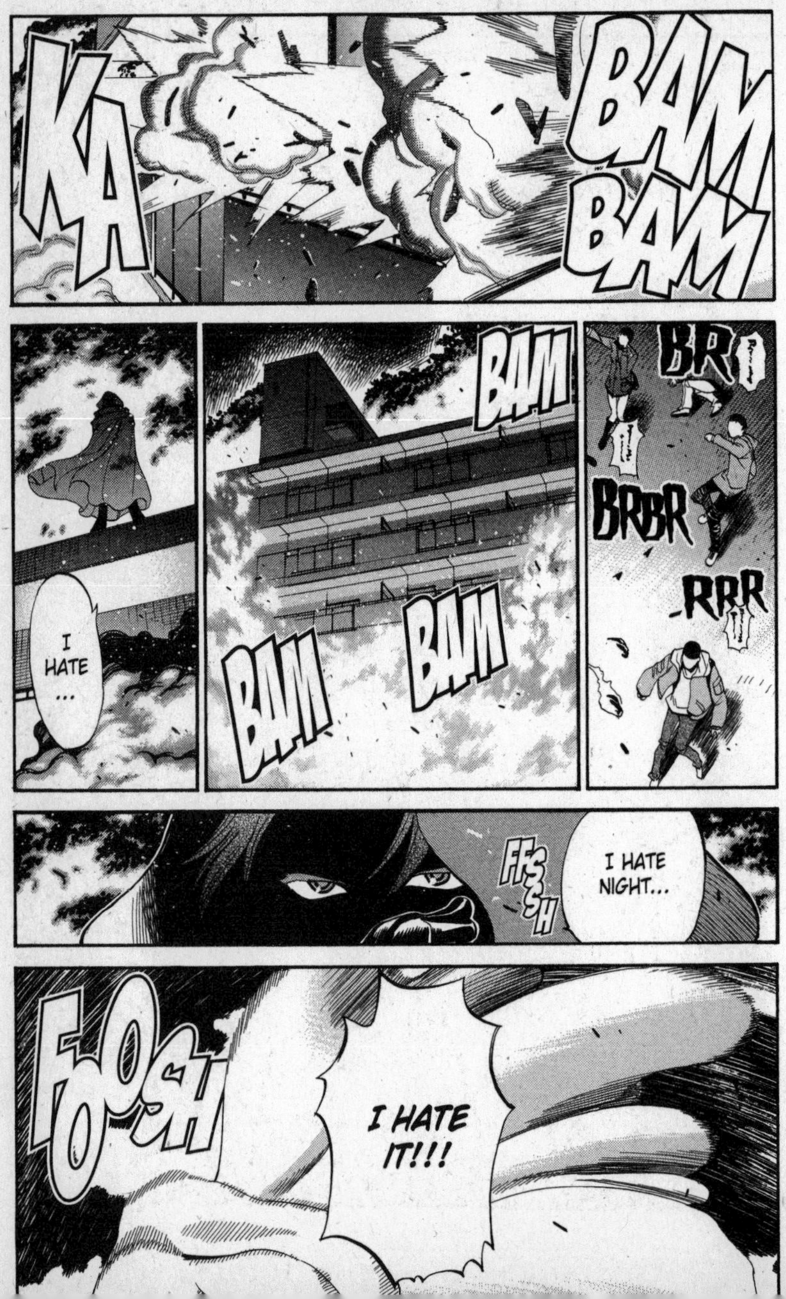
BAM BAM
KA
BR
BRBR
RRR
BAM
BAM
BAM
I HATE ...
I HATE NIGHT...
FFSSH
I HATE IT!!!
FOOSH

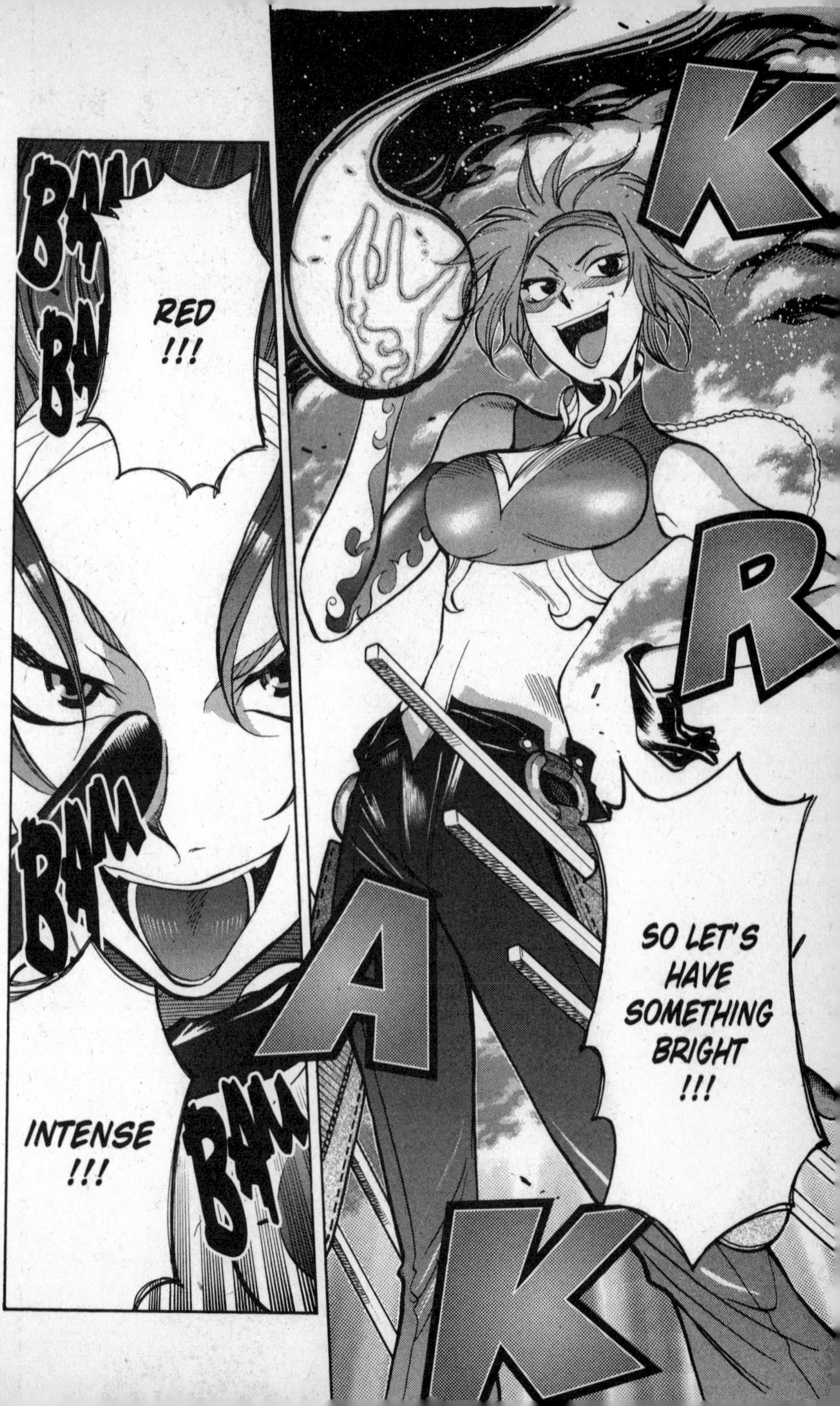
KRAK
SO LET'S HAVE SOMETHING BRIGHT !!!
BAM BAM
RED !!!
BAM
BAM
INTENSE !!!

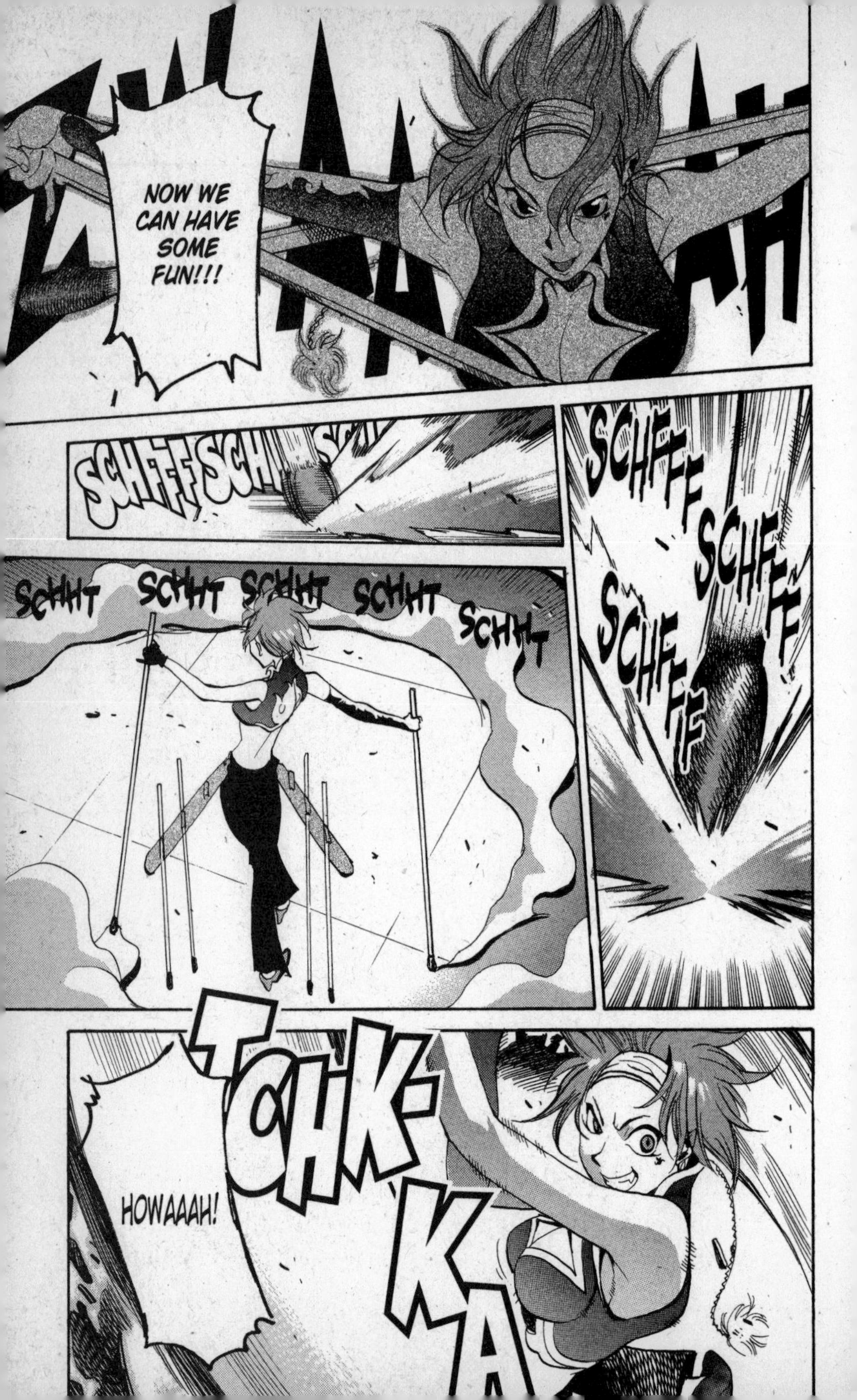

ZAAAAAAHH
NOW WE CAN HAVE SOME FUN!!!
SCHFFFF SCHFFFF SCHFFFF
SCHFFF SCHFF
SCHHT SCHHT SCHHT SCHHT SCHHT
TCHK-KA
HOWAAAH!

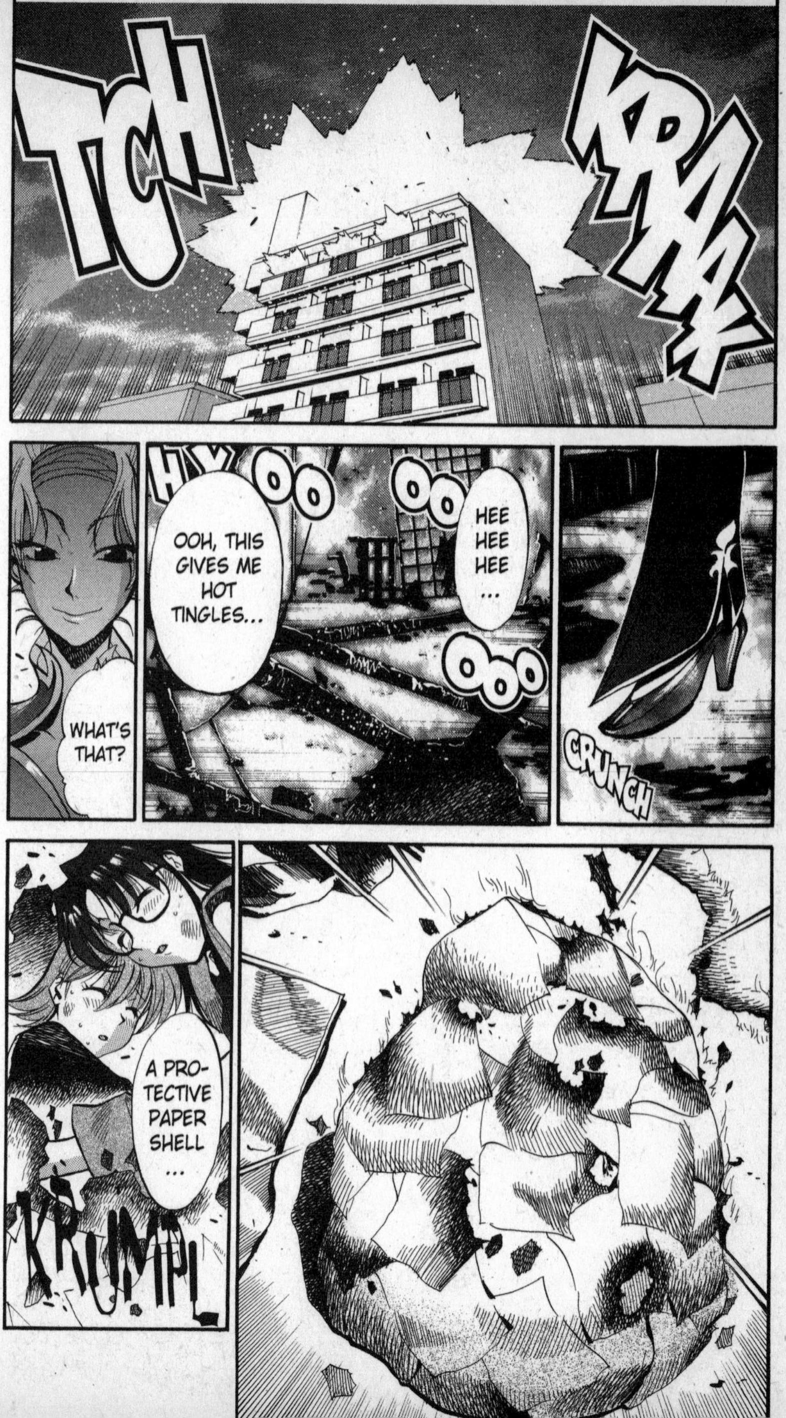
KRAAK
TCH
CRUNCH
HEE HEE HEE ...
OOO
HYOOOOOO
OOH, THIS GIVES ME HOT TINGLES...
WHAT'S THAT?
A PRO-TECTIVE PAPER SHELL ...
KRUMPL

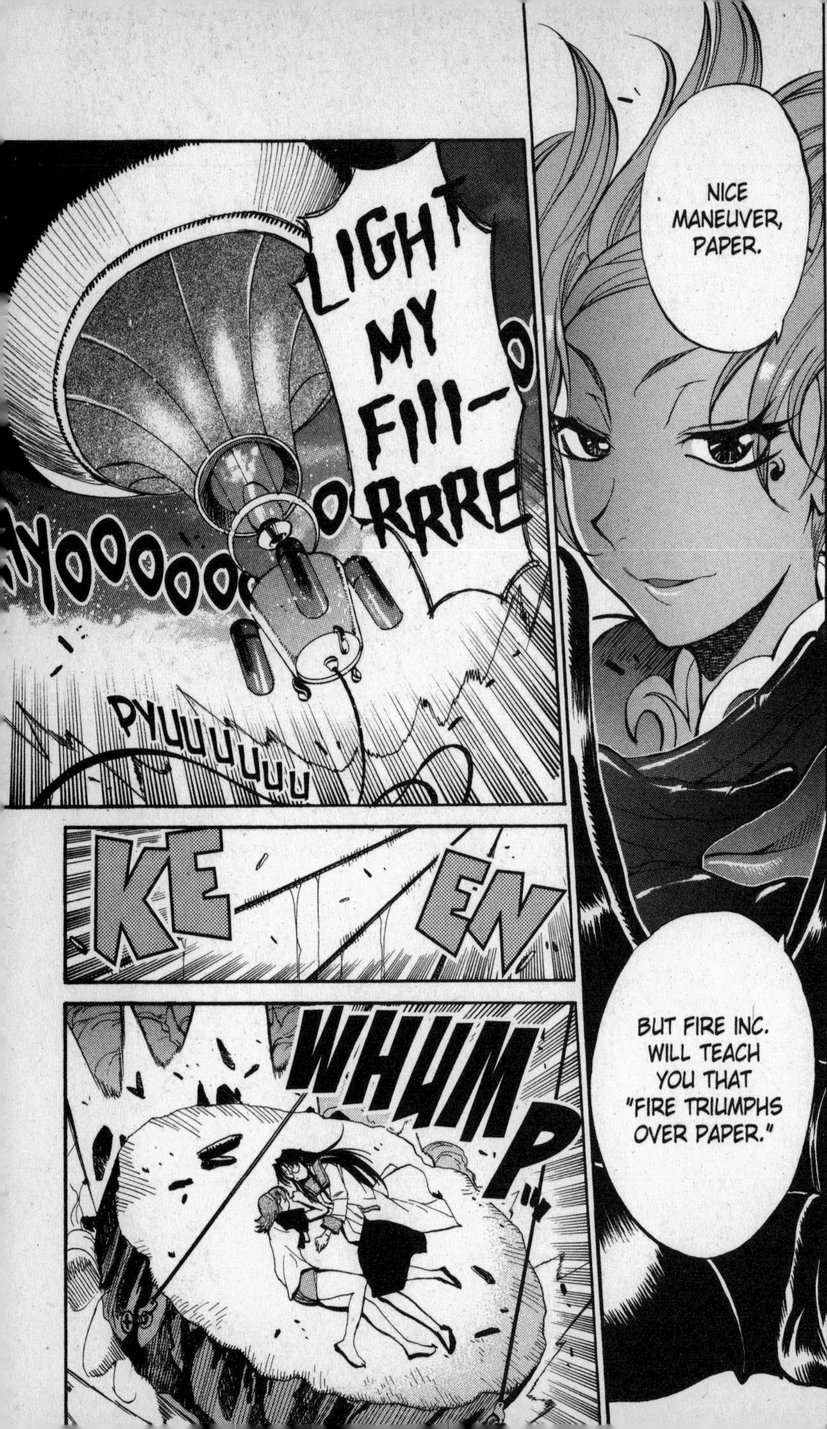
NICE MANEUVER, PAPER.
BUT FIRE INC. WILL TEACH YOU THAT "FIRE TRIUMPHS OVER PAPER."
LIGHT MY FIII-O-RRRE
...YOOOOOO
PYUUUUUUU
KE EN
WHUMP..

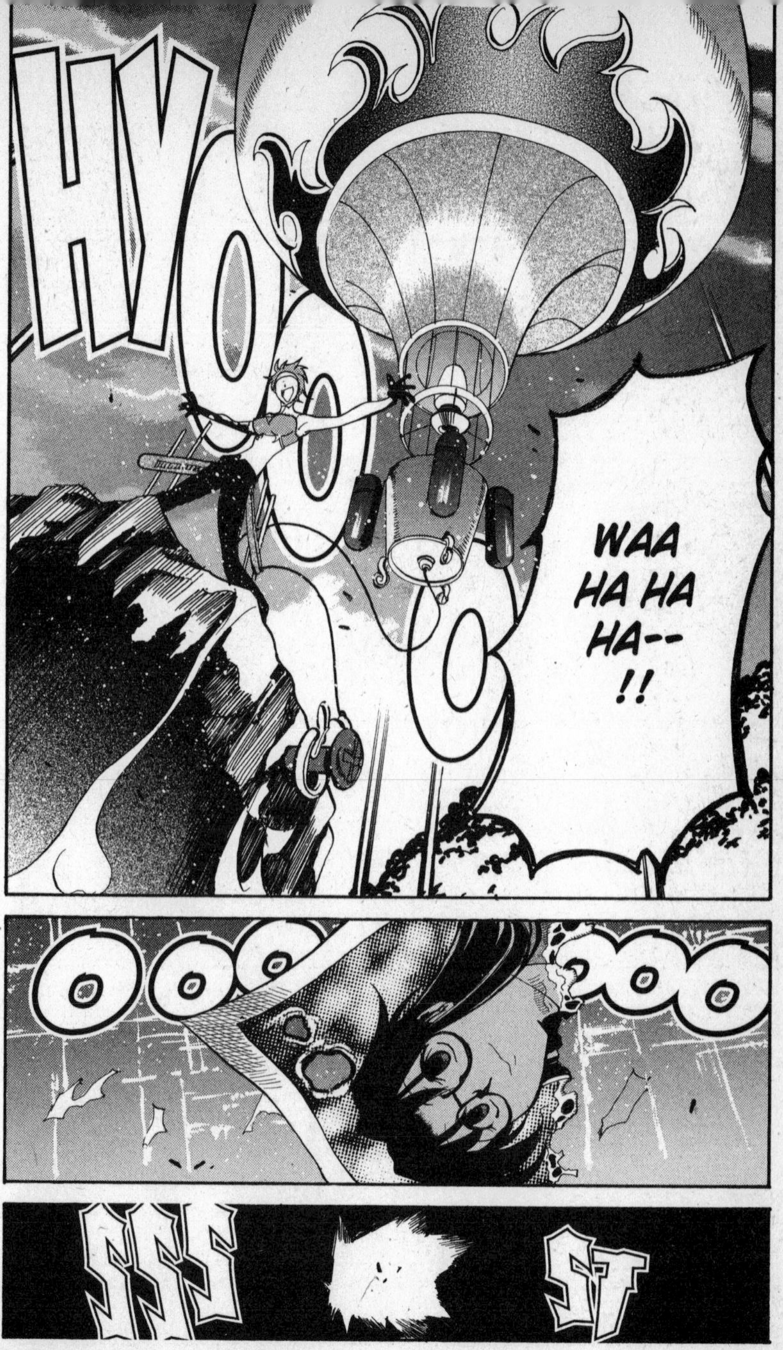
WAA HA HA HA-- !!
HYO
OOOOOO
SSS
ST

EPISODE FIVE

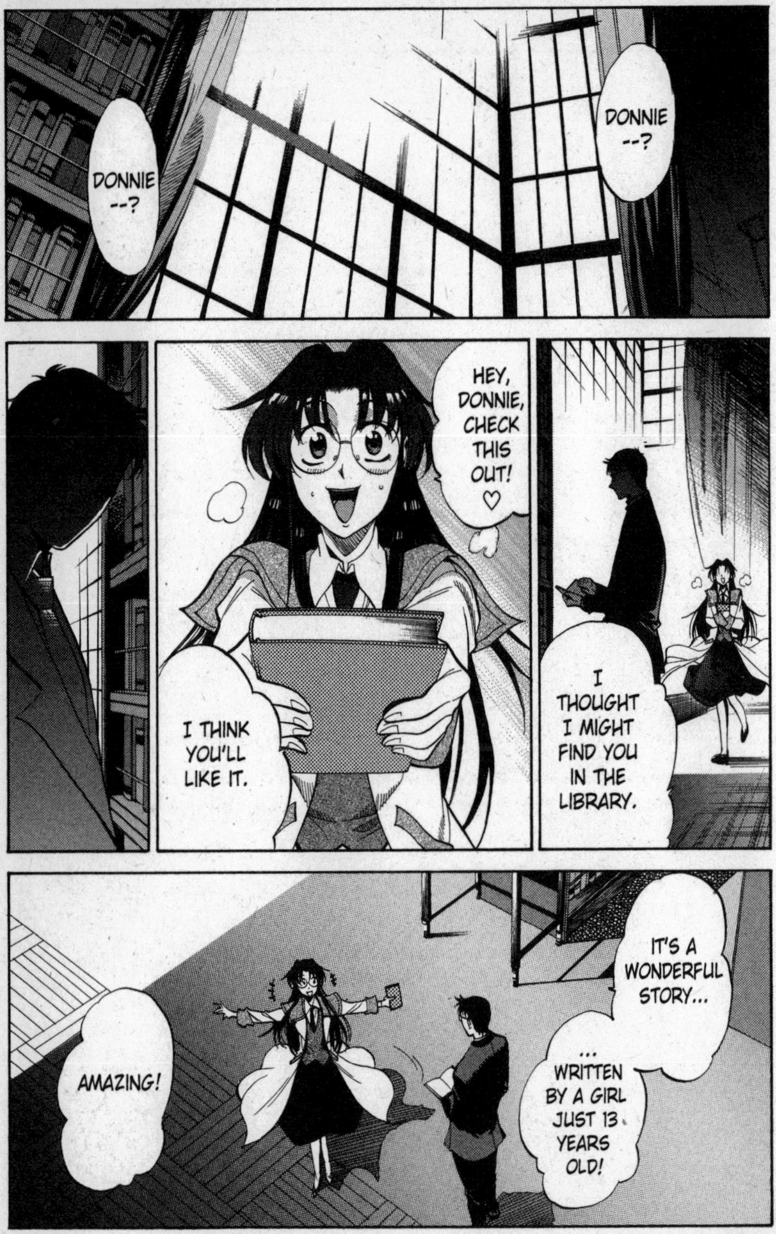
DONNIE --?
DONNIE --?
I THOUGHT I MIGHT FIND YOU IN THE LIBRARY.
HEY, DONNIE, CHECK THIS OUT! ♡
I THINK YOU'LL LIKE IT.
IT'S A WONDERFUL STORY...
... WRITTEN BY A GIRL JUST 13 YEARS OLD!
AMAZING!

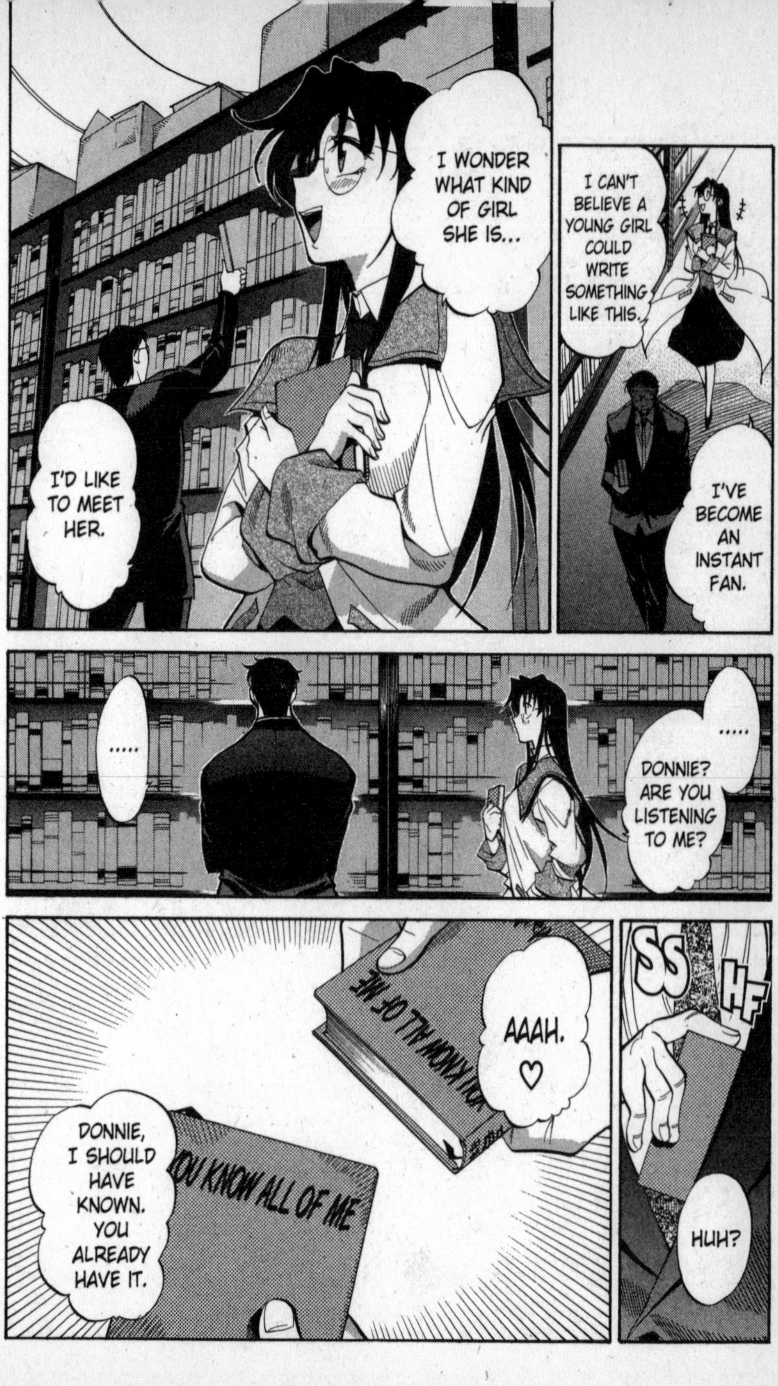
I CAN'T BELIEVE A YOUNG GIRL COULD WRITE SOMETHING LIKE THIS.
I'VE BECOME AN INSTANT FAN.
I WONDER WHAT KIND OF GIRL SHE IS...
I'D LIKE TO MEET HER.
.....
DONNIE? ARE YOU LISTENING TO ME?
.....
SSHF
HUH?
AAAH. ♡
YOU KNOW ALL OF ME
DONNIE, I SHOULD HAVE KNOWN. YOU ALREADY HAVE IT.
YOU KNOW ALL OF ME

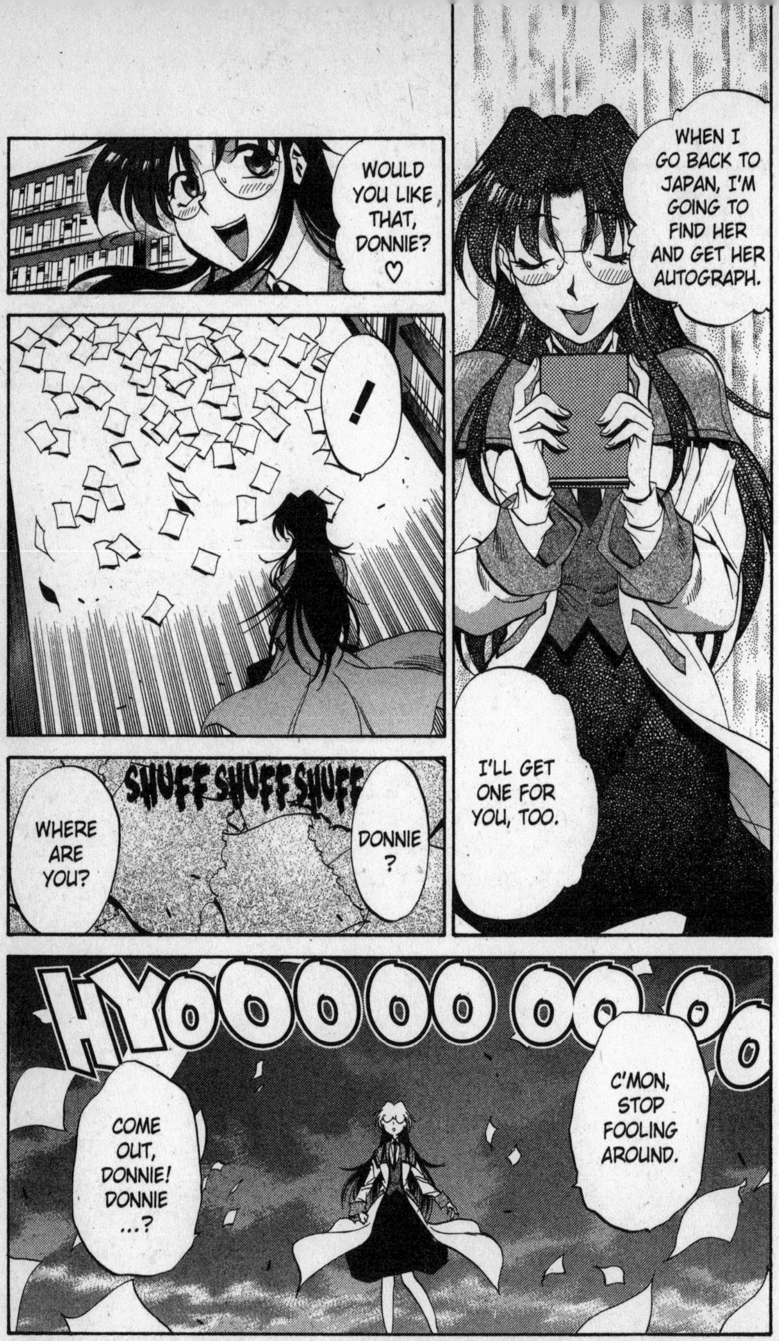
WHEN I GO BACK TO JAPAN, I'M GOING TO FIND HER AND GET HER AUTOGRAPH.
I'LL GET ONE FOR YOU, TOO.
WOULD YOU LIKE THAT, DONNIE? ♡
!
DONNIE ?
SHUFF SHUFF SHUFF
WHERE ARE YOU?
HYOOOOO OO OO
C'MON, STOP FOOLING AROUND.
COME OUT, DONNIE! DONNIE ...?

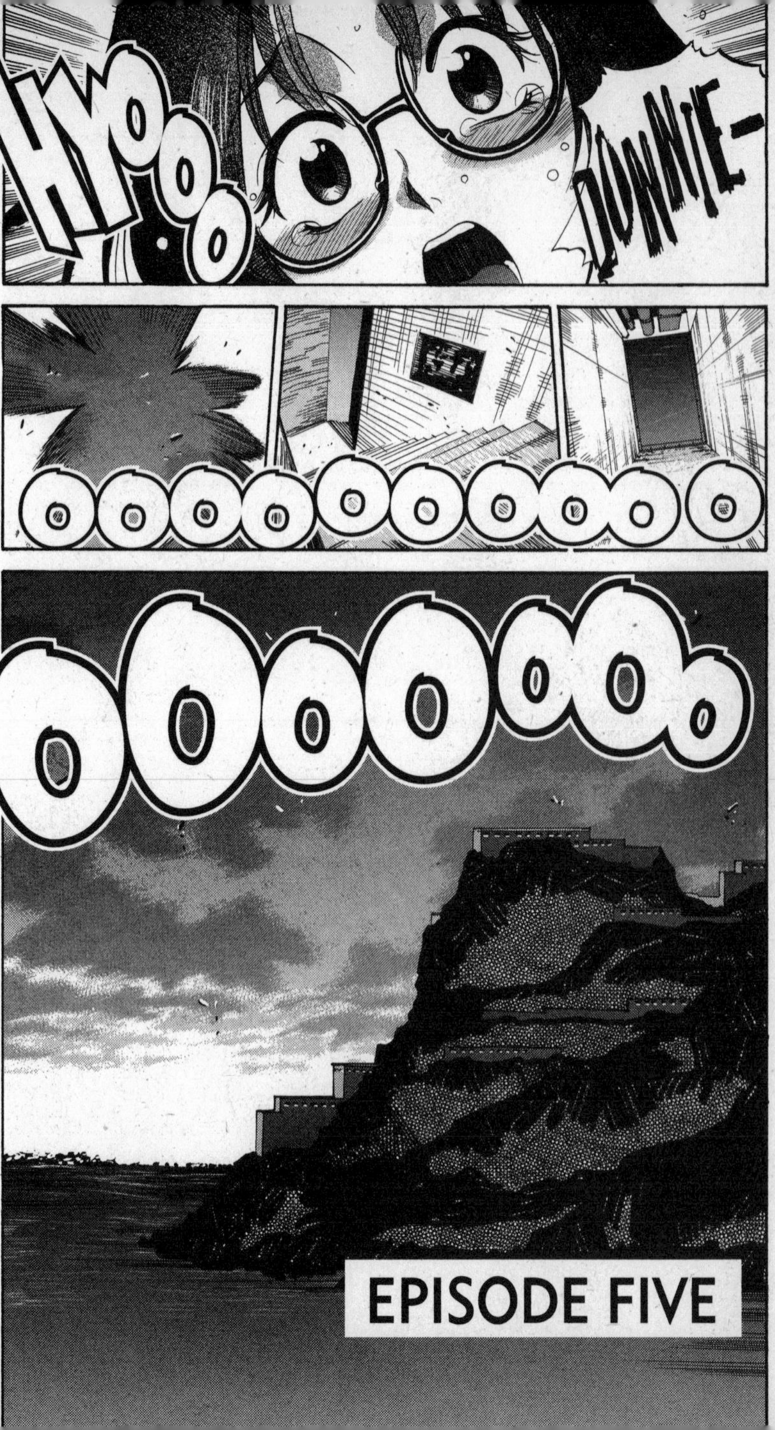
DONNIE-
HYOOOO
OOOOOOOOOO
OOOOOOO
EPISODE FIVE

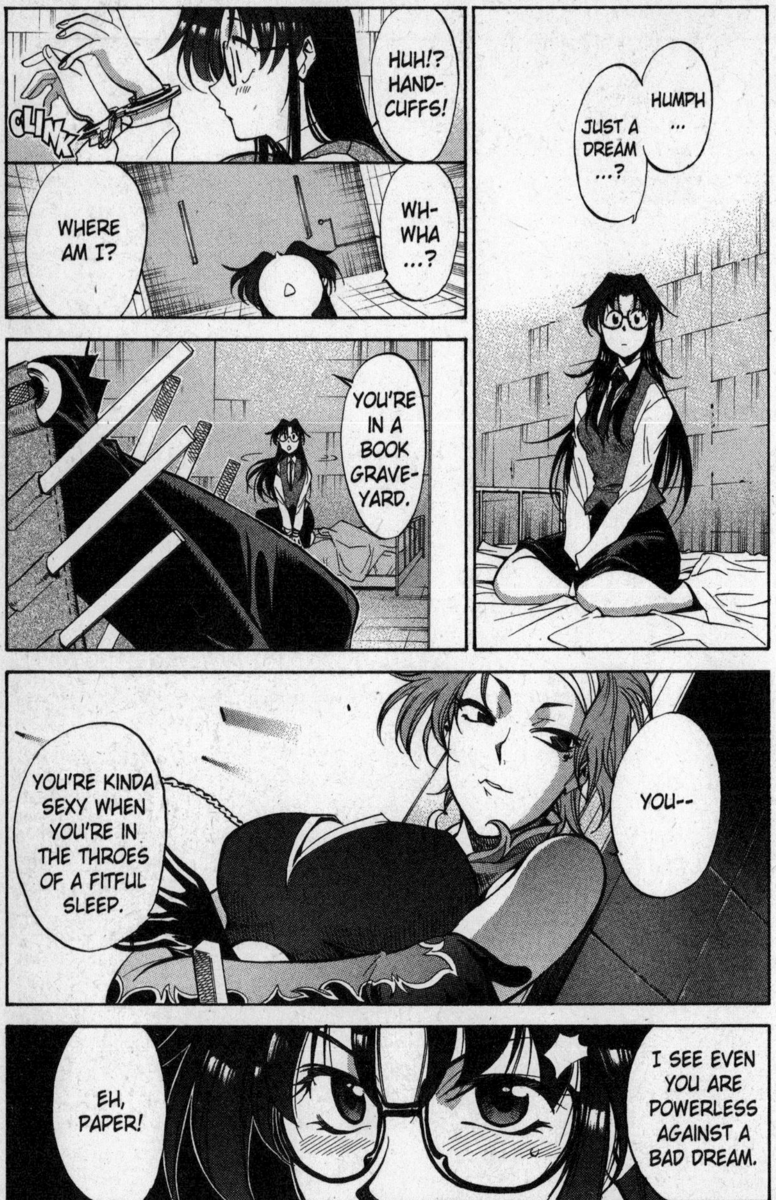
HUMPH ...
JUST A DREAM ...?
HUH!? HAND-CUFFS!
CLINK
WH-WHA ...?
WHERE AM I?
YOU'RE IN A BOOK GRAVE-YARD.
YOU--
YOU'RE KINDA SEXY WHEN YOU'RE IN THE THROES OF A FITFUL SLEEP.
I SEE EVEN YOU ARE POWERLESS AGAINST A BAD DREAM.
EH, PAPER!

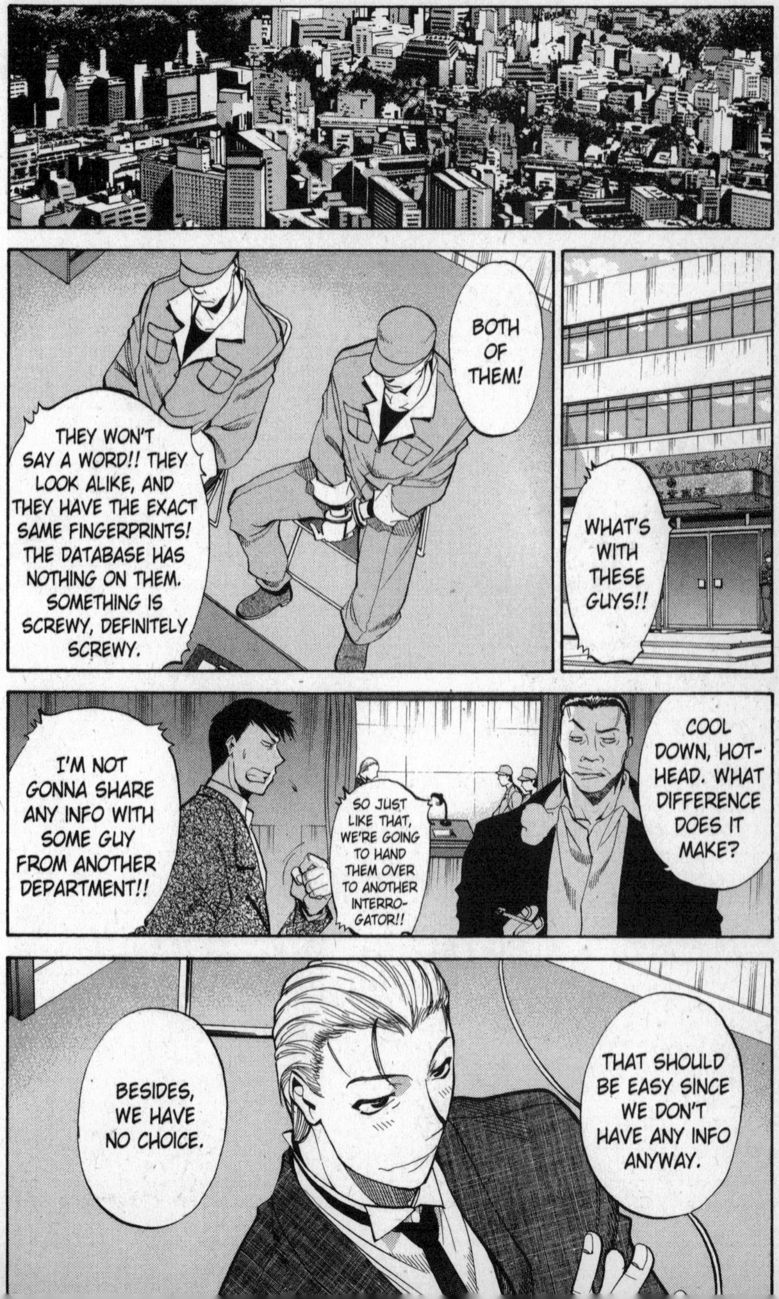
WHAT'S WITH THESE GUYS!!
BOTH OF THEM!
THEY WON'T SAY A WORD!! THEY LOOK ALIKE, AND THEY HAVE THE EXACT SAME FINGERPRINTS! THE DATABASE HAS NOTHING ON THEM. SOMETHING IS SCREWY, DEFINITELY SCREWY.
COOL DOWN, HOT-HEAD. WHAT DIFFERENCE DOES IT MAKE?
SO JUST LIKE THAT, WE'RE GOING TO HAND THEM OVER TO ANOTHER INTERRO-GATOR!!
I'M NOT GONNA SHARE ANY INFO WITH SOME GUY FROM ANOTHER DEPARTMENT!!
THAT SHOULD BE EASY SINCE WE DON'T HAVE ANY INFO ANYWAY.
BESIDES, WE HAVE NO CHOICE.

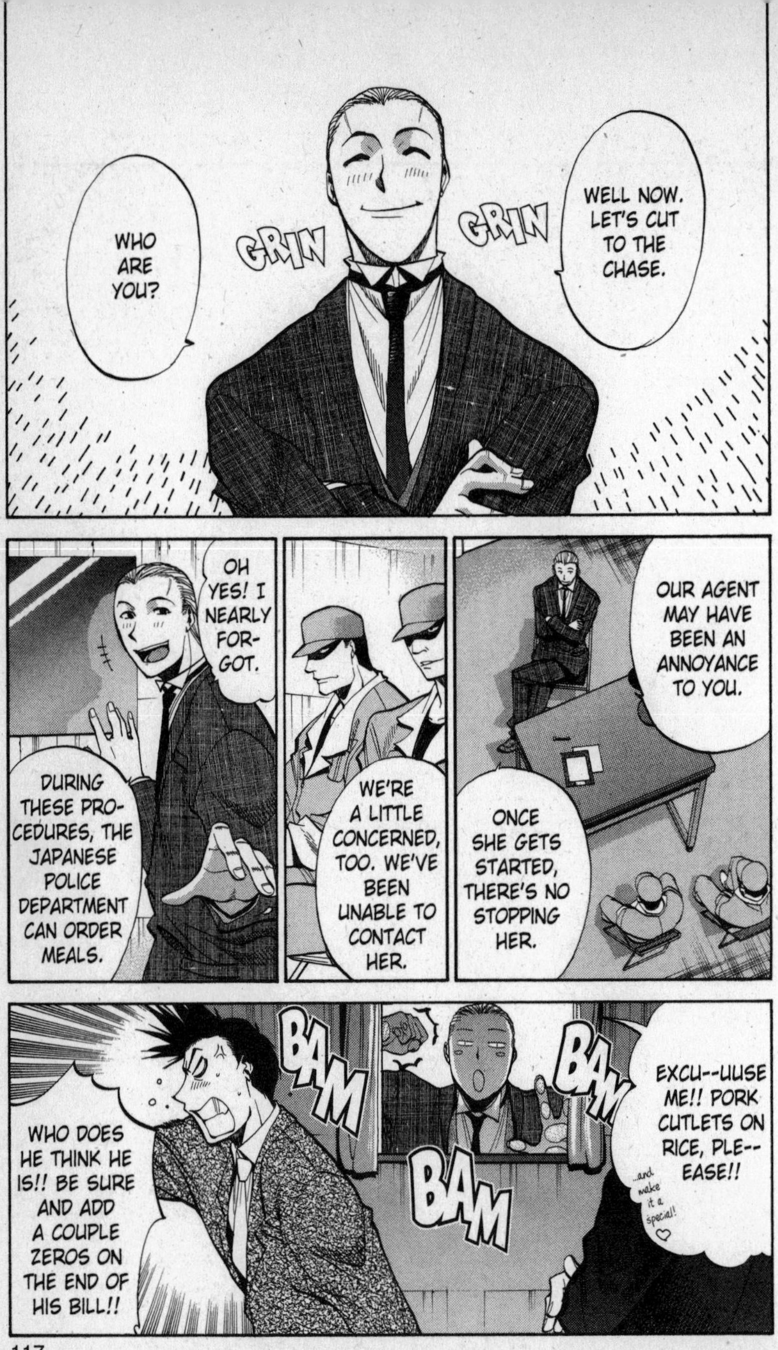
WELL NOW. LET'S CUT TO THE CHASE.
GRIN
GRIN
WHO ARE YOU?
OUR AGENT MAY HAVE BEEN AN ANNOYANCE TO YOU.
ONCE SHE GETS STARTED, THERE'S NO STOPPING HER.
WE'RE A LITTLE CONCERNED, TOO. WE'VE BEEN UNABLE TO CONTACT HER.
OH YES! I NEARLY FOR-GOT.
DURING THESE PRO-CEDURES, THE JAPANESE POLICE DEPARTMENT CAN ORDER MEALS.
EXCU--UUSE ME!! PORK CUTLETS ON RICE, PLE--EASE!!
...and make it a special!! ♡
BAM
BAM
BAM
WHO DOES HE THINK HE IS!! BE SURE AND ADD A COUPLE ZEROS ON THE END OF HIS BILL!!

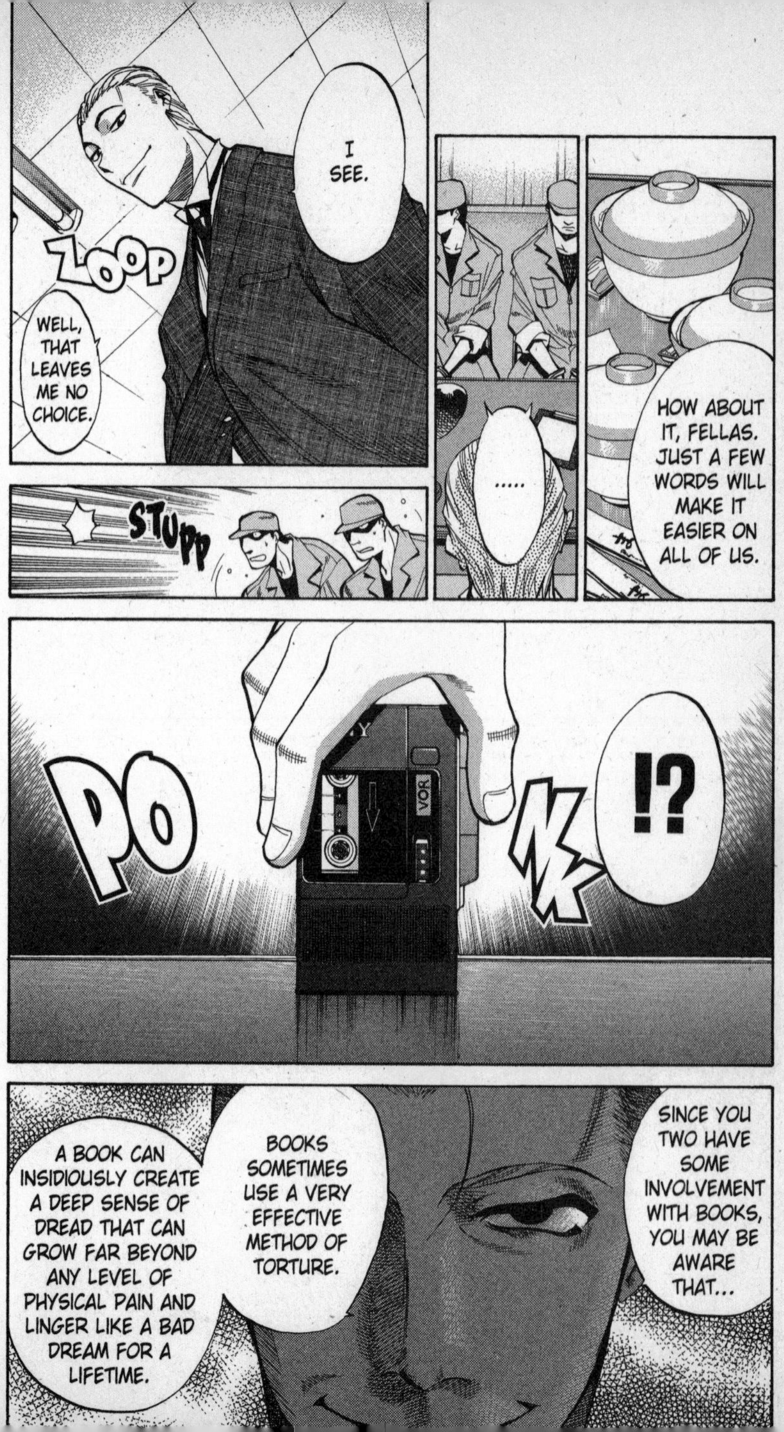
HOW ABOUT IT, FELLAS. JUST A FEW WORDS WILL MAKE IT EASIER ON ALL OF US.
.....
I SEE.
ZOOP
WELL, THAT LEAVES ME NO CHOICE.
STUPP
!?
NK
PO
SINCE YOU TWO HAVE SOME INVOLVEMENT WITH BOOKS, YOU MAY BE AWARE THAT...
BOOKS SOMETIMES USE A VERY EFFECTIVE METHOD OF TORTURE.
A BOOK CAN INSIDIOUSLY CREATE A DEEP SENSE OF DREAD THAT CAN GROW FAR BEYOND ANY LEVEL OF PHYSICAL PAIN AND LINGER LIKE A BAD DREAM FOR A LIFETIME.

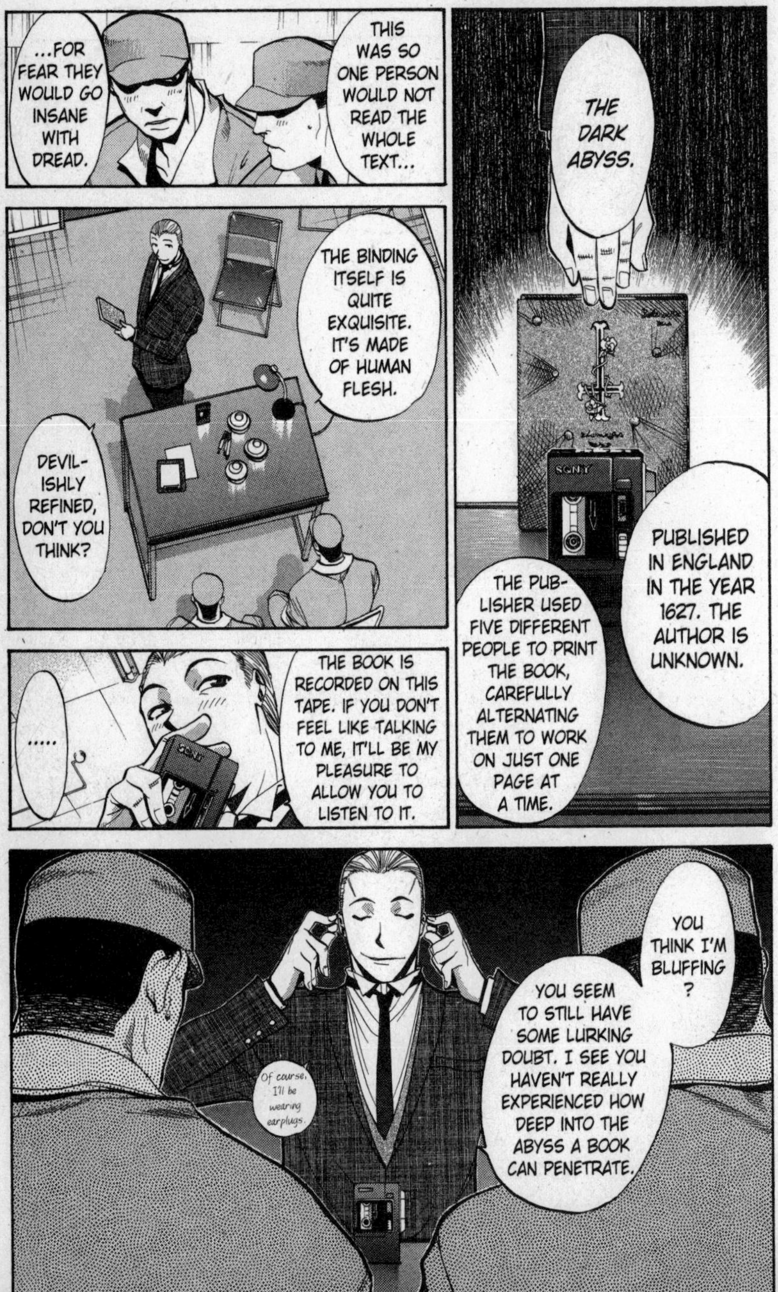
THE DARK ABYSS.
PUBLISHED IN ENGLAND IN THE YEAR 1627. THE AUTHOR IS UNKNOWN.
THE PUB-LISHER USED FIVE DIFFERENT PEOPLE TO PRINT THE BOOK, CAREFULLY ALTERNATING THEM TO WORK ON JUST ONE PAGE AT A TIME.
THIS WAS SO ONE PERSON WOULD NOT READ THE WHOLE TEXT...
...FOR FEAR THEY WOULD GO INSANE WITH DREAD.
THE BINDING ITSELF IS QUITE EXQUISITE. IT'S MADE OF HUMAN FLESH.
DEVIL-ISHLY REFINED, DON'T YOU THINK?
THE BOOK IS RECORDED ON THIS TAPE. IF YOU DON'T FEEL LIKE TALKING TO ME, IT'LL BE MY PLEASURE TO ALLOW YOU TO LISTEN TO IT.
.....
YOU THINK I'M BLUFFING ?
YOU SEEM TO STILL HAVE SOME LURKING DOUBT. I SEE YOU HAVEN'T REALLY EXPERIENCED HOW DEEP INTO THE ABYSS A BOOK CAN PENETRATE.
Of course, I'll be wearing earplugs.

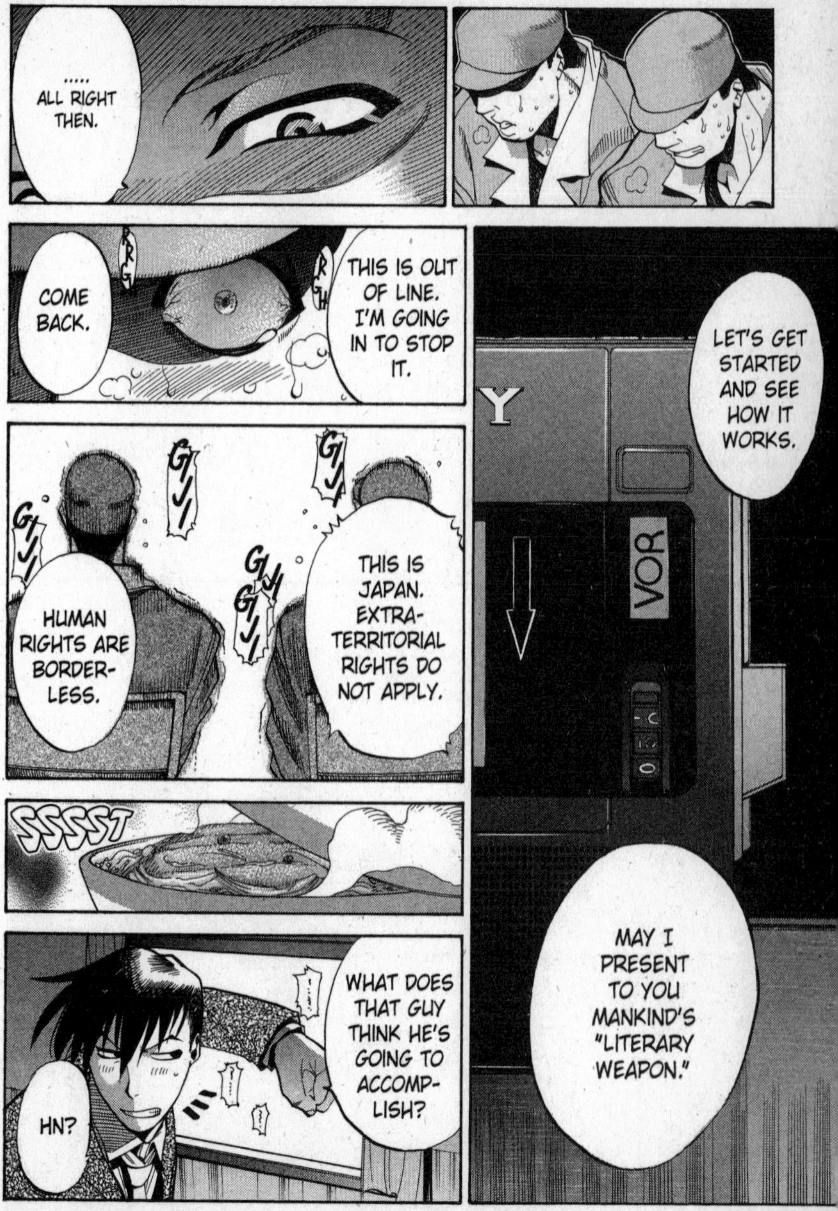
.....
ALL RIGHT THEN.
LET'S GET STARTED AND SEE HOW IT WORKS.
Y
VOR
MAY I PRESENT TO YOU MANKIND'S "LITERARY WEAPON."
RGH
THIS IS OUT OF LINE. I'M GOING IN TO STOP IT.
RRGH
COME BACK.
GIJI
THIS IS JAPAN. EXTRA-TERRITORIAL RIGHTS DO NOT APPLY.
GIJI GIJI
GIJI
GIJI
HUMAN RIGHTS ARE BORDER-LESS.
SSSST
WHAT DOES THAT GUY THINK HE'S GOING TO ACCOMP-LISH?
HN?

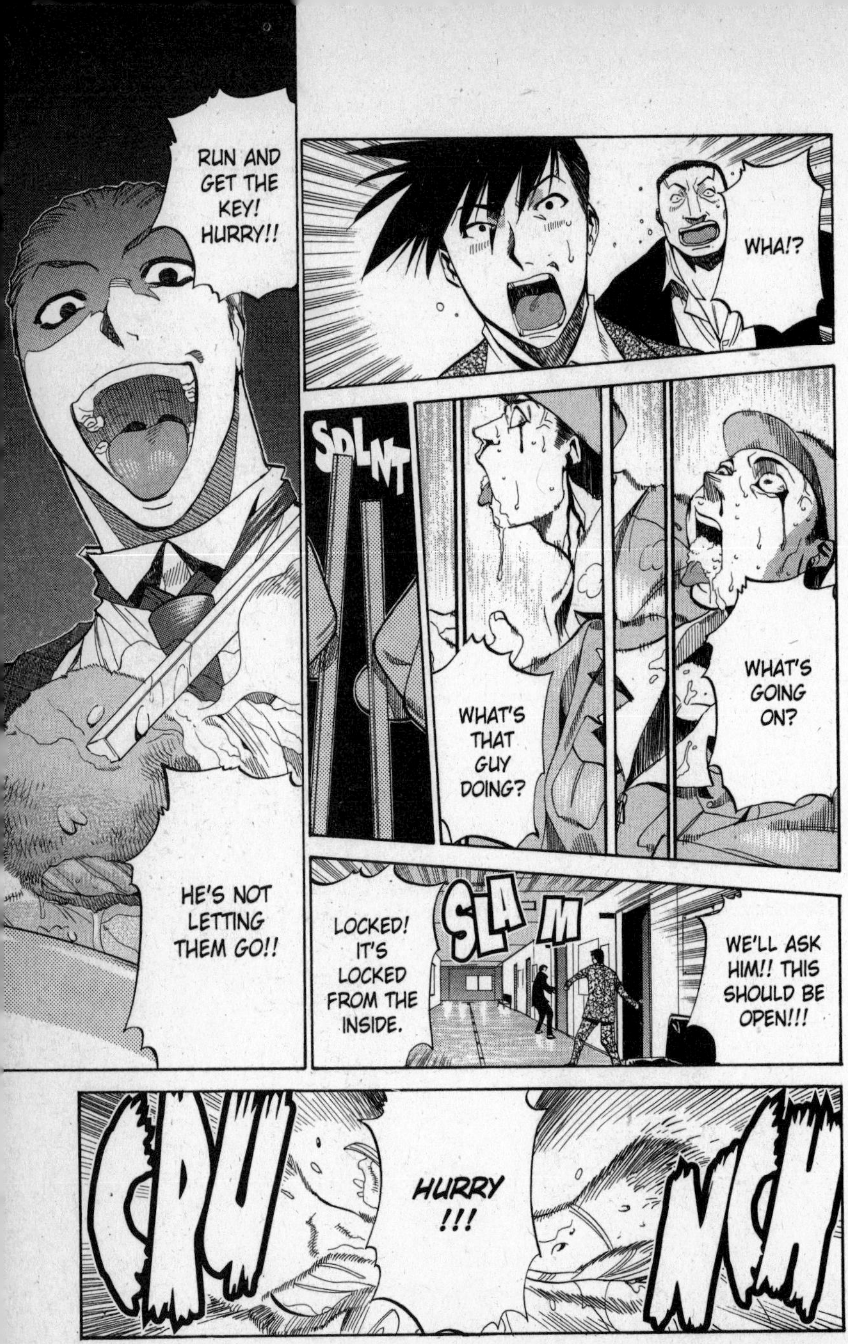
WHA!?
WHAT'S GOING ON?
WHAT'S THAT GUY DOING?
SPLNT
WE'LL ASK HIM!! THIS SHOULD BE OPEN!!!
SLAM
LOCKED! IT'S LOCKED FROM THE INSIDE.
RUN AND GET THE KEY! HURRY!!
HE'S NOT LETTING THEM GO!!
CRUNCH
HURRY !!!

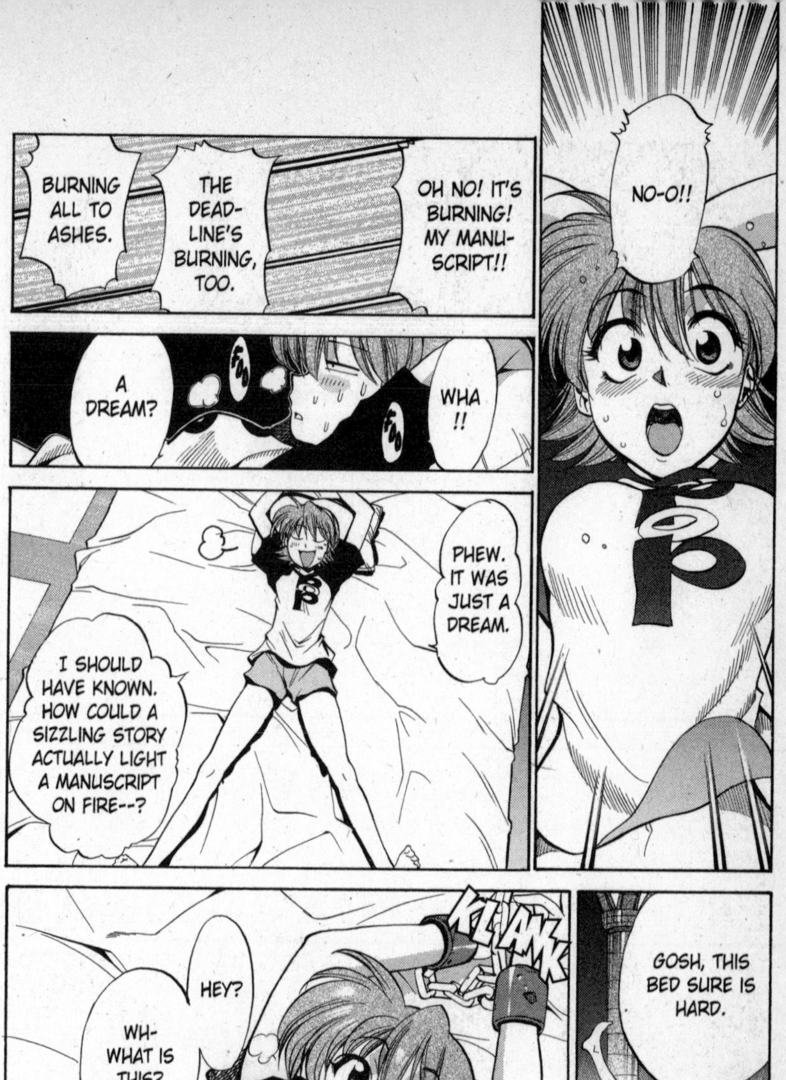
NO-O!!
OH NO! IT'S BURNING! MY MANU-SCRIPT!!
THE DEAD-LINE'S BURNING, TOO.
BURNING ALL TO ASHES.
WHA !!
FOO
FOO
A DREAM?
PHEW. IT WAS JUST A DREAM.
I SHOULD HAVE KNOWN. HOW COULD A SIZZLING STORY ACTUALLY LIGHT A MANUSCRIPT ON FIRE--?
GOSH, THIS BED SURE IS HARD.
THUD
UMPH!
KLANK
HEY?
WH-WHAT IS THIS?

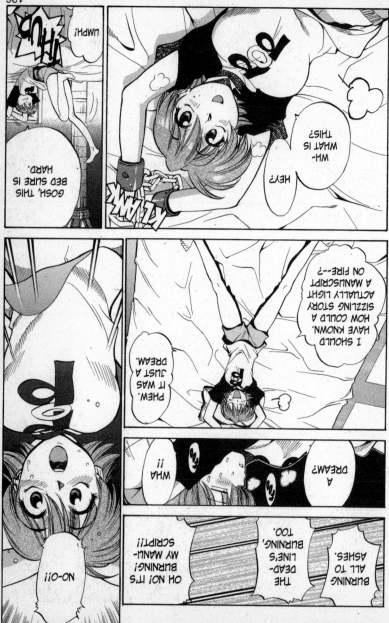

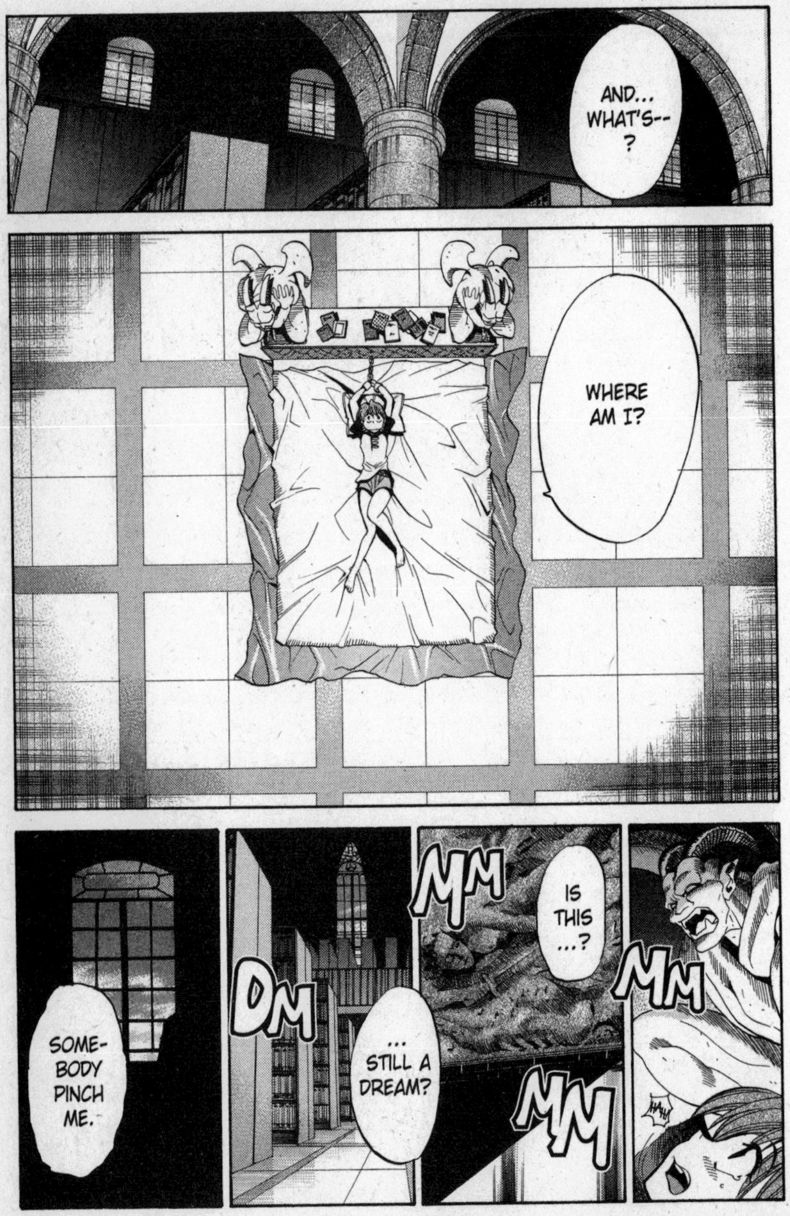
AND... WHAT'S-- ?
WHERE AM I?
MM
MM
HAH
IS THIS ...?
MM
... STILL A DREAM?
DM
SOME-BODY PINCH ME.

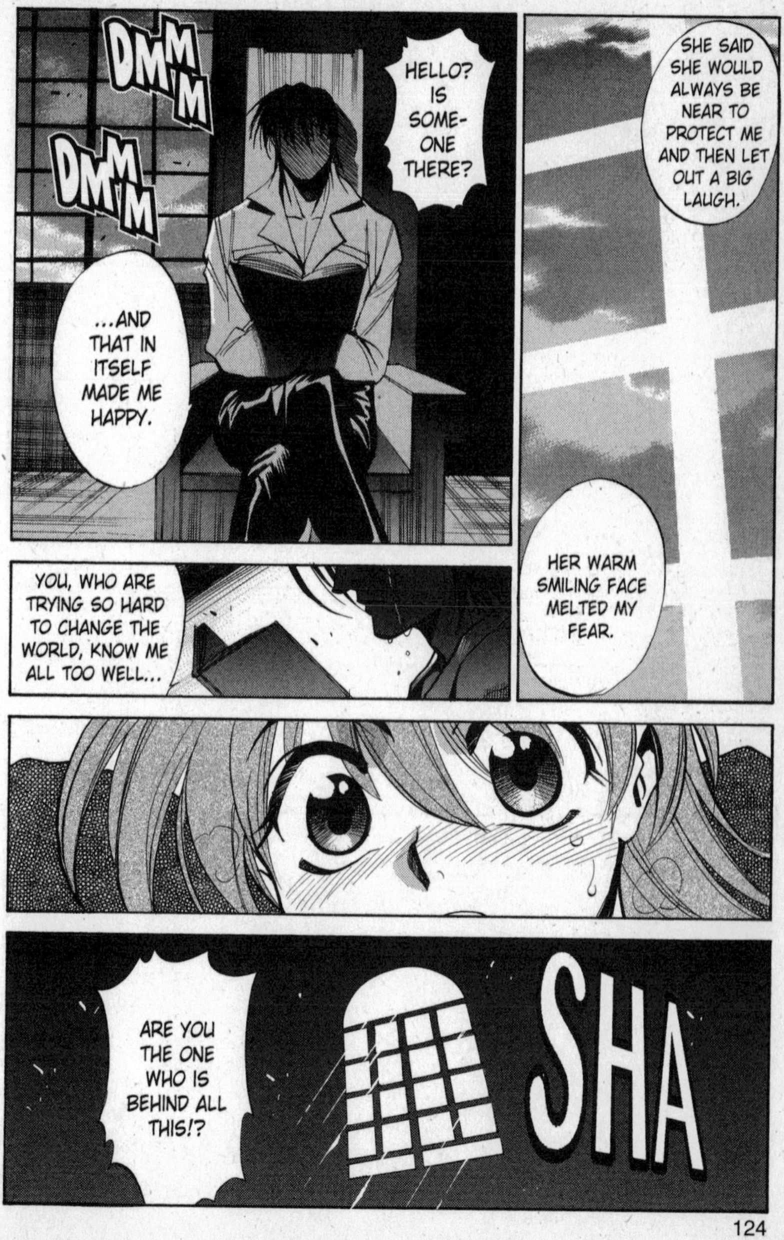
SHE SAID SHE WOULD ALWAYS BE NEAR TO PROTECT ME AND THEN LET OUT A BIG LAUGH.
HER WARM SMILING FACE MELTED MY FEAR.
HELLO? IS SOME-ONE THERE?
DMMM
DMMM
...AND THAT IN ITSELF MADE ME HAPPY.
YOU, WHO ARE TRYING SO HARD TO CHANGE THE WORLD, KNOW ME ALL TOO WELL...
SHA
ARE YOU THE ONE WHO IS BEHIND ALL THIS!?

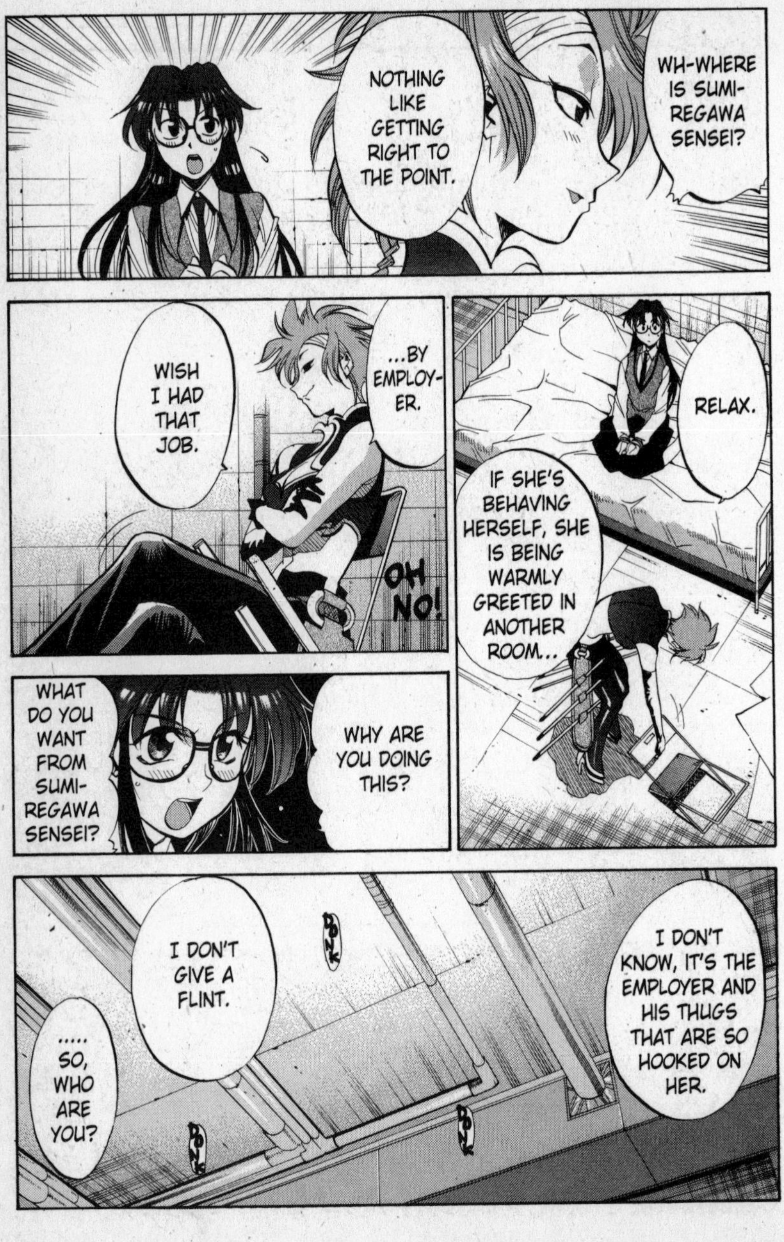
WH-WHERE IS SUMI-REGAWA SENSEI?
NOTHING LIKE GETTING RIGHT TO THE POINT.
RELAX.
IF SHE'S BEHAVING HERSELF, SHE IS BEING WARMLY GREETED IN ANOTHER ROOM...
...BY EMPLOY-ER.
WISH I HAD THAT JOB.
OH NO!
WHY ARE YOU DOING THIS?
WHAT DO YOU WANT FROM SUMI-REGAWA SENSEI?
I DON'T KNOW, IT'S THE EMPLOYER AND HIS THUGS THAT ARE SO HOOKED ON HER.
DONK
I DON'T GIVE A FLINT.
DONK
DONK
..... SO, WHO ARE YOU?

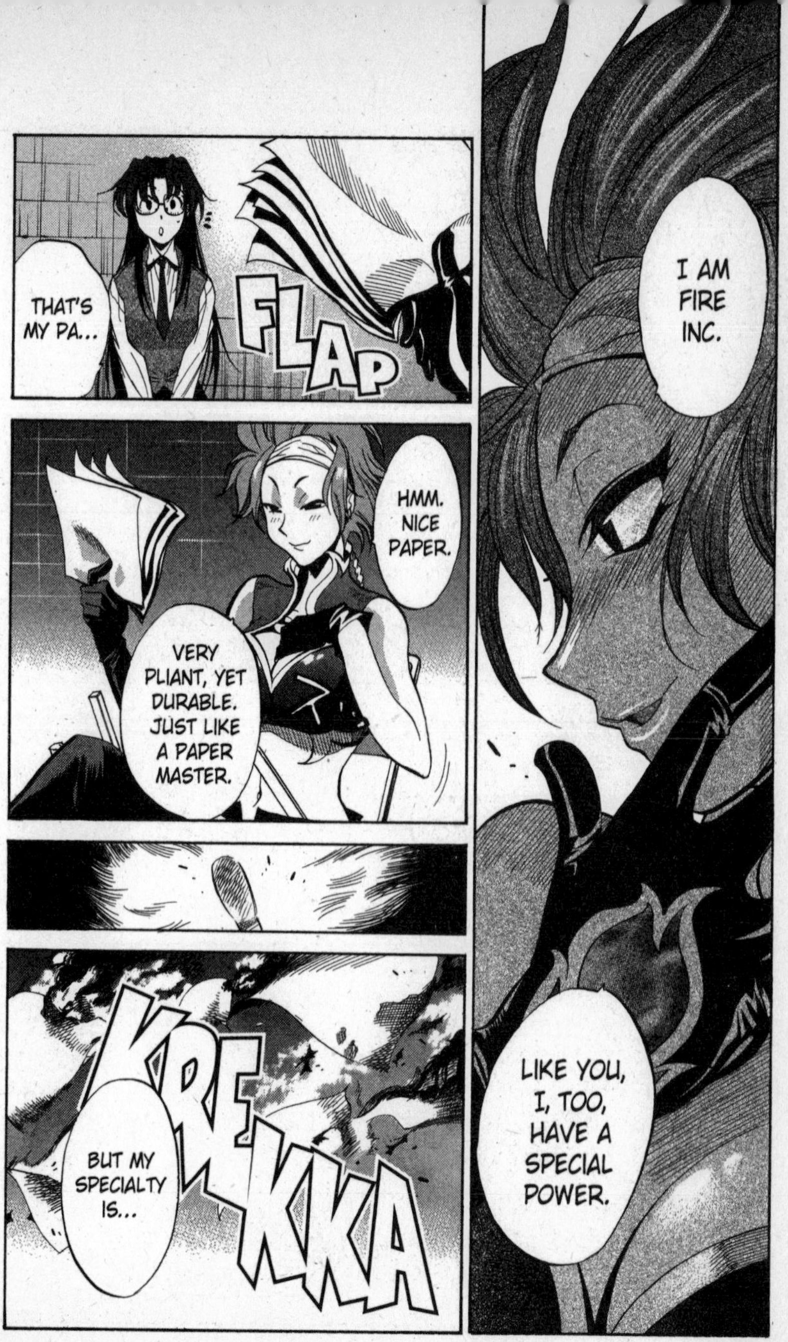
I AM FIRE INC.
LIKE YOU, I, TOO, HAVE A SPECIAL POWER.
THAT'S MY PA...
FLAP
HMM. NICE PAPER.
VERY PLIANT, YET DURABLE. JUST LIKE A PAPER MASTER.
KRE KKA
BUT MY SPECIALTY IS...

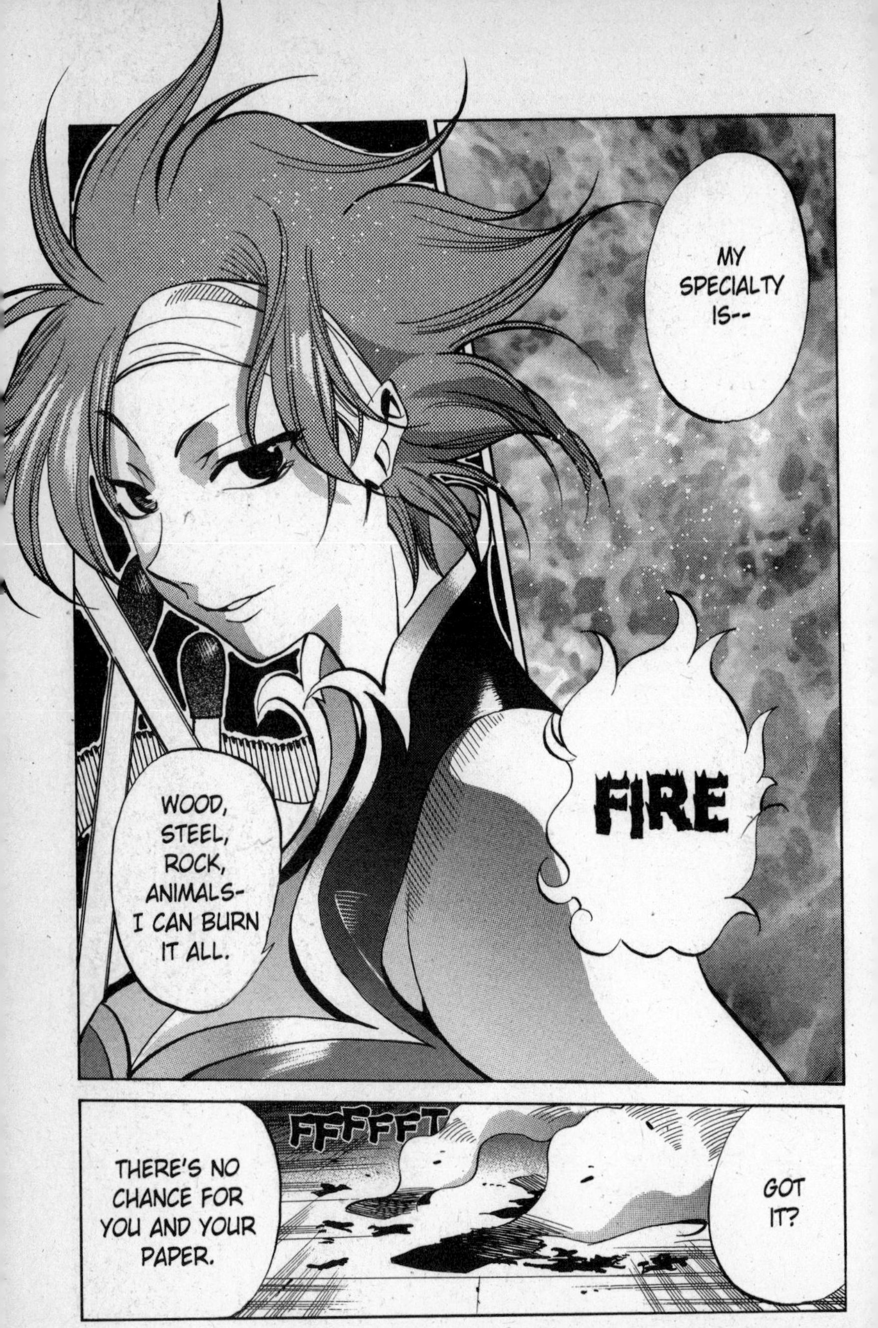
MY SPECIALTY IS--
FIRE
WOOD, STEEL, ROCK, ANIMALS- I CAN BURN IT ALL.
GOT IT?
FFFFFT
THERE'S NO CHANCE FOR YOU AND YOUR PAPER.

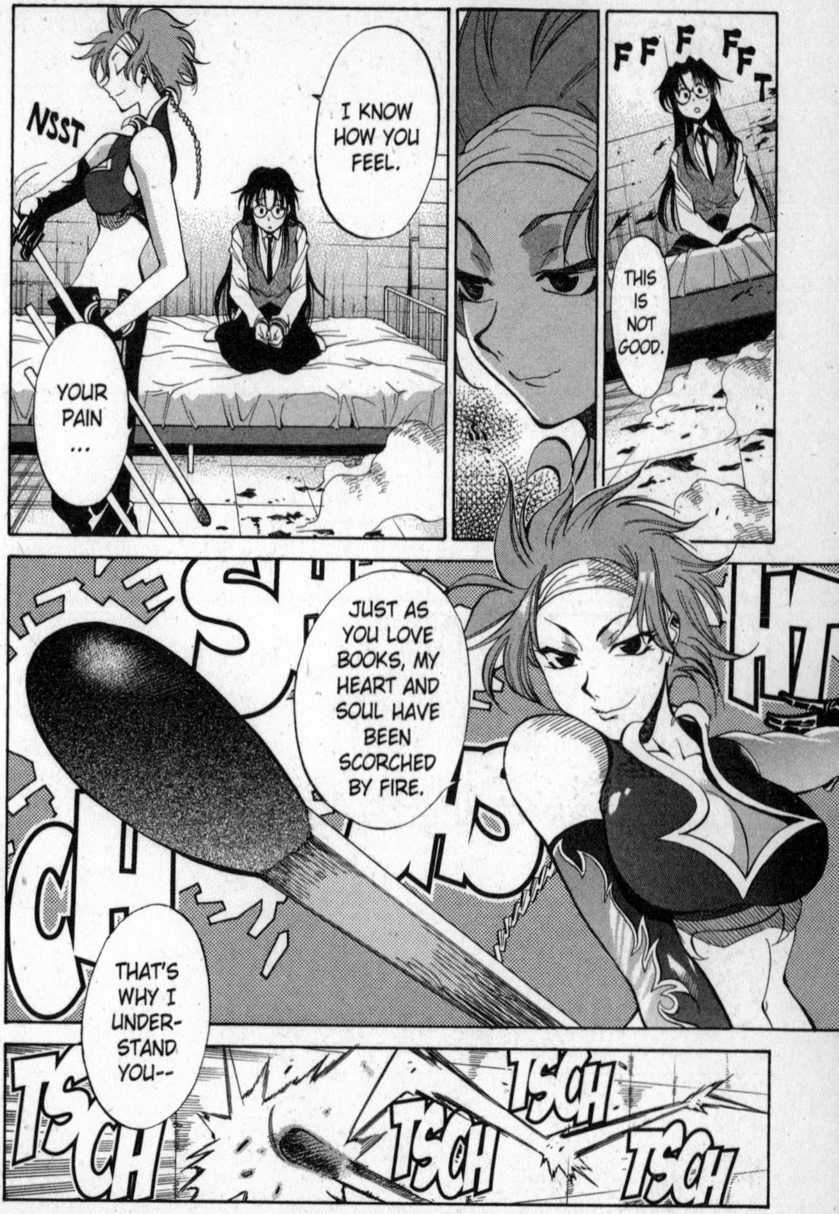
F F F FFT
THIS IS NOT GOOD.
I KNOW HOW YOU FEEL.
NSST
YOUR PAIN ...
JUST AS YOU LOVE BOOKS, MY HEART AND SOUL HAVE BEEN SCORCHED BY FIRE.
THAT'S WHY I UNDER-STAND YOU--
TSCH
TSCH
TSCH
TSCH

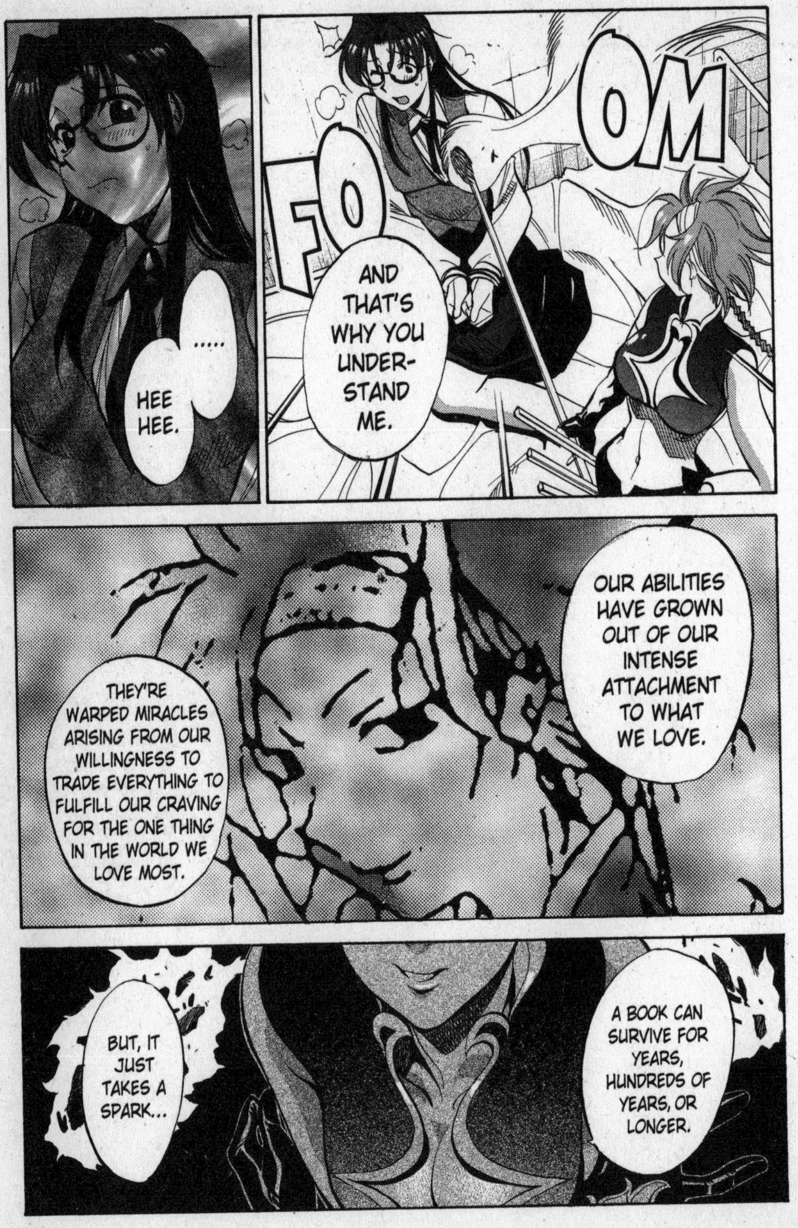
FOOM
AND THAT'S WHY YOU UNDER-STAND ME.
.....
HEE HEE.
OUR ABILITIES HAVE GROWN OUT OF OUR INTENSE ATTACHMENT TO WHAT WE LOVE.
THEY'RE WARPED MIRACLES ARISING FROM OUR WILLINGNESS TO TRADE EVERYTHING TO FULFILL OUR CRAVING FOR THE ONE THING IN THE WORLD WE LOVE MOST.
A BOOK CAN SURVIVE FOR YEARS, HUNDREDS OF YEARS, OR LONGER.
BUT, IT JUST TAKES A SPARK...

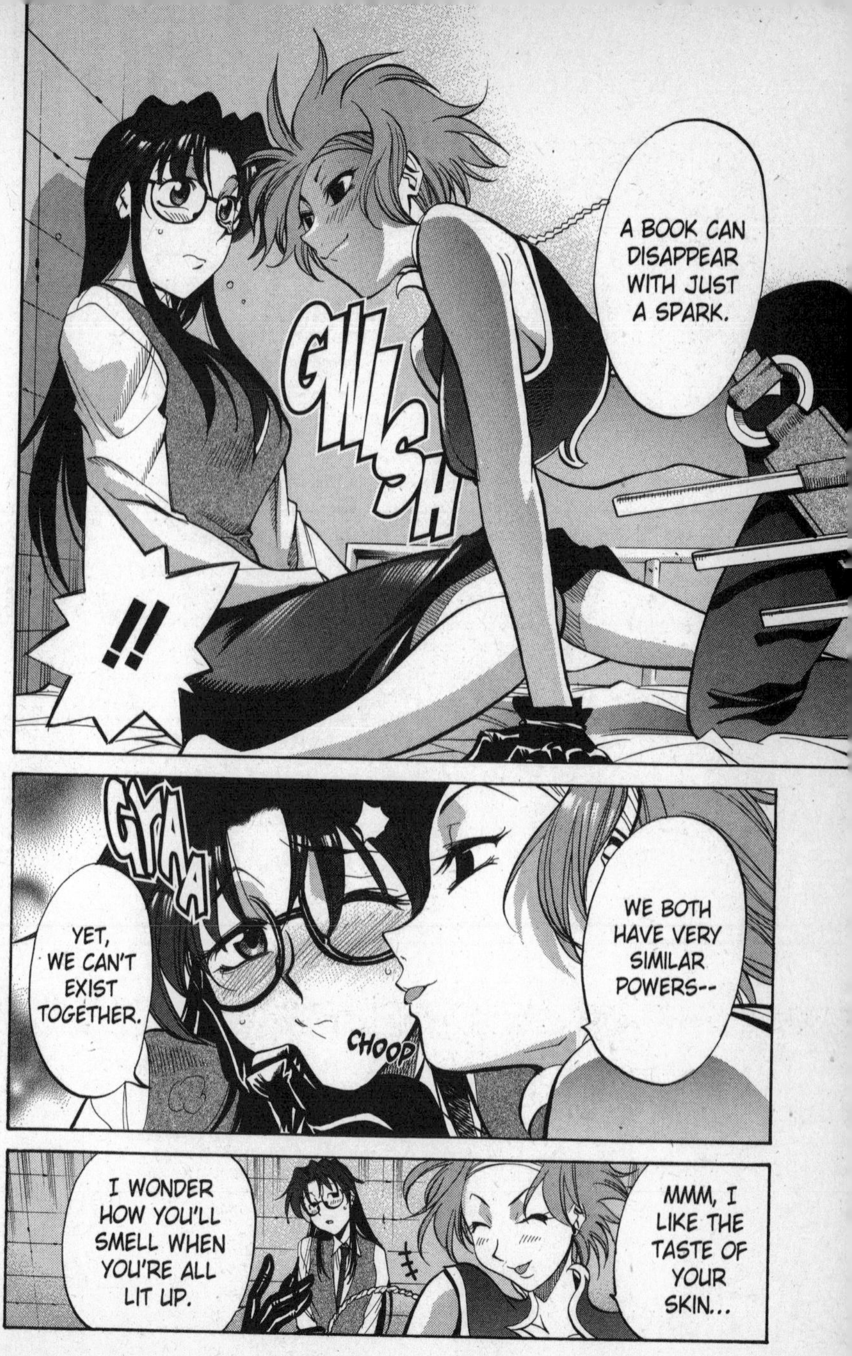
A BOOK CAN DISAPPEAR WITH JUST A SPARK.
GWISH
!!
WE BOTH HAVE VERY SIMILAR POWERS--
GYAA
YET, WE CAN'T EXIST TOGETHER.
CHOOP
MMM, I LIKE THE TASTE OF YOUR SKIN...
I WONDER HOW YOU'LL SMELL WHEN YOU'RE ALL LIT UP.

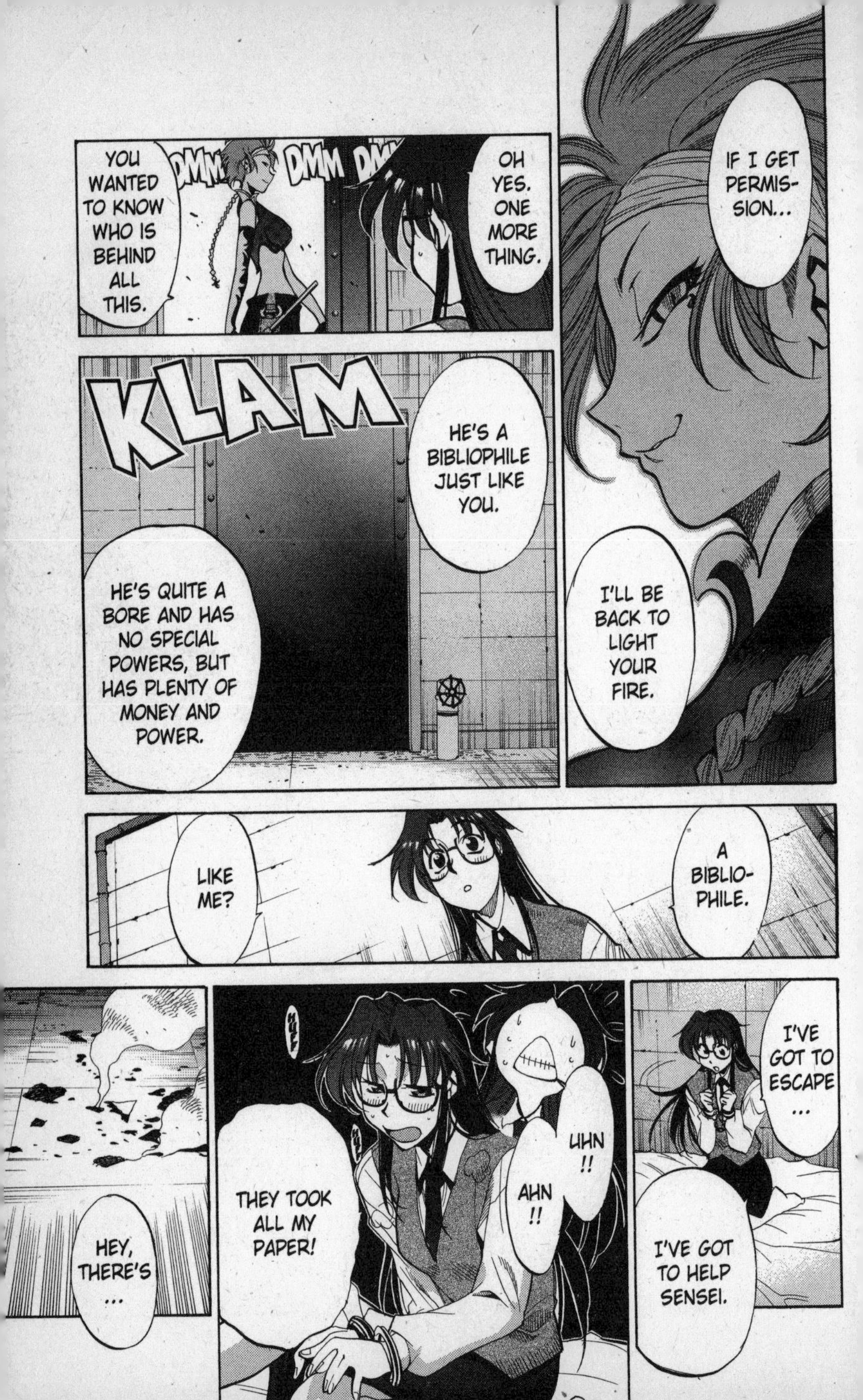
IF I GET PERMISSION...
I'LL BE BACK TO LIGHT YOUR FIRE.
OH YES. ONE MORE THING.
DMM DMM DMM
YOU WANTED TO KNOW WHO IS BEHIND ALL THIS.
HE'S A BIBLIOPHILE JUST LIKE YOU.
HE'S QUITE A BORE AND HAS NO SPECIAL POWERS, BUT HAS PLENTY OF MONEY AND POWER.
KLAM
A BIBLIO-PHILE.
LIKE ME?
I'VE GOT TO ESCAPE...
I'VE GOT TO HELP SENSEI.
UHN !!
AHN !!
HUFF
HUFF
THEY TOOK ALL MY PAPER!
HEY, THERE'S...

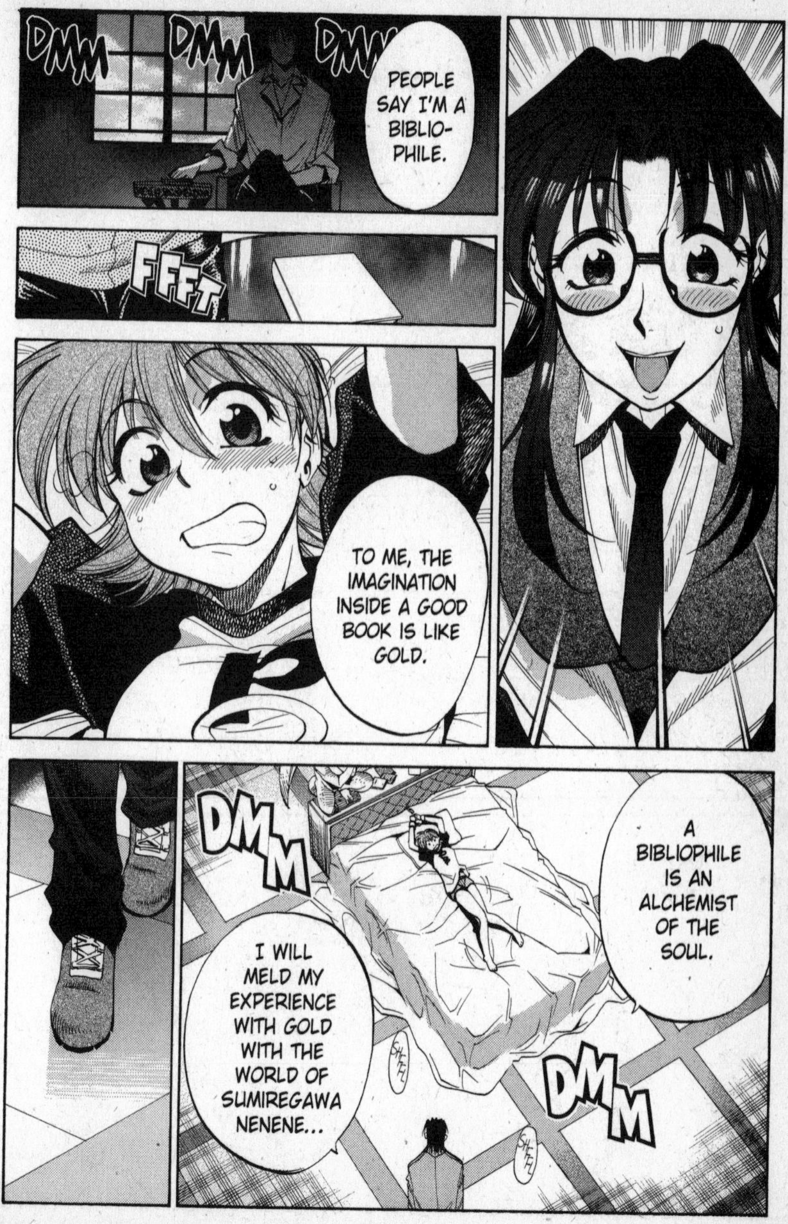
DMM DMM DMM
PEOPLE SAY I'M A BIBLIO-PHILE.
FFFT
TO ME, THE IMAGINATION INSIDE A GOOD BOOK IS LIKE GOLD.
A BIBLIOPHILE IS AN ALCHEMIST OF THE SOUL.
DMM
I WILL MELD MY EXPERIENCE WITH GOLD WITH THE WORLD OF SUMIREGAWA NENENE...
SHFFL
DMM
SHFFL

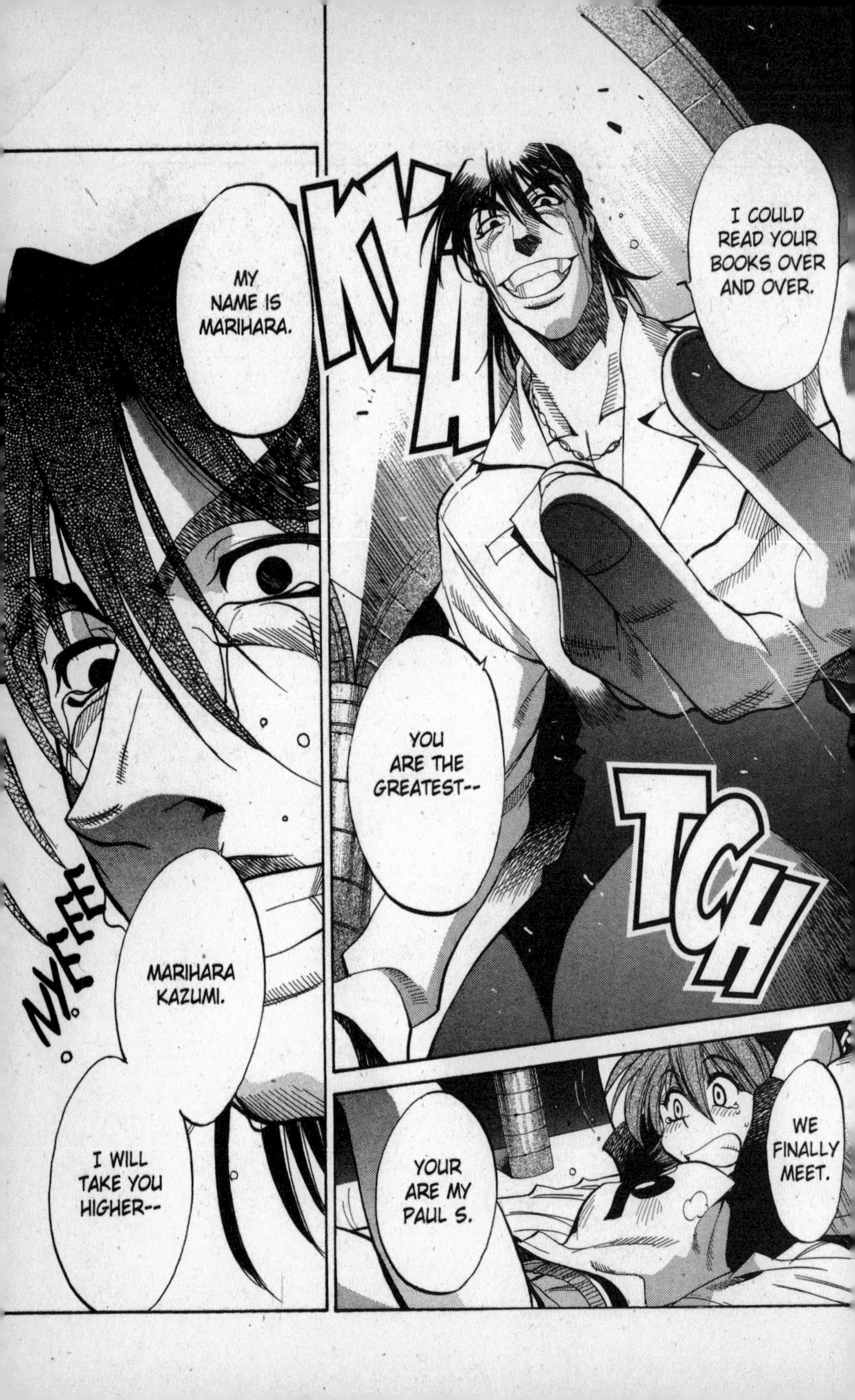
I COULD READ YOUR BOOKS OVER AND OVER.
KYA
YOU ARE THE GREATEST--
TCH
WE FINALLY MEET.
YOUR ARE MY PAUL S.
MY NAME IS MARIHARA.
MARIHARA KAZUMI.
NYEEE
I WILL TAKE YOU HIGHER--

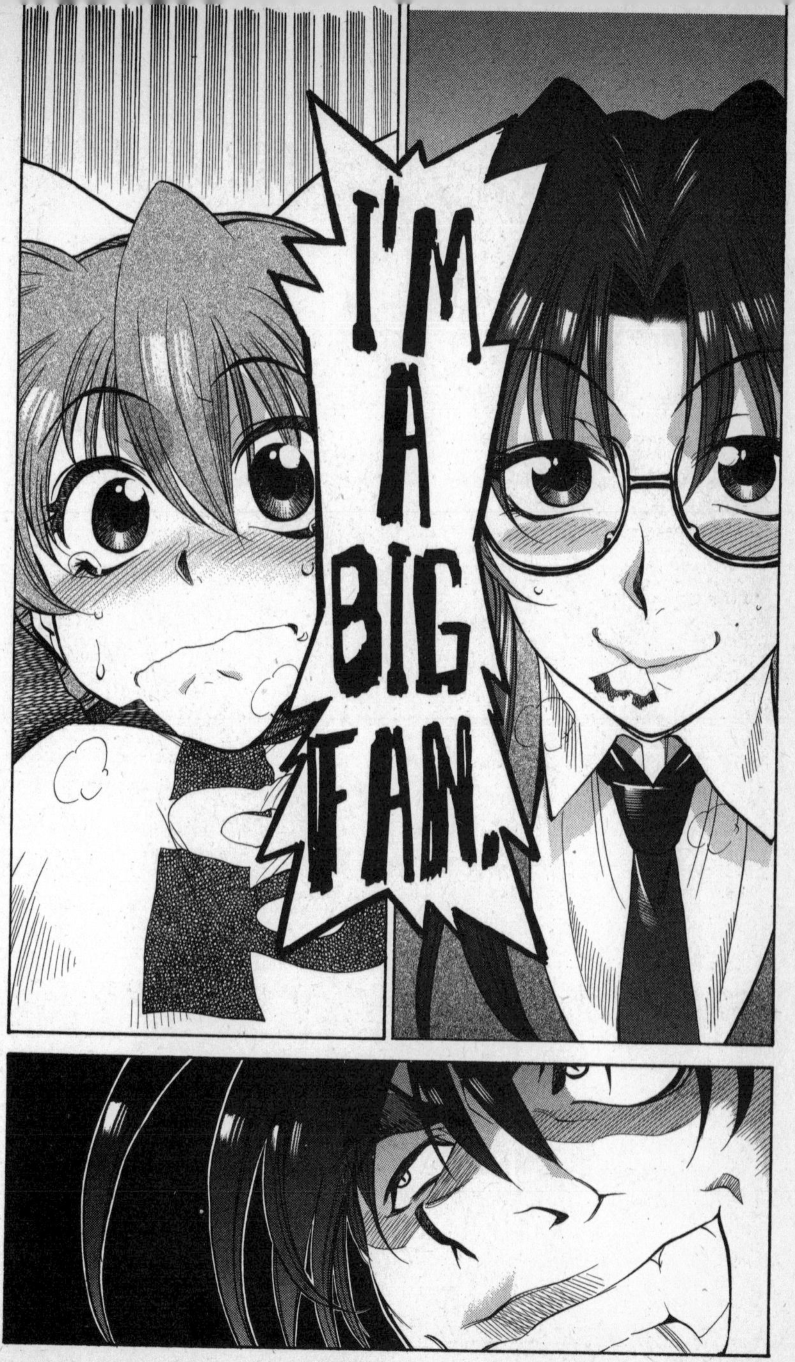
I'M A BIG FAN.

EPISODE SIX

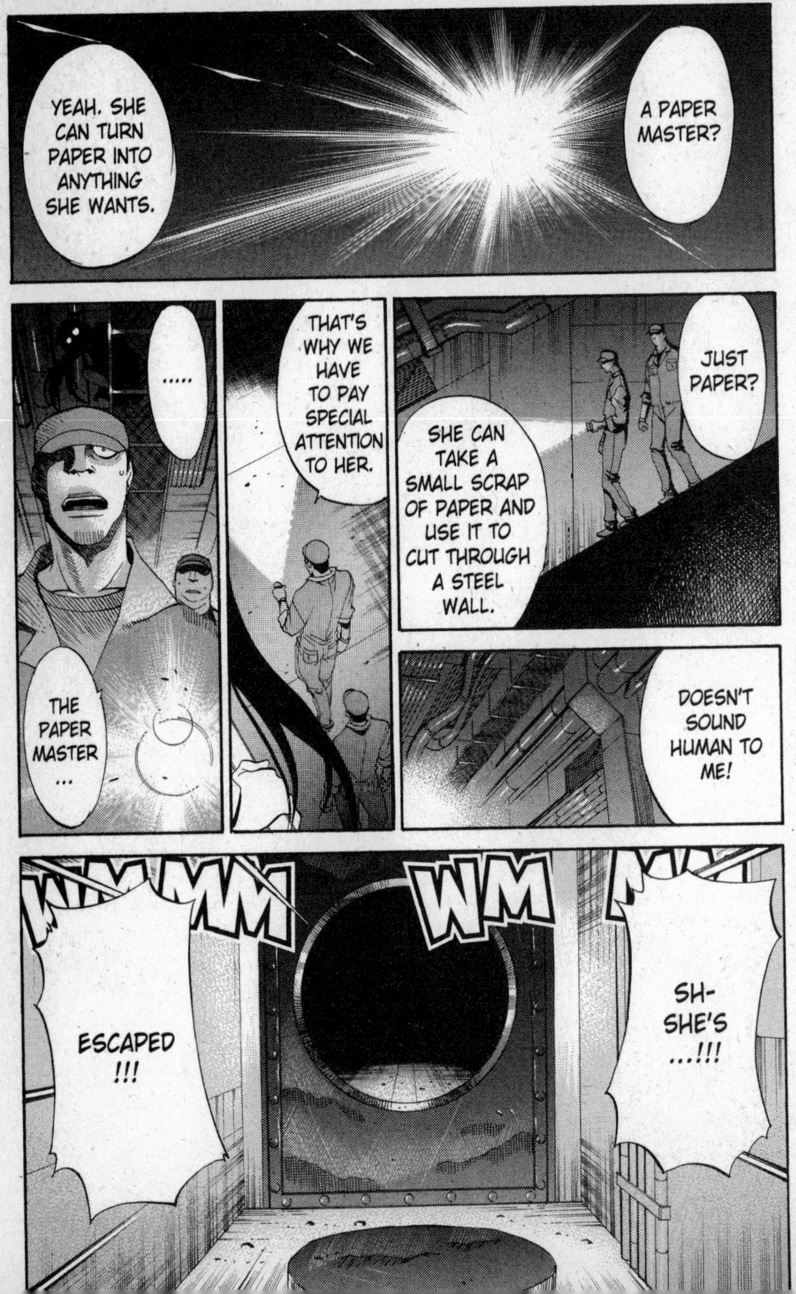
A PAPER MASTER?
YEAH. SHE CAN TURN PAPER INTO ANYTHING SHE WANTS.
JUST PAPER?
SHE CAN TAKE A SMALL SCRAP OF PAPER AND USE IT TO CUT THROUGH A STEEL WALL.
THAT'S WHY WE HAVE TO PAY SPECIAL ATTENTION TO HER.
.....
THE PAPER MASTER ...
DOESN'T SOUND HUMAN TO ME!
WM
SH- SHE'S ...!!!
ESCAPED !!!

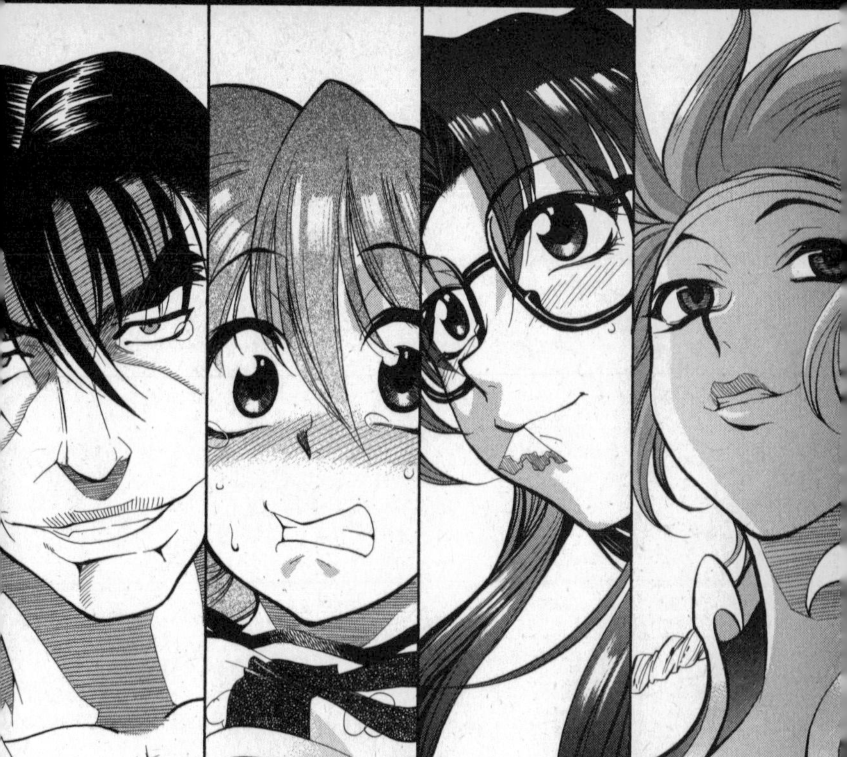

EPISODE SIX

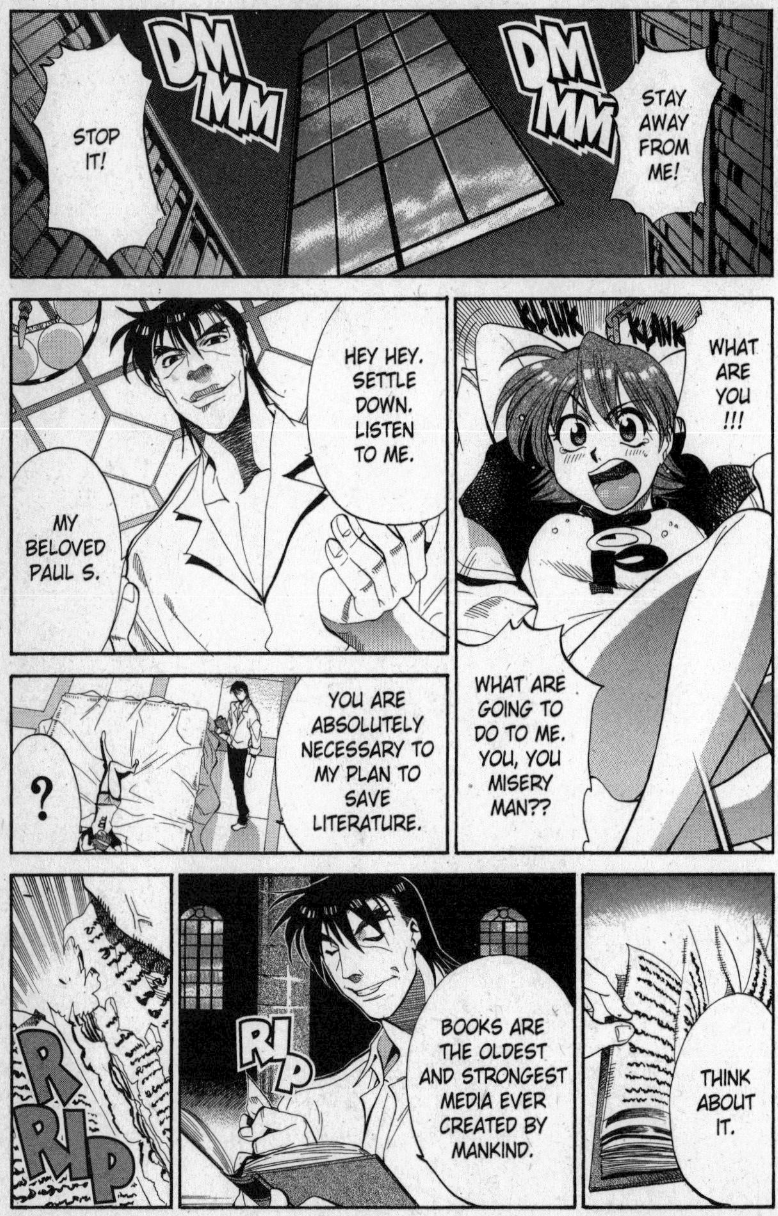
STAY AWAY FROM ME!
DM MM
DM MM
STOP IT!
SLINK
KLANK
WHAT ARE YOU !!!
WHAT ARE GOING TO DO TO ME. YOU, YOU MISERY MAN??
HEY HEY. SETTLE DOWN. LISTEN TO ME.
MY BELOVED PAUL S.
YOU ARE ABSOLUTELY NECESSARY TO MY PLAN TO SAVE LITERATURE.
?
THINK ABOUT IT.
RIP
BOOKS ARE THE OLDEST AND STRONGEST MEDIA EVER CREATED BY MANKIND.
RRIP

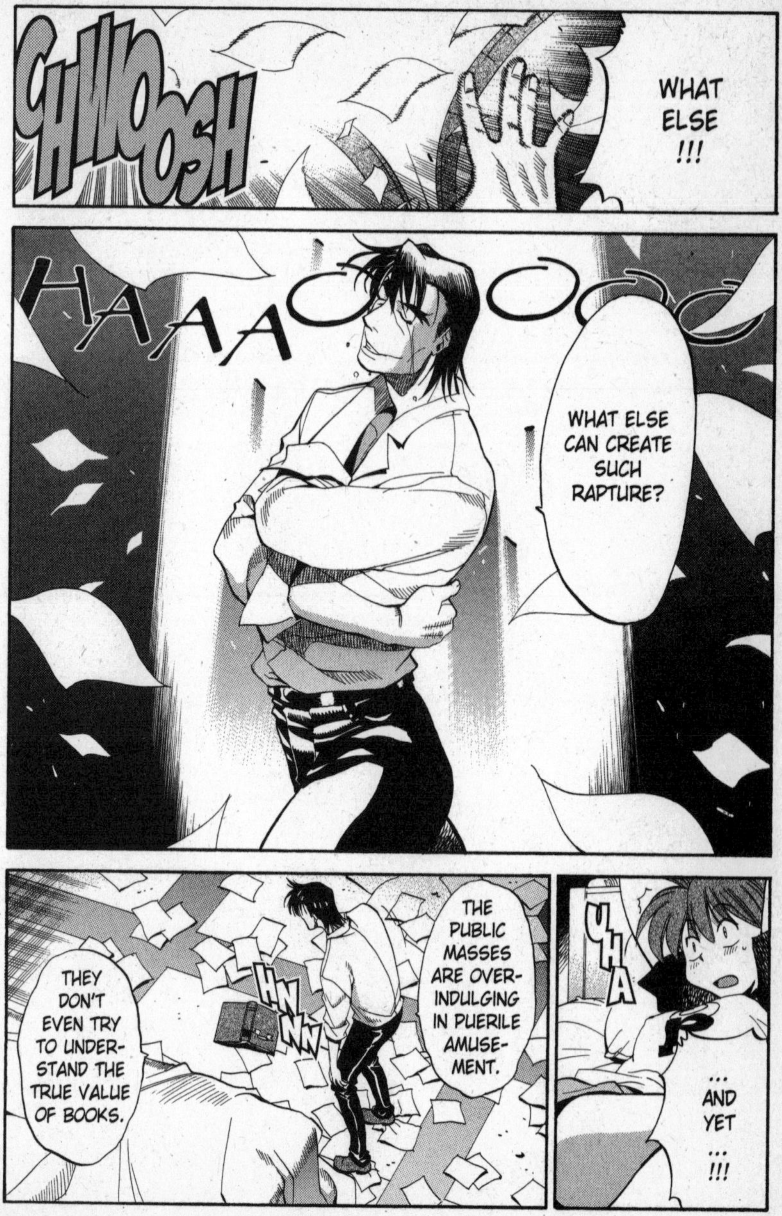
WHAT ELSE !!!
CHWOOSH
WHAT ELSE CAN CREATE SUCH RAPTURE?
HAAAOOOOO
UHA
...AND YET...!!!
THE PUBLIC MASSES ARE OVER-INDULGING IN PUERILE AMUSE-MENT.
HNNN
THEY DON'T EVEN TRY TO UNDER-STAND THE TRUE VALUE OF BOOKS.

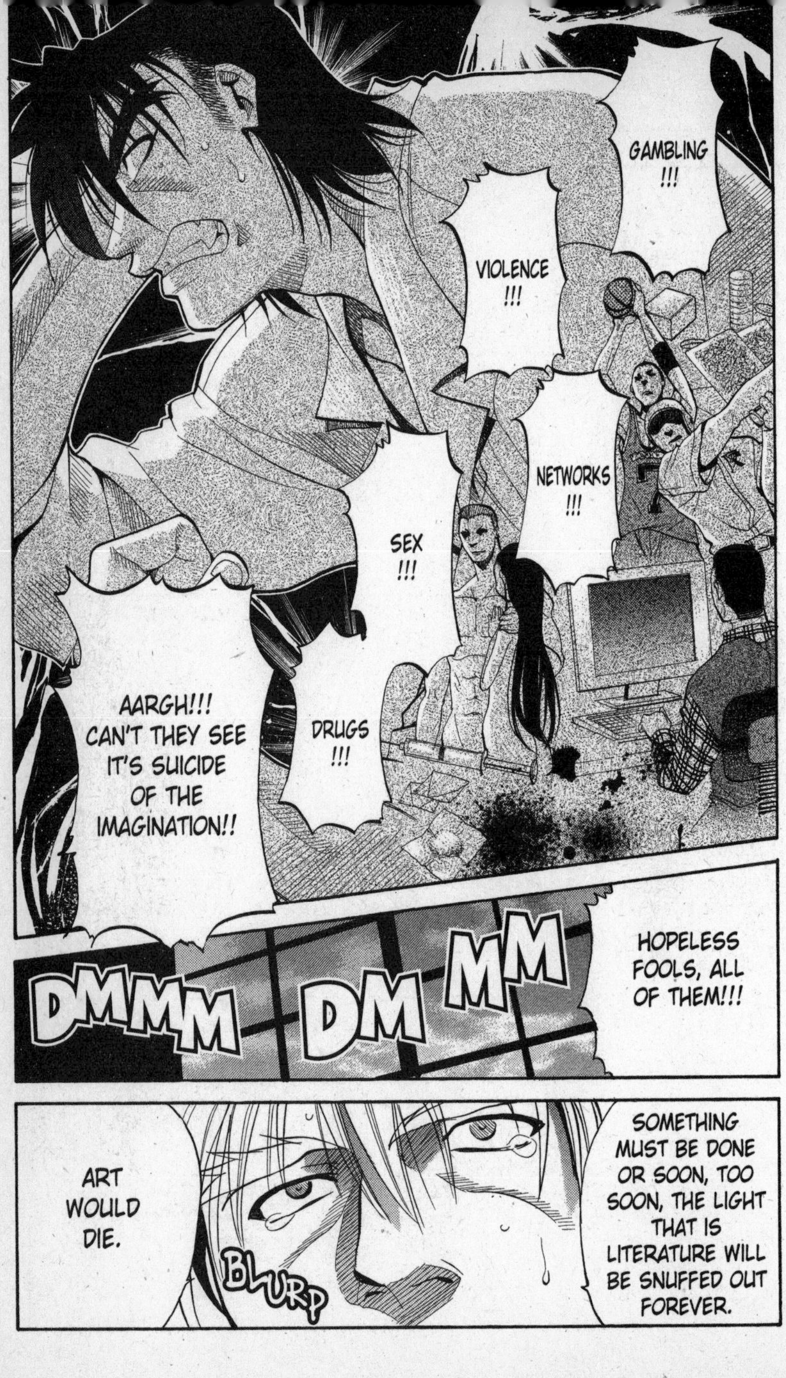
GAMBLING !!!
VIOLENCE !!!
NETWORKS !!!
SEX !!!
DRUGS !!!
AARGH!!! CAN'T THEY SEE IT'S SUICIDE OF THE IMAGINATION!!
HOPELESS FOOLS, ALL OF THEM!!!
DMMM DM MM
SOMETHING MUST BE DONE OR SOON, TOO SOON, THE LIGHT THAT IS LITERATURE WILL BE SNUFFED OUT FOREVER.
ART WOULD DIE.
BLURP

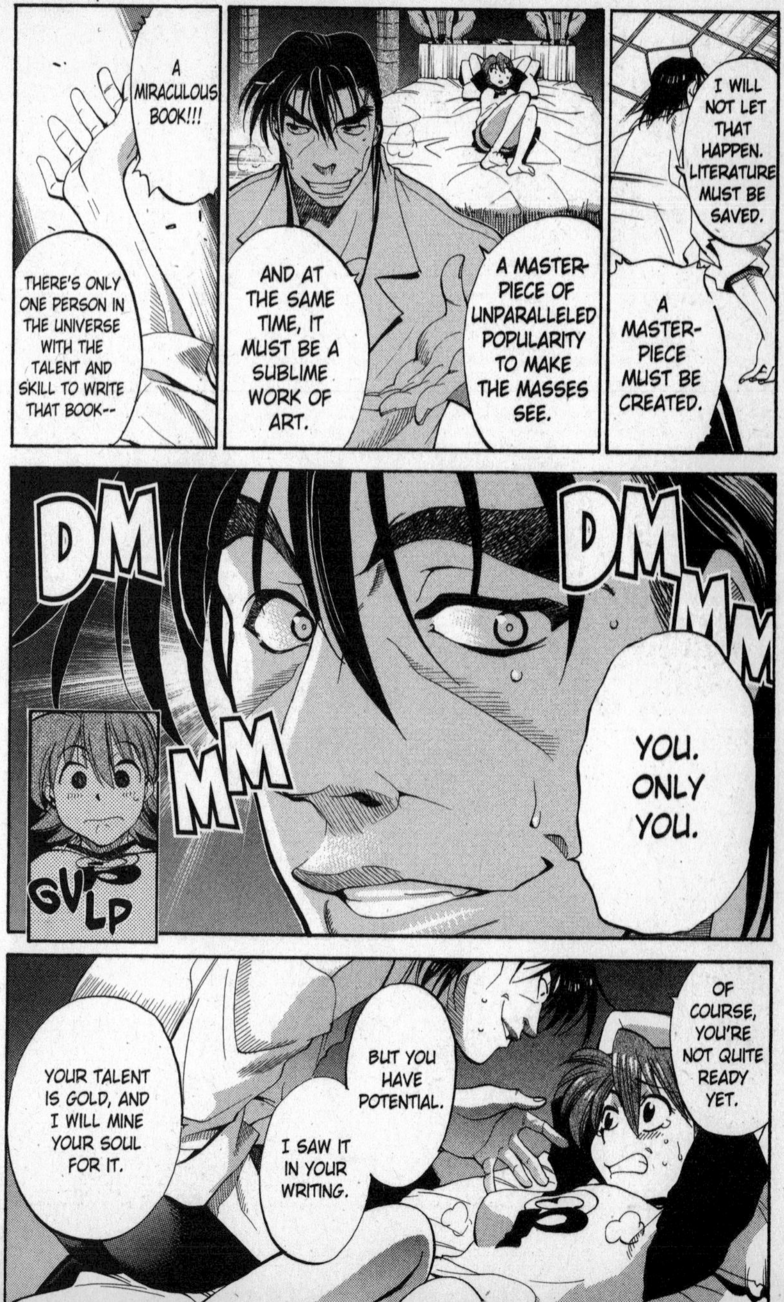
I WILL NOT LET THAT HAPPEN. LITERATURE MUST BE SAVED.
A MASTER-PIECE MUST BE CREATED.
A MASTER-PIECE OF UNPARALLELED POPULARITY TO MAKE THE MASSES SEE.
AND AT THE SAME TIME, IT MUST BE A SUBLIME WORK OF ART.
A MIRACULOUS BOOK!!!
THERE'S ONLY ONE PERSON IN THE UNIVERSE WITH THE TALENT AND SKILL TO WRITE THAT BOOK--
DM MMM
DM MMM
YOU. ONLY YOU.
GULP
OF COURSE, YOU'RE NOT QUITE READY YET.
BUT YOU HAVE POTENTIAL.
I SAW IT IN YOUR WRITING.
YOUR TALENT IS GOLD, AND I WILL MINE YOUR SOUL FOR IT.

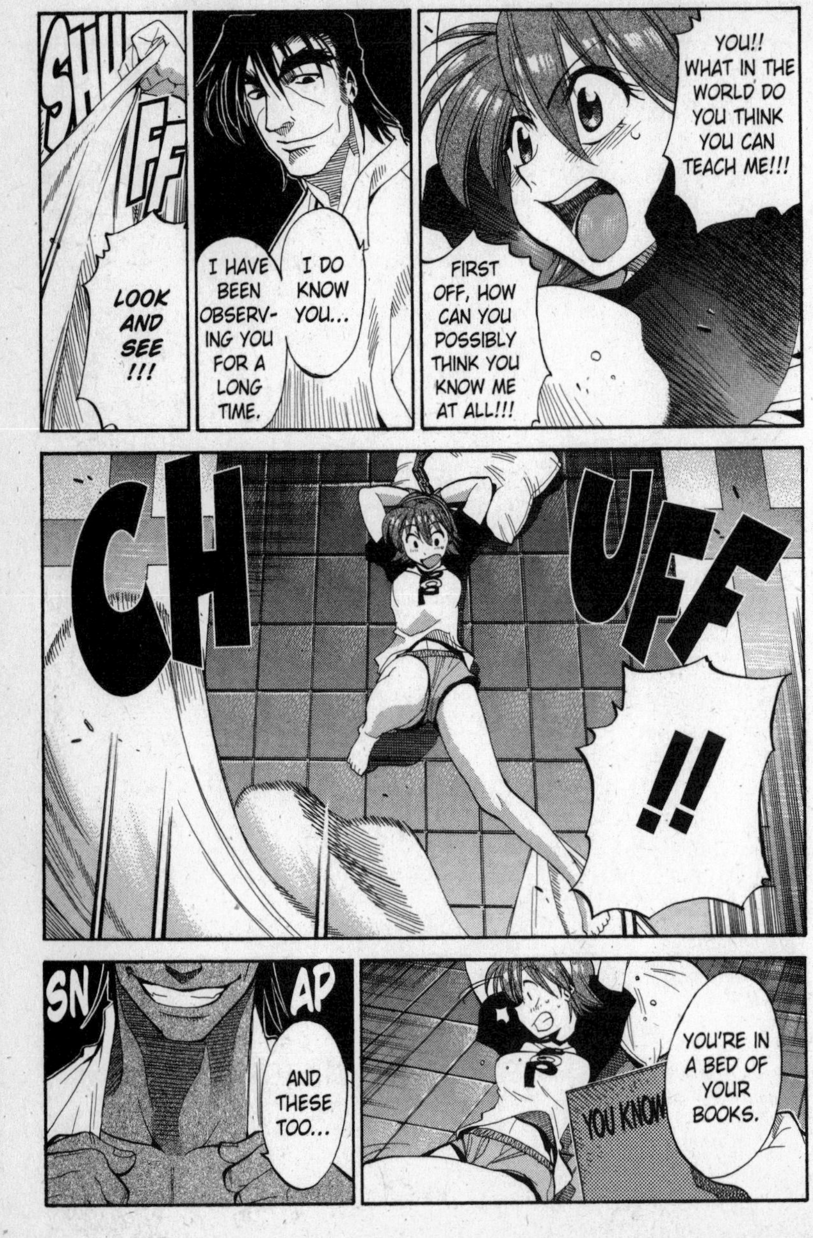
YOU!! WHAT IN THE WORLD DO YOU THINK YOU CAN TEACH ME!!!
FIRST OFF, HOW CAN YOU POSSIBLY THINK YOU KNOW ME AT ALL!!!
I DO KNOW YOU...
I HAVE BEEN OBSERVING YOU FOR A LONG TIME.
SHUFF
LOOK AND SEE !!!
UFF
CH
!!
YOU'RE IN A BED OF YOUR BOOKS.
YOU KNOW
SNAP
AND THESE TOO...

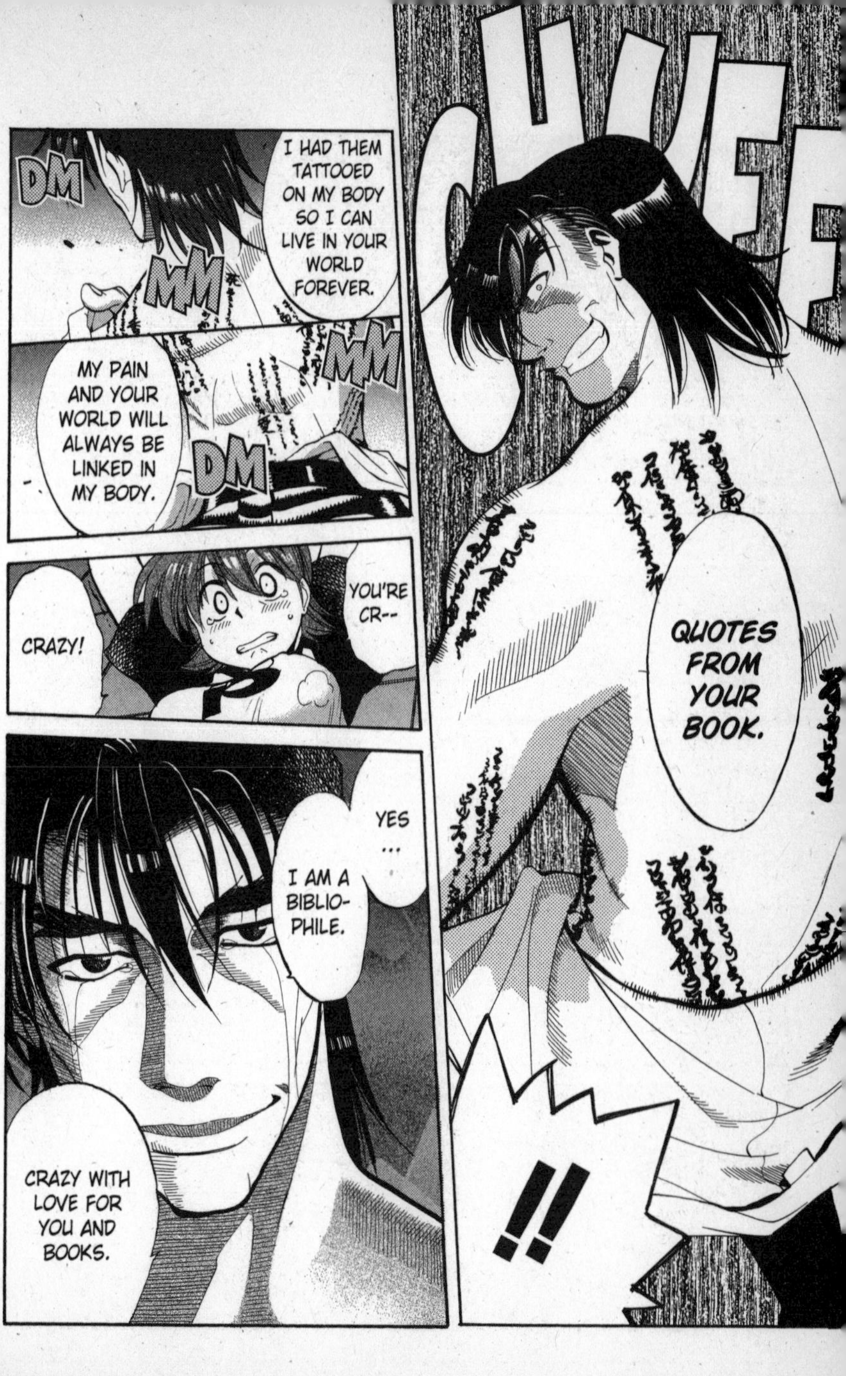
QUOTES FROM YOUR BOOK.
!!
I HAD THEM TATTOOED ON MY BODY SO I CAN LIVE IN YOUR WORLD FOREVER.
DM
MM
MM
MY PAIN AND YOUR WORLD WILL ALWAYS BE LINKED IN MY BODY.
DM
YOU'RE CR--
CRAZY!
YES ...
I AM A BIBLIO-PHILE.
CRAZY WITH LOVE FOR YOU AND BOOKS.

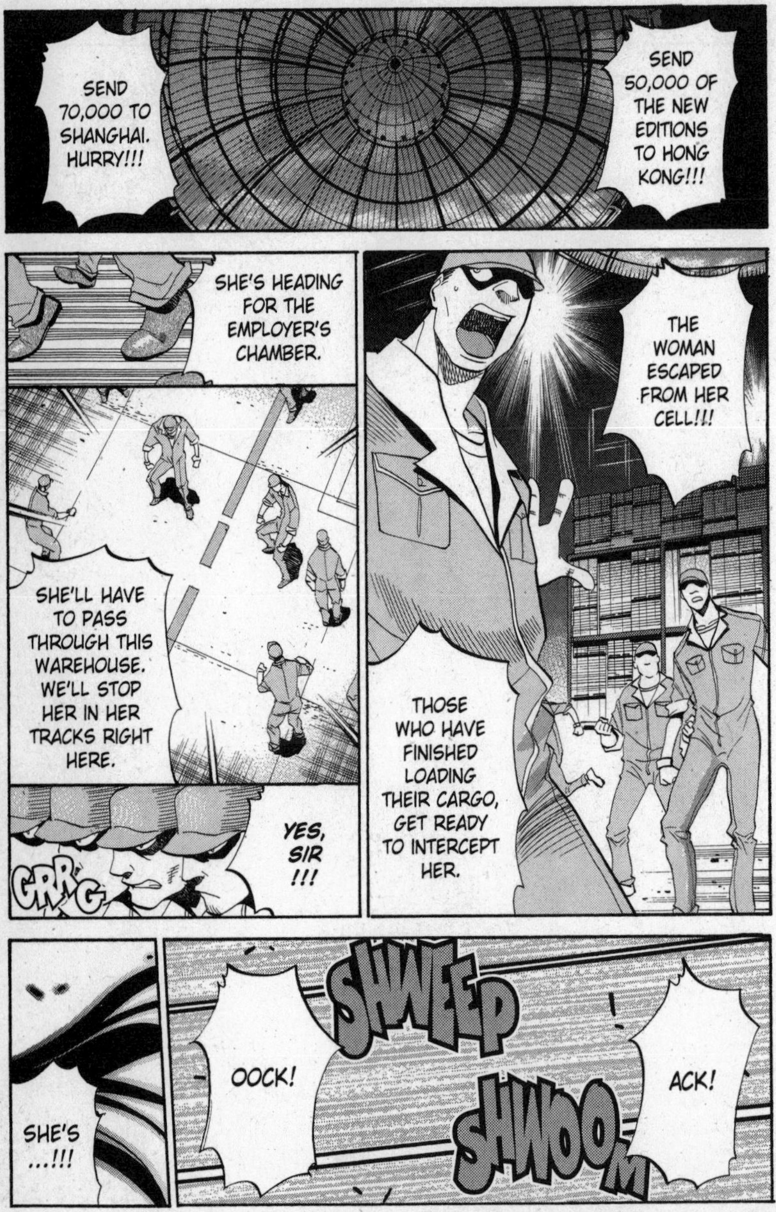
SEND 50,000 OF THE NEW EDITIONS TO HONG KONG!!!
SEND 70,000 TO SHANGHAI. HURRY!!!
THE WOMAN ESCAPED FROM HER CELL!!!
THOSE WHO HAVE FINISHED LOADING THEIR CARGO, GET READY TO INTERCEPT HER.
SHE'S HEADING FOR THE EMPLOYER'S CHAMBER.
SHE'LL HAVE TO PASS THROUGH THIS WAREHOUSE. WE'LL STOP HER IN HER TRACKS RIGHT HERE.
YES, SIR !!!
GRRG
ACK!
SHWEEP
SHWOOM
OOCK!
SHE'S ...!!!

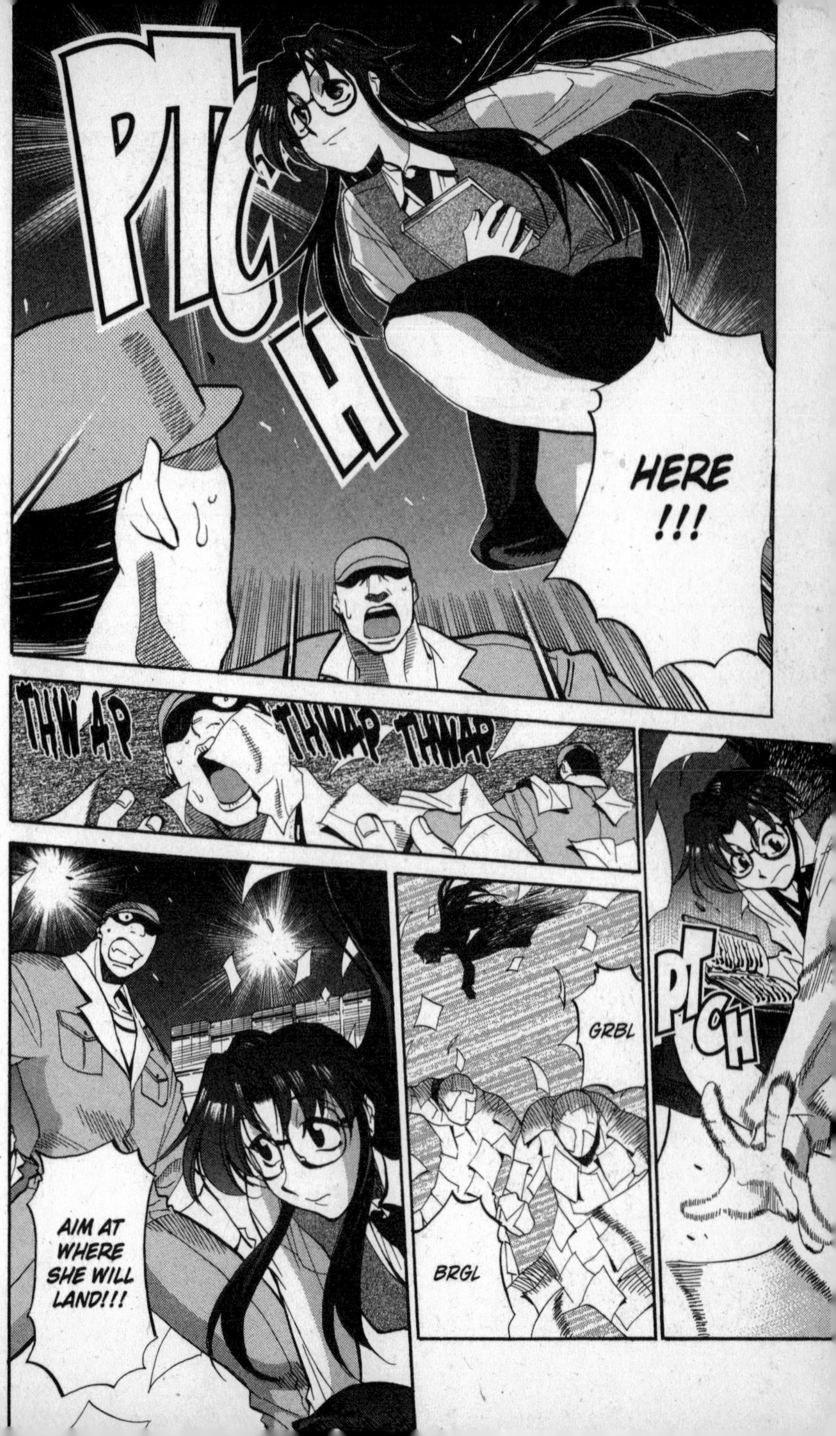
PTCH
HERE !!!
THWAP THWAP THWAP
PTCH
GRBL
BRGL
AIM AT WHERE SHE WILL LAND!!!

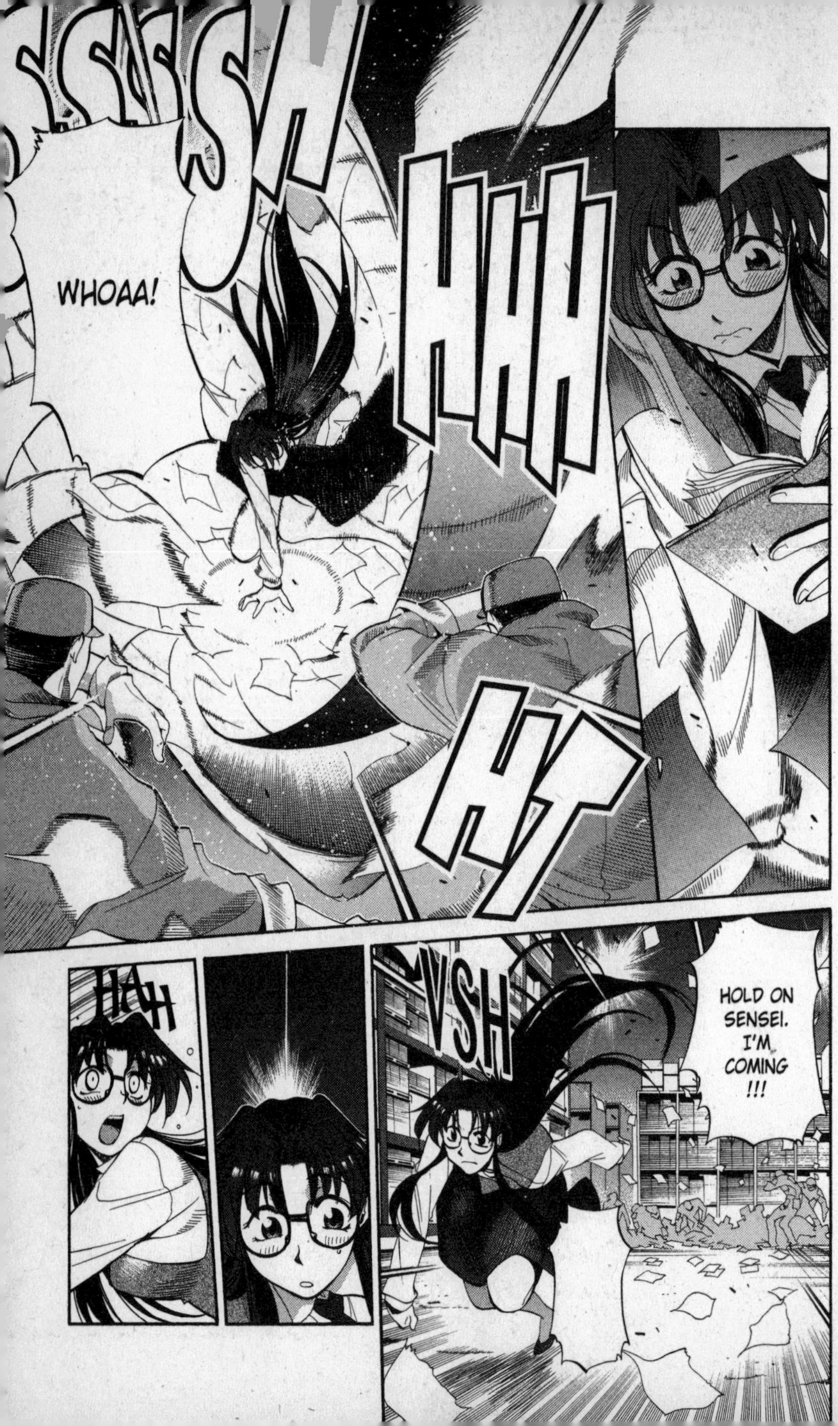
SFASH
HHHA
HT
WHOAA!
HOLD ON SENSEI. I'M COMING !!!
VSH
HAH

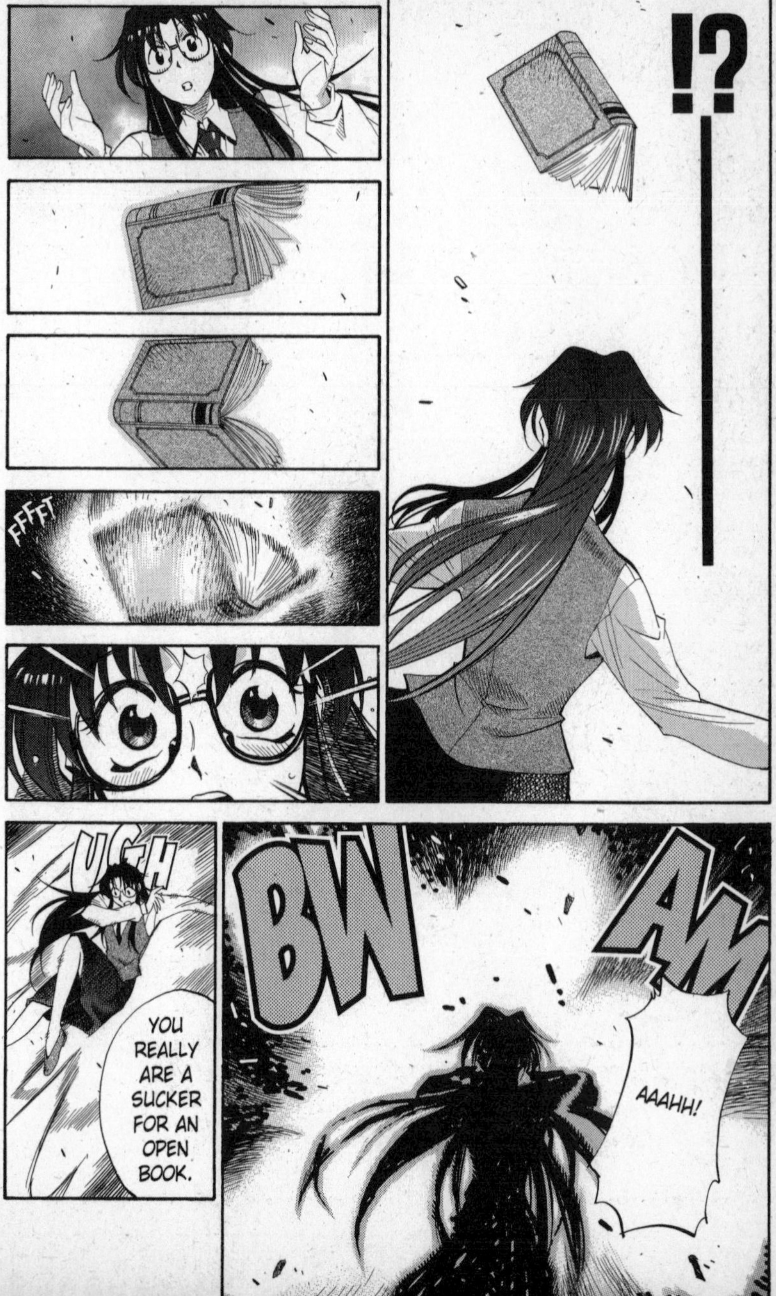
!?
FFFFT
BWAM
AAAHH!
UGH
YOU REALLY ARE A SUCKER FOR AN OPEN BOOK.

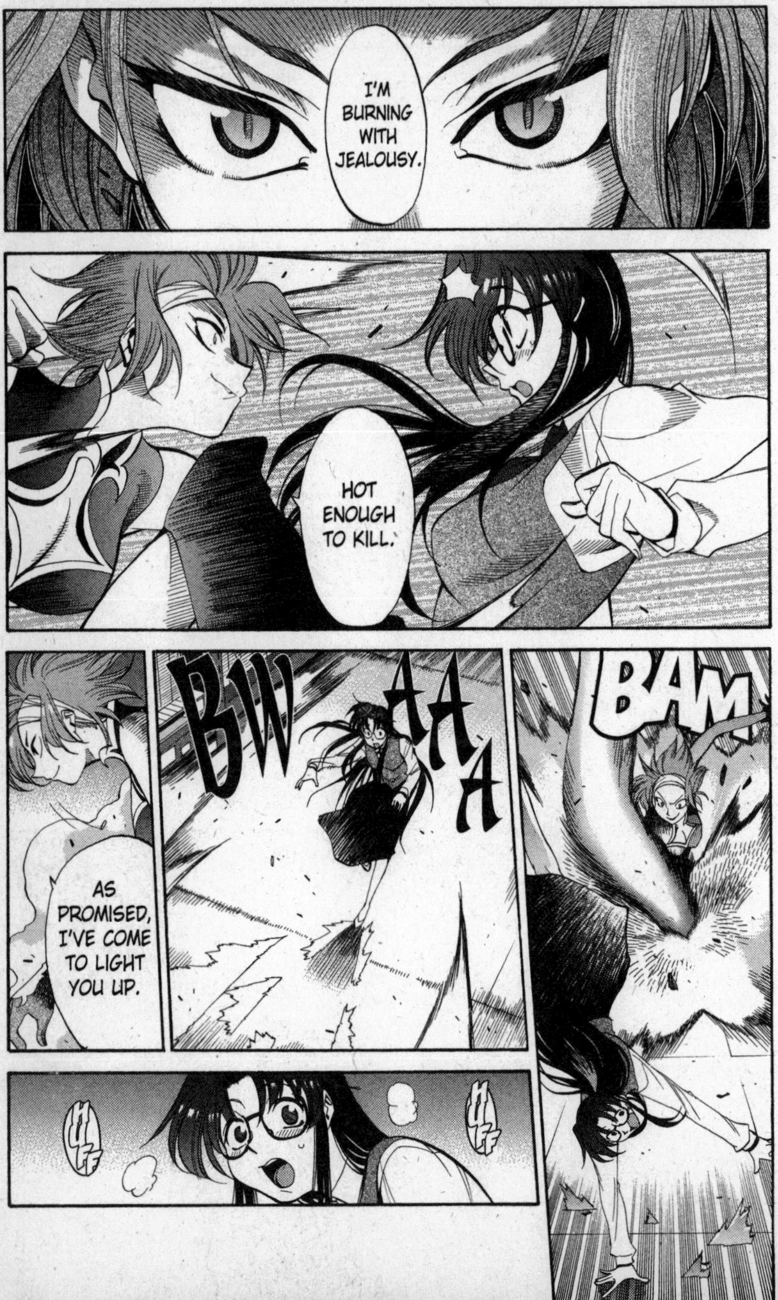
I'M BURNING WITH JEALOUSY.
HOT ENOUGH TO KILL.
BAM
BWAAA
AS PROMISED, I'VE COME TO LIGHT YOU UP.
HUFF
HUFF

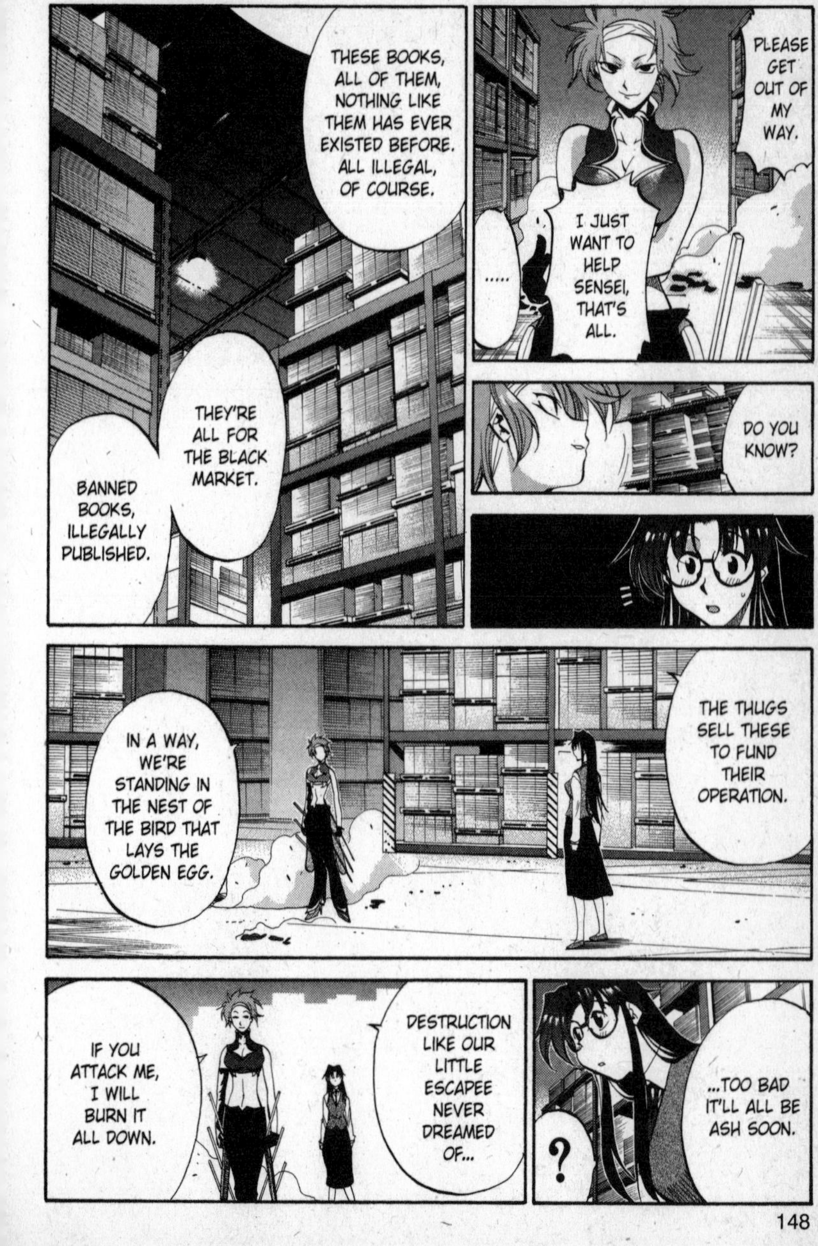
PLEASE GET OUT OF MY WAY.
I JUST WANT TO HELP SENSEI, THAT'S ALL.
.....
DO YOU KNOW?
THESE BOOKS, ALL OF THEM, NOTHING LIKE THEM HAS EVER EXISTED BEFORE. ALL ILLEGAL, OF COURSE.
THEY'RE ALL FOR THE BLACK MARKET.
BANNED BOOKS, ILLEGALLY PUBLISHED.
THE THUGS SELL THESE TO FUND THEIR OPERATION.
IN A WAY, WE'RE STANDING IN THE NEST OF THE BIRD THAT LAYS THE GOLDEN EGG.
...TOO BAD IT'LL ALL BE ASH SOON.
?
DESTRUCTION LIKE OUR LITTLE ESCAPEE NEVER DREAMED OF...
IF YOU ATTACK ME, I WILL BURN IT ALL DOWN.

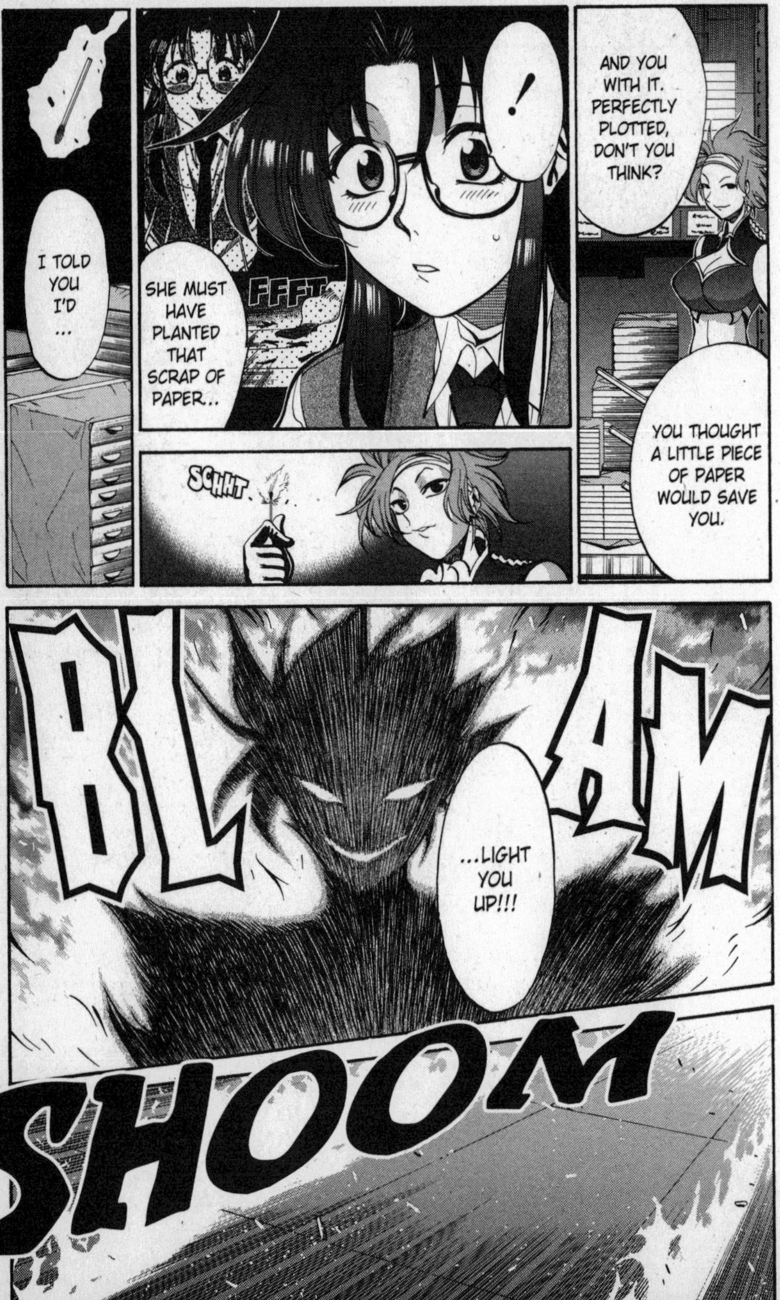
AND YOU WITH IT. PERFECTLY PLOTTED, DON'T YOU THINK?
YOU THOUGHT A LITTLE PIECE OF PAPER WOULD SAVE YOU.
!
SHE MUST HAVE PLANTED THAT SCRAP OF PAPER...
FFFT
SCHHT
I TOLD YOU I'D ...
BLAM
...LIGHT YOU UP!!!
SHOOM

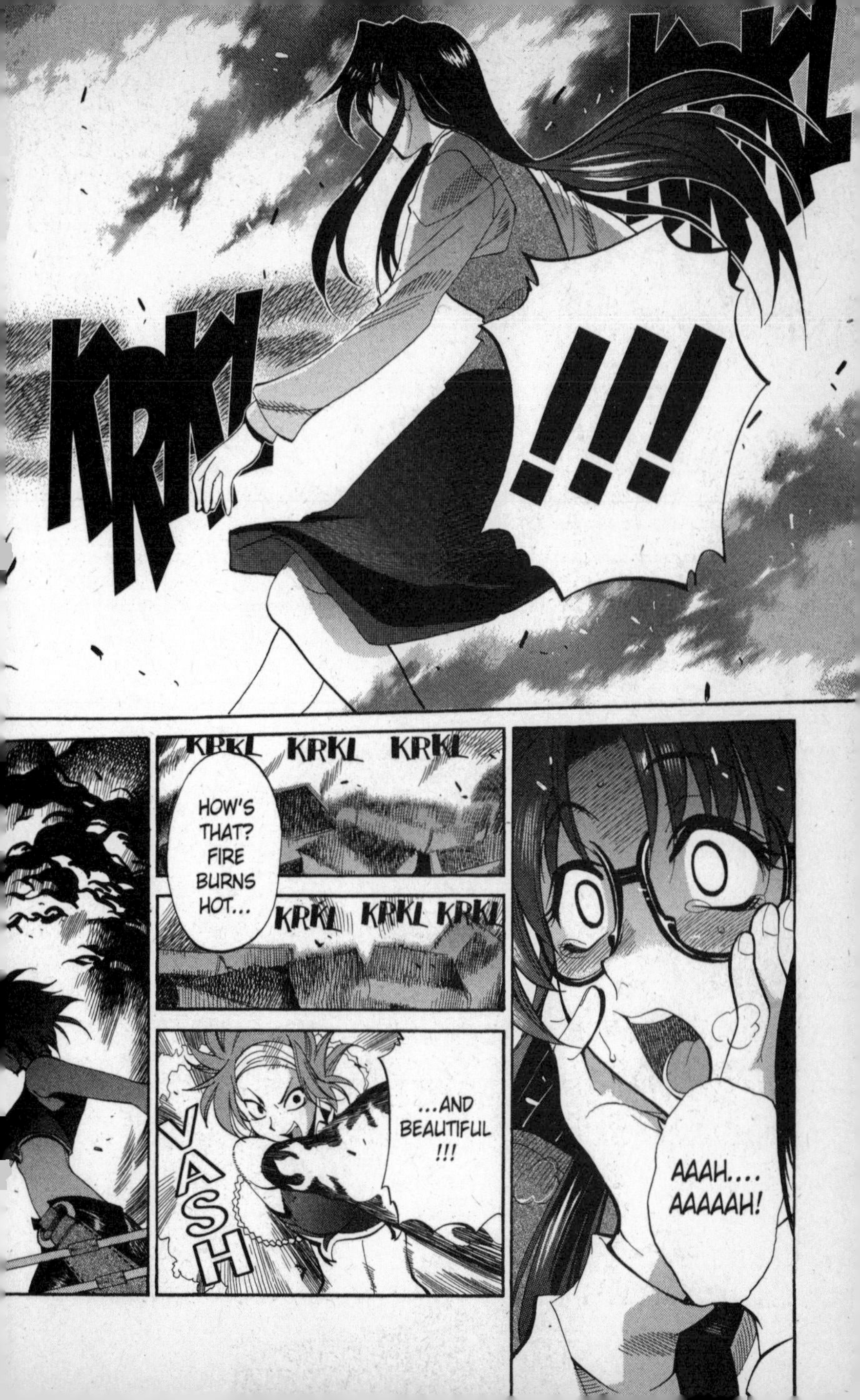
KRKL
!!!
KRKL
AAAH.... AAAAAH!
KRKL KRKL KRKL
HOW'S THAT? FIRE BURNS HOT...
KRKL KRKL KRKL
...AND BEAUTIFUL !!!
VASH

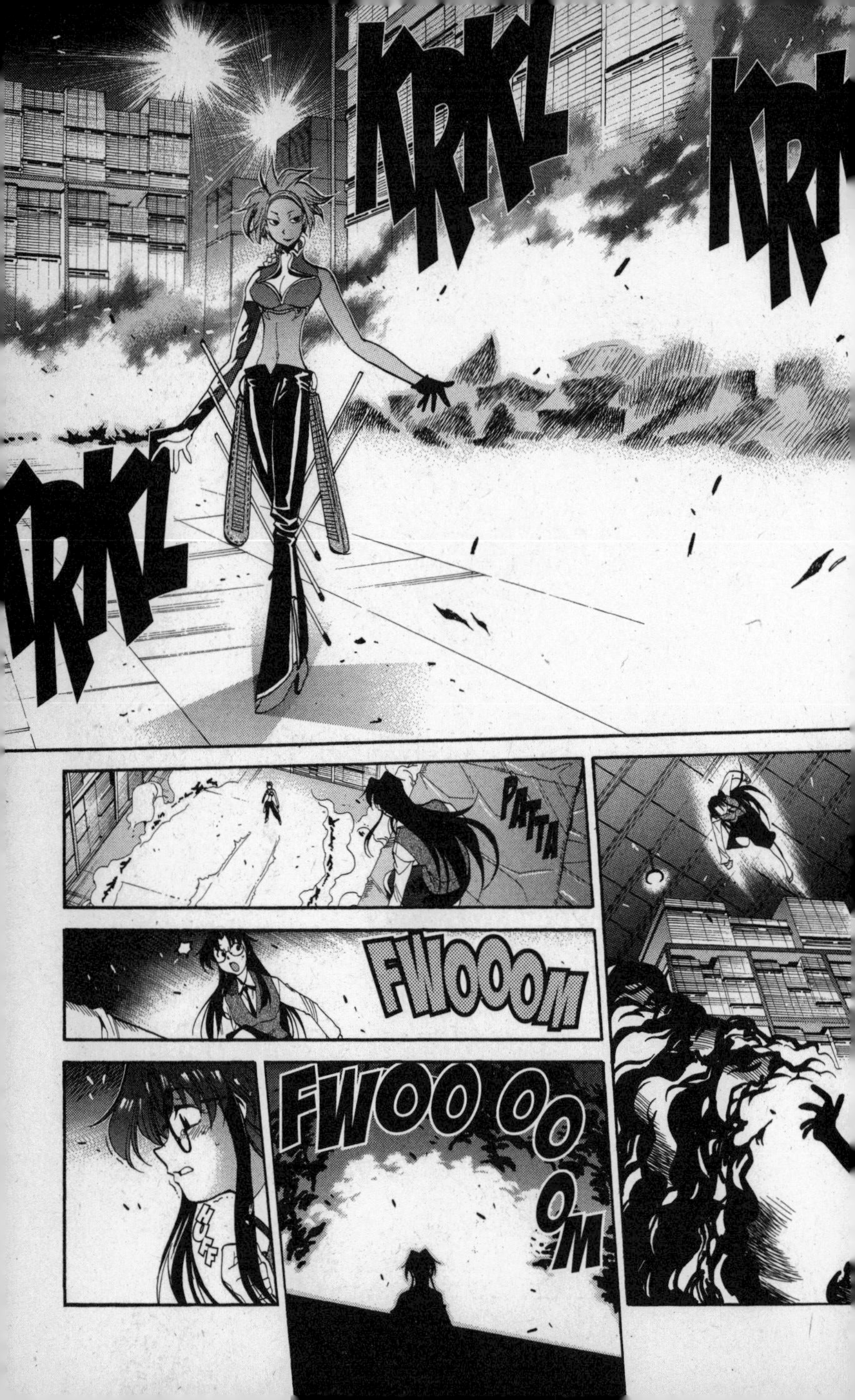
KRKL
PATTA
FWOOOM
FWOO OO OM
HUFF

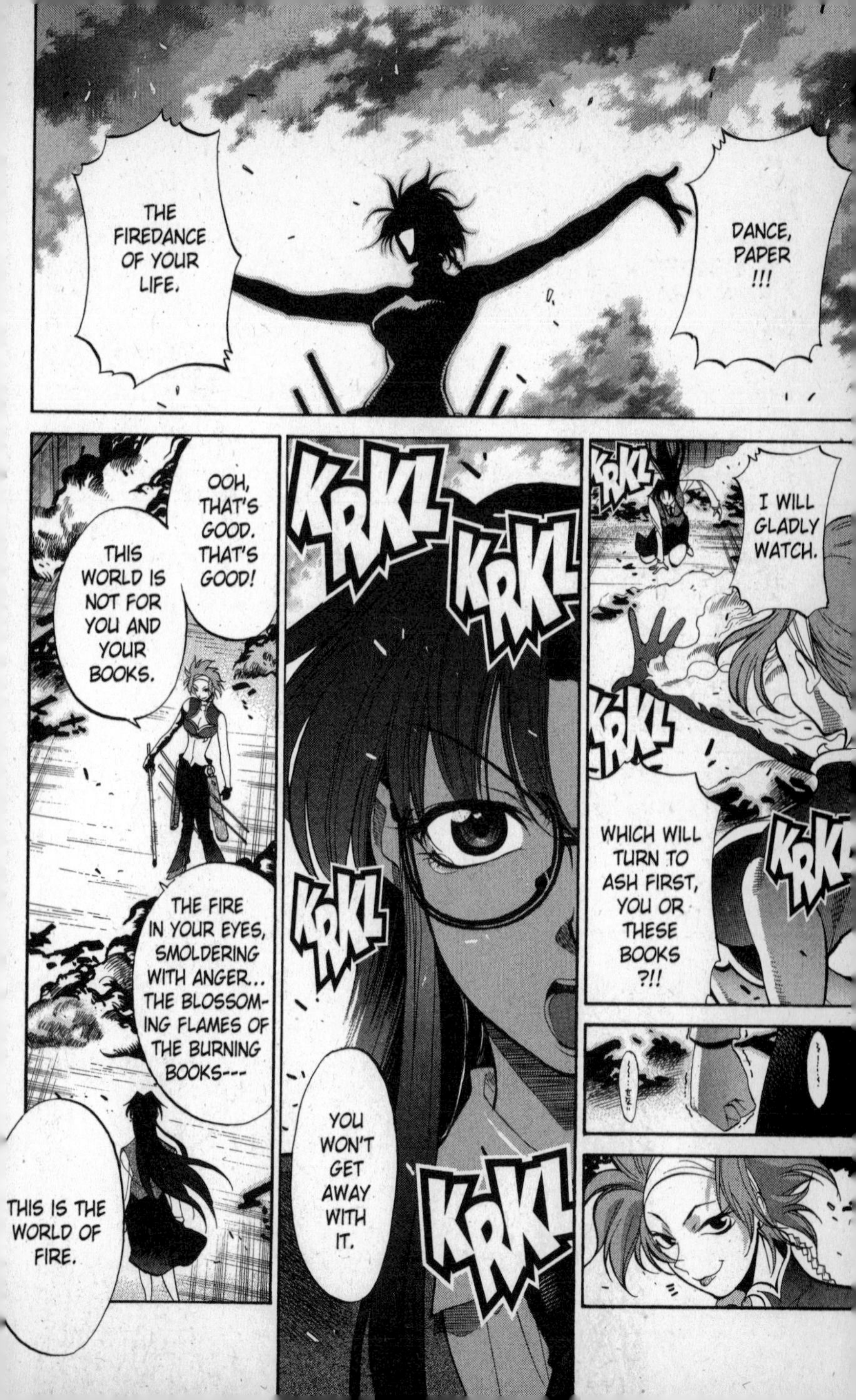
DANCE, PAPER !!!
THE FIREDANCE OF YOUR LIFE.
I WILL GLADLY WATCH.
KRKL
KRKL
WHICH WILL TURN TO ASH FIRST, YOU OR THESE BOOKS ?!!
KRKL
KRKL
KRKL
KRKL
YOU WON'T GET AWAY WITH IT.
KRKL
OOH, THAT'S GOOD. THAT'S GOOD!
THIS WORLD IS NOT FOR YOU AND YOUR BOOKS.
THE FIRE IN YOUR EYES, SMOLDERING WITH ANGER... THE BLOSSOMING FLAMES OF THE BURNING BOOKS---
THIS IS THE WORLD OF FIRE.

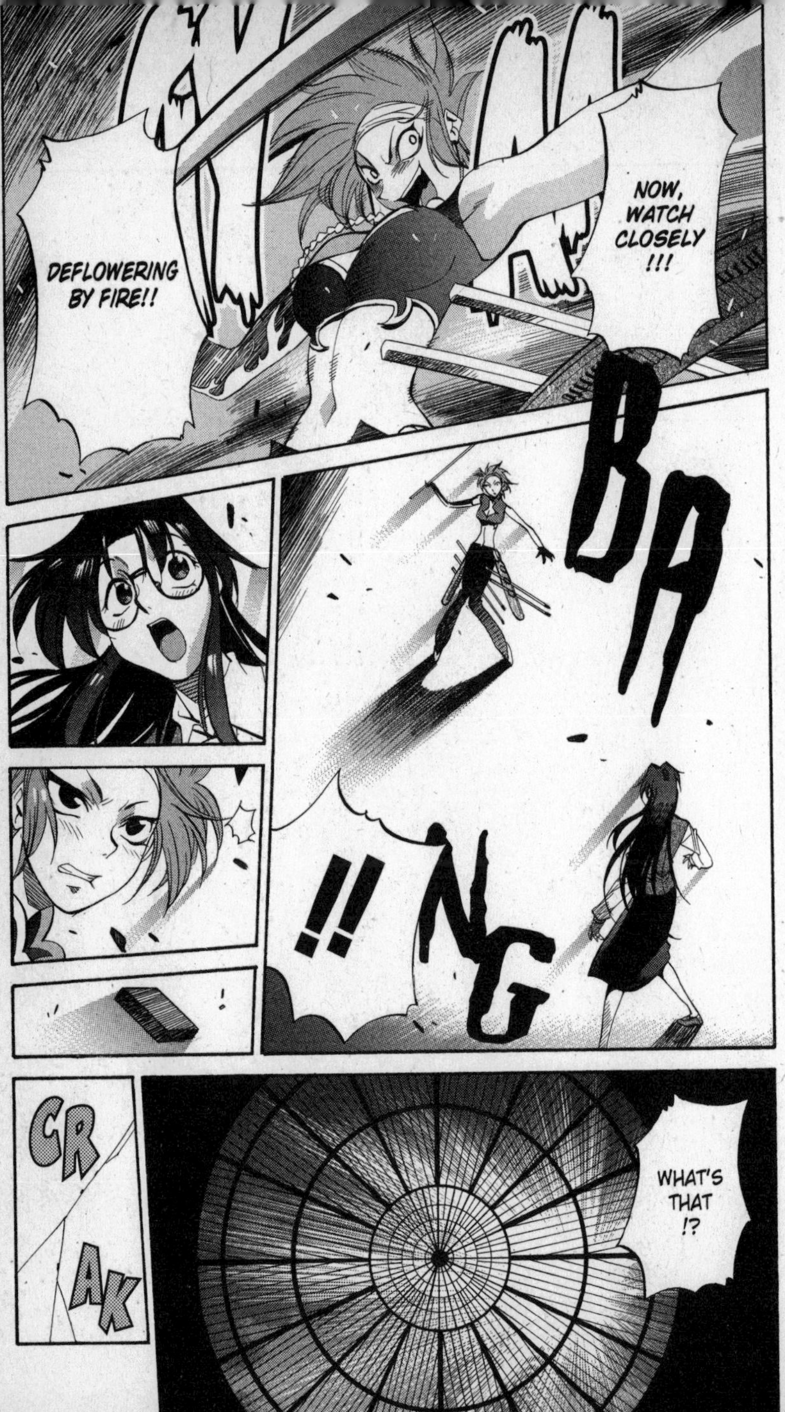
NOW, WATCH CLOSELY !!!
DEFLOWERING BY FIRE!!
BANG!!
WHAT'S THAT !?
CRAK

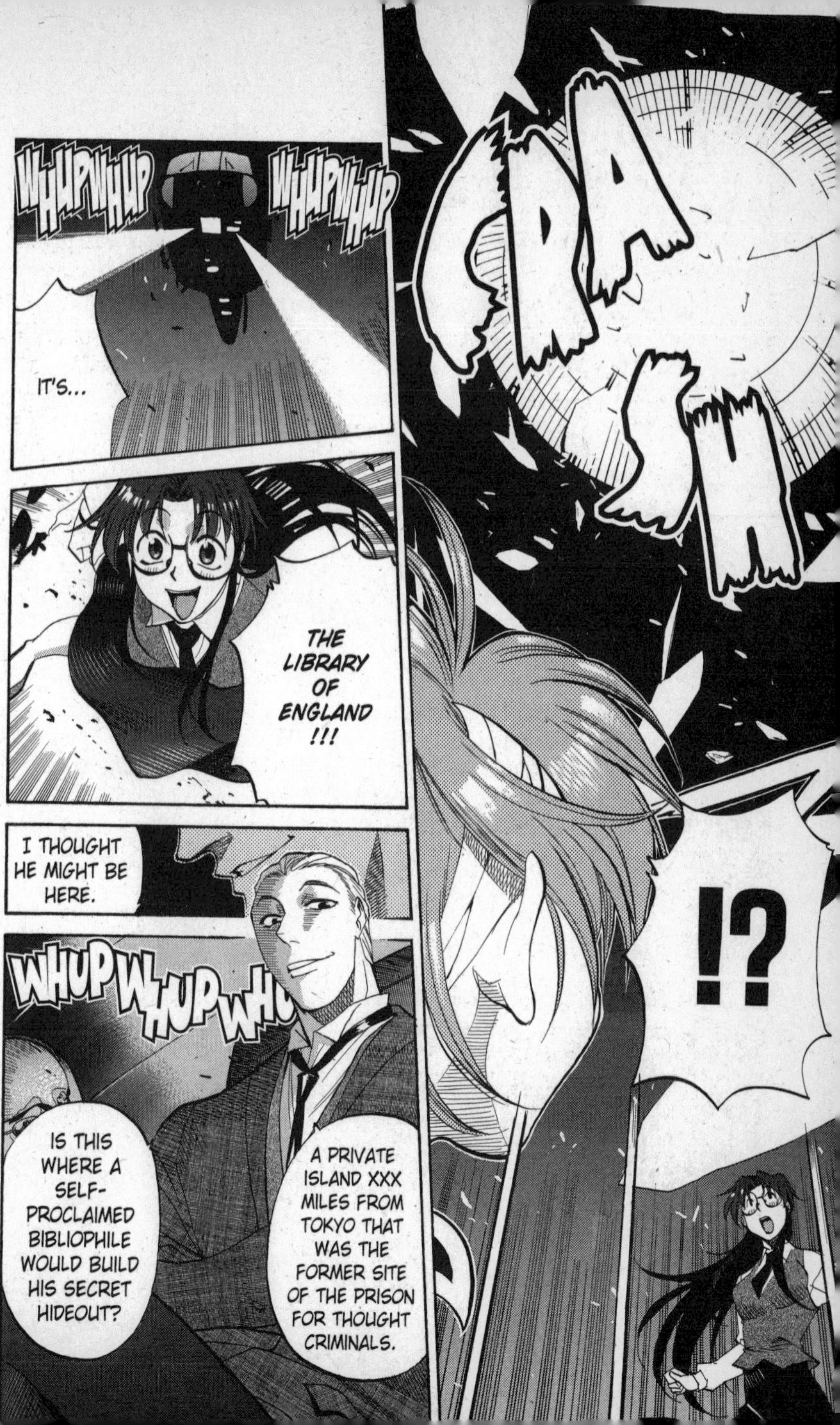
RASH
!?
WHUPWHUP
WHUPWHUP
IT'S...
THE LIBRARY OF ENGLAND !!!
I THOUGHT HE MIGHT BE HERE.
WHUPWHUPWHU
A PRIVATE ISLAND XXX MILES FROM TOKYO THAT WAS THE FORMER SITE OF THE PRISON FOR THOUGHT CRIMINALS.
IS THIS WHERE A SELF-PROCLAIMED BIBLIOPHILE WOULD BUILD HIS SECRET HIDEOUT?

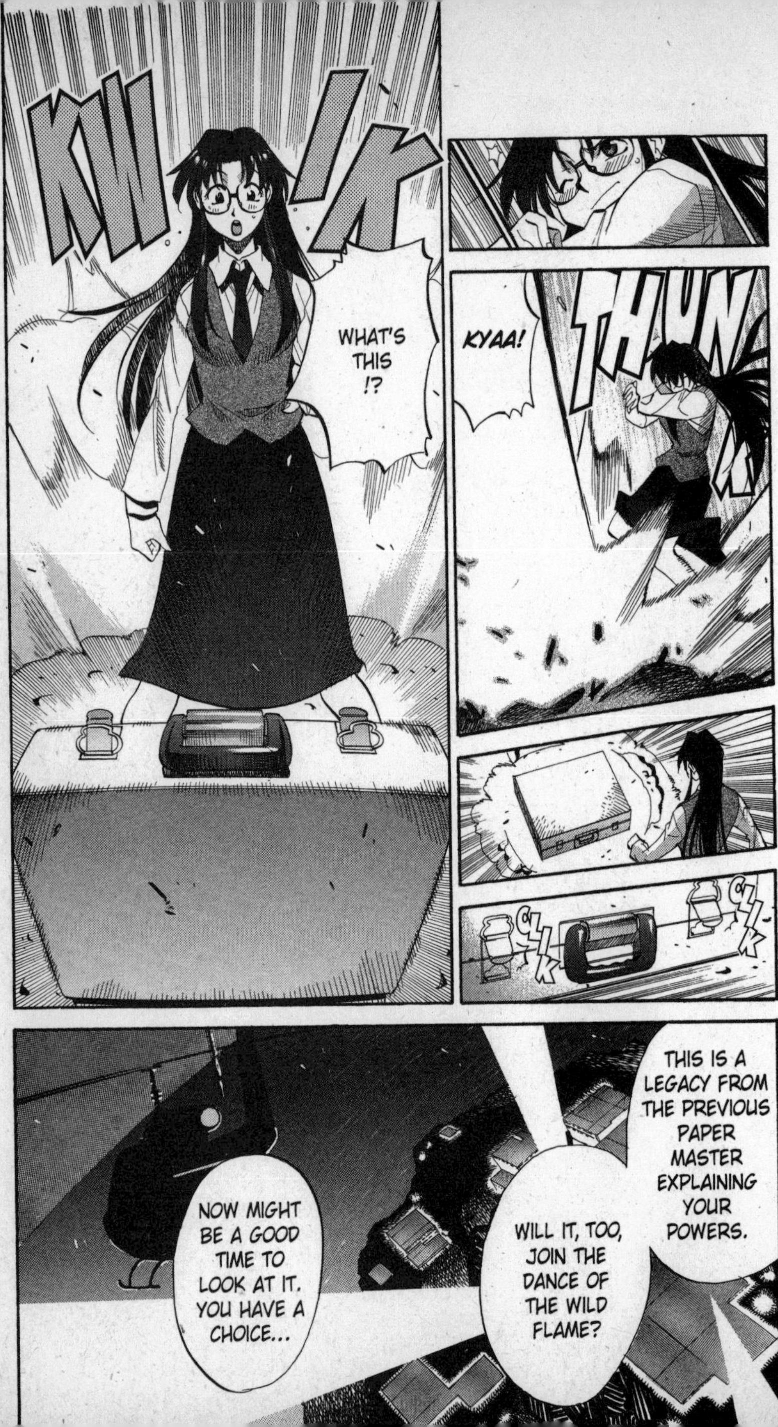
THUNK
KYAA!
CLIK
CLIK
KWIK
WHAT'S THIS !?
THIS IS A LEGACY FROM THE PREVIOUS PAPER MASTER EXPLAINING YOUR POWERS.
WILL IT, TOO, JOIN THE DANCE OF THE WILD FLAME?
NOW MIGHT BE A GOOD TIME TO LOOK AT IT. YOU HAVE A CHOICE...

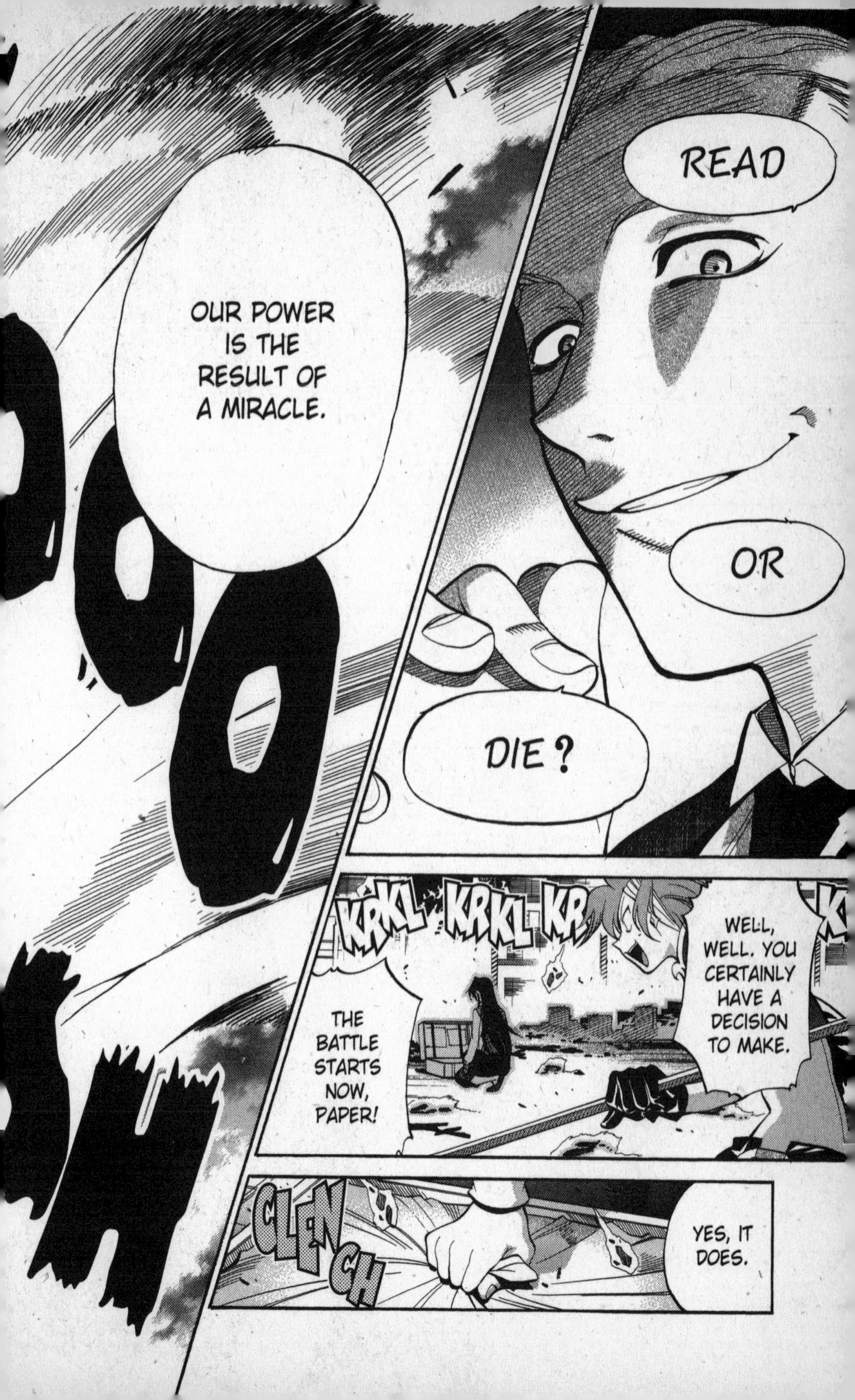
READ
OR
DIE ?
OUR POWER IS THE RESULT OF A MIRACLE.
WELL, WELL. YOU CERTAINLY HAVE A DECISION TO MAKE.
KRKL KRKL KR
THE BATTLE STARTS NOW, PAPER!
YES, IT DOES.
CLENCH

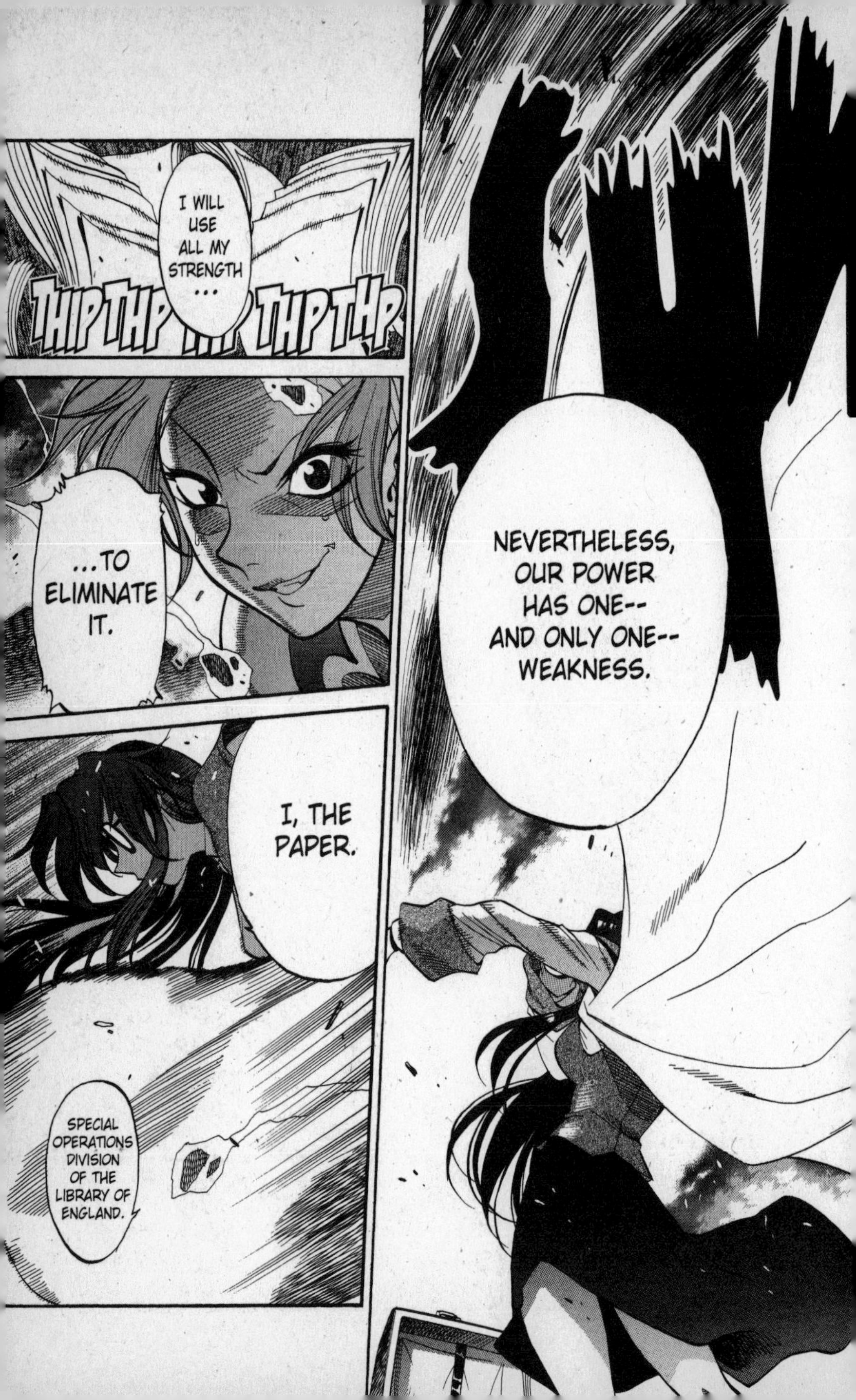
NEVERTHELESS, OUR POWER HAS ONE-- AND ONLY ONE-- WEAKNESS.
I WILL USE ALL MY STRENGTH ...
THIP THP THP THP THP
...TO ELIMINATE IT.
I, THE PAPER.
SPECIAL OPERATIONS DIVISION OF THE LIBRARY OF ENGLAND.

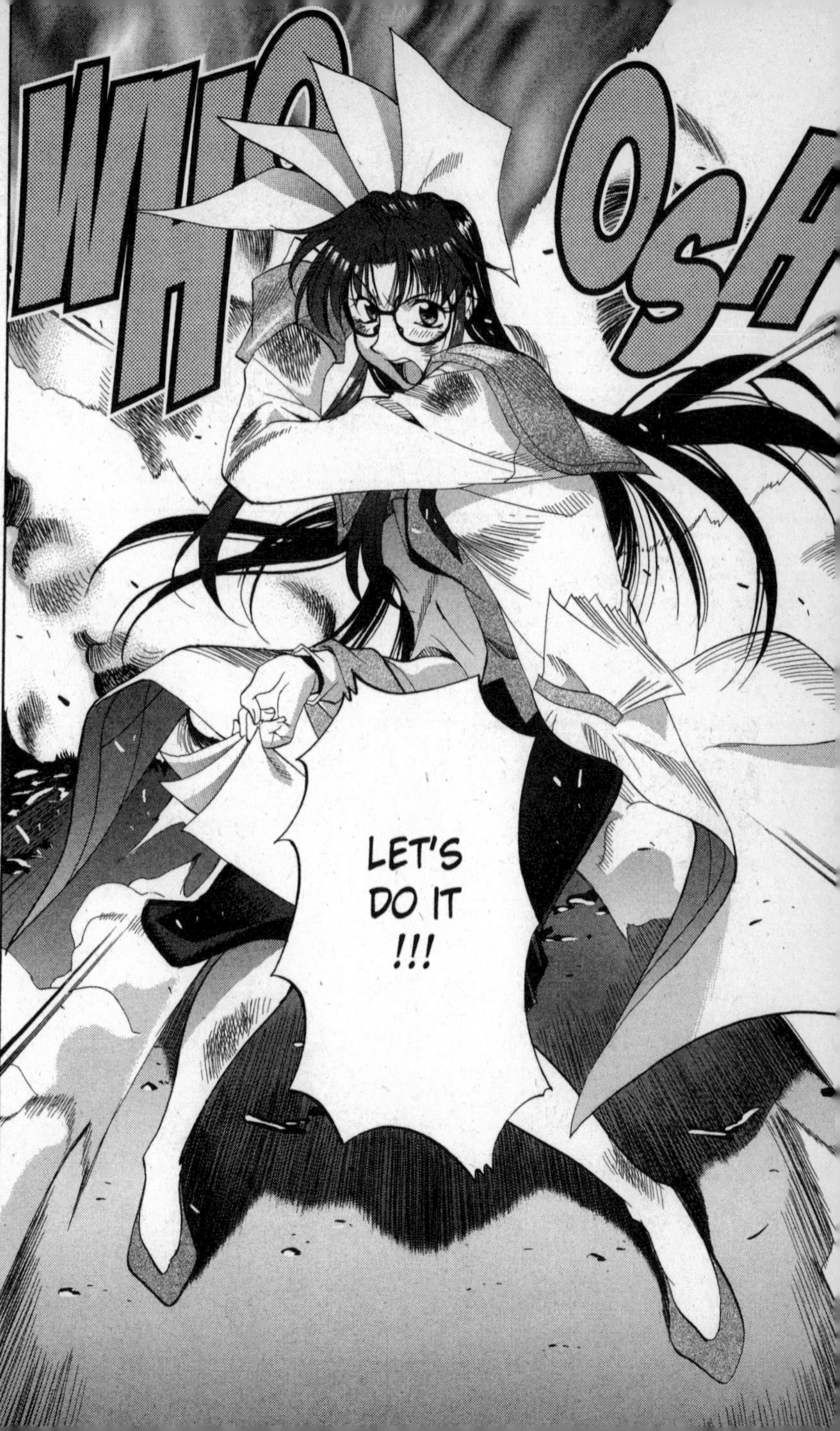
LET'S DO IT !!!

EPISODE SEVEN

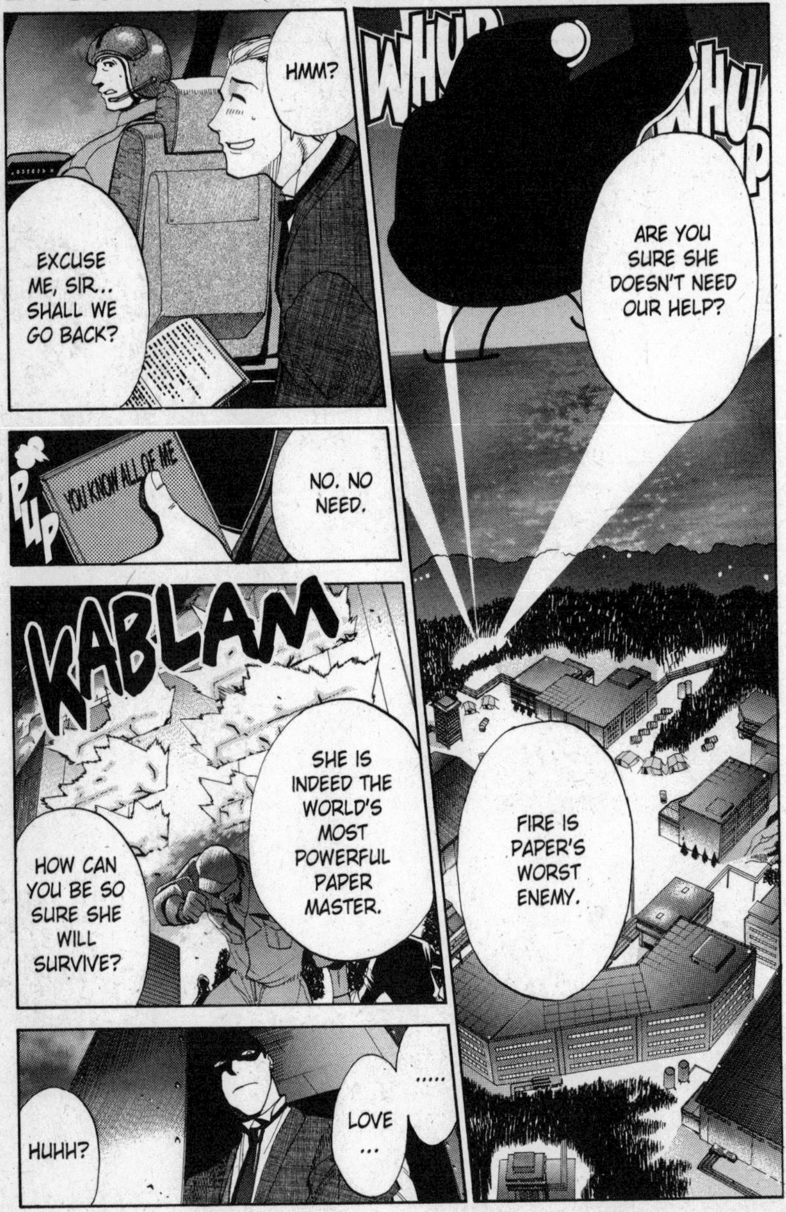
WHUP
WHUP
ARE YOU SURE SHE DOESN'T NEED OUR HELP?
FIRE IS PAPER'S WORST ENEMY.
HMM?
EXCUSE ME, SIR... SHALL WE GO BACK?
PUP
YOU KNOW ALL OF ME
NO. NO NEED.
KABLAM
SHE IS INDEED THE WORLD'S MOST POWERFUL PAPER MASTER.
HOW CAN YOU BE SO SURE SHE WILL SURVIVE?
.....
LOVE ...
HUHH?

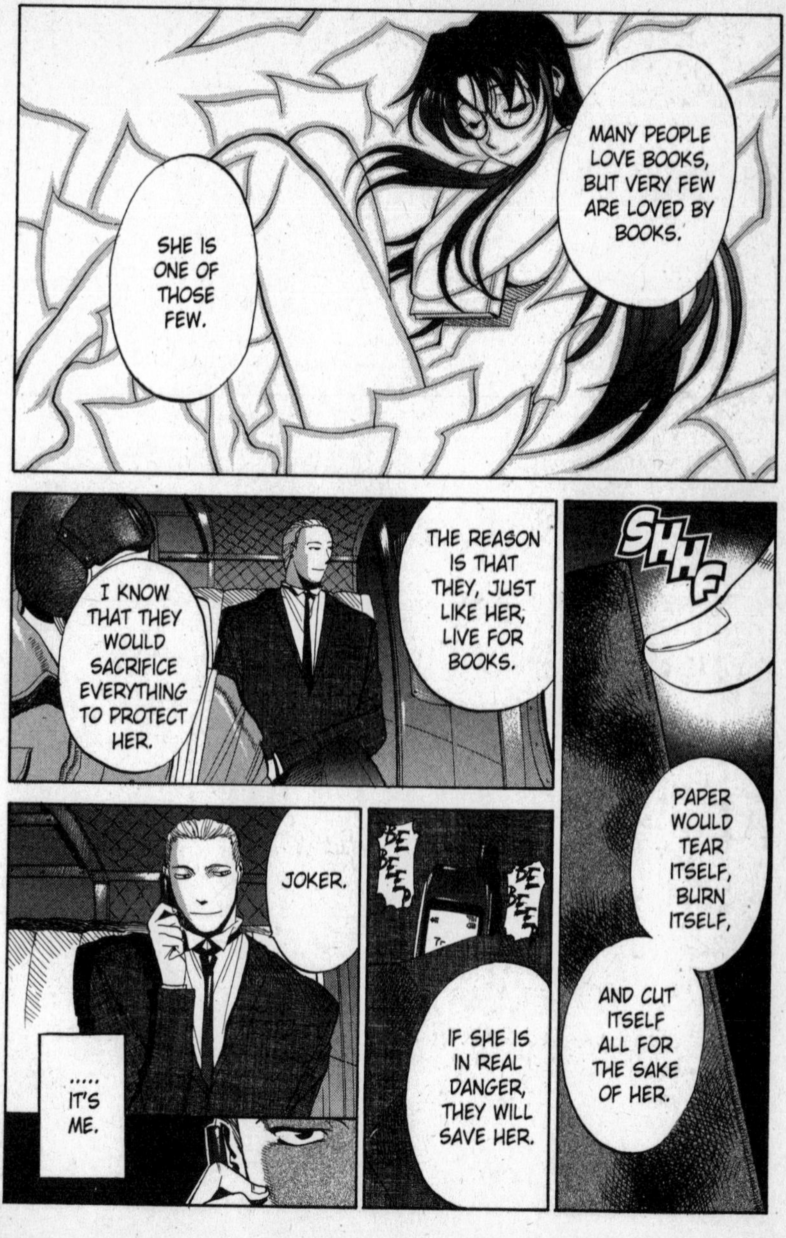
MANY PEOPLE LOVE BOOKS, BUT VERY FEW ARE LOVED BY BOOKS.
SHE IS ONE OF THOSE FEW.
SHHF
PAPER WOULD TEAR ITSELF, BURN ITSELF,
AND CUT ITSELF ALL FOR THE SAKE OF HER.
THE REASON IS THAT THEY, JUST LIKE HER, LIVE FOR BOOKS.
I KNOW THAT THEY WOULD SACRIFICE EVERYTHING TO PROTECT HER.
BE BEEP
DE BEEP
IF SHE IS IN REAL DANGER, THEY WILL SAVE HER.
JOKER.
..... IT'S ME.

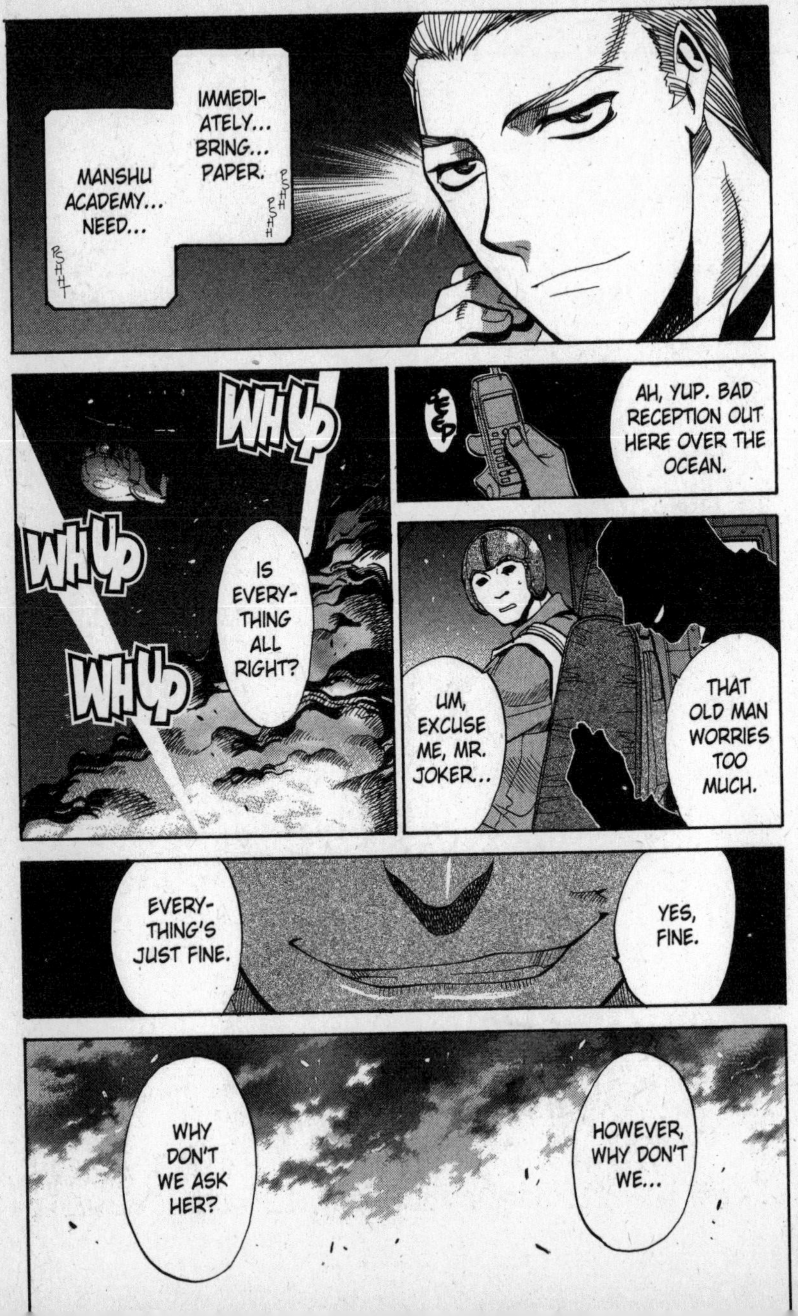
IMMEDI-ATELY... BRING... PAPER.
PSHH PSHH
MANSHU ACADEMY... NEED...
PSHHT
AH, YUP. BAD RECEPTION OUT HERE OVER THE OCEAN.
BEEP
THAT OLD MAN WORRIES TOO MUCH.
UM, EXCUSE ME, MR. JOKER...
WHUP
IS EVERY-THING ALL RIGHT?
WHUP
WHUP
YES, FINE.
EVERY-THING'S JUST FINE.
HOWEVER, WHY DON'T WE...
WHY DON'T WE ASK HER?

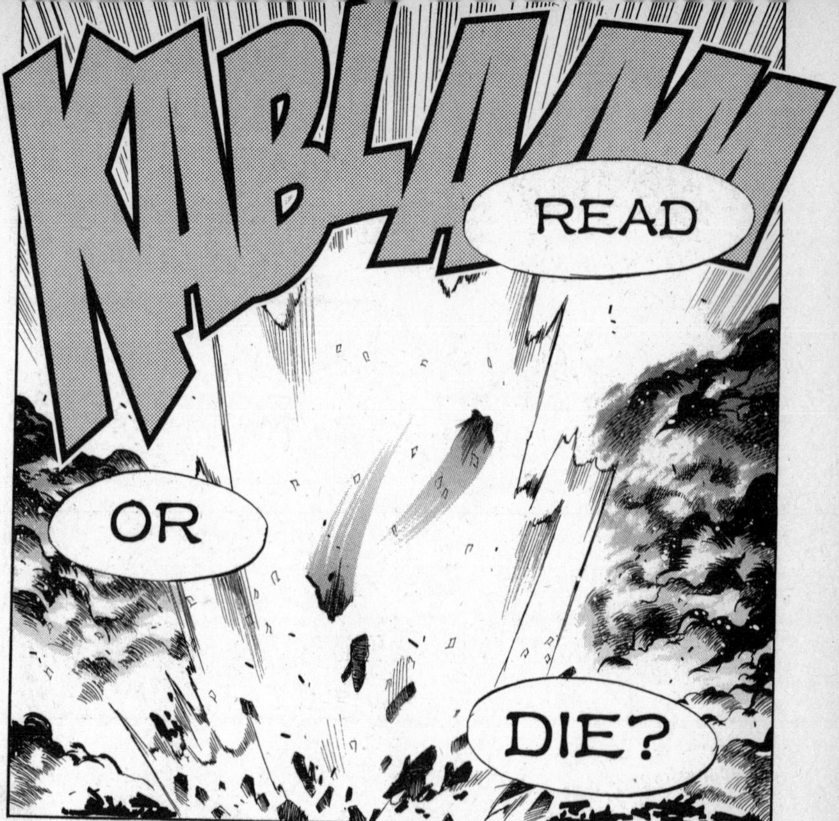
KABLAM
READ
OR
DIE?

EPISODE SEVEN

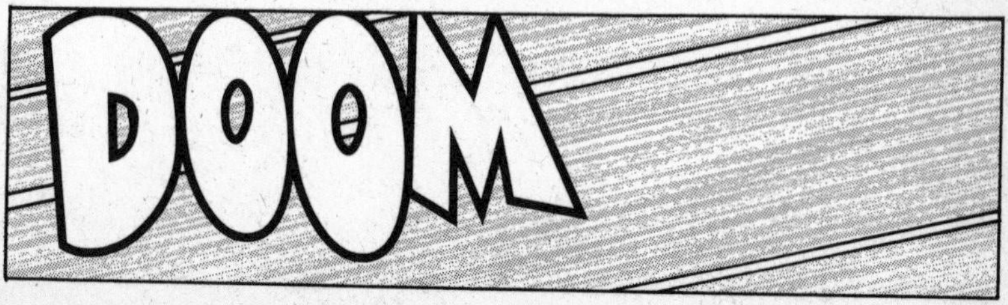
DOOM

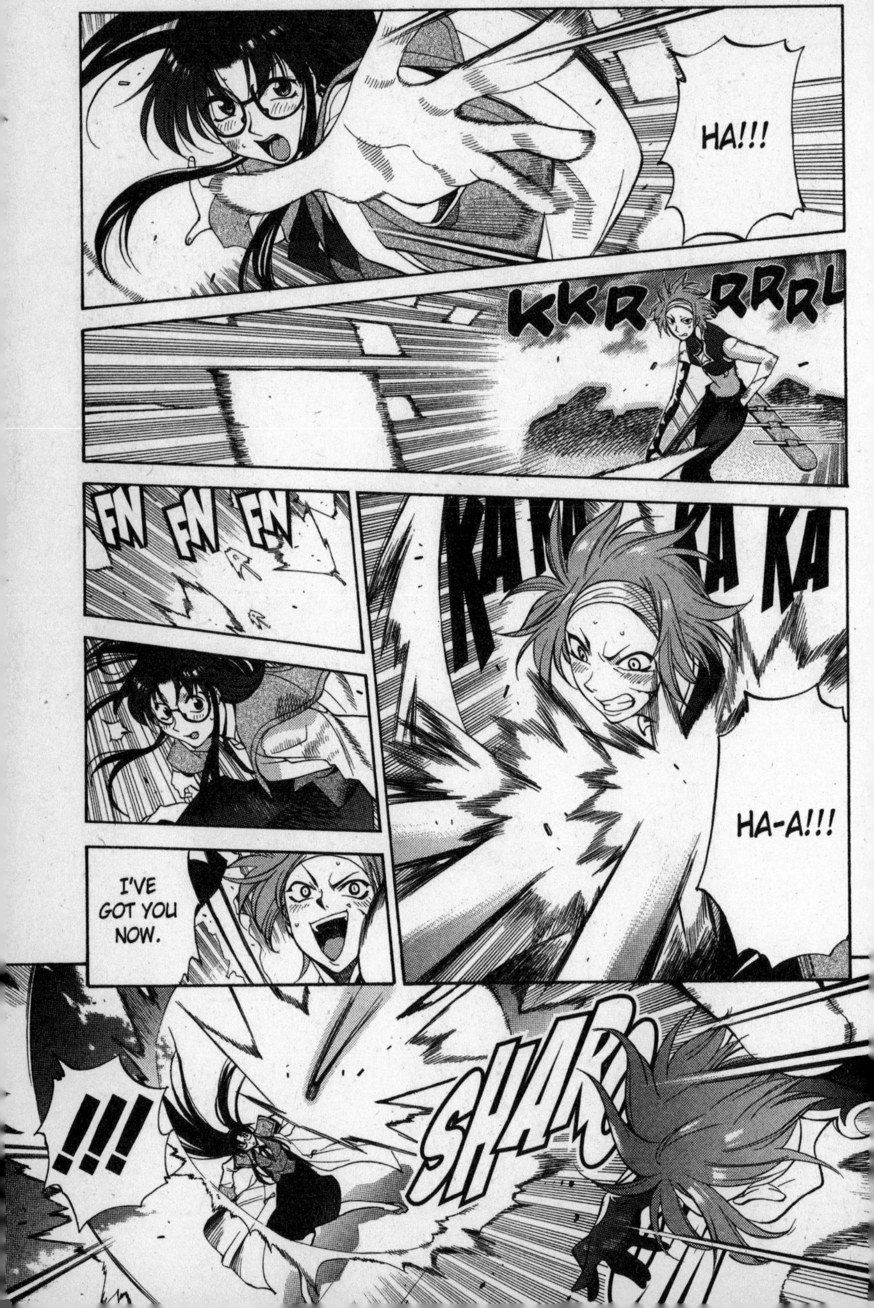
HA!!!
KKR RRRL
KA KA KA KA KA
HA-A!!!
FN FN FN
I'VE GOT YOU NOW.
SHAK
!!!

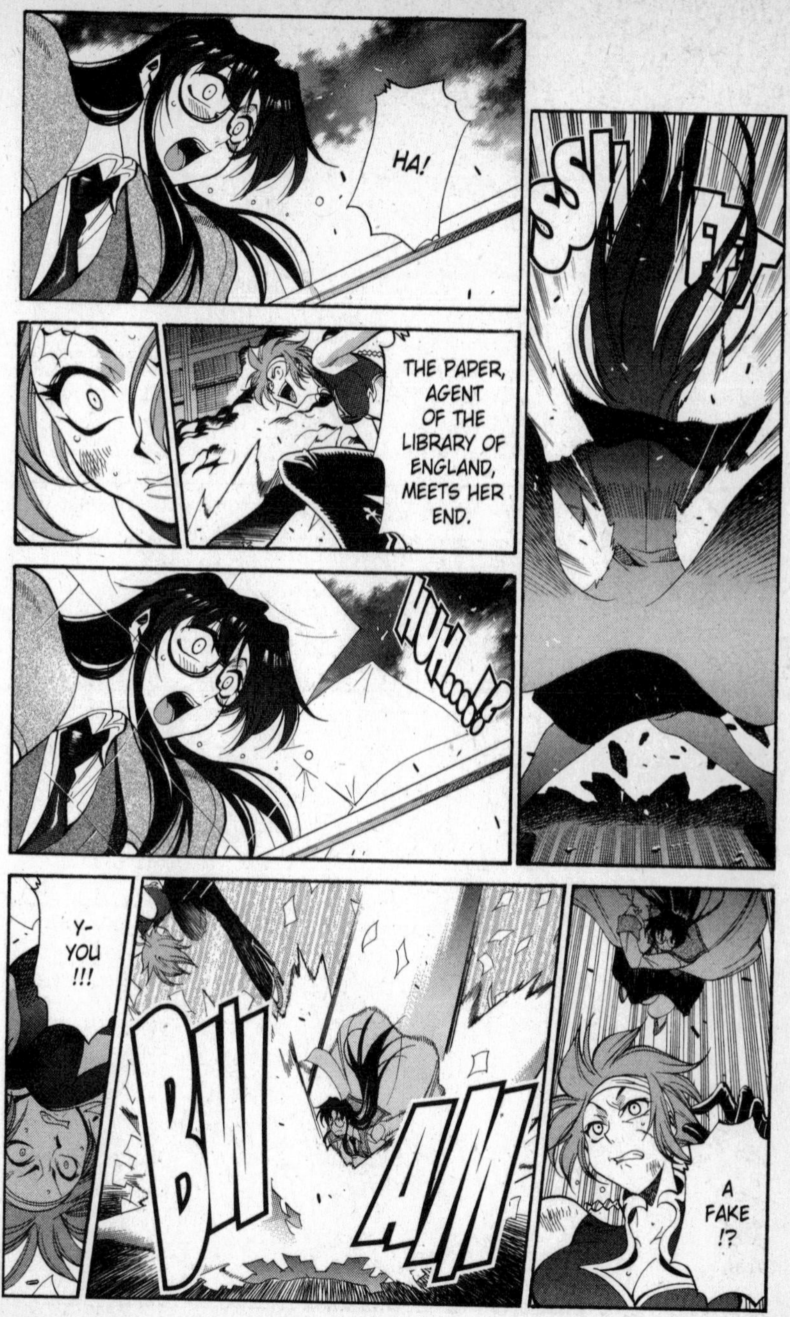
HA!
THE PAPER, AGENT OF THE LIBRARY OF ENGLAND, MEETS HER END.
HUH...!?
A FAKE !?
BWAM
Y-YOU !!!

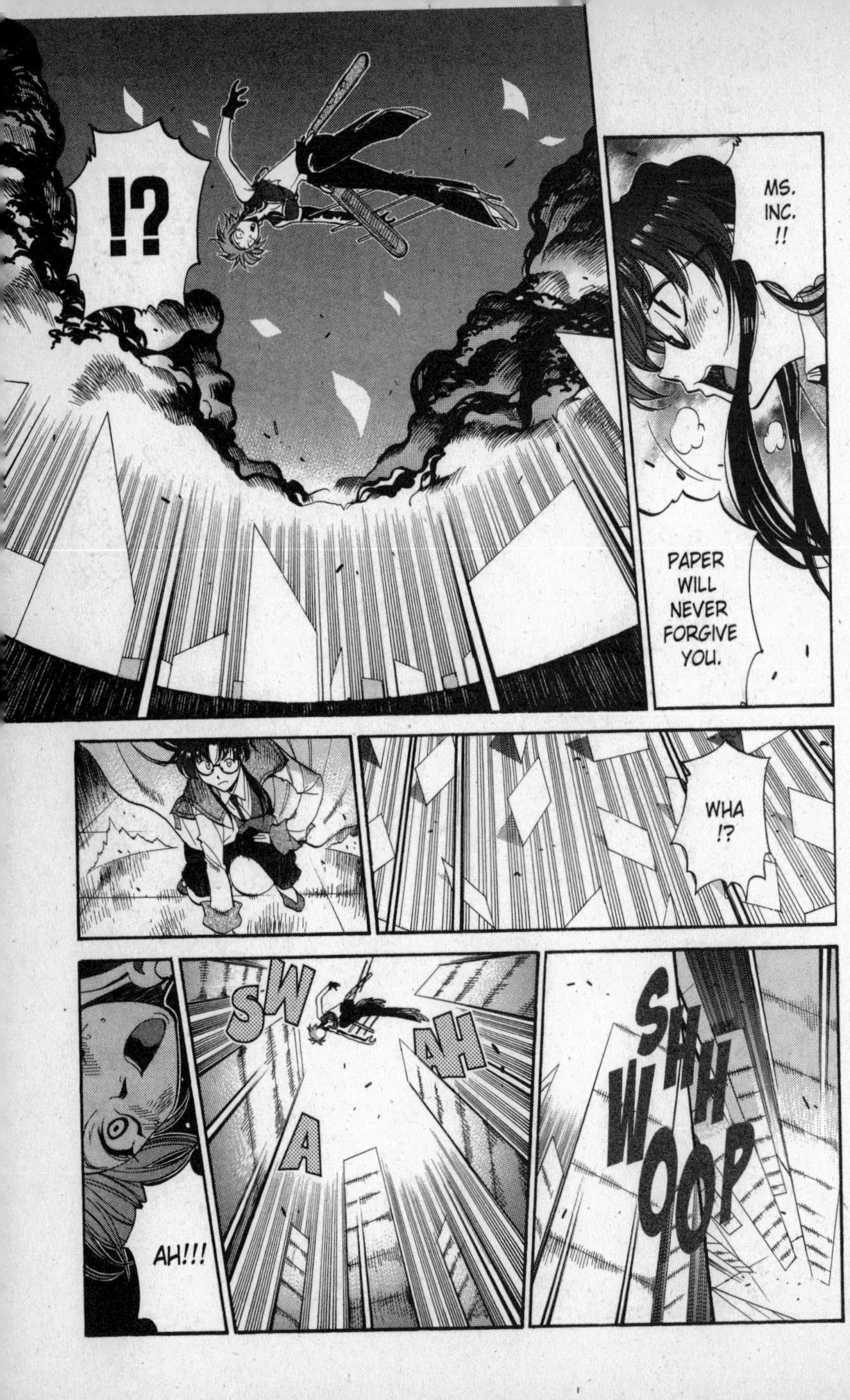
MS. INC. !!
PAPER WILL NEVER FORGIVE YOU.
!?
WHA !?
SHHWOOP
SWAAH
AH!!!

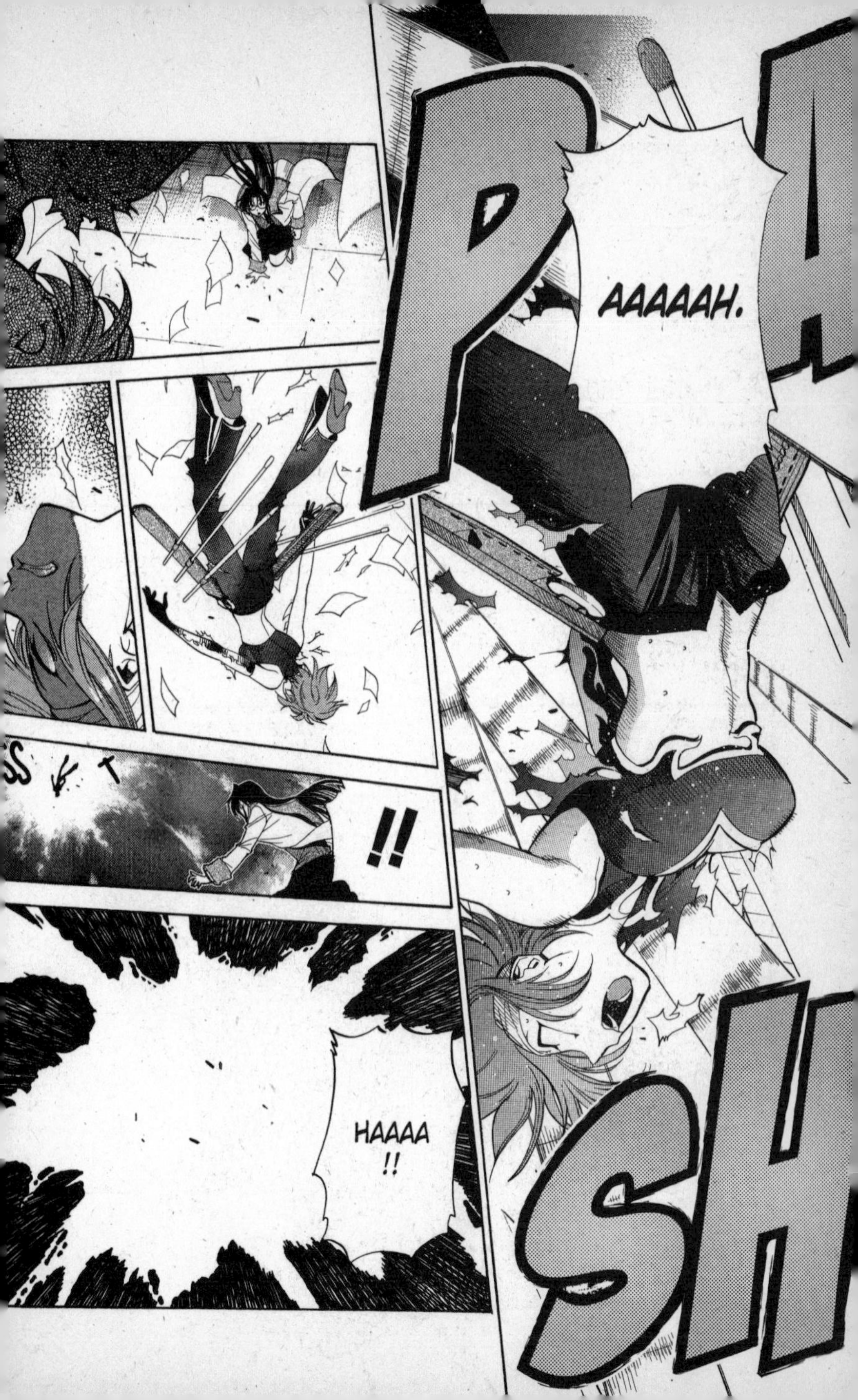
PA
AAAAAH.
SH
!!
HAAAA !!

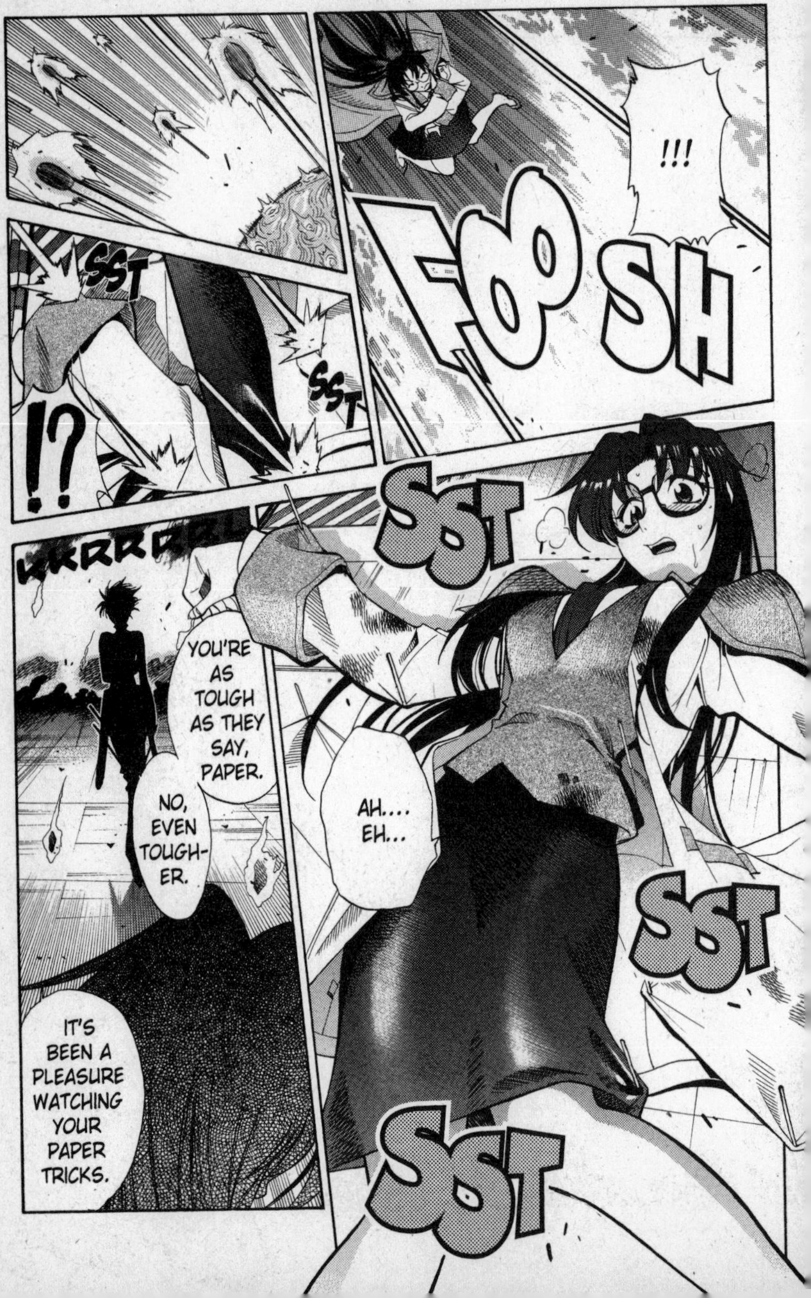
!!!
FOOSH
SST
SST
!?
SST
KRRRRRL
AH.... EH...
YOU'RE AS TOUGH AS THEY SAY, PAPER.
NO, EVEN TOUGHER.
SST
IT'S BEEN A PLEASURE WATCHING YOUR PAPER TRICKS.
SST

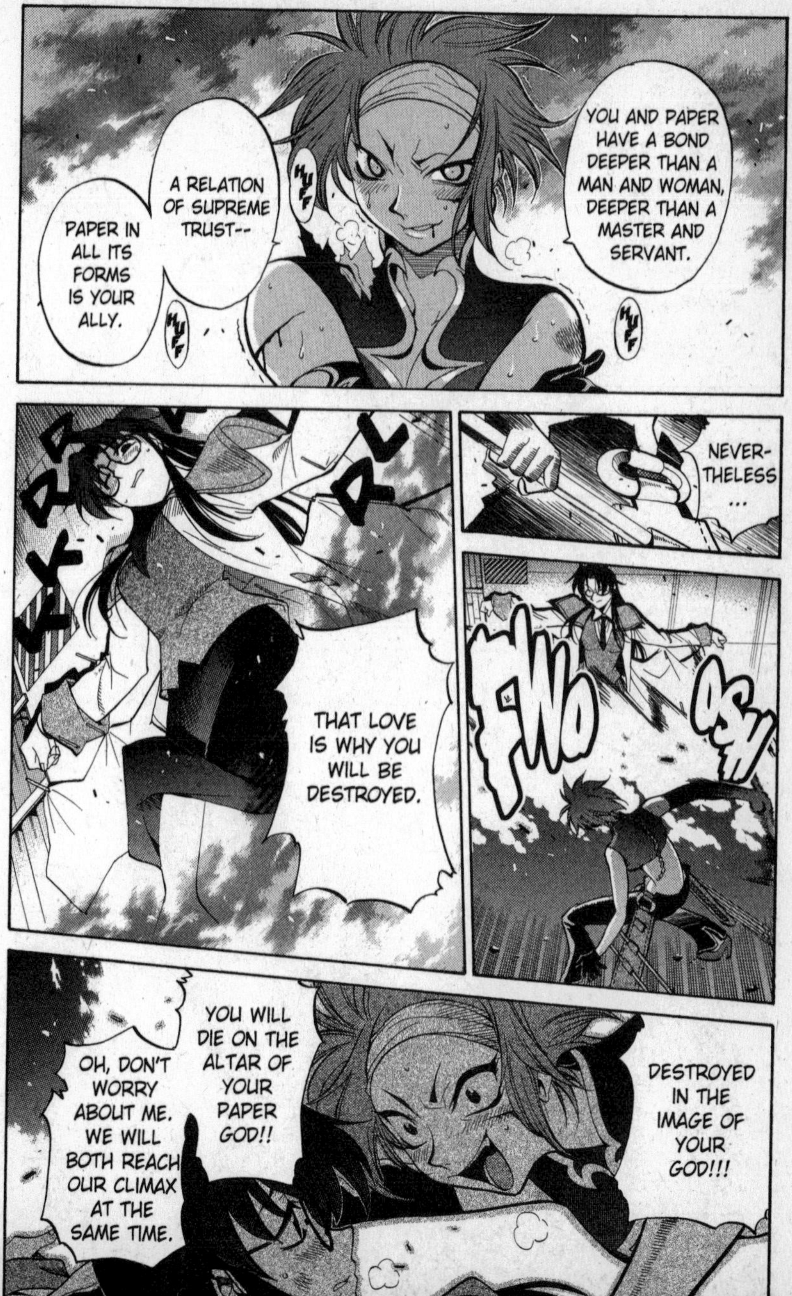
YOU AND PAPER HAVE A BOND DEEPER THAN A MAN AND WOMAN, DEEPER THAN A MASTER AND SERVANT.
HUFF
HUFF
A RELATION OF SUPREME TRUST--
PAPER IN ALL ITS FORMS IS YOUR ALLY.
HUFF
NEVER-THELESS ...
FWOOSH
THAT LOVE IS WHY YOU WILL BE DESTROYED.
DESTROYED IN THE IMAGE OF YOUR GOD!!!
YOU WILL DIE ON THE ALTAR OF YOUR PAPER GOD!!
OH, DON'T WORRY ABOUT ME. WE WILL BOTH REACH OUR CLIMAX AT THE SAME TIME.

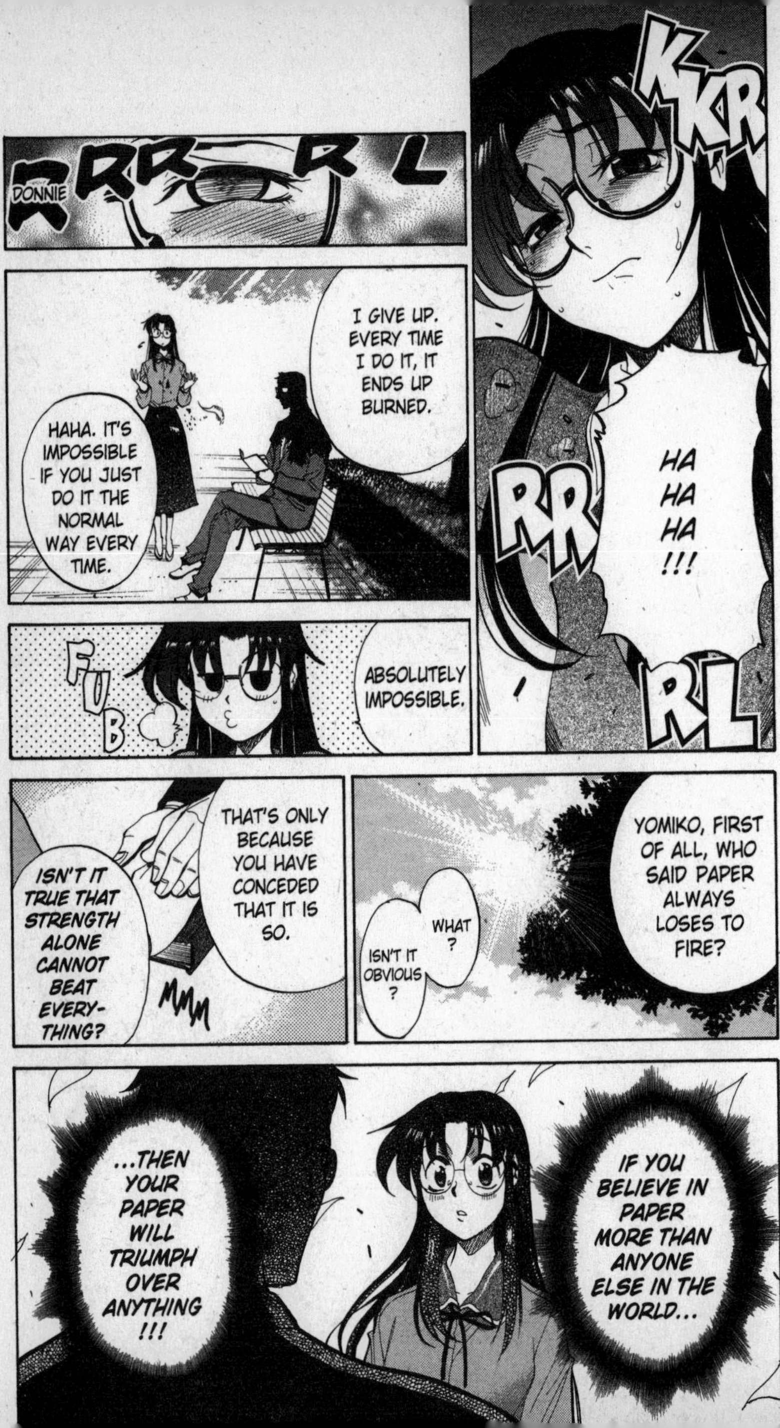
KKR
HA HA HA !!!
RR
RL
RRR-R L
DONNIE
I GIVE UP. EVERY TIME I DO IT, IT ENDS UP BURNED.
HAHA. IT'S IMPOSSIBLE IF YOU JUST DO IT THE NORMAL WAY EVERY TIME.
ABSOLUTELY IMPOSSIBLE.
FUB
YOMIKO, FIRST OF ALL, WHO SAID PAPER ALWAYS LOSES TO FIRE?
WHAT?
ISN'T IT OBVIOUS?
THAT'S ONLY BECAUSE YOU HAVE CONCEDED THAT IT IS SO.
ISN'T IT TRUE THAT STRENGTH ALONE CANNOT BEAT EVERY-THING?
MMM
IF YOU BELIEVE IN PAPER MORE THAN ANYONE ELSE IN THE WORLD...
...THEN YOUR PAPER WILL TRIUMPH OVER ANYTHING !!!

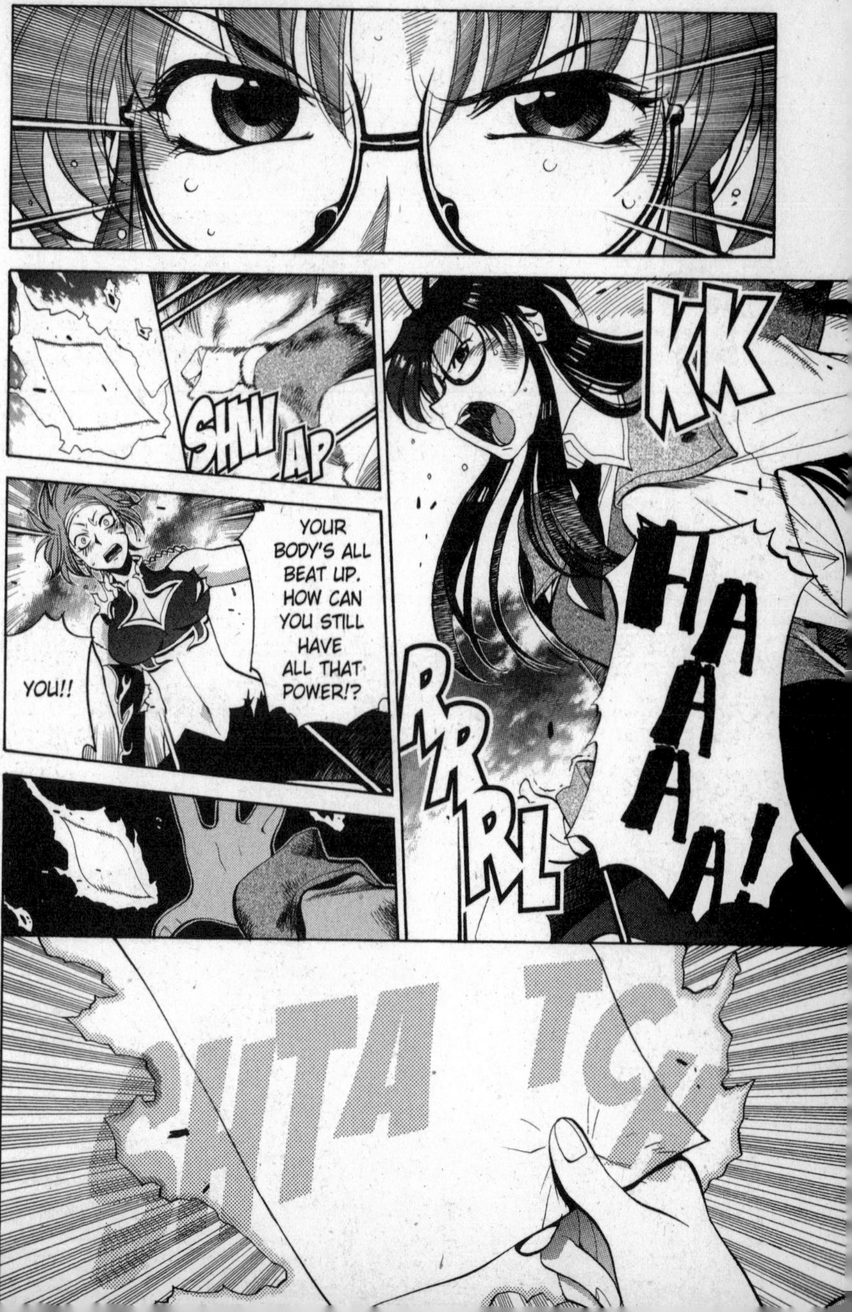
KK
HAAAAA!
RRRL
SHWAP
YOUR BODY'S ALL BEAT UP. HOW CAN YOU STILL HAVE ALL THAT POWER!?
YOU!!
HITA TCH

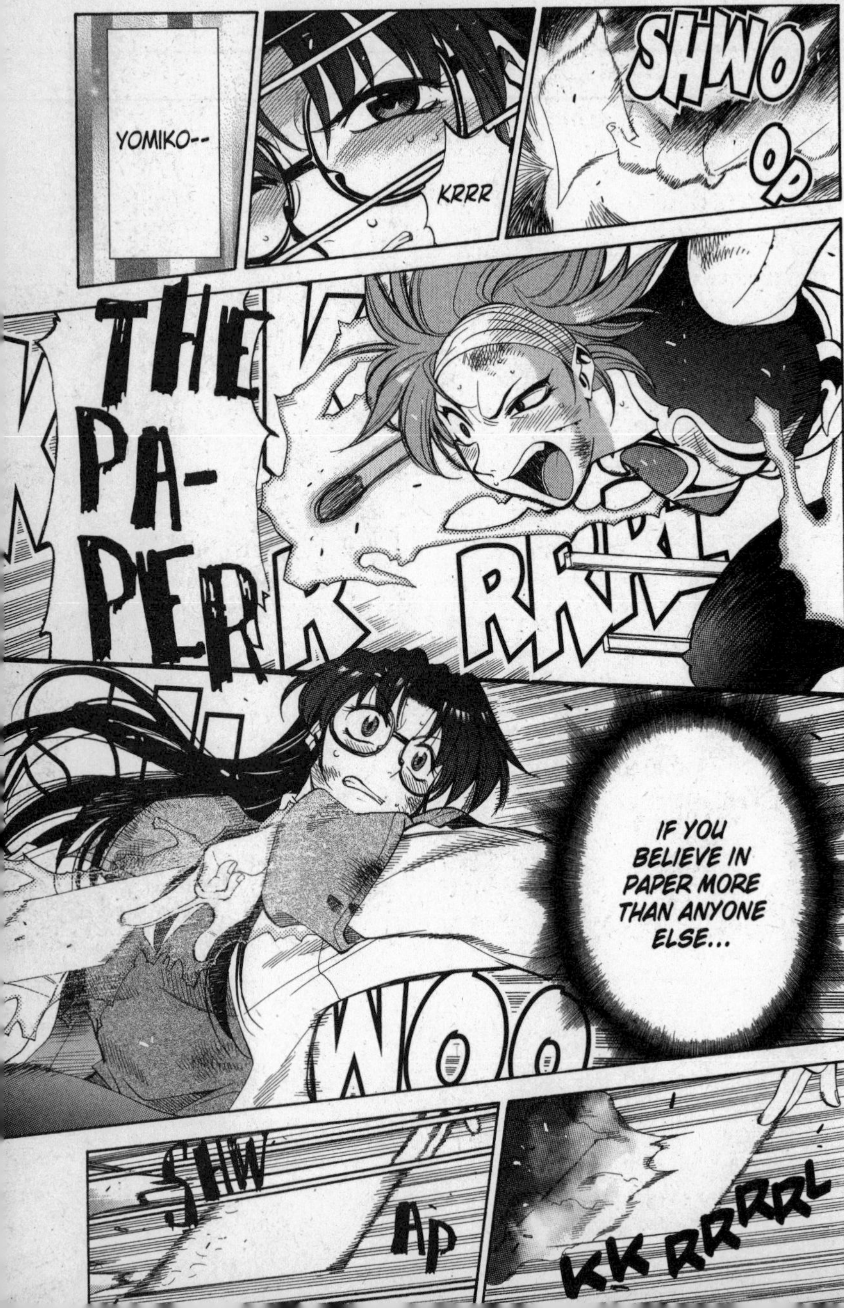
SHWO OP
KRRR
YOMIKO--
THE PA-PER
IF YOU BELIEVE IN PAPER MORE THAN ANYONE ELSE...
WOO
KK RRRRL
SHW AP

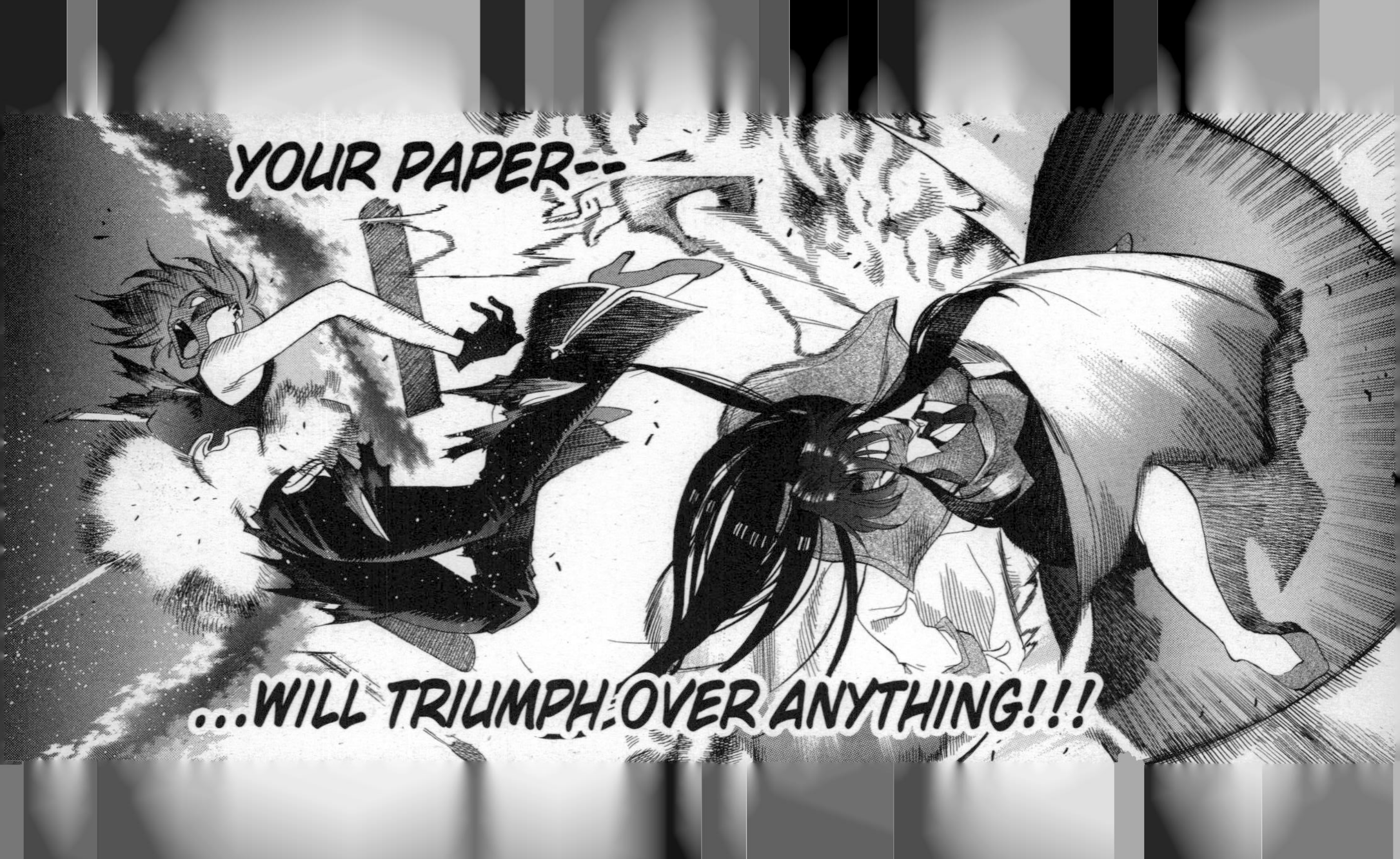
YOUR PAPER--
...WILL TRIUMPH OVER ANYTHING!!!

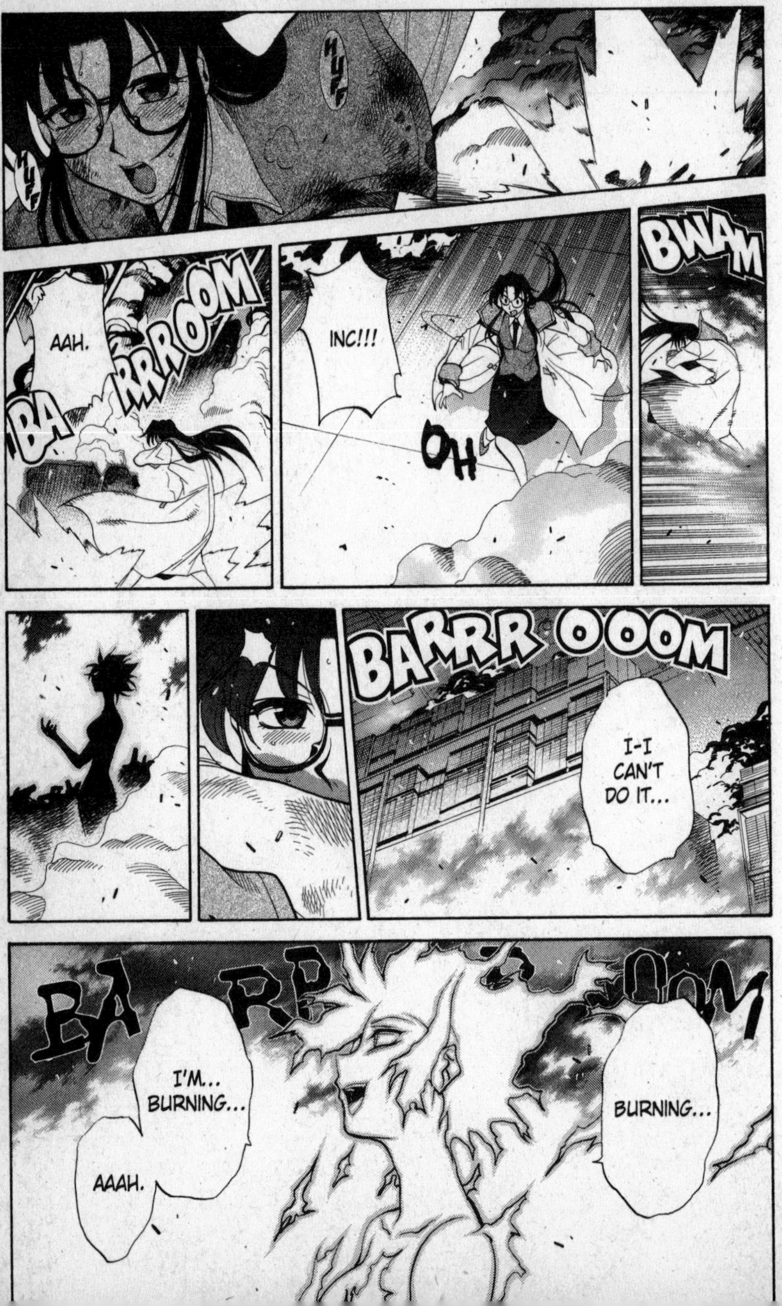
BWAM
INC!!!
OH
BA RRROOM
AAH.
BARRR OOOM
I-I CAN'T DO IT...
BURNING...
I'M... BURNING...
AAAH.

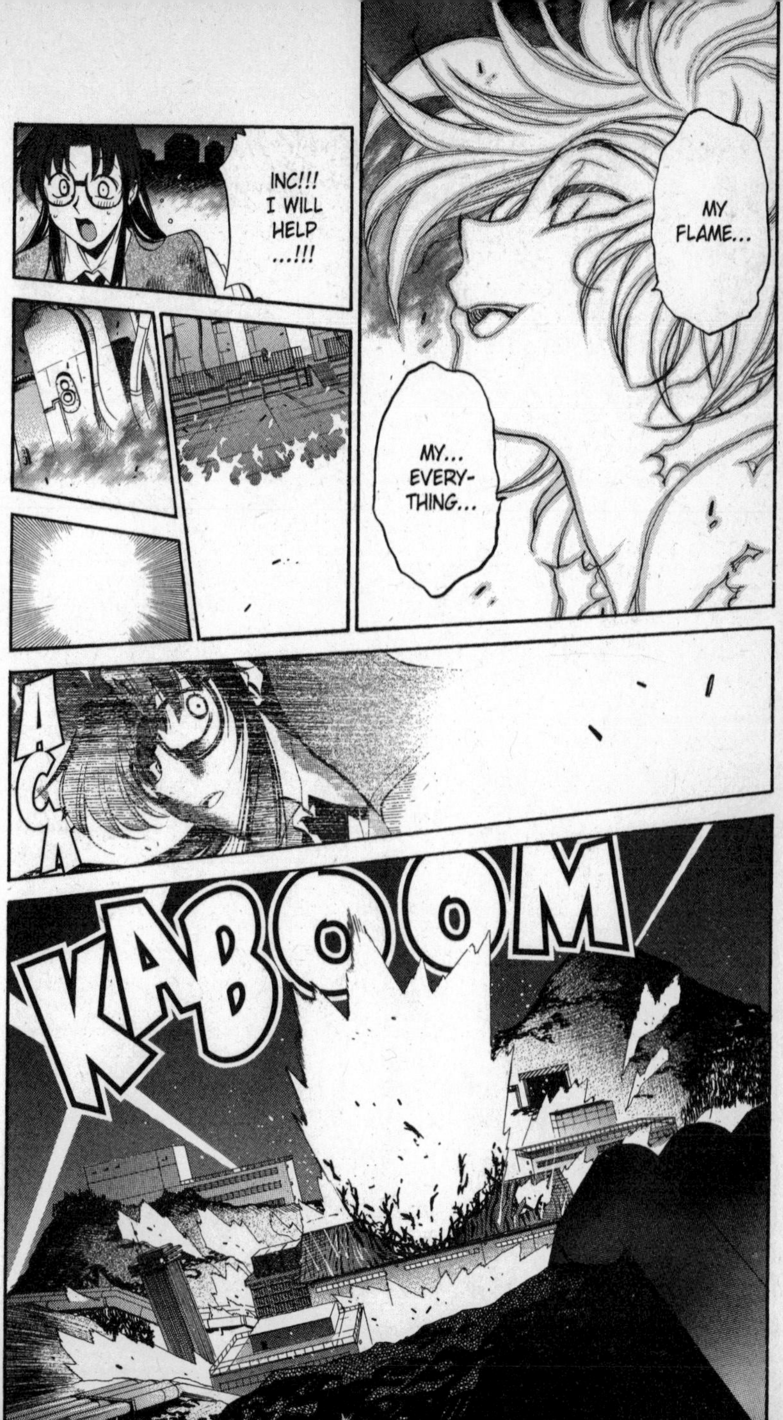
MY FLAME...
MY... EVERYTHING...
INC!!! I WILL HELP ...!!!
ACK
KABOOM

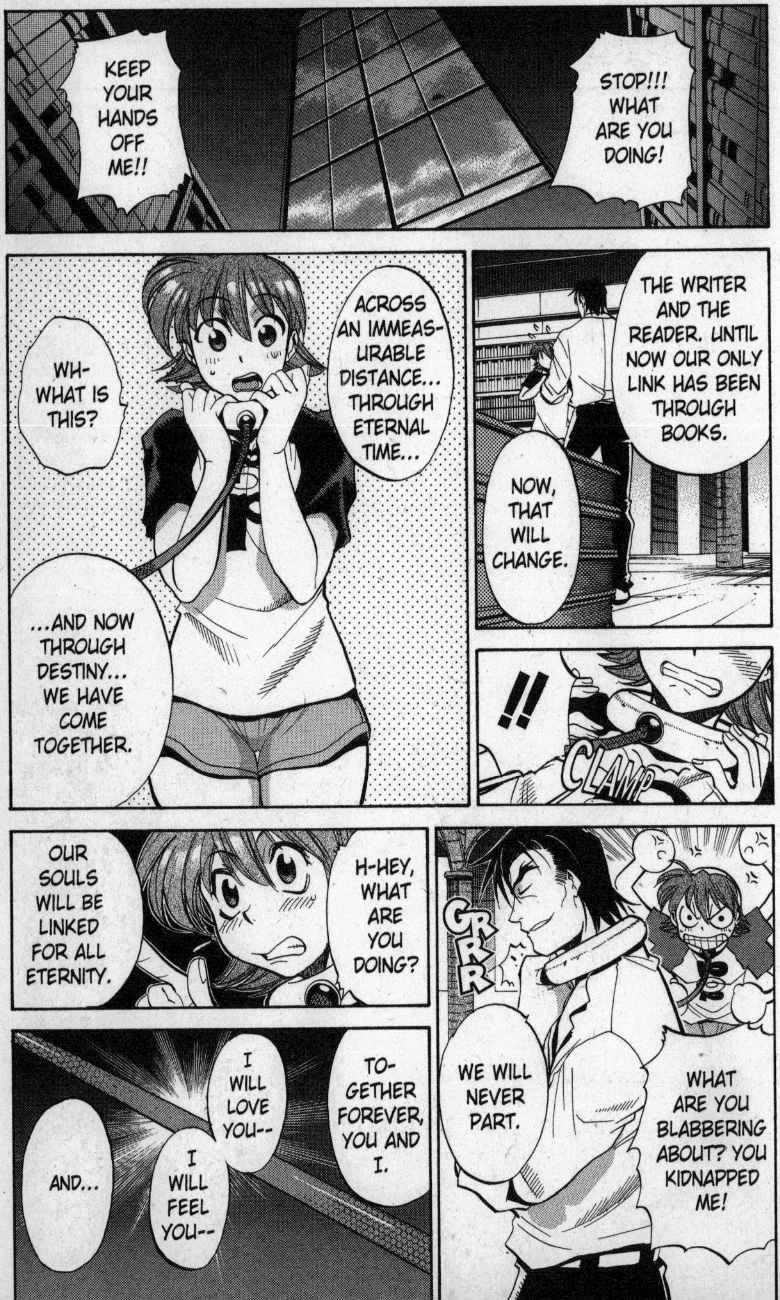
STOP!!! WHAT ARE YOU DOING!
KEEP YOUR HANDS OFF ME!!
THE WRITER AND THE READER. UNTIL NOW OUR ONLY LINK HAS BEEN THROUGH BOOKS.
NOW, THAT WILL CHANGE.
!!
CLAMP
ACROSS AN IMMEASURABLE DISTANCE... THROUGH ETERNAL TIME...
WH-WHAT IS THIS?
...AND NOW THROUGH DESTINY... WE HAVE COME TOGETHER.
GRRR
WE WILL NEVER PART.
WHAT ARE YOU BLABBERING ABOUT? YOU KIDNAPPED ME!
H-HEY, WHAT ARE YOU DOING?
OUR SOULS WILL BE LINKED FOR ALL ETERNITY.
TO-GETHER FOREVER, YOU AND I.
I WILL LOVE YOU--
I WILL FEEL YOU--
AND...

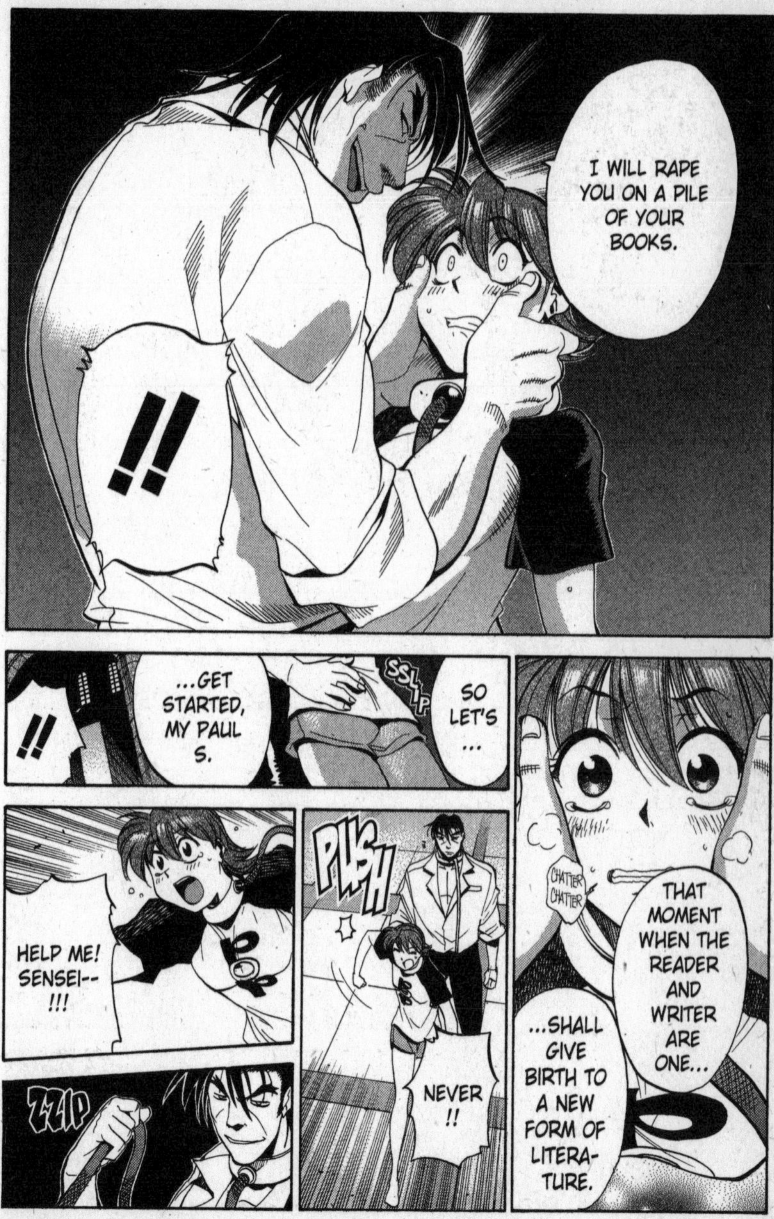
I WILL RAPE YOU ON A PILE OF YOUR BOOKS.
!!
CHATTER CHATTER
THAT MOMENT WHEN THE READER AND WRITER ARE ONE...
...SHALL GIVE BIRTH TO A NEW FORM OF LITERA-TURE.
SO LET'S ...
SSLIP
...GET STARTED, MY PAUL S.
!!
PUSH
NEVER !!
HELP ME! SENSEI-- !!!
ZZIP

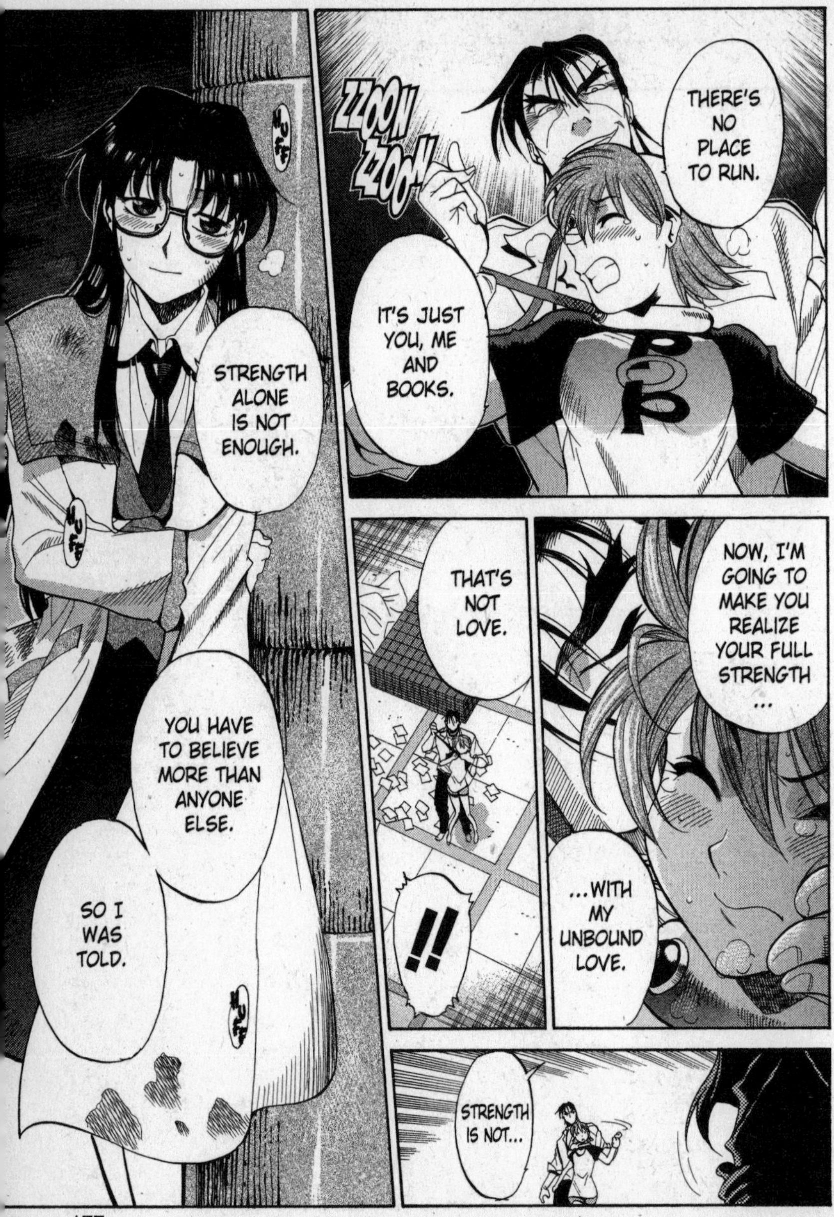
THERE'S NO PLACE TO RUN.
ZZOON ZZOON
IT'S JUST YOU, ME AND BOOKS.
NOW, I'M GOING TO MAKE YOU REALIZE YOUR FULL STRENGTH ...
...WITH MY UNBOUND LOVE.
THAT'S NOT LOVE.
!!
STRENGTH IS NOT...
HUFF
STRENGTH ALONE IS NOT ENOUGH.
HUFF
YOU HAVE TO BELIEVE MORE THAN ANYONE ELSE.
SO I WAS TOLD.
HUFF

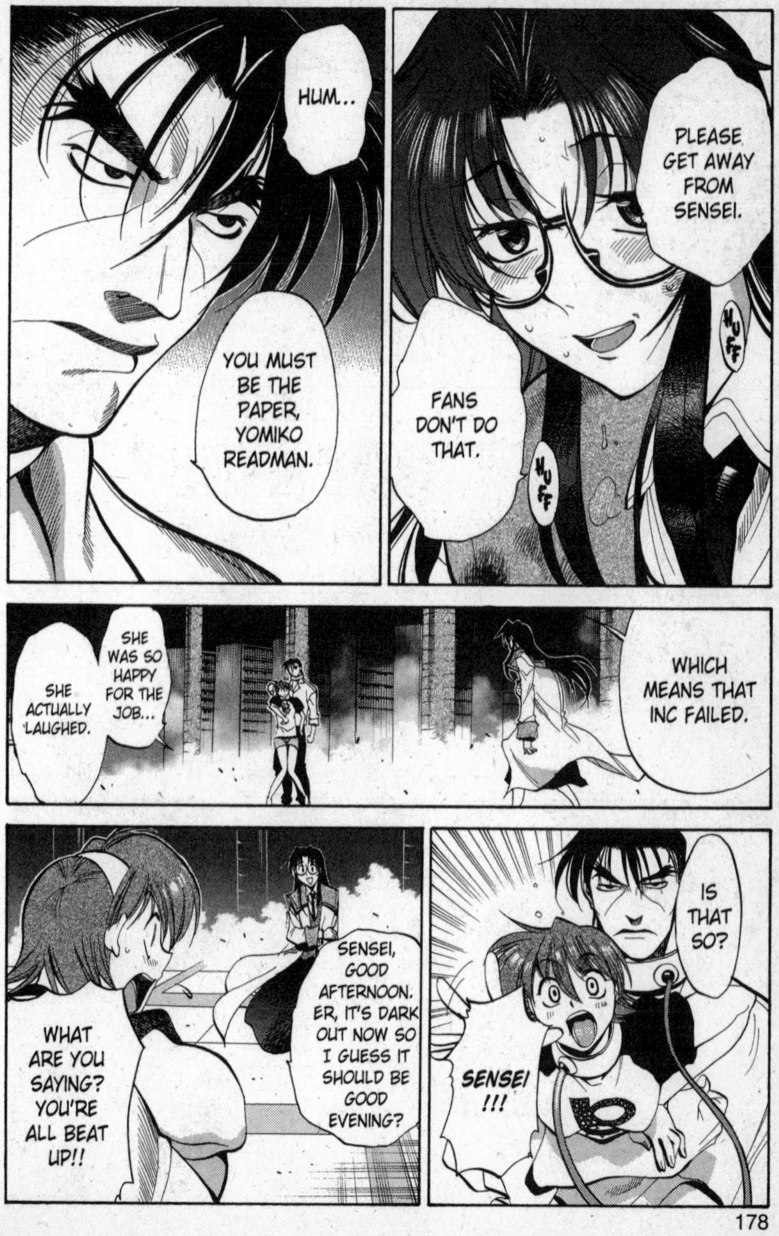
PLEASE GET AWAY FROM SENSEI.
HUFF
FANS DON'T DO THAT.
HUFF
HUM...
YOU MUST BE THE PAPER, YOMIKO READMAN.
WHICH MEANS THAT INC FAILED.
SHE WAS SO HAPPY FOR THE JOB...
SHE ACTUALLY LAUGHED.
IS THAT SO?
SENSEI!!!
SENSEI, GOOD AFTERNOON. ER, IT'S DARK OUT NOW SO I GUESS IT SHOULD BE GOOD EVENING?
WHAT ARE YOU SAYING? YOU'RE ALL BEAT UP!!

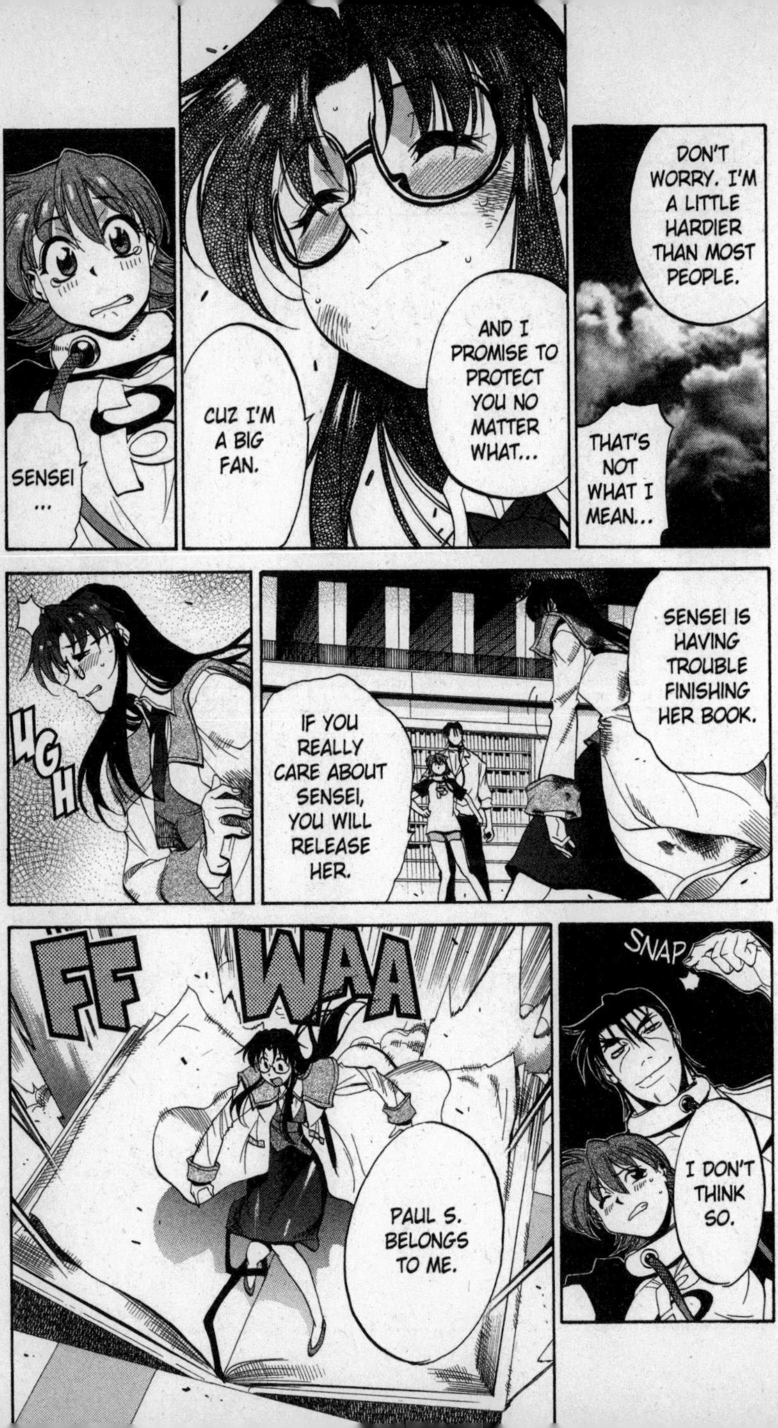
DON'T WORRY. I'M A LITTLE HARDIER THAN MOST PEOPLE.
THAT'S NOT WHAT I MEAN...
AND I PROMISE TO PROTECT YOU NO MATTER WHAT...
CUZ I'M A BIG FAN.
SENSEI ...
SENSEI IS HAVING TROUBLE FINISHING HER BOOK.
IF YOU REALLY CARE ABOUT SENSEI, YOU WILL RELEASE HER.
UGH
SNAP
I DON'T THINK SO.
WAA
FF
PAUL S. BELONGS TO ME.

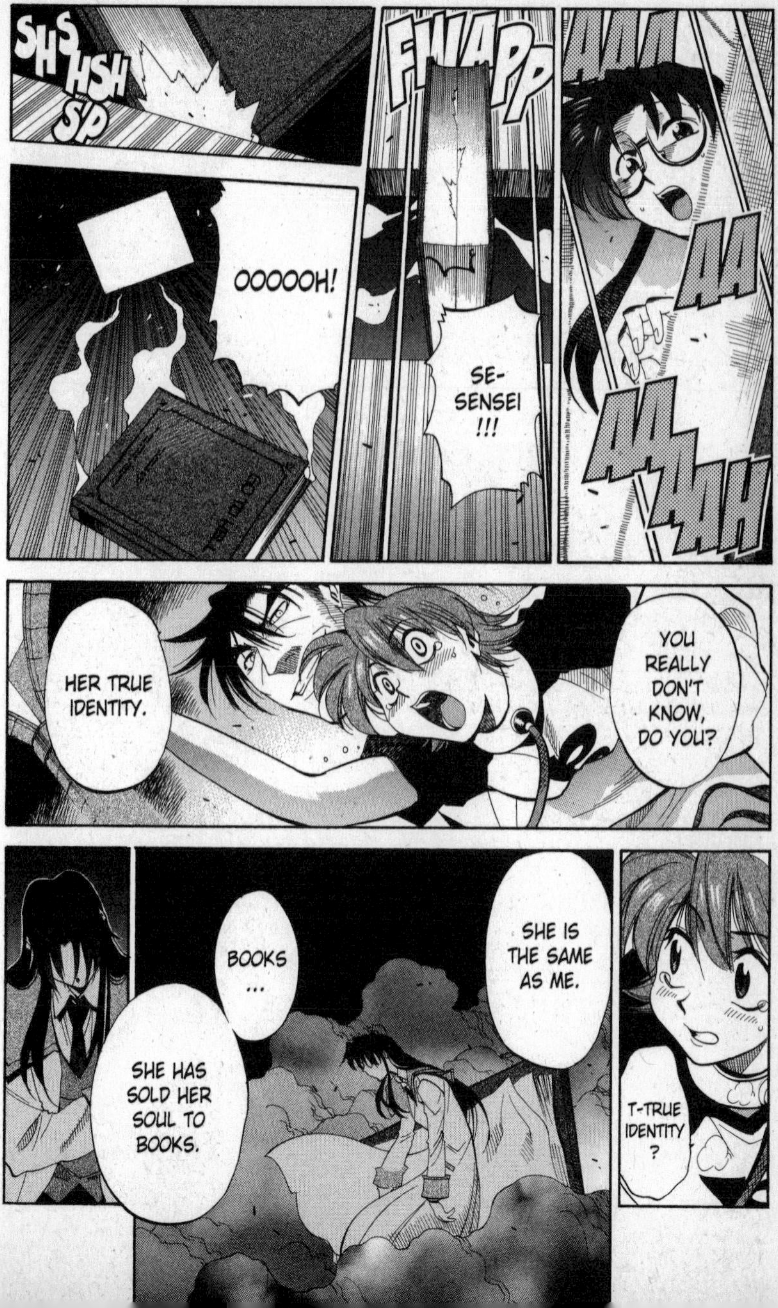
AAAA
AA
AAAAH
FWAPP
SE-SENSEI!!!
SHSHSH SP
OOOOOH!
YOU REALLY DON'T KNOW, DO YOU?
HER TRUE IDENTITY.
T-TRUE IDENTITY?
SHE IS THE SAME AS ME.
BOOKS...
SHE HAS SOLD HER SOUL TO BOOKS.

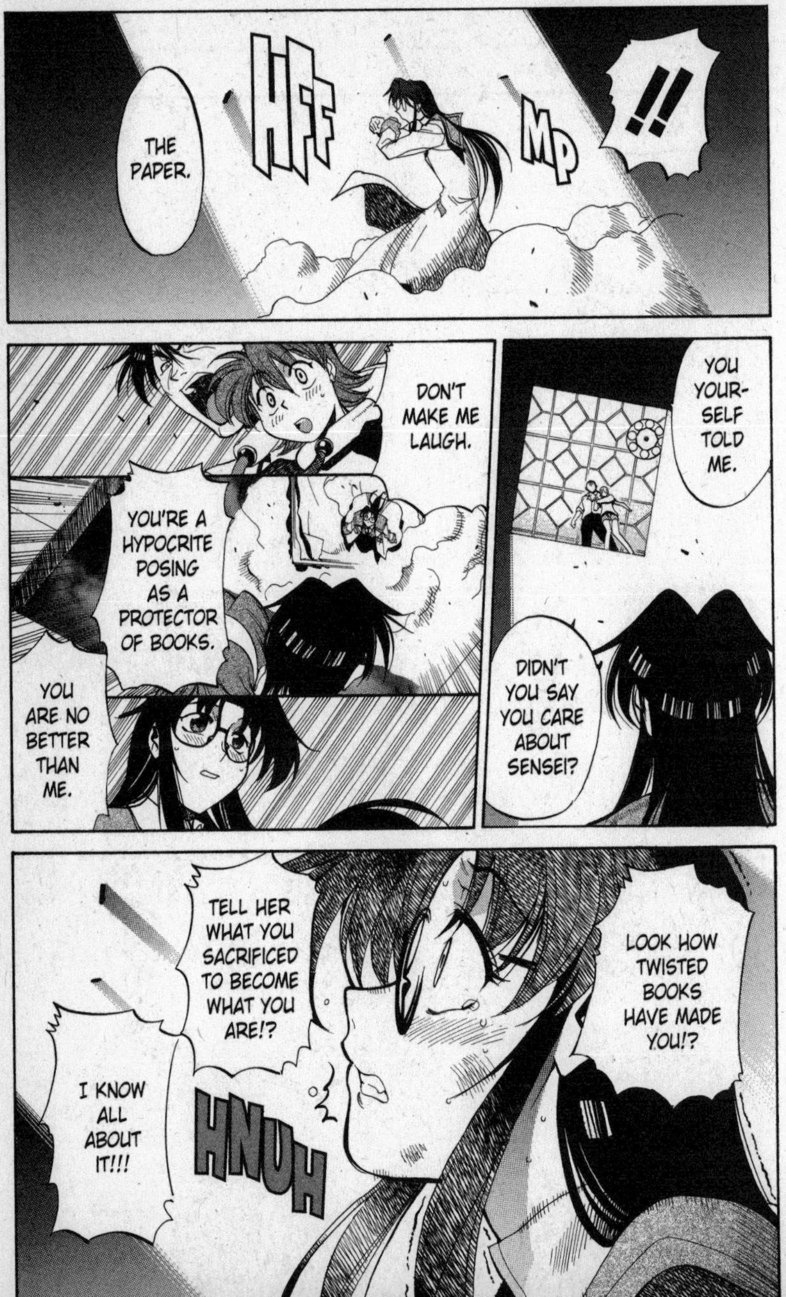
!!
MP
HFF
THE PAPER.
YOU YOURSELF TOLD ME.
DIDN'T YOU SAY YOU CARE ABOUT SENSEI?
DON'T MAKE ME LAUGH.
YOU'RE A HYPOCRITE POSING AS A PROTECTOR OF BOOKS.
YOU ARE NO BETTER THAN ME.
LOOK HOW TWISTED BOOKS HAVE MADE YOU!?
TELL HER WHAT YOU SACRIFICED TO BECOME WHAT YOU ARE!?
HNUH
I KNOW ALL ABOUT IT!!!

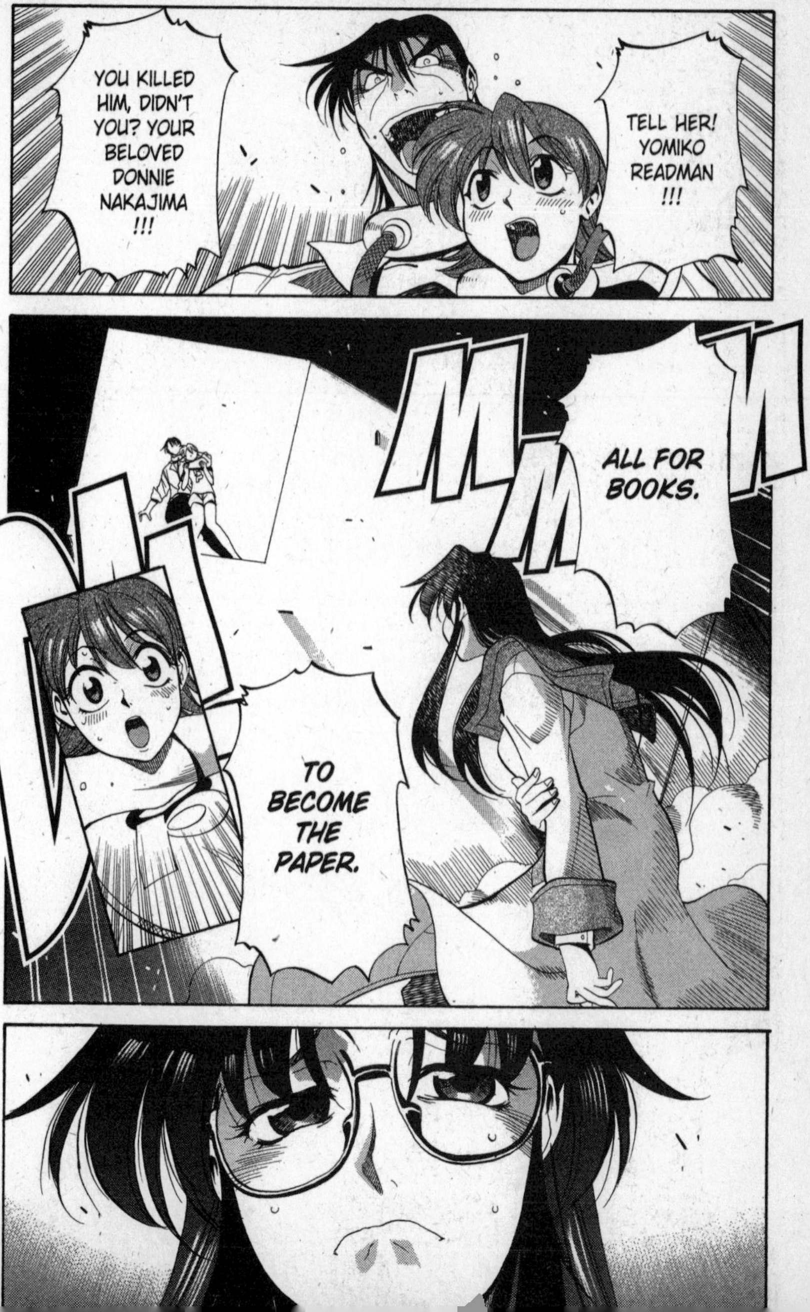
TELL HER! YOMIKO READMAN !!!
YOU KILLED HIM, DIDN'T YOU? YOUR BELOVED DONNIE NAKAJIMA !!!
ALL FOR BOOKS.
TO BECOME THE PAPER.

EPISODE EIGHT

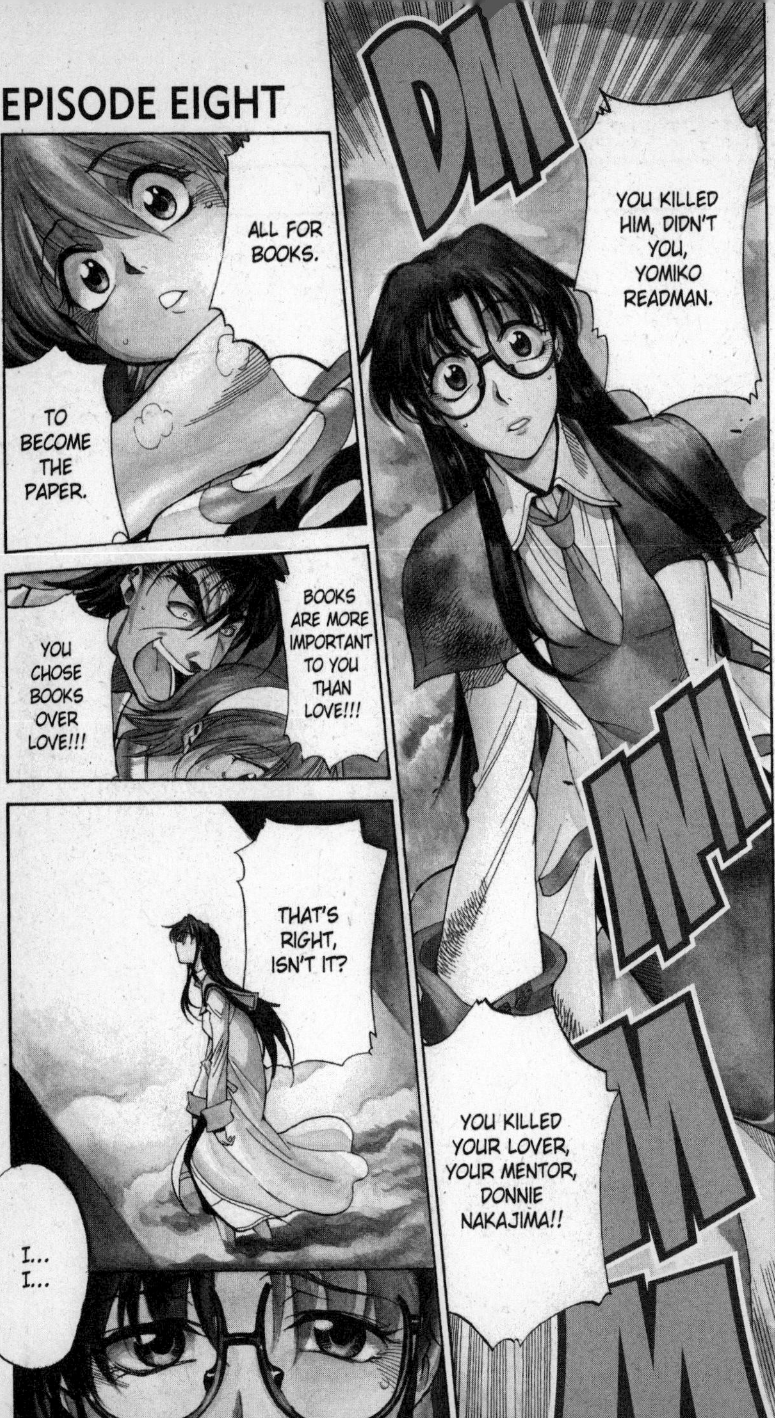
DM
YOU KILLED HIM, DIDN'T YOU, YOMIKO READMAN.
MM
MM
YOU KILLED YOUR LOVER, YOUR MENTOR, DONNIE NAKAJIMA!!
ALL FOR BOOKS.
TO BECOME THE PAPER.
BOOKS ARE MORE IMPORTANT TO YOU THAN LOVE!!!
YOU CHOSE BOOKS OVER LOVE!!!
THAT'S RIGHT, ISN'T IT?
I... I...

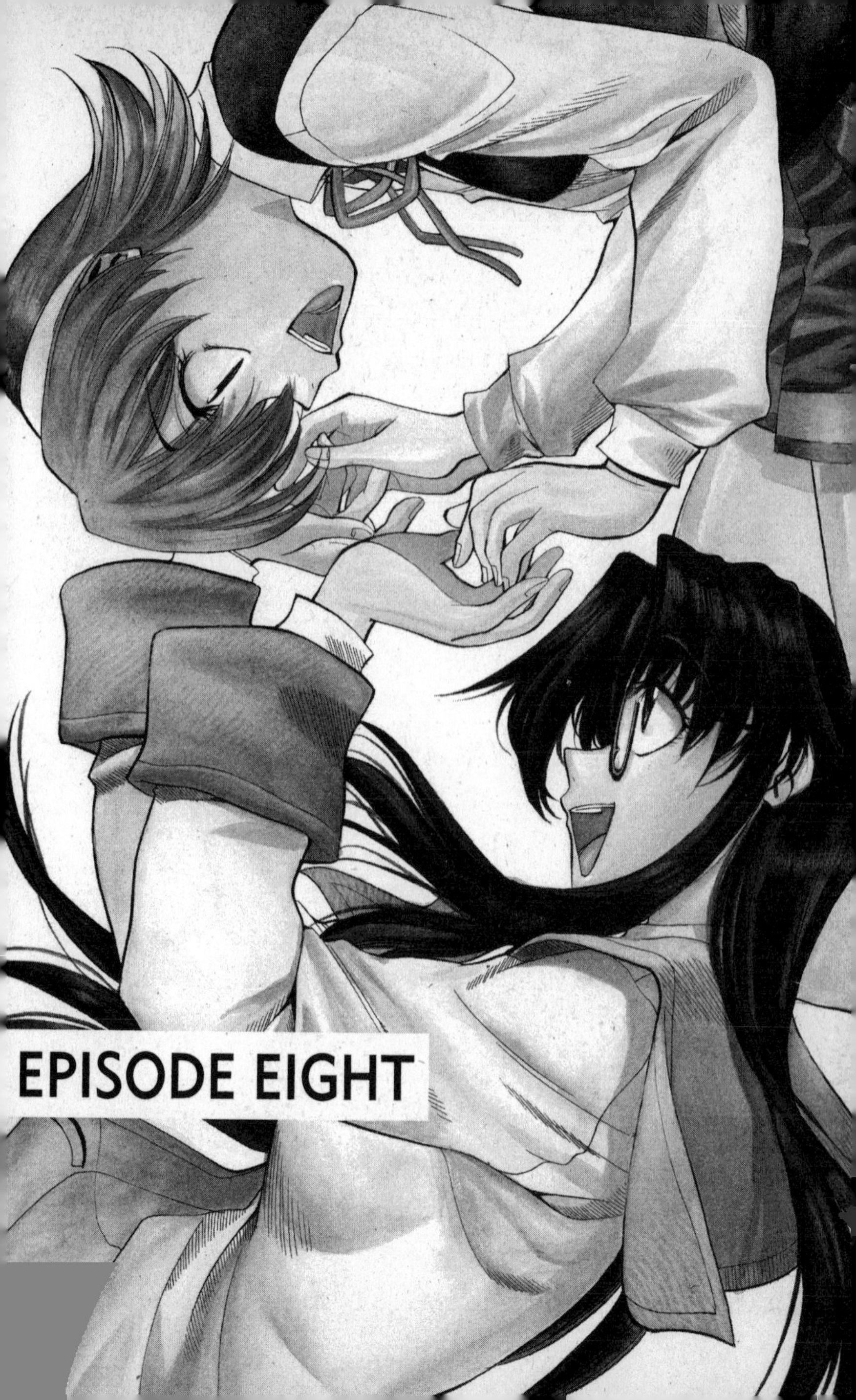
EPISODE EIGHT

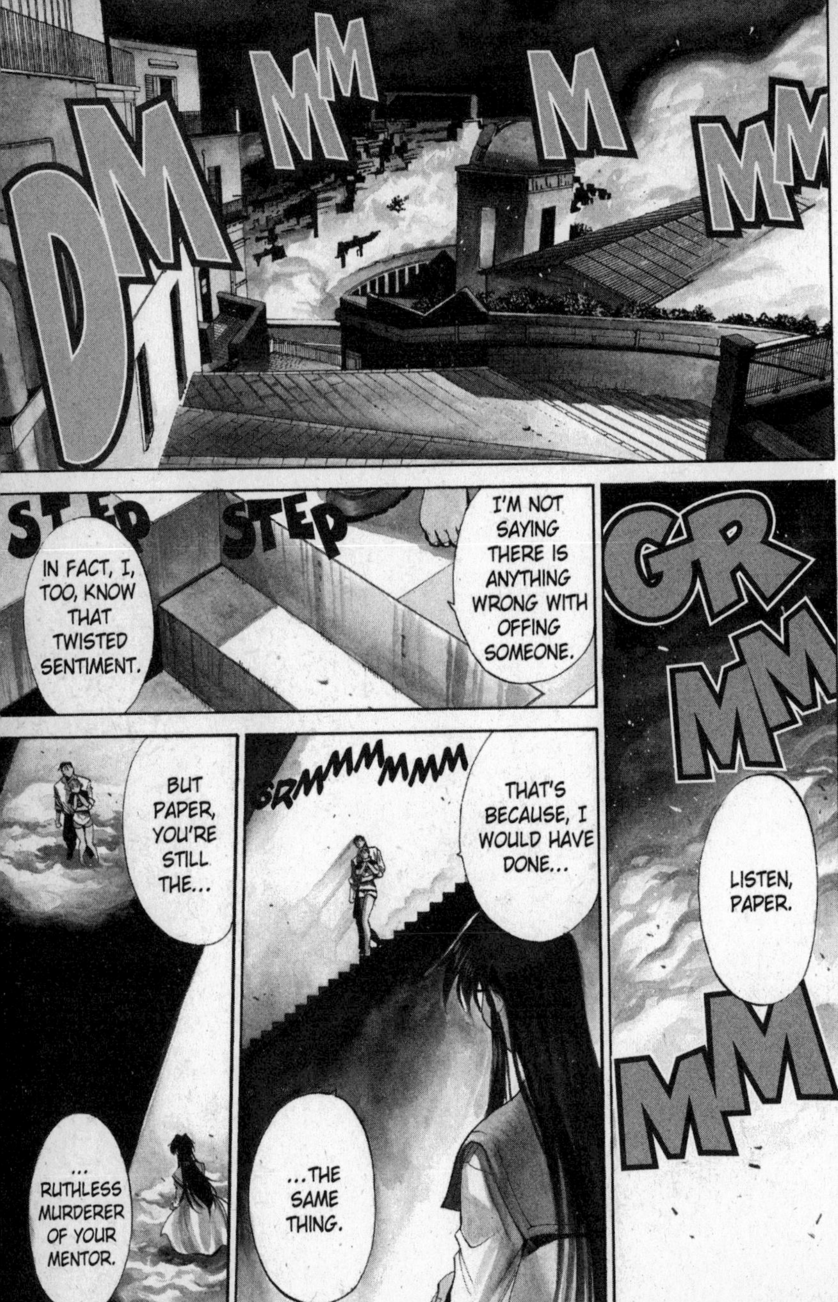
DMMMMMMM
GRMMMM
LISTEN, PAPER.
I'M NOT SAYING THERE IS ANYTHING WRONG WITH OFFING SOMEONE.
STEP
STEP
IN FACT, I, TOO, KNOW THAT TWISTED SENTIMENT.
SRMMMMMMM
THAT'S BECAUSE, I WOULD HAVE DONE...
...THE SAME THING.
BUT PAPER, YOU'RE STILL THE...
... RUTHLESS MURDERER OF YOUR MENTOR.

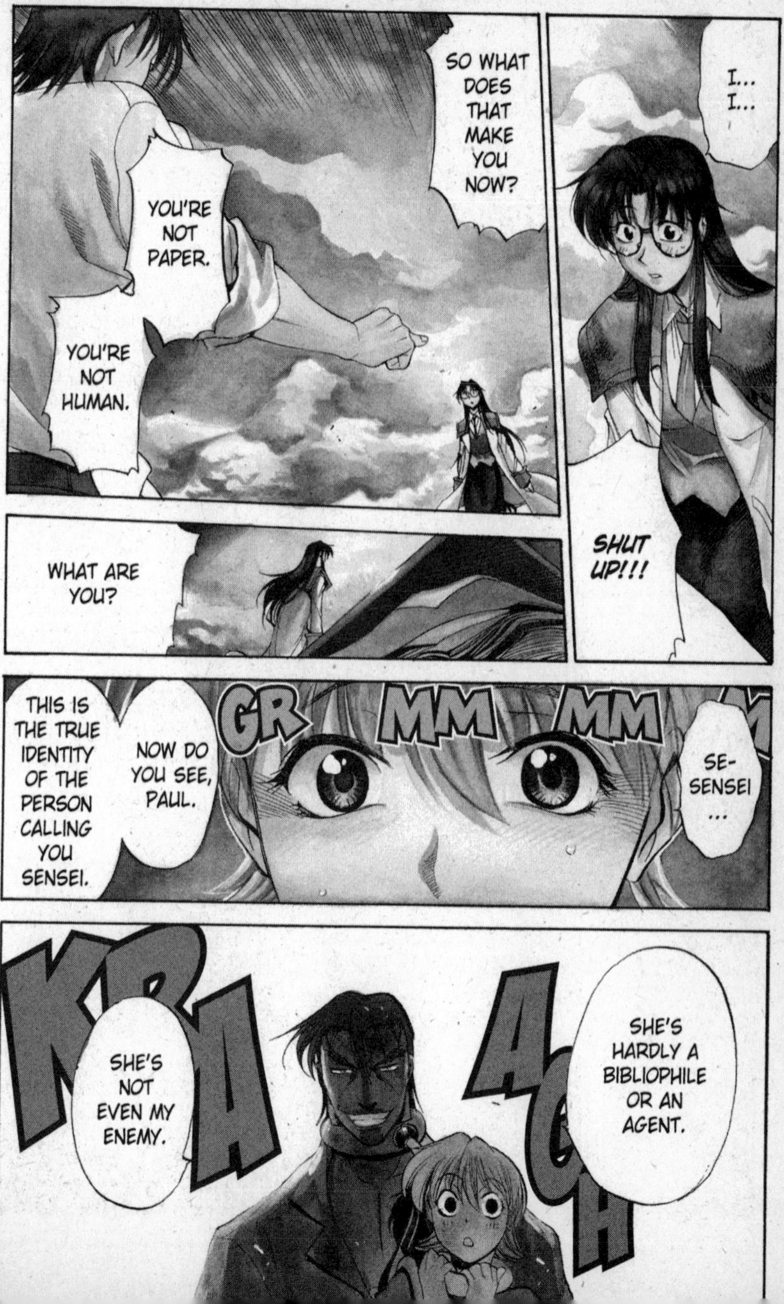
I...
I...
SHUT UP!!!
SO WHAT DOES THAT MAKE YOU NOW?
YOU'RE NOT PAPER.
YOU'RE NOT HUMAN.
WHAT ARE YOU?
SE-SENSEI...
GR MM MM
NOW DO YOU SEE, PAUL.
THIS IS THE TRUE IDENTITY OF THE PERSON CALLING YOU SENSEI.
SHE'S HARDLY A BIBLIOPHILE OR AN AGENT.
AGH
KRA
SHE'S NOT EVEN MY ENEMY.

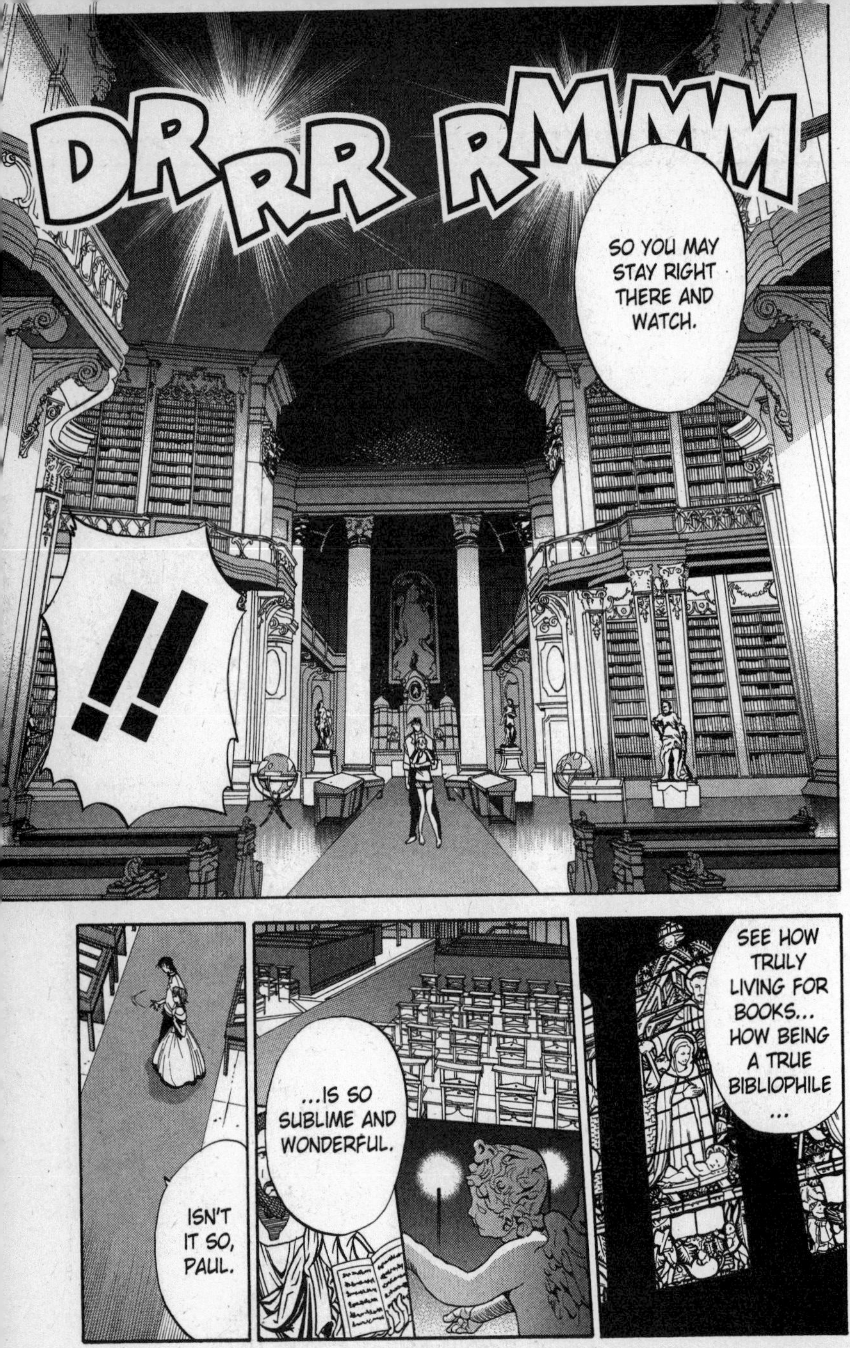
DRRR RMMM
SO YOU MAY STAY RIGHT THERE AND WATCH.
!!
SEE HOW TRULY LIVING FOR BOOKS... HOW BEING A TRUE BIBLIOPHILE ...
...IS SO SUBLIME AND WONDERFUL.
ISN'T IT SO, PAUL.

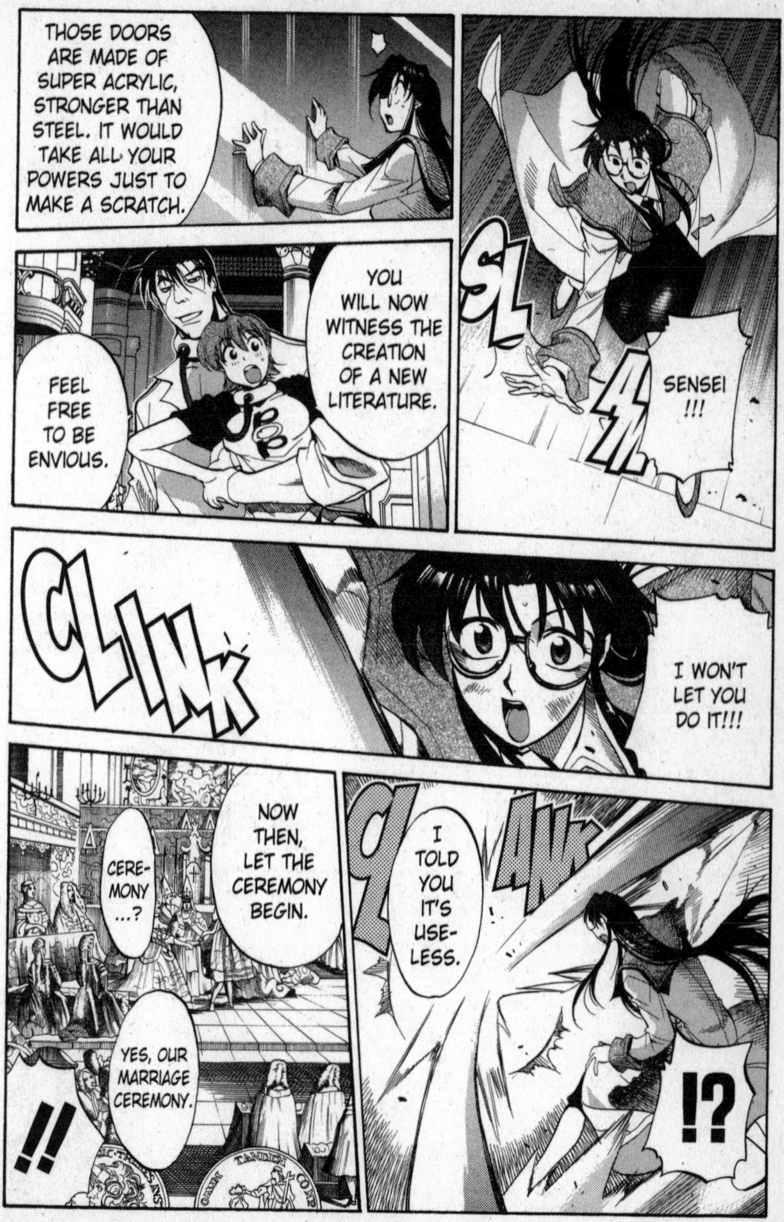
SL
A
SENSEI !!!
THOSE DOORS ARE MADE OF SUPER ACRYLIC, STRONGER THAN STEEL. IT WOULD TAKE ALL YOUR POWERS JUST TO MAKE A SCRATCH.
YOU WILL NOW WITNESS THE CREATION OF A NEW LITERATURE.
FEEL FREE TO BE ENVIOUS.
I WON'T LET YOU DO IT!!!
CLINK
CL
ANK
I TOLD YOU IT'S USE-LESS.
!?
NOW THEN, LET THE CEREMONY BEGIN.
CERE-MONY ...?
YES, OUR MARRIAGE CEREMONY.
!!

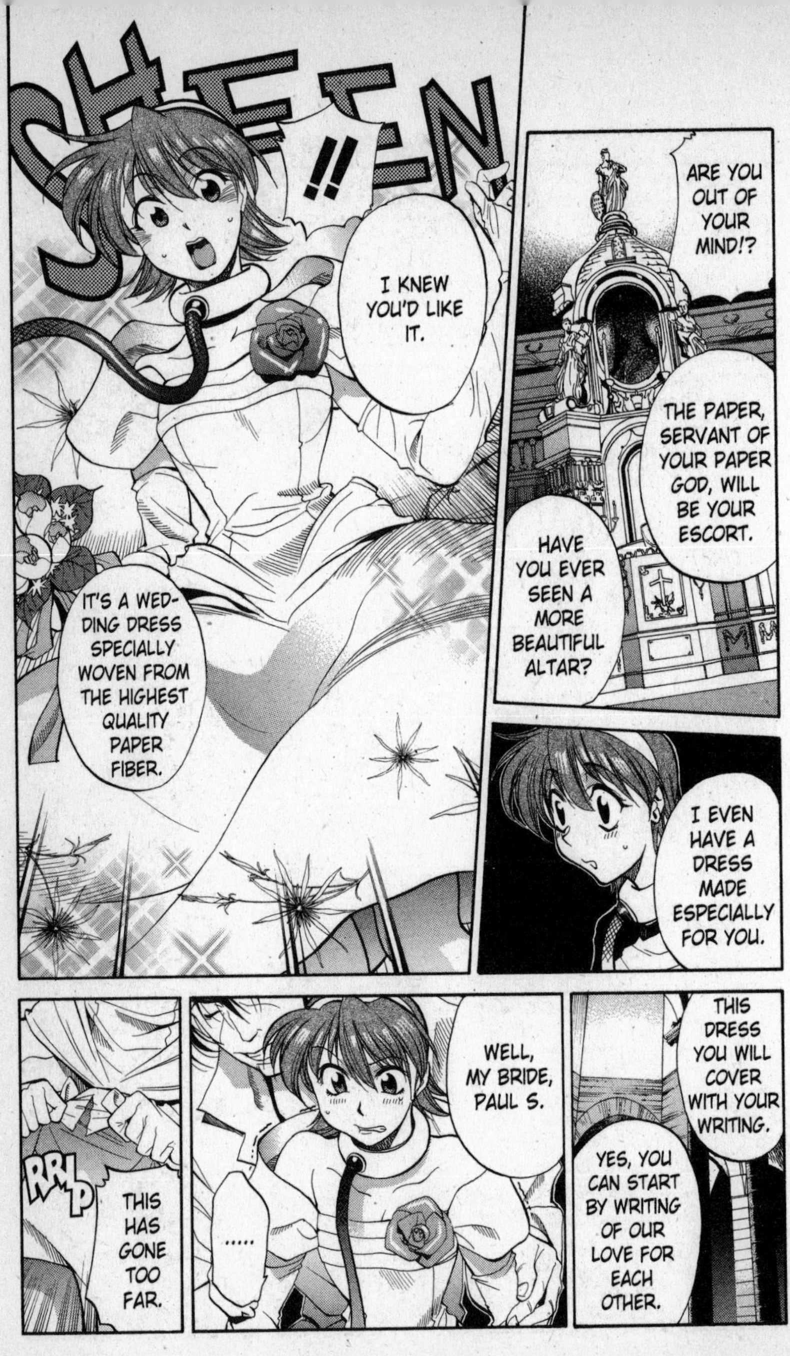
ARE YOU OUT OF YOUR MIND!?
THE PAPER, SERVANT OF YOUR PAPER GOD, WILL BE YOUR ESCORT.
HAVE YOU EVER SEEN A MORE BEAUTIFUL ALTAR?
I EVEN HAVE A DRESS MADE ESPECIALLY FOR YOU.
SHEEEN!!
I KNEW YOU'D LIKE IT.
IT'S A WEDDING DRESS SPECIALLY WOVEN FROM THE HIGHEST QUALITY PAPER FIBER.
THIS DRESS YOU WILL COVER WITH YOUR WRITING.
YES, YOU CAN START BY WRITING OF OUR LOVE FOR EACH OTHER.
WELL, MY BRIDE, PAUL S.
.....
RRIP
THIS HAS GONE TOO FAR.

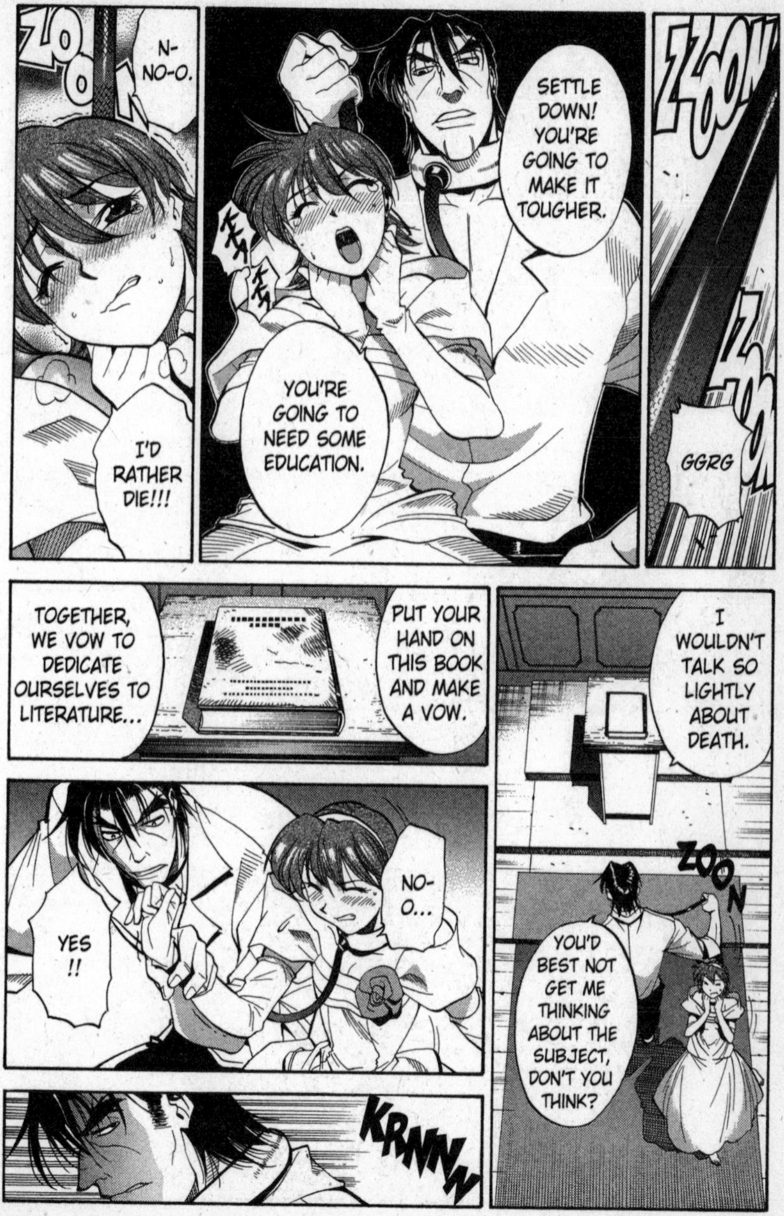
ZZOON
GGRG
ZOOOM
SETTLE DOWN! YOU'RE GOING TO MAKE IT TOUGHER.
YOU'RE GOING TO NEED SOME EDUCATION.
ZOOO
N- NO-O.
I'D RATHER DIE!!!
I WOULDN'T TALK SO LIGHTLY ABOUT DEATH.
PUT YOUR HAND ON THIS BOOK AND MAKE A VOW.
TOGETHER, WE VOW TO DEDICATE OURSELVES TO LITERATURE...
YES !!
NO- O...
ZOON
YOU'D BEST NOT GET ME THINKING ABOUT THE SUBJECT, DON'T YOU THINK?
KRNNN

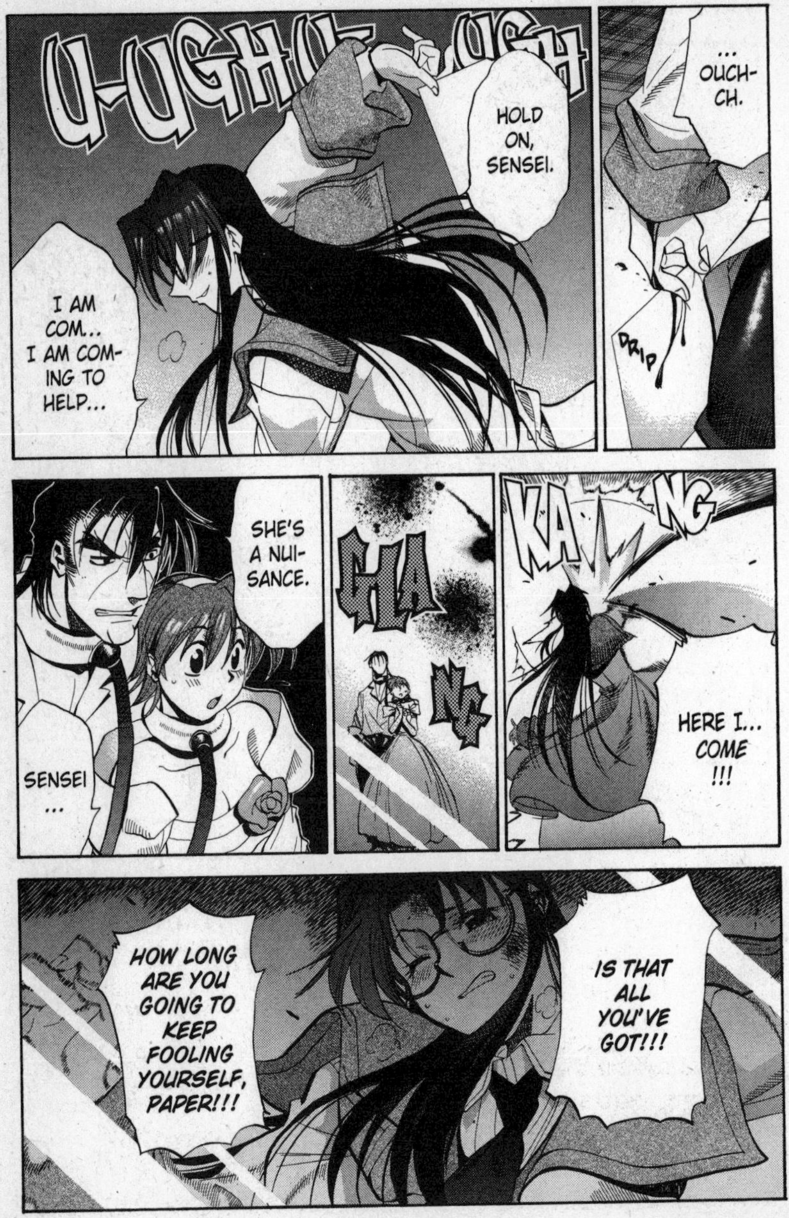
... OUCH-CH.
DRIP
U-UGH! ...UGH
HOLD ON, SENSEI.
I AM COM... I AM COMING TO HELP...
KA NG
HERE I... COME!!!
CHA
NG
SHE'S A NUISANCE.
SENSEI ...
IS THAT ALL YOU'VE GOT!!!
HOW LONG ARE YOU GOING TO KEEP FOOLING YOURSELF, PAPER!!!

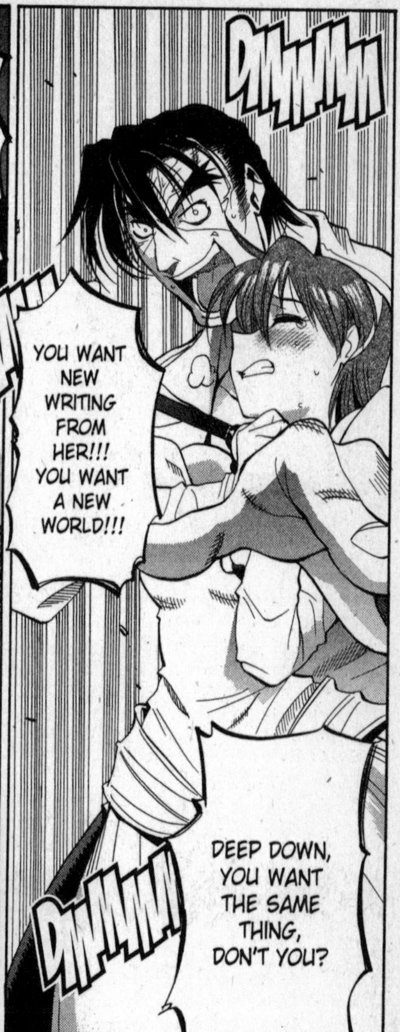
DMMMMM
YOU WANT NEW WRITING FROM HER!!! YOU WANT A NEW WORLD!!!
DMMMMM
DEEP DOWN, YOU WANT THE SAME THING, DON'T YOU?
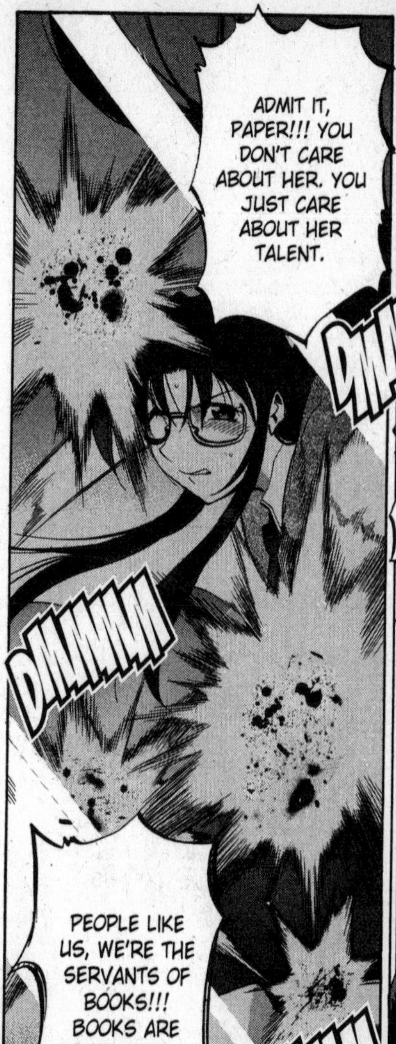
ADMIT IT, PAPER!!! YOU DON'T CARE ABOUT HER. YOU JUST CARE ABOUT HER TALENT.
DMMMMM
PEOPLE LIKE US, WE'RE THE SERVANTS OF BOOKS!!! BOOKS ARE EVERYTHING TO US!!!
DMMMMM

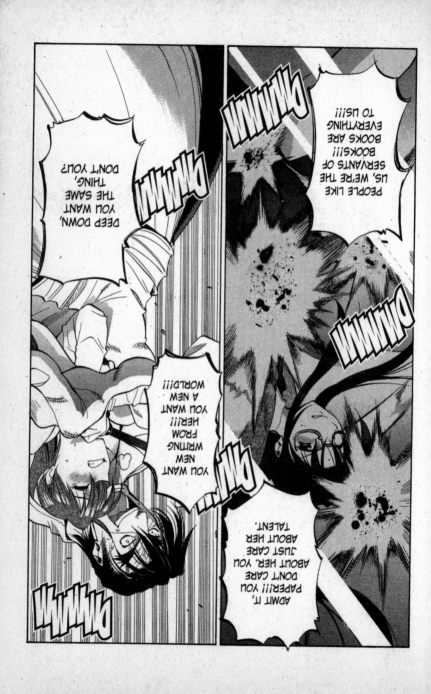

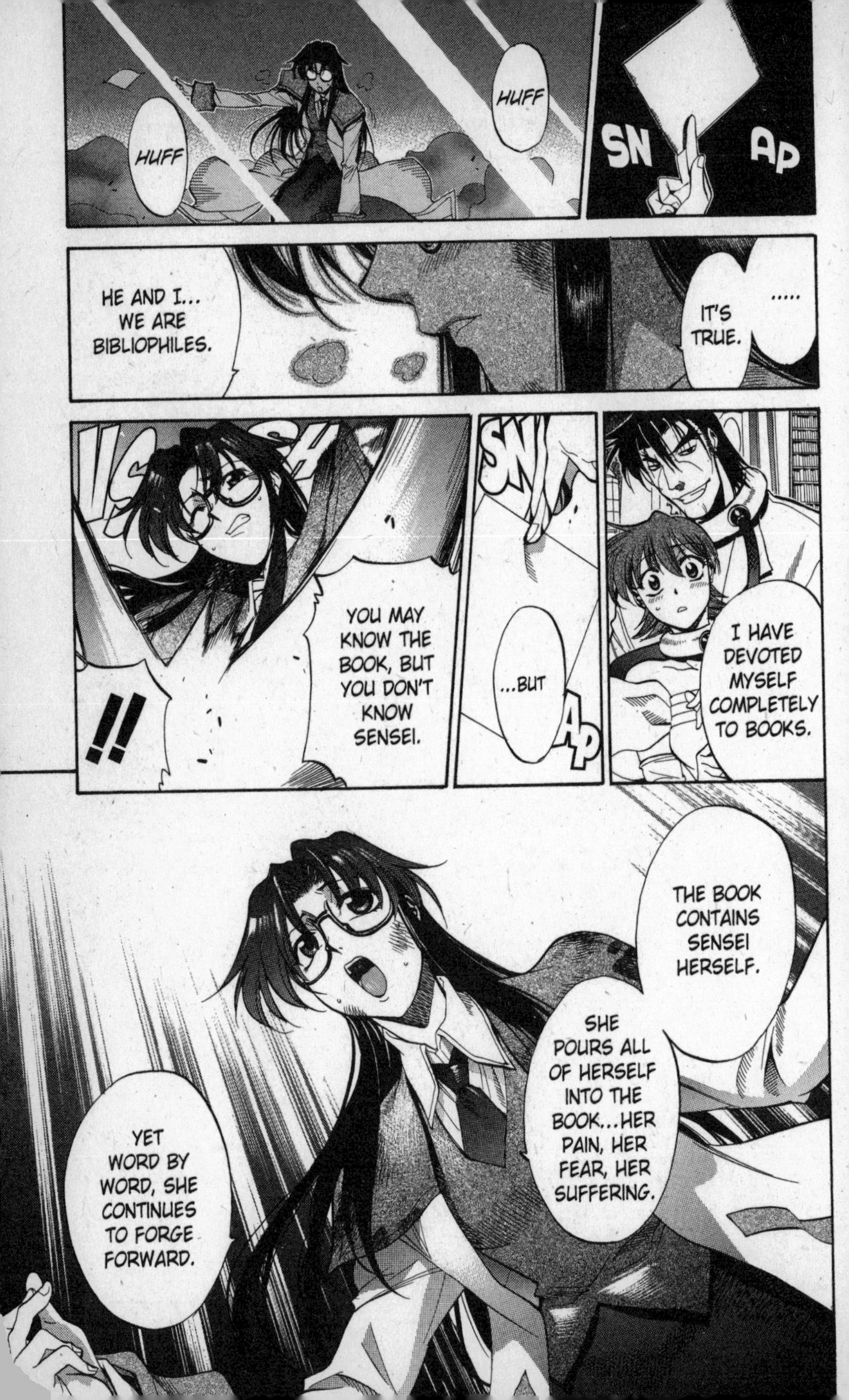
SN
AP
HUFF
HUFF
.....
IT'S TRUE.
HE AND I... WE ARE BIBLIOPHILES.
I HAVE DEVOTED MYSELF COMPLETELY TO BOOKS.
SN
AP
...BUT
YOU MAY KNOW THE BOOK, BUT YOU DON'T KNOW SENSEI.
!!
THE BOOK CONTAINS SENSEI HERSELF.
SHE POURS ALL OF HERSELF INTO THE BOOK...HER PAIN, HER FEAR, HER SUFFERING.
YET WORD BY WORD, SHE CONTINUES TO FORGE FORWARD.

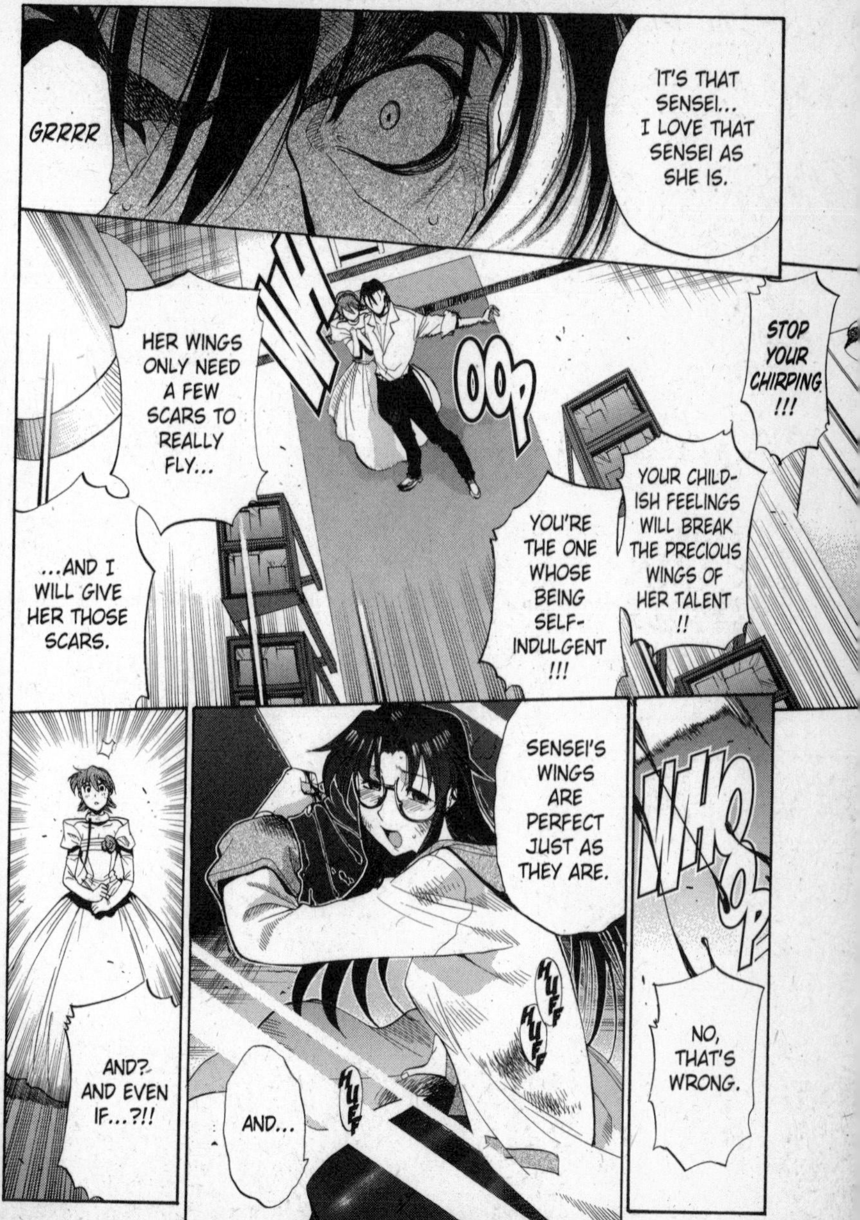
IT'S THAT SENSEI... I LOVE THAT SENSEI AS SHE IS.
GRRRR
STOP YOUR CHIRPING !!!
YOUR CHILDISH FEELINGS WILL BREAK THE PRECIOUS WINGS OF HER TALENT !!
YOU'RE THE ONE WHOSE BEING SELF-INDULGENT !!!
WHOOP
HER WINGS ONLY NEED A FEW SCARS TO REALLY FLY...
...AND I WILL GIVE HER THOSE SCARS.
WHOOP
NO, THAT'S WRONG.
SENSEI'S WINGS ARE PERFECT JUST AS THEY ARE.
HUFF
HUFF
HUFF
AND...
AND? AND EVEN IF...?!!

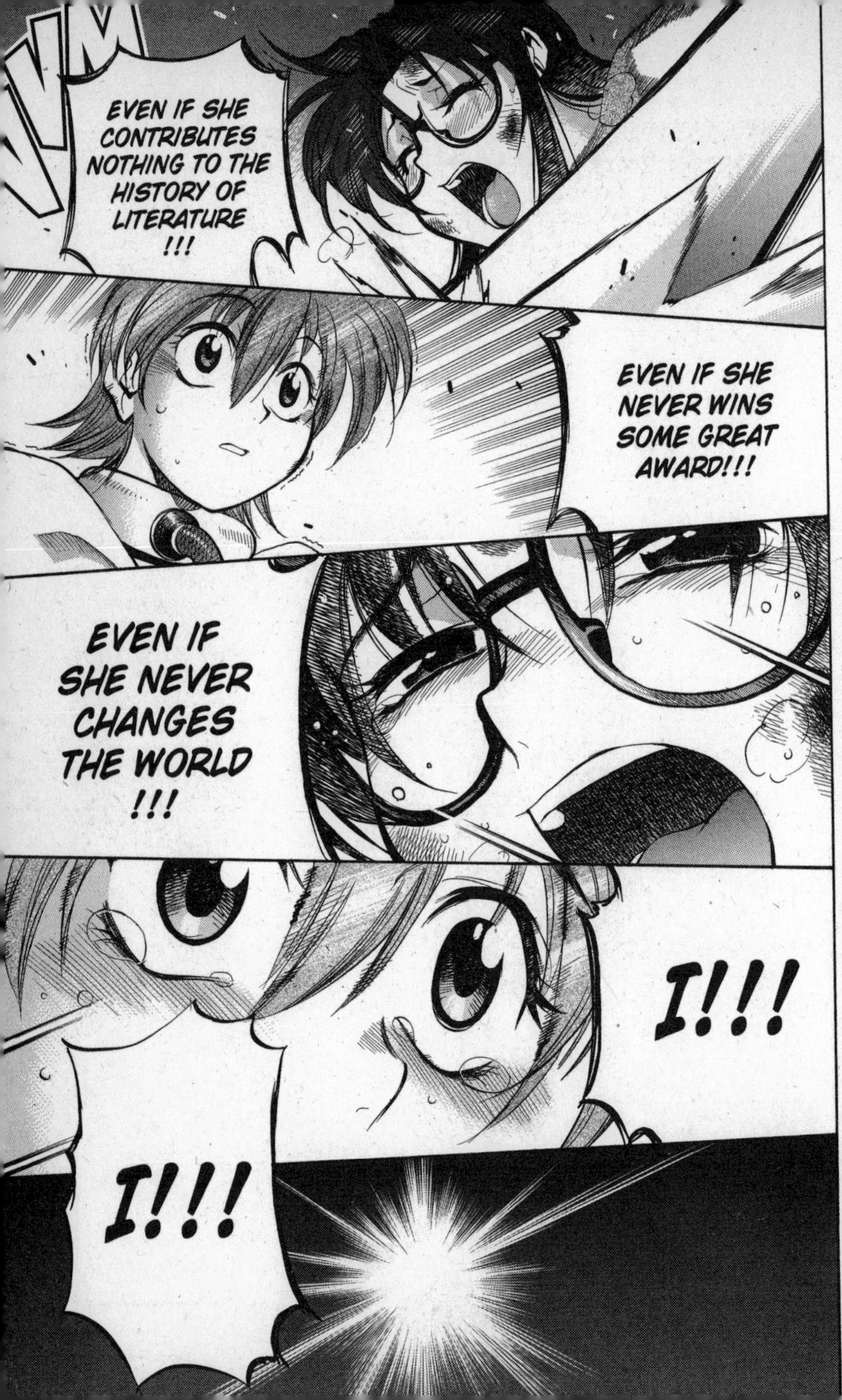
EVEN IF SHE CONTRIBUTES NOTHING TO THE HISTORY OF LITERATURE !!!
EVEN IF SHE NEVER WINS SOME GREAT AWARD!!!
EVEN IF SHE NEVER CHANGES THE WORLD !!!
I!!!
I!!!

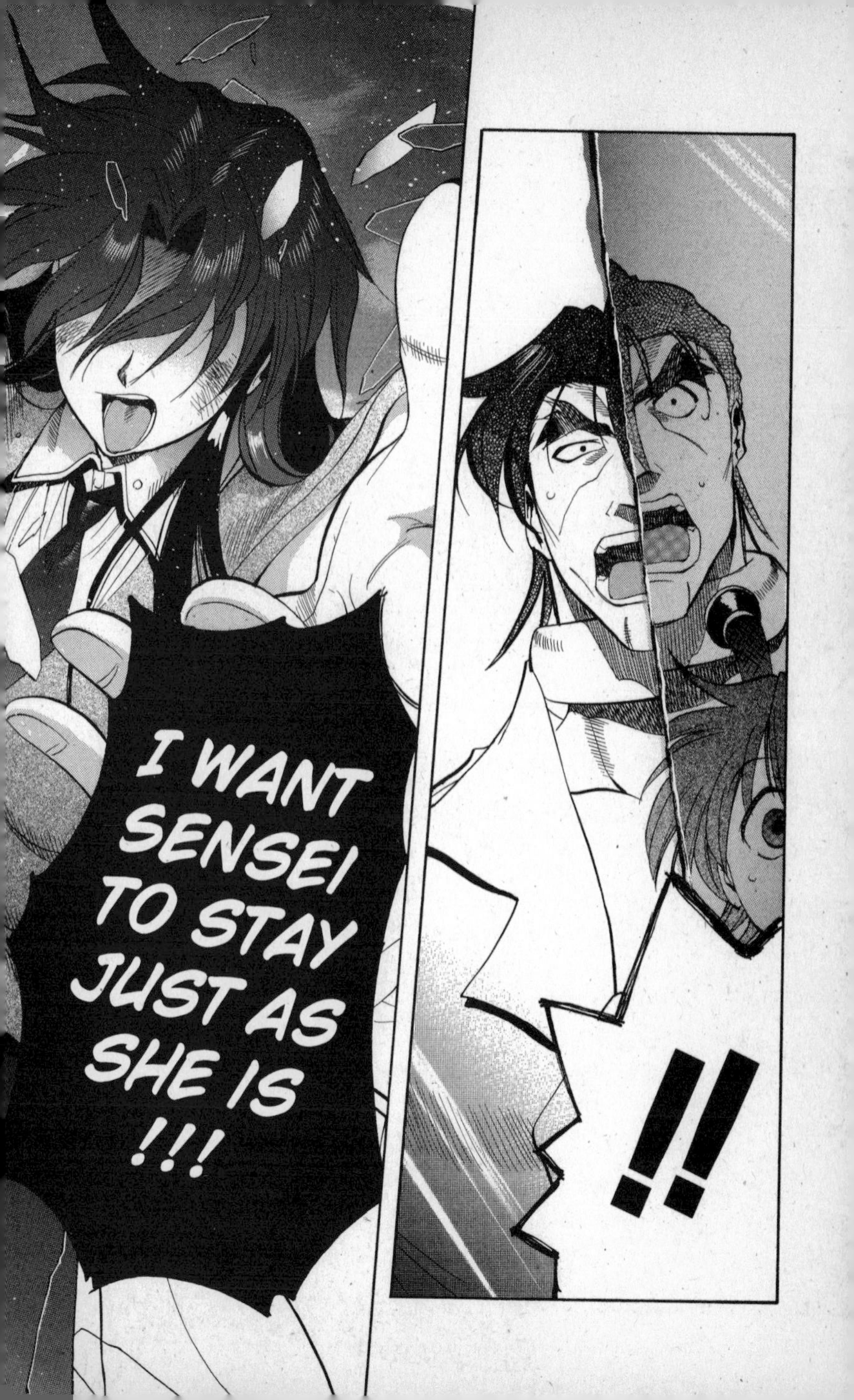
!!
I WANT SENSEI TO STAY JUST AS SHE IS !!!

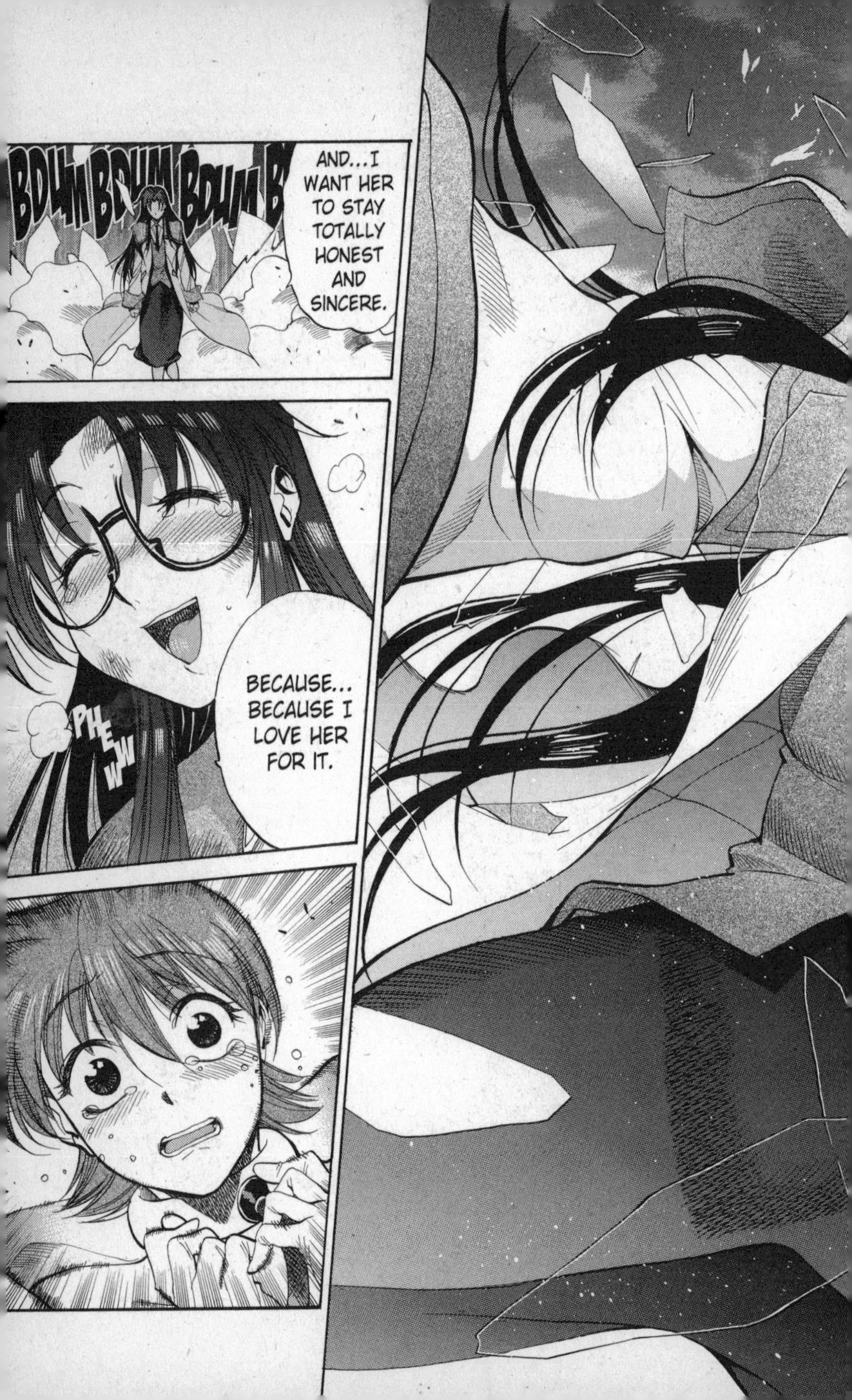
AND...I WANT HER TO STAY TOTALLY HONEST AND SINCERE.
BDUM BDUM BDUM B
BECAUSE... BECAUSE I LOVE HER FOR IT.
PHEWW

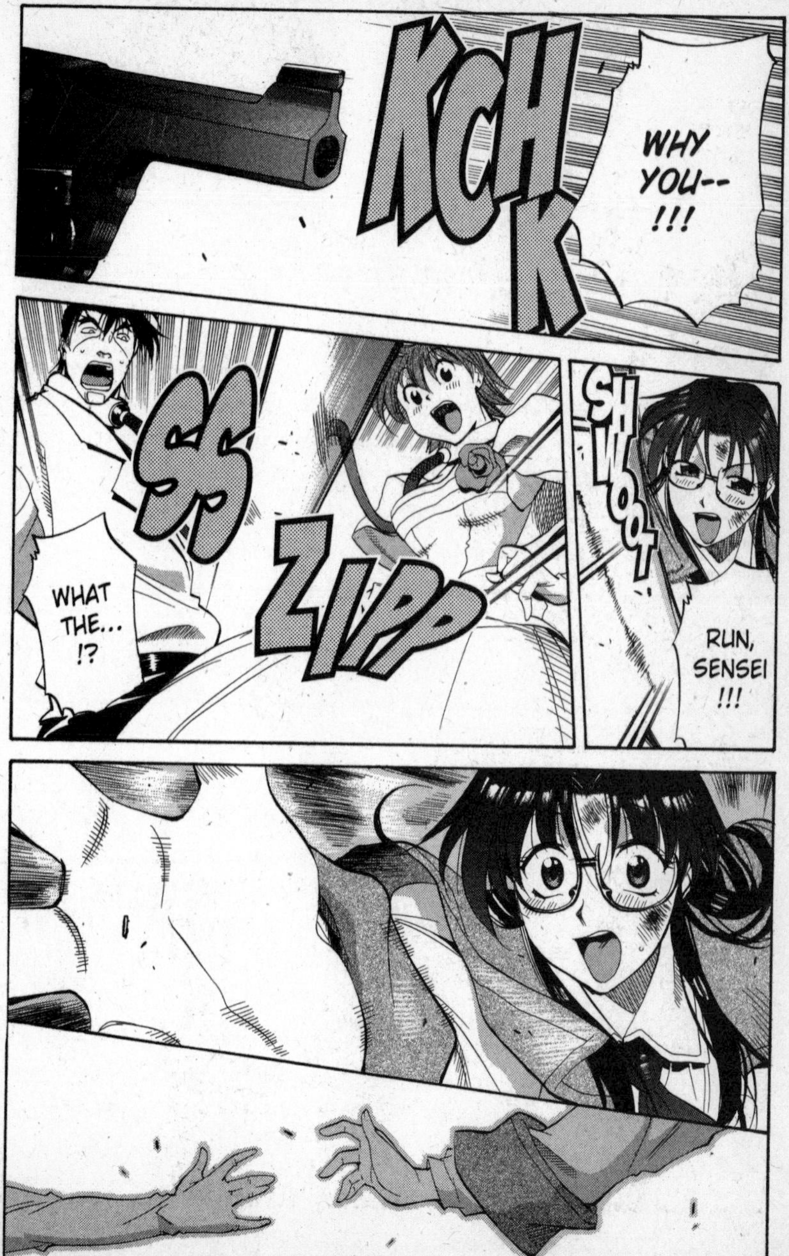
WHY YOU-- !!!
KCHK
RUN, SENSEI !!!
SHWOOT
ZIPP
SS
WHAT THE... !?

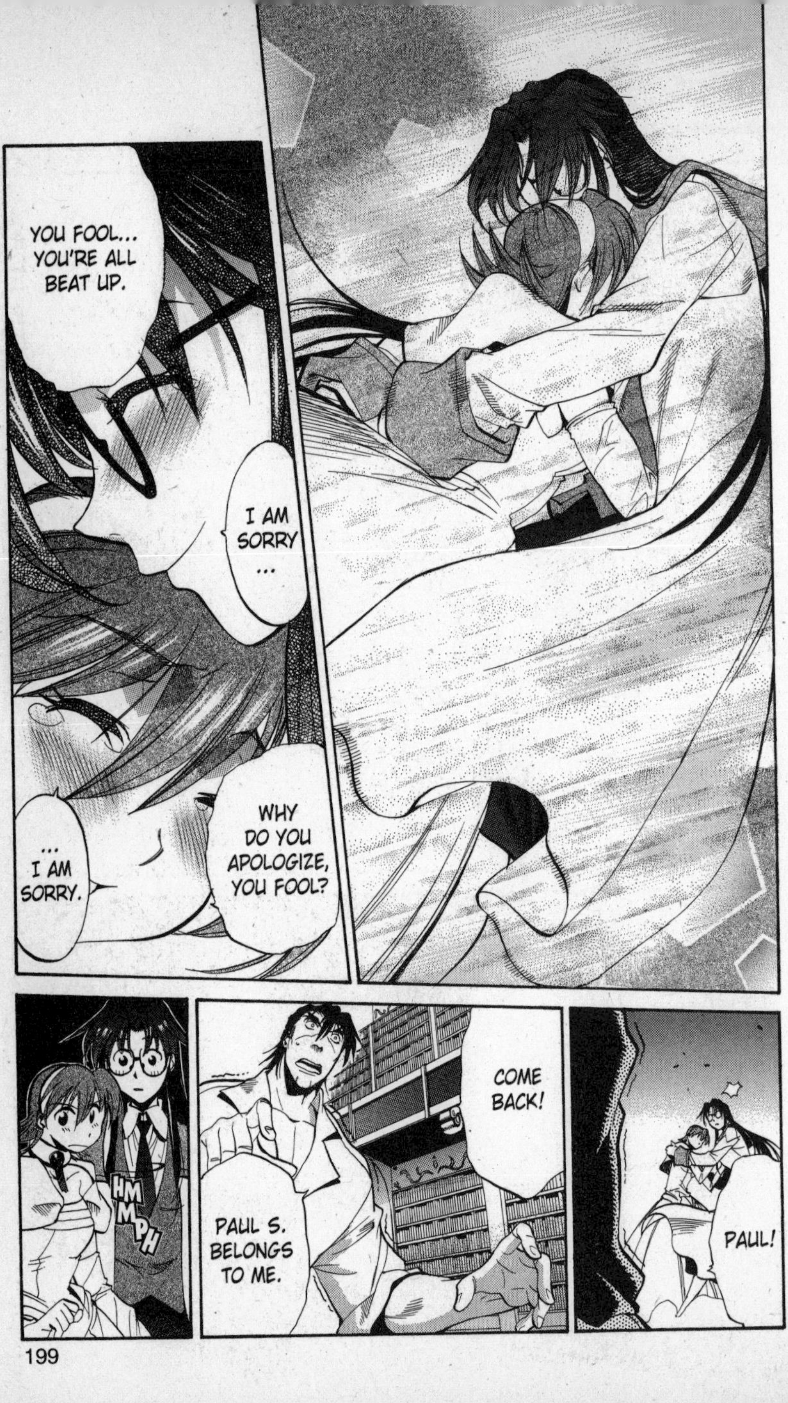
YOU FOOL... YOU'RE ALL BEAT UP.
I AM SORRY ...
WHY DO YOU APOLOGIZE, YOU FOOL?
... I AM SORRY.
PAUL!
COME BACK!
PAUL S. BELONGS TO ME.
HMMPH

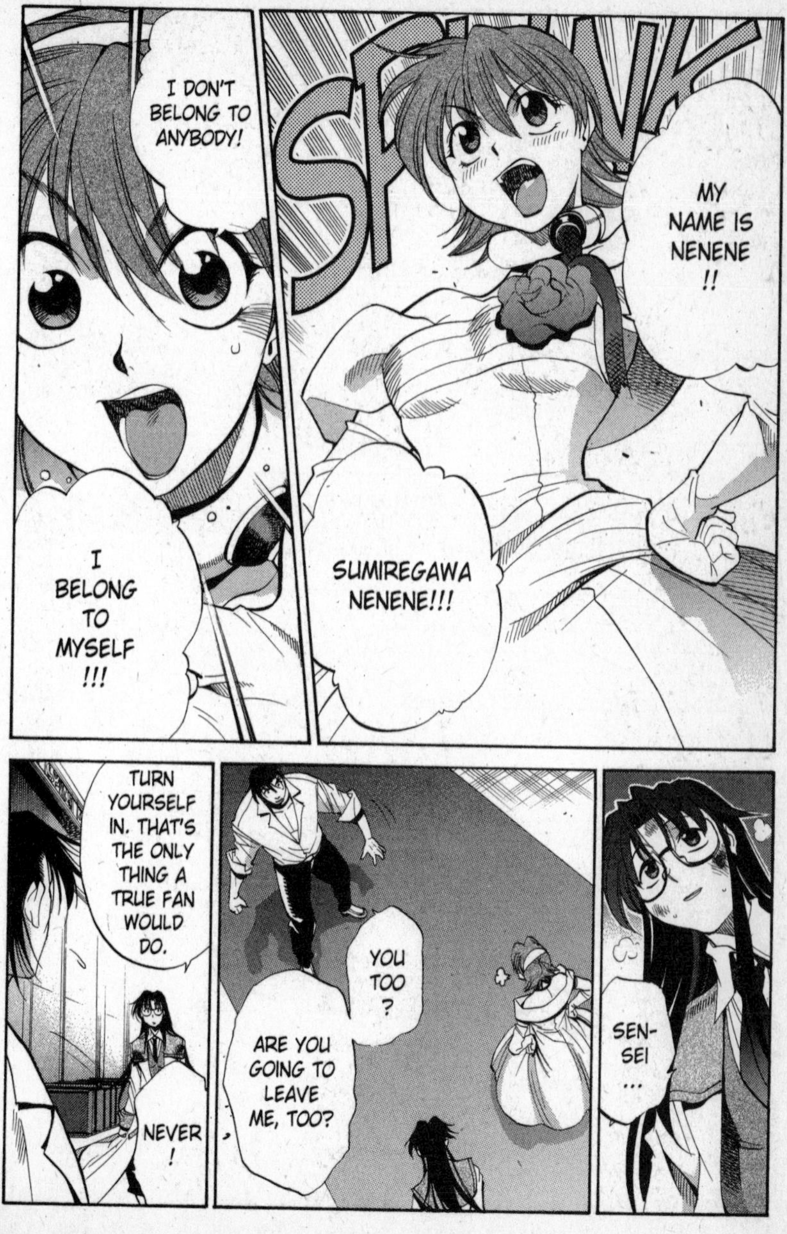
MY NAME IS NENENE !!
SUMIREGAWA NENENE!!!
I DON'T BELONG TO ANYBODY!
I BELONG TO MYSELF !!!
SEN-SEI ...
YOU TOO ?
ARE YOU GOING TO LEAVE ME, TOO?
TURN YOURSELF IN. THAT'S THE ONLY THING A TRUE FAN WOULD DO.
NEVER !

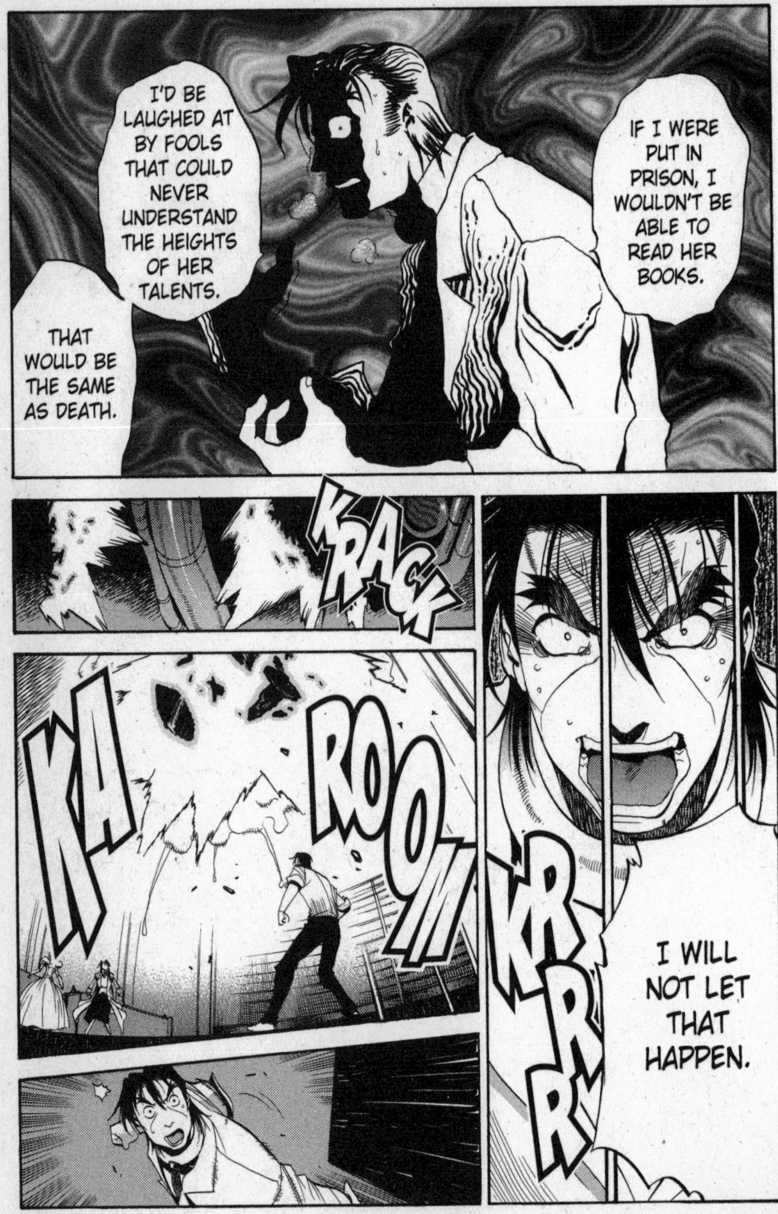
IF I WERE PUT IN PRISON, I WOULDN'T BE ABLE TO READ HER BOOKS.
I'D BE LAUGHED AT BY FOOLS THAT COULD NEVER UNDERSTAND THE HEIGHTS OF HER TALENTS.
THAT WOULD BE THE SAME AS DEATH.
KRRR
I WILL NOT LET THAT HAPPEN.
KRACK
KA
ROOOM

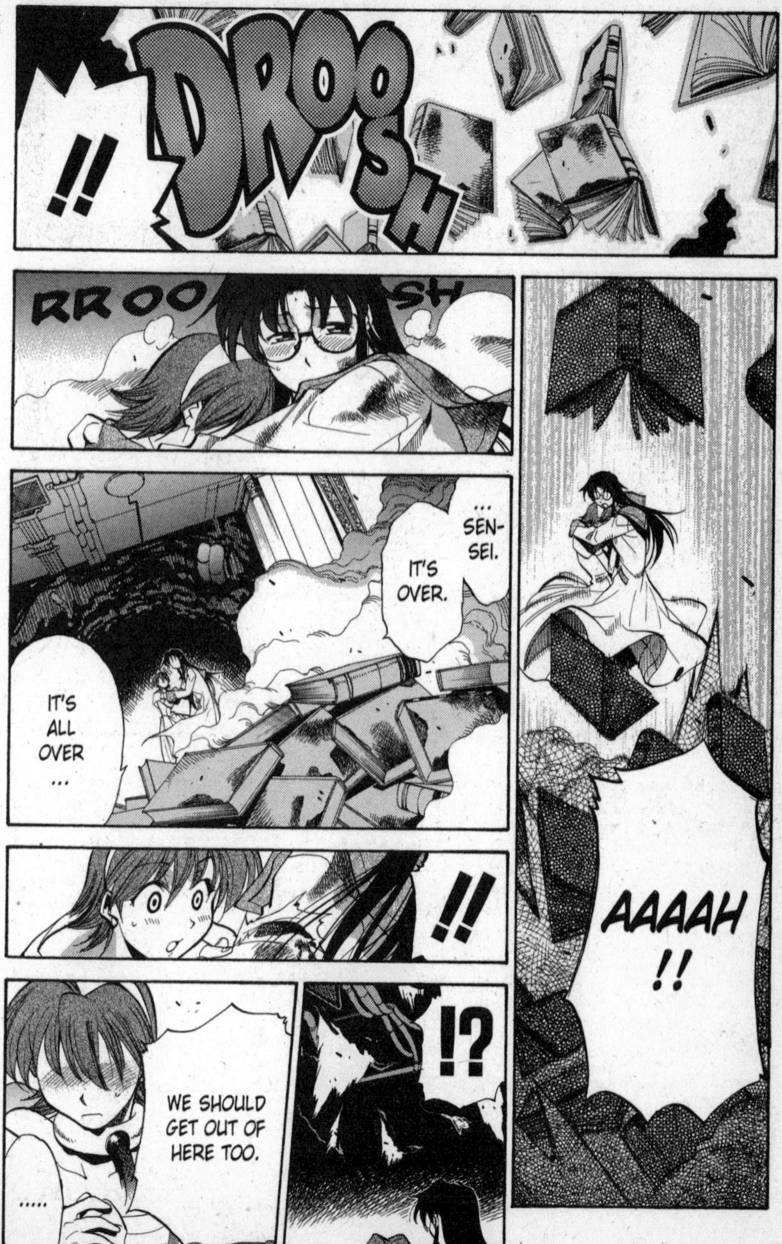
DROOSH !!
AAAAH !!
RROOSH
... SEN-SEI.
IT'S OVER.
IT'S ALL OVER ...
!!
!?
WE SHOULD GET OUT OF HERE TOO.
.....

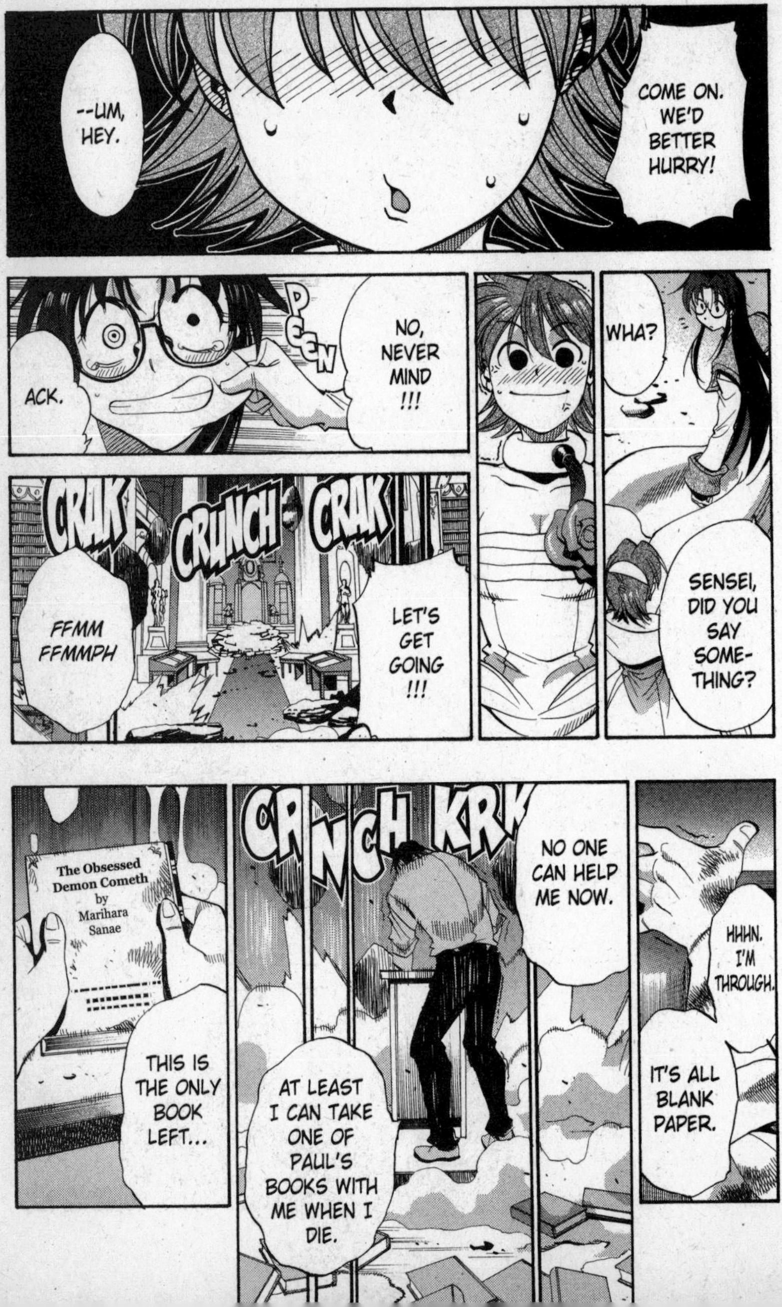
COME ON. WE'D BETTER HURRY!
--UM, HEY.
WHA?
SENSEI, DID YOU SAY SOME-THING?
NO, NEVER MIND !!!
PEEN
ACK.
CRAK
CRUNCH
CRAK
LET'S GET GOING !!!
FFMM FFMMPH
HHHN. I'M THROUGH.
IT'S ALL BLANK PAPER.
CRNCH KRK
NO ONE CAN HELP ME NOW.
AT LEAST I CAN TAKE ONE OF PAUL'S BOOKS WITH ME WHEN I DIE.
The Obsessed Demon Cometh by Marihara Sanae
THIS IS THE ONLY BOOK LEFT...

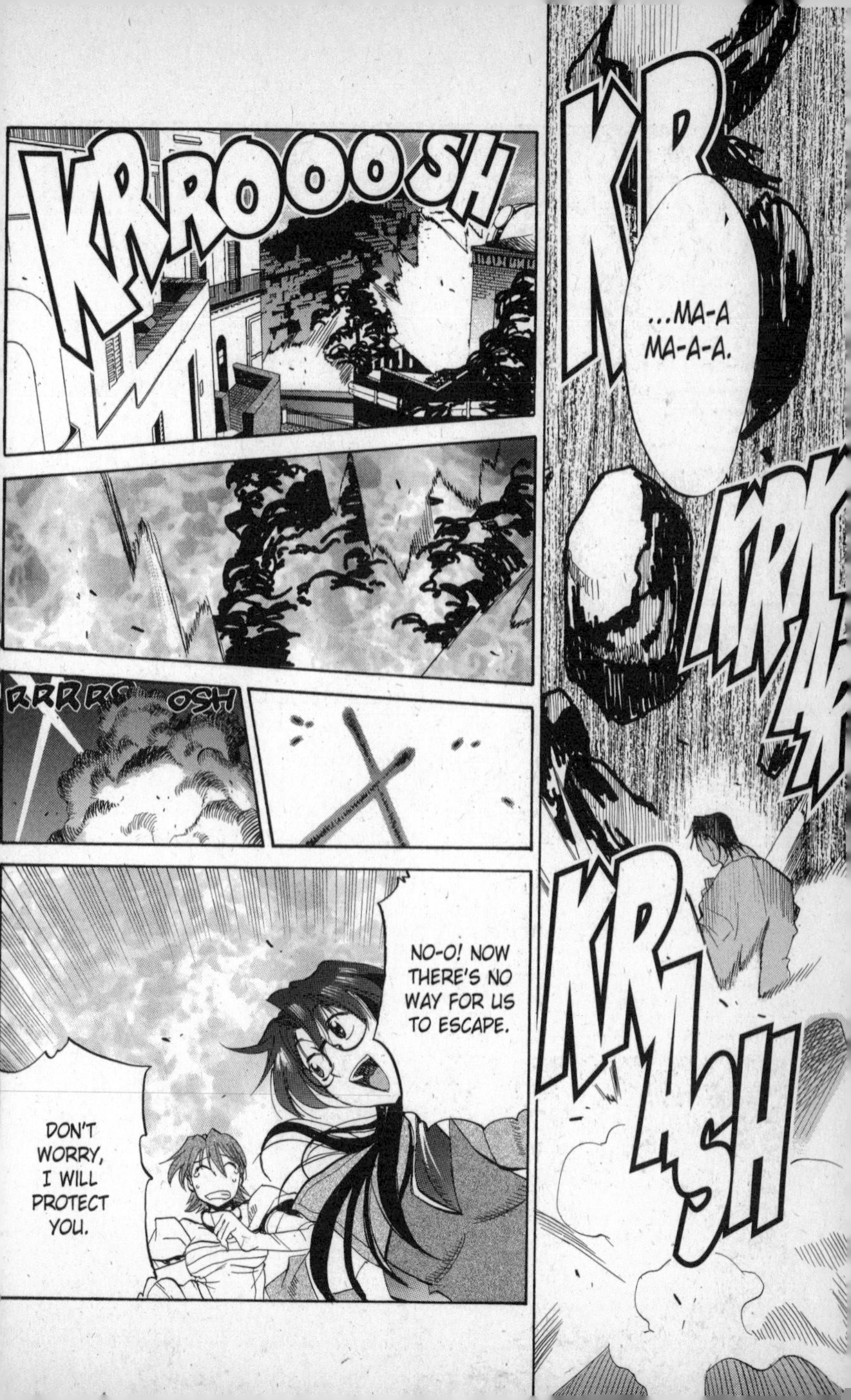
KR
...MA-A
MA-A-A.
KRAK
KRASH
KRROOOSH
RRRRS OSH
NO-O! NOW THERE'S NO WAY FOR US TO ESCAPE.
DON'T WORRY, I WILL PROTECT YOU.

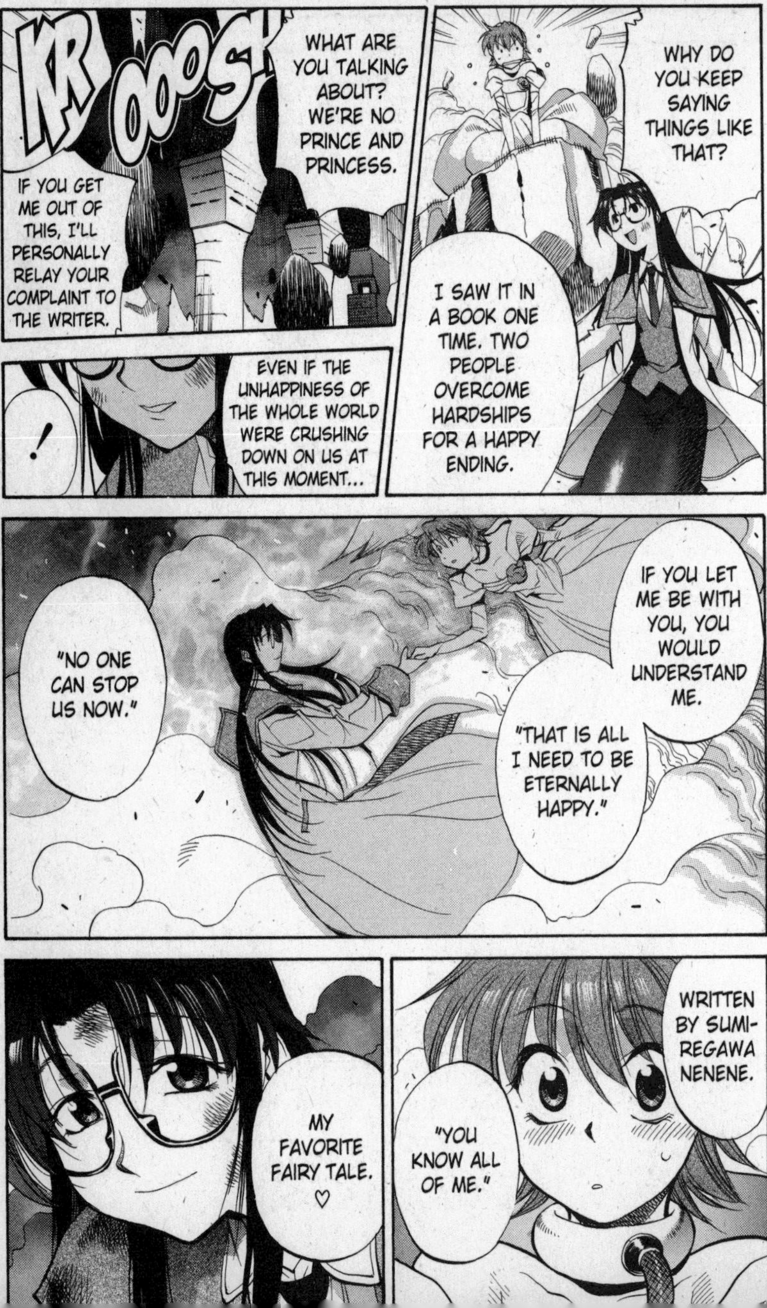
WHY DO YOU KEEP SAYING THINGS LIKE THAT?
I SAW IT IN A BOOK ONE TIME. TWO PEOPLE OVERCOME HARDSHIPS FOR A HAPPY ENDING.
WHAT ARE YOU TALKING ABOUT? WE'RE NO PRINCE AND PRINCESS.
KR OOOSH
IF YOU GET ME OUT OF THIS, I'LL PERSONALLY RELAY YOUR COMPLAINT TO THE WRITER.
EVEN IF THE UNHAPPINESS OF THE WHOLE WORLD WERE CRUSHING DOWN ON US AT THIS MOMENT...
!
IF YOU LET ME BE WITH YOU, YOU WOULD UNDERSTAND ME.
"THAT IS ALL I NEED TO BE ETERNALLY HAPPY."
"NO ONE CAN STOP US NOW."
WRITTEN BY SUMI-REGAWA NENENE.
"YOU KNOW ALL OF ME."
MY FAVORITE FAIRY TALE. ♡

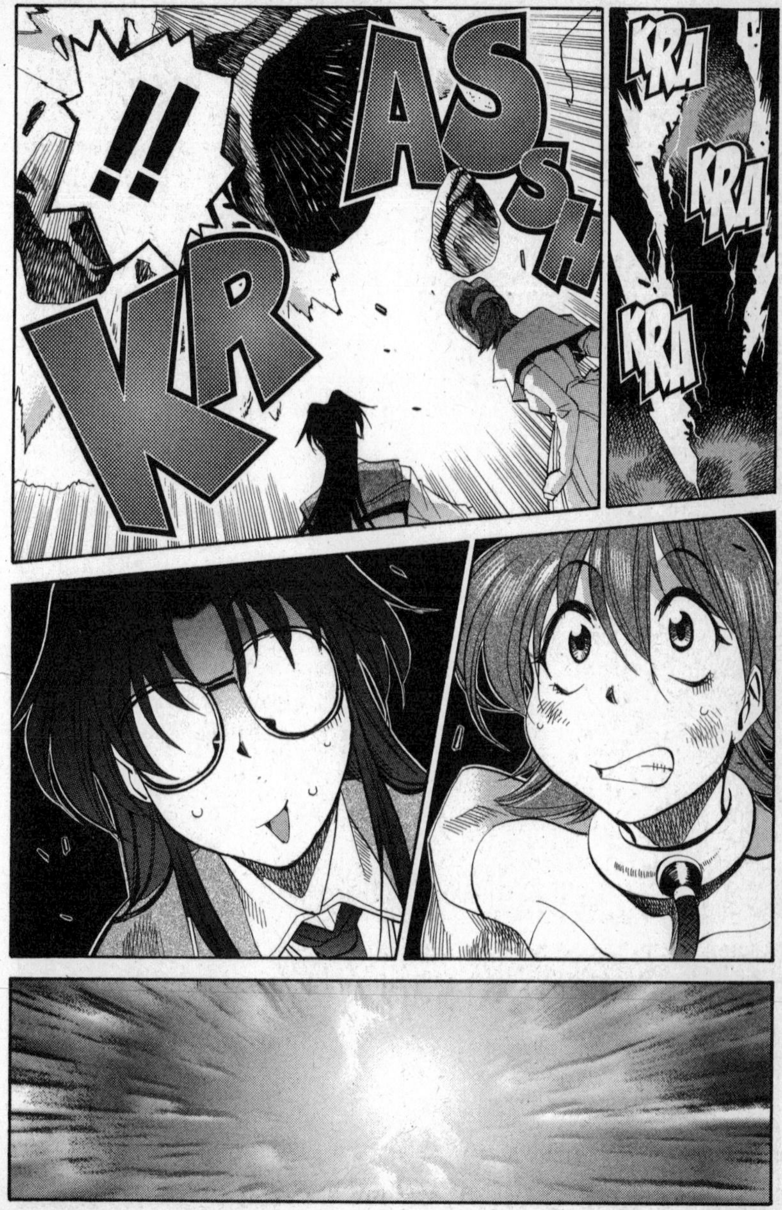
KRA
KRA
KRA
KRASH!!

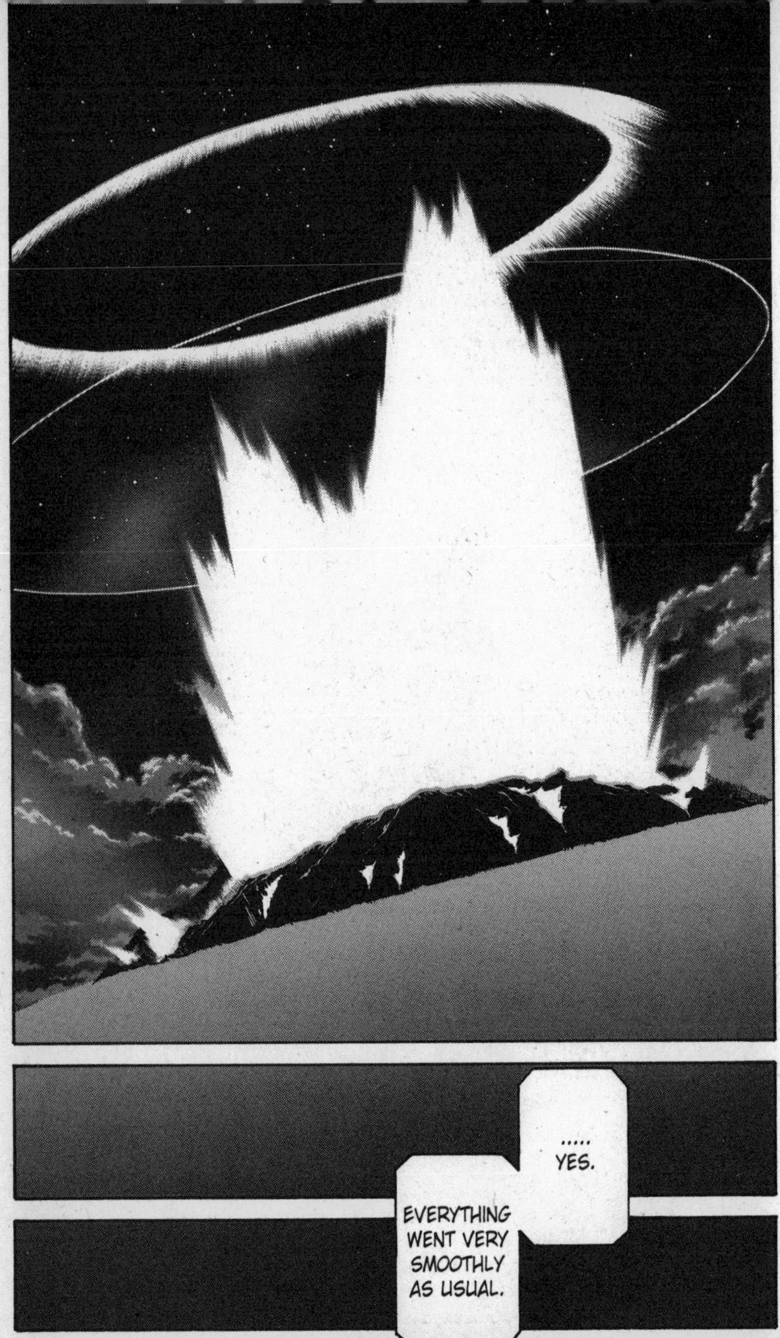

..... YES.
EVERYTHING WENT VERY SMOOTHLY AS USUAL.

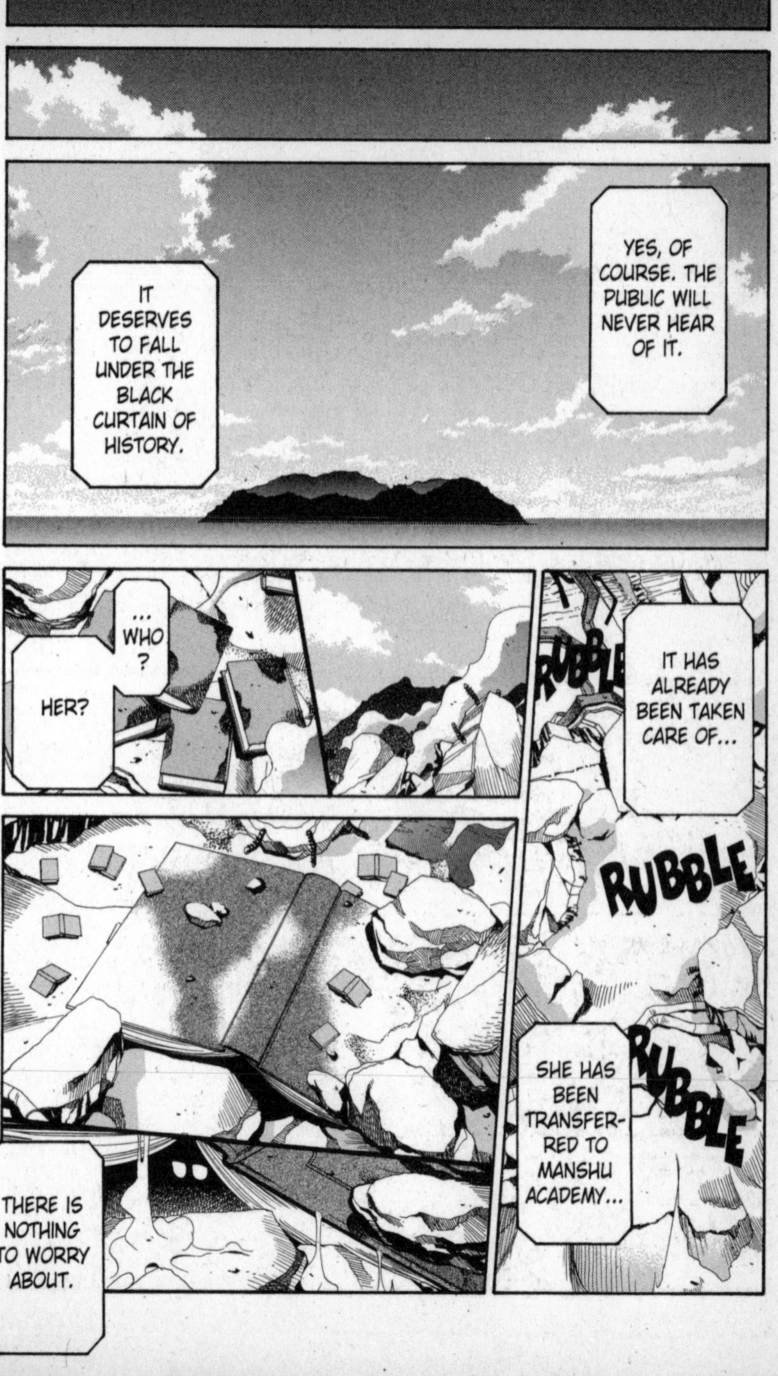
YES, OF COURSE. THE PUBLIC WILL NEVER HEAR OF IT.
IT DESERVES TO FALL UNDER THE BLACK CURTAIN OF HISTORY.
IT HAS ALREADY BEEN TAKEN CARE OF...
RUBBLE
RUBBLE
RUBBLE
SHE HAS BEEN TRANSFER-RED TO MANSHU ACADEMY...
...WHO?
HER?
THERE IS NOTHING TO WORRY ABOUT.

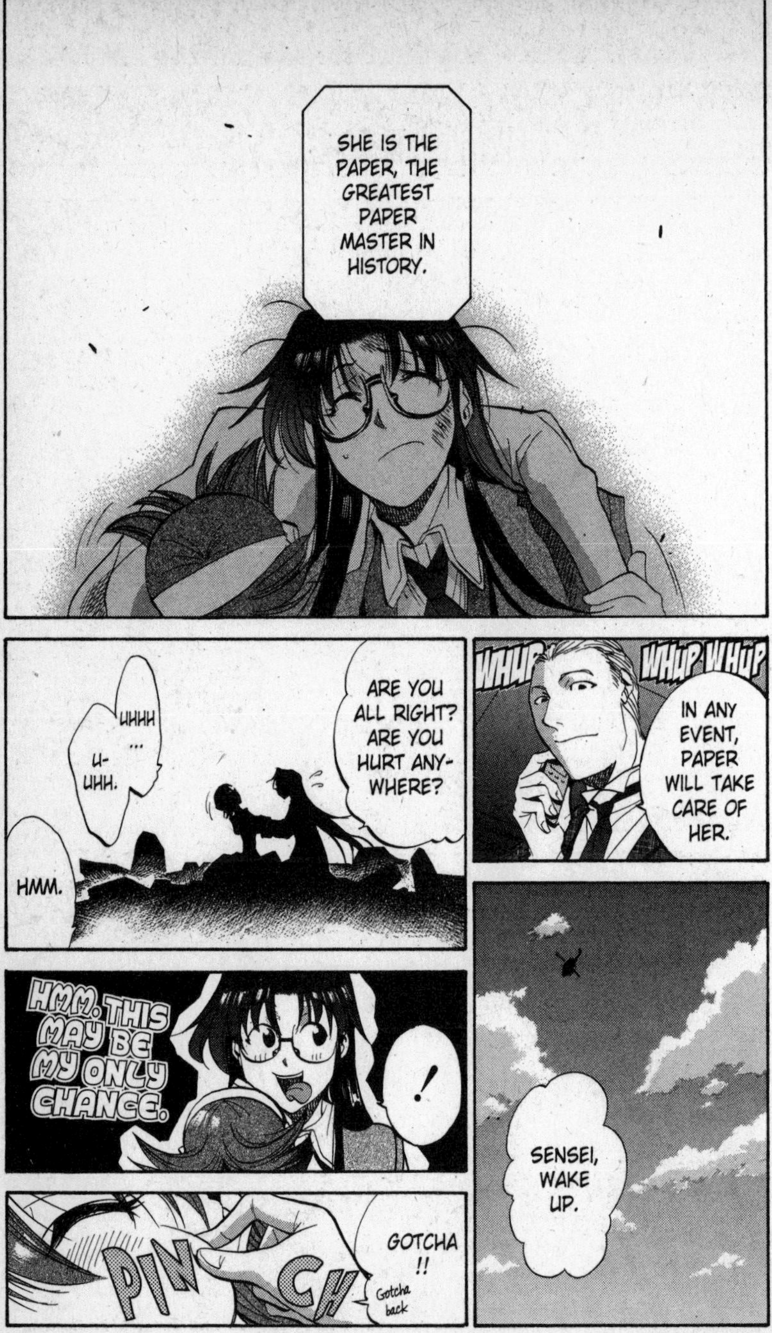
SHE IS THE PAPER, THE GREATEST PAPER MASTER IN HISTORY.
WHUP WHUP WHUP
IN ANY EVENT, PAPER WILL TAKE CARE OF HER.
ARE YOU ALL RIGHT? ARE YOU HURT ANY-WHERE?
UHHH ... U-UHH.
HMM.
SENSEI, WAKE UP.
HMM. THIS MAY BE MY ONLY CHANCE.
!
GOTCHA !!
PINCH
Gotcha back

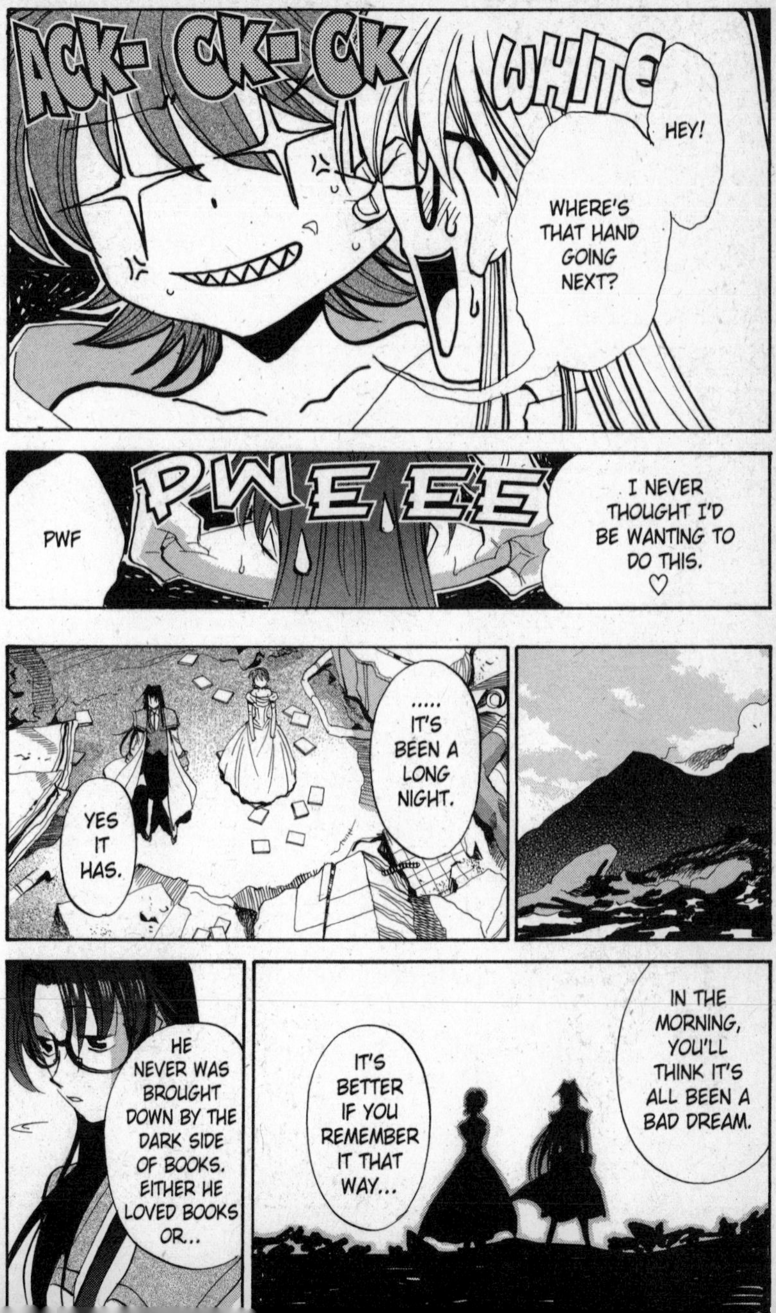
HEY!
WHITE
WHERE'S THAT HAND GOING NEXT?
ACK-CK-CK
I NEVER THOUGHT I'D BE WANTING TO DO THIS. ♡
PWEEE
PWF
..... IT'S BEEN A LONG NIGHT.
YES IT HAS.
IN THE MORNING, YOU'LL THINK IT'S ALL BEEN A BAD DREAM.
IT'S BETTER IF YOU REMEMBER IT THAT WAY...
HE NEVER WAS BROUGHT DOWN BY THE DARK SIDE OF BOOKS. EITHER HE LOVED BOOKS OR...

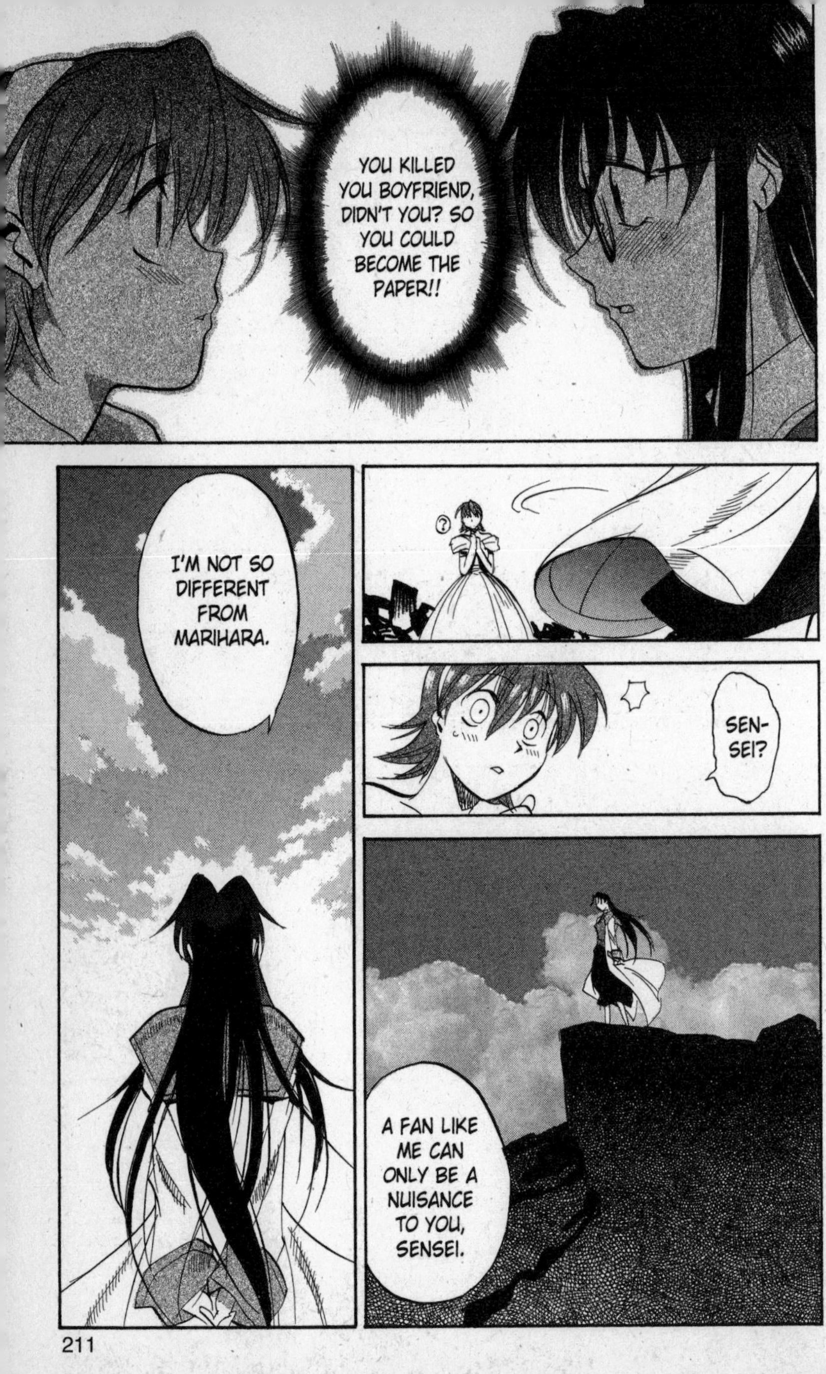
YOU KILLED YOU BOYFRIEND, DIDN'T YOU? SO YOU COULD BECOME THE PAPER!!
?
SEN-SEI?
A FAN LIKE ME CAN ONLY BE A NUISANCE TO YOU, SENSEI.
I'M NOT SO DIFFERENT FROM MARIHARA.

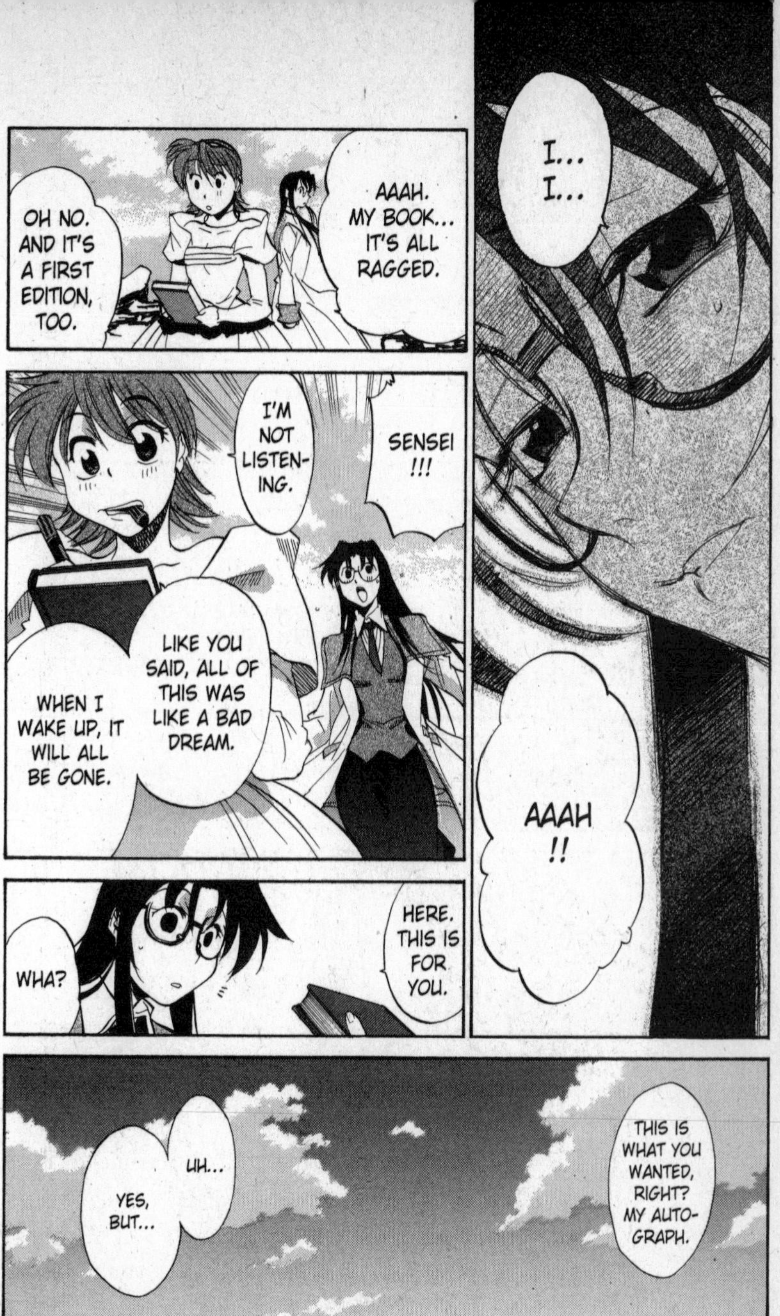
I...
I...
AAAH
!!
AAAH.
MY BOOK...
IT'S ALL
RAGGED.
OH NO.
AND IT'S
A FIRST
EDITION,
TOO.
SENSEI
!!!
I'M
NOT
LISTEN-
ING.
LIKE YOU
SAID, ALL OF
THIS WAS
LIKE A BAD
DREAM.
WHEN I
WAKE UP, IT
WILL ALL
BE GONE.
HERE.
THIS IS
FOR
YOU.
WHA?
THIS IS
WHAT YOU
WANTED,
RIGHT?
MY AUTO-
GRAPH.
UH...
YES,
BUT...

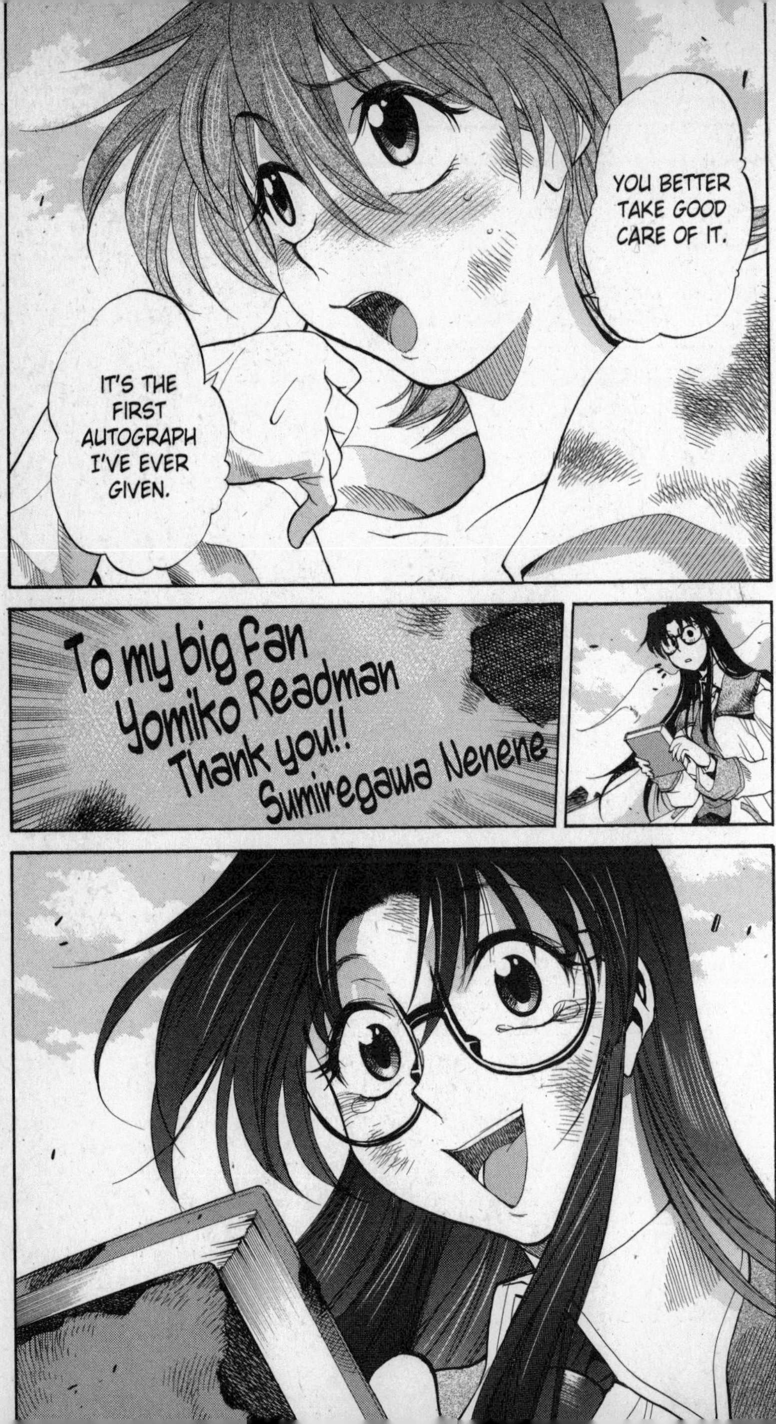
YOU BETTER TAKE GOOD CARE OF IT.
IT'S THE FIRST AUTOGRAPH I'VE EVER GIVEN.
To my big fan
Yomiko Readman
Thank you!!
Sumiregawa Nenene

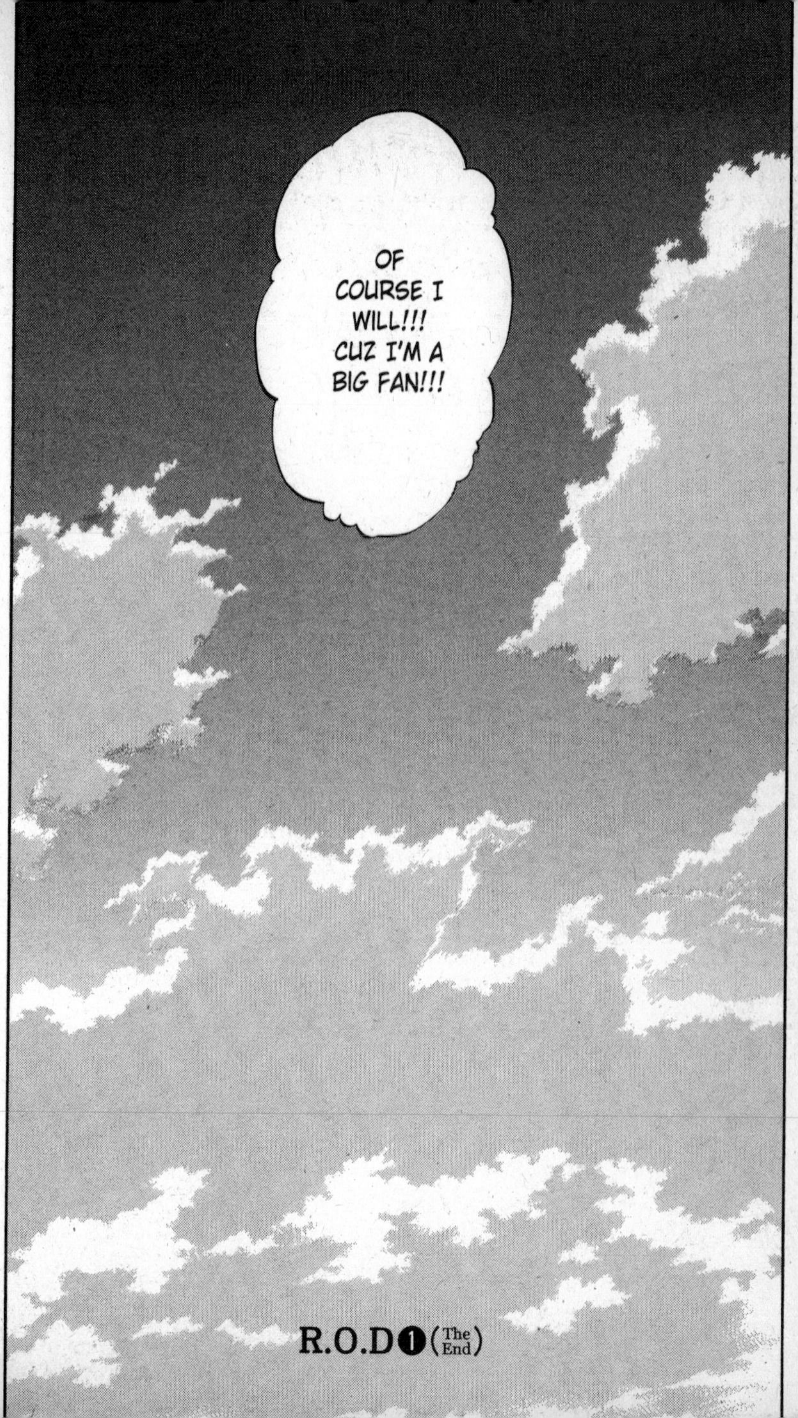
OF COURSE I WILL!!! CUZ I'M A BIG FAN!!!
R.O.D 1 (The End)

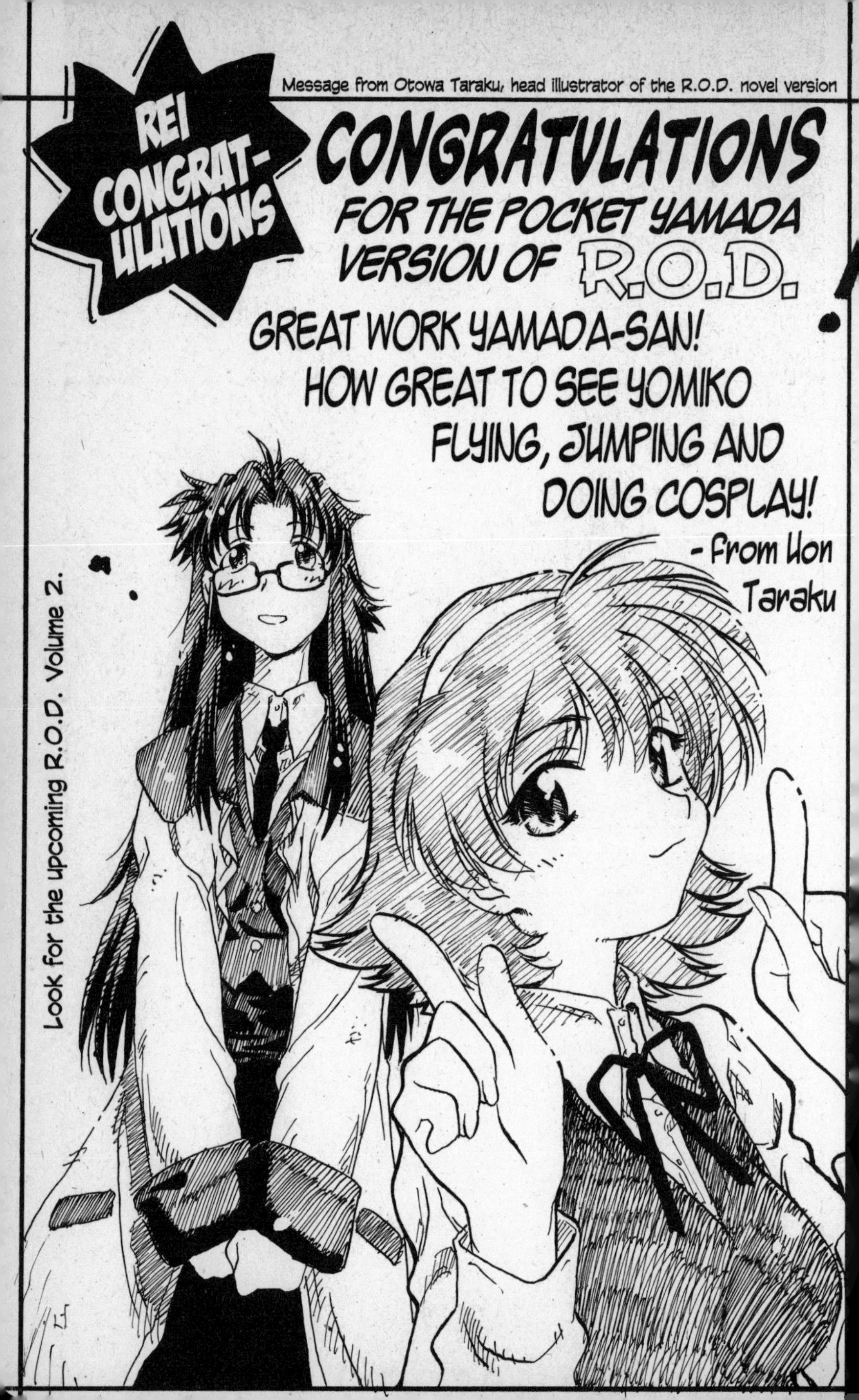
Message from Otowa Taraku, head illustrator of the R.O.D. novel version
REI CONGRAT-ULATIONS
CONGRATULATIONS FOR THE POCKET YAMADA VERSION OF R.O.D.!
GREAT WORK YAMADA-SAN! HOW GREAT TO SEE YOMIKO FLYING, JUMPING AND DOING COSPLAY!
- from Uon Taraku
Look for the upcoming R.O.D. Volume 2.

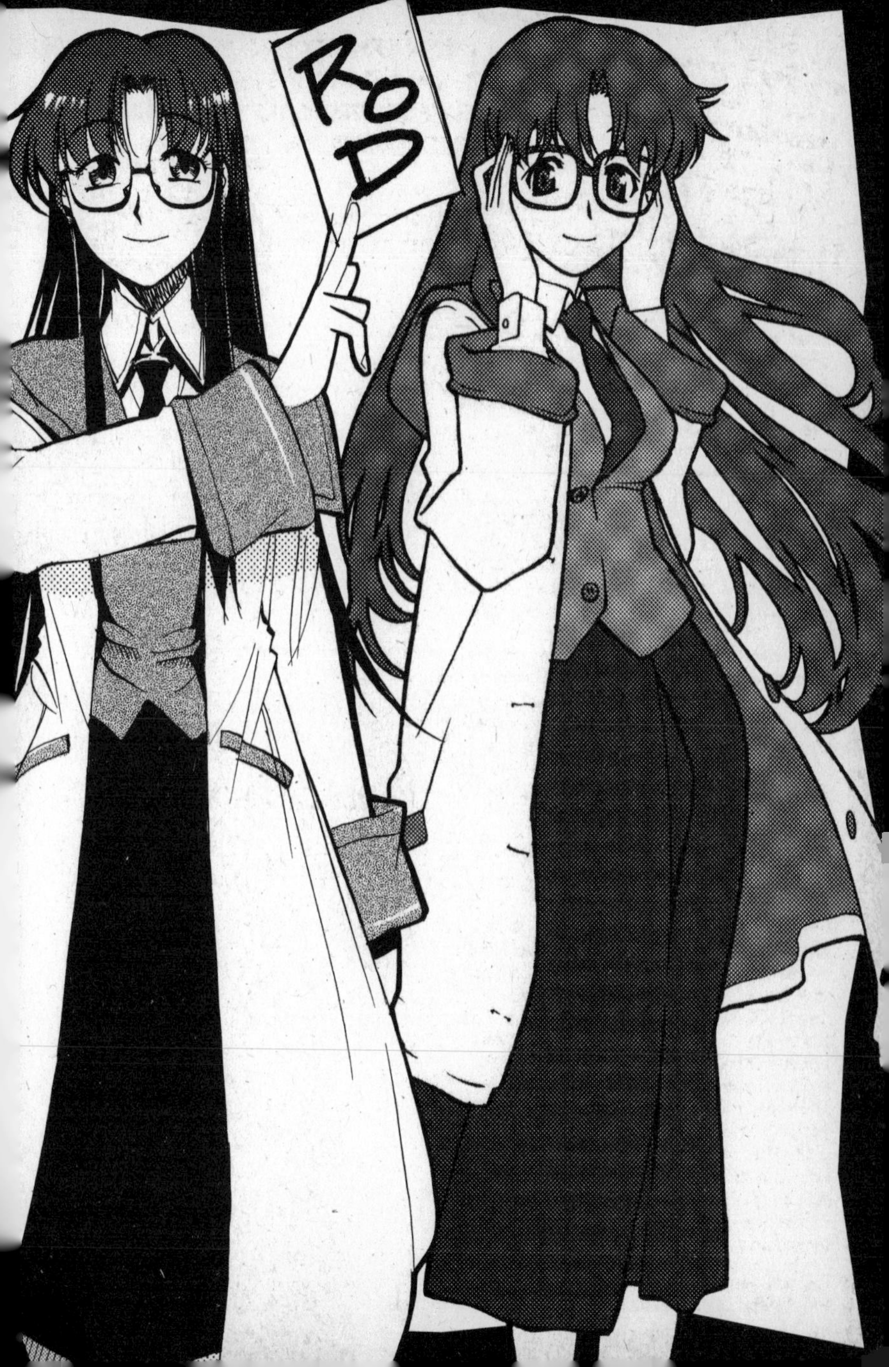
ROD

ULTRA ULTRA READER KING YOMIOH

SPECIAL EXHIBITION TO CELEBRATE PUBLICATION OF VOLUME 1 OF THE NOVELIZED R.O.D. THREE GORGEOUS GUESTS TO TITILLATE HARD-CORE READERS, THE ULTRA YOMIO.

By Kurata Hideyuki

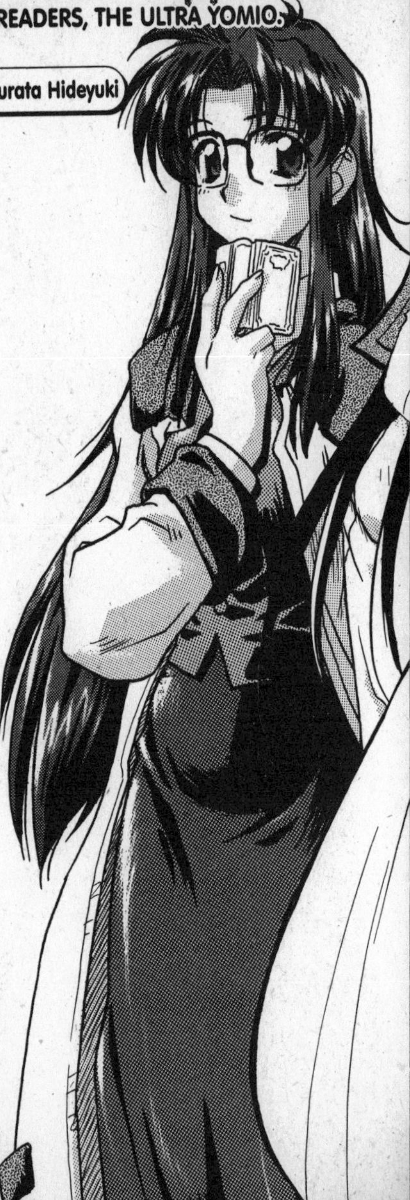

Hey everyone! This Yomio page is a sort of ***dream bridge*** where the writer gets to cross over for direct contact with the readers. The main purpose of this page is to display drawings from the various media where R.O.D. has appeared with the express aim of ***creating desire*** to buy more R.O.D. publications. For what it's worth, I might add that some of my favorites are "Jojo", "North Star" and "Boy's School". Here I present to you a page to exhibit illustrations from the (Ultra Jump) R.O.D. series. I've brought some ***exceptional guests***, who are also friends, to celebrate this initial publication in the novelized series. On the right are three versions of Yomiko from various media that can only be seen together right here. The character on the left is Yomiko drawn by Uon Taraku, the head illustrator of the novelized version. On the far right is the character design by Ishihama Masashi, general production supervisor of the anime version. In the center is the Yamada Shutaro's Yomiko for this novelized version. Publisher Shueisha might call these the ***three sirens*** of the ROD media. Note ***how similar they look*** and how they give full play to Yomiko's key features, her glasses and coat. But I've drifted from the main topic. This is my first publication for Shueisha Comics, and I'm already rambling. It has been 16 years since I saw pages like this for the two volumes of ***Ihara Daisuke's*** Hokuto no Ken (Fist of the North Star). Ihara and I went to the same middle school and were both members of the school ***kendo club***. I've been jealous ever since and now, finally, feel some ***satisfaction***. For you first time readers, don't worry if it looks like I'm almost out of writing space yet still haven't said anything. This is how it always is! Lastly, I want to give a ***huge thanks*** to all of the staff who helped bring this volume to publication.

Illustrations:
Hao Taraku, Yamada Shutaro, Ishihama Masashi

CONGRATULATORY POSTCARDS FROM THE ANIME STAFF

THANKS FOR ALL YOUR WORK! WHEN THE ROYALTIES COME IN, LET'S HAVE A CRAB FEAST!

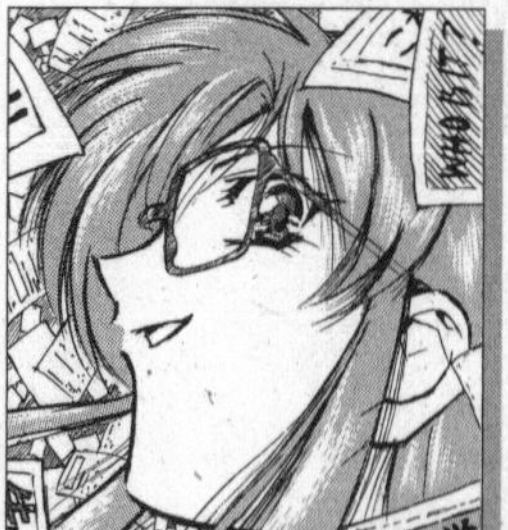
MÔ NANTE
ITTE YOIYARA
GOMENNASAI

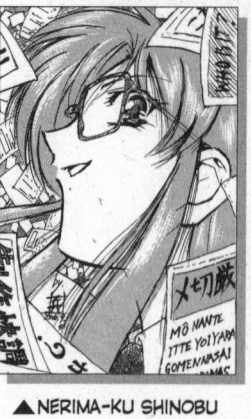

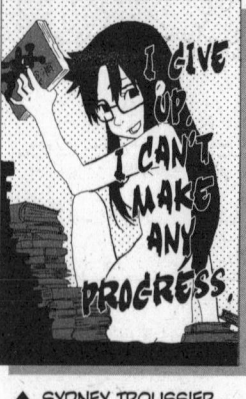

▲NERIMA-KU SHINOBU

Can't really say who it is. The paper flying around contains a cry from the soul. At times like that, just think "*John Woo*"!

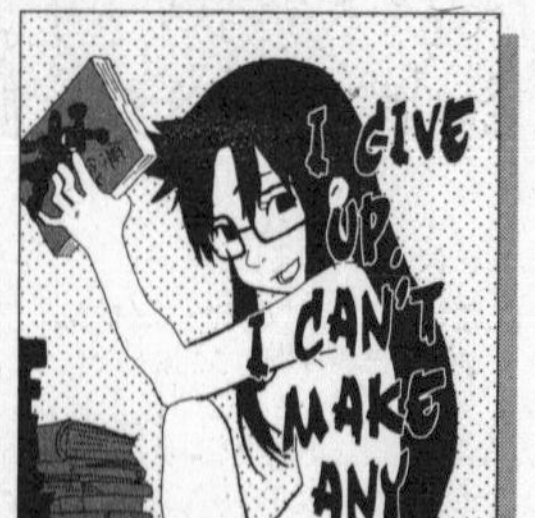
I GIVE UP. I CAN'T MAKE ANY PROGRESS.

▲ SYDNEY TROUSSIER

Ooh, completely naked! Not sure what this means, but what the hey, anyway! The book in her hand is "The Obscene Shadow".

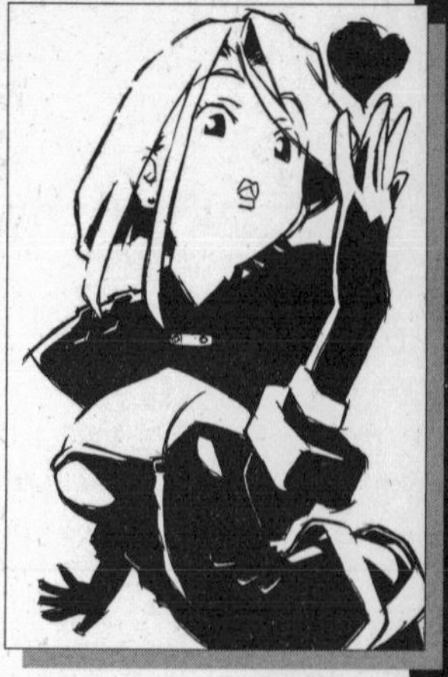

▲ SUGINAMI-KU ISHIHAMA

This is Nancy, pal of the anime Yomiko. Ishihama says, with a big laugh, "It's OK to make her nipples as big as ***CD singles***".

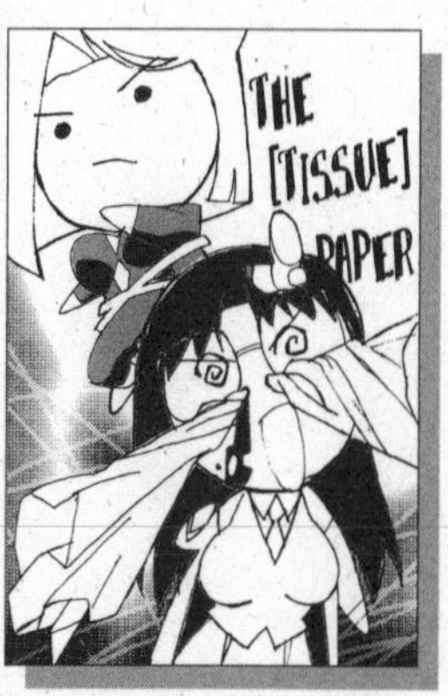
THE [TISSUE] PAPER

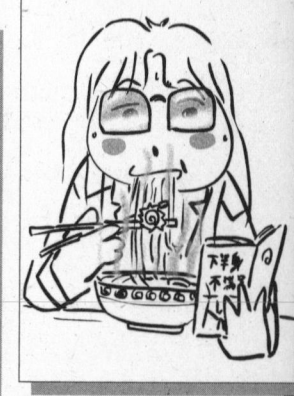

▲ NERIMA-KU TATCHII

This is what the anime version is like. Blood and violence! Hey ***Wachowski***, this is the quintessence of Japanimation!

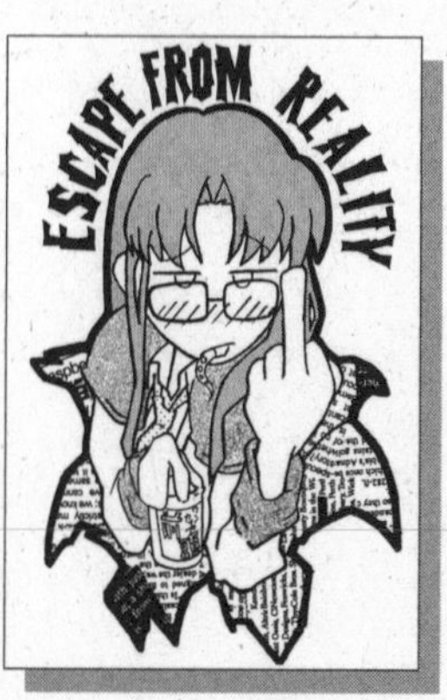
ESCAPE FROM REALITY

▲EDOGAWA-KU CHIKACHAYU

Am I wrong or will most people see this as the cry of the soul? If so, let's go out and drink away the stress!

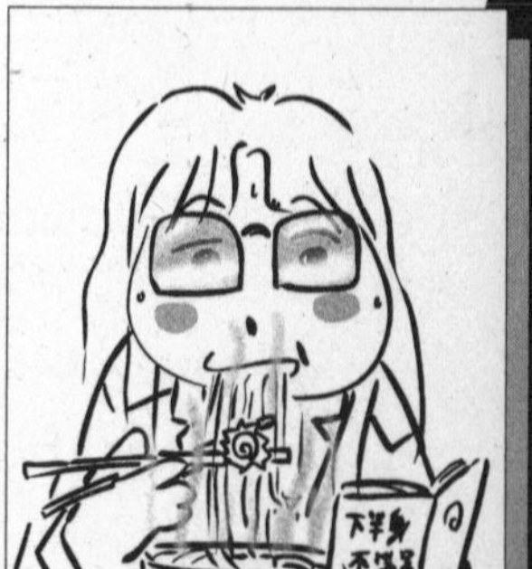

▲DARUMA OSHO OF SHIMANE

When you're finished, come to the faculty room.

Read or Die
Vol. 1

STORY BY **HIDEYUKI KURATA**
ART BY **SHUTARO YAMADA**

English Translation and Adaptation/Steve Ballati
Touch-up Art & Lettering/Mark McMurray
Cover & Graphic Design/Janet Piercy
Editor/Urian Brown

Managing Editor/Annette Roman
Director of Production/Noboru Watanabe
VP of Publishing/Alvin Lu
Sr. Director of Acquisitions/Rika Inouye
VP of Sales & Marketing/Liza Coppola
Publisher/Hyoe Narita

R.O.D -READ OR DIE- © 2000 by Hideyuki Kurata, Shutaro Yamada
All rights reserved. First published in Japan in 2000 by SHUEISHA Inc., Tokyo.
English translation rights in the United States of America
and Canada arranged by SHUEISHA Inc.
The stories, characters and incidents mentioned in
this publication are entirely fictional.

Printed in the U.S.A.

Published by VIZ Media, LLC
P.O. Box 77010
San Francisco, CA 94107

10 9 8 7 6 5 4 3 2 1
First printing, March 2006

www.viz.com

PARENTAL ADVISORY
READ OR DIE is rated T+ for Older Teen
and is recommended for ages16 and up.
This book contains violence.

store.viz.com

The Evolution of Science... The Downfall of Man?

Based on the hit movie from Katsuhiro Otomo

STEAMBOY

Meet Ray Steam, a resourceful young inventor whose father and grandfather have harnessed the ultimate energy source that will transform the world for better or worse!

Their *Journey.*
Your **Adventure.**

Join Edward and Alphonse as they continue their quest for the Philosopher's Stone and a return to normalcy.

Fullmetal Alchemist: The Land of Sand

The Elric brothers get their identity stolen. Now it's Alphonse and Edward vs. Alphonse and Edward: the ultimate alchemist smackdown!

$9.99
paperback

Fullmetal Alchemist: The Abducted Alchemist

Alphonse and Edward get caught up in a string of terrorist bombings. Can they stop the reign of terror before they become suspects?

Full-length FULLMETAL ALCHEMIST novels now available.

Buy yours today at store.viz.com!

FULLMETAL ALCHEMIST

VIZ media
www.viz.com
store.viz.com

© Hiromu Arakawa, Makoto Inoue/SQUARE ENIX
Cover art subject to change.

LOVE MANGA?   LET US KNOW!

☐ Please do NOT send me information about VIZ Media products, news and events, special offers, or other information.

☐ Please do NOT send me information from VIZ Media's trusted business partners.

Name: _____

Address: _____

City:_____ State:_____ Zip:_____

E-mail: _____

☐ Male ☐ Female   Date of Birth (mm/dd/yyyy): __/__/____ (Under 13? Parental consent required)

What race/ethnicity do you consider yourself? (check all that apply)

☐ White/Caucasian   ☐ Black/African American   ☐ Hispanic/Latino

☐ Asian/Pacific Islander   ☐ Native American/Alaskan Native ☐ Other: _____

What VIZ Media title(s) did you purchase? (indicate title(s) purchased) _____

_____

What other VIZ Media titles do you own? _____

_____

Reason for purchase: (check all that apply)

☐ Special offer   ☐ Favorite title / author / artist / genre

☐ Gift   ☐ Recommendation   ☐ Collection

☐ Read excerpt in VIZ Media manga sampler   ☐ Other _____

Where did you make your purchase? (please check one)

☐ Comic store   ☐ Bookstore   ☐ Grocery Store

☐ Convention   ☐ Newsstand   ☐ Video Game Store

☐ Online (site:_____)   ☐ Other _____

How many manga titles have you purchased in the last year? How many were VIZ Media titles? (please check one from each column)

MANGA	VIZ Media
☐ None	☐ None
☐ 1 – 4	☐ 1 – 4
☐ 5 – 10	☐ 5 – 10
☐ 11+	☐ 11+

How much influence do special promotions and gifts-with-purchase have on the titles you buy? (please circle, with 5 being great influence and 1 being none)

1 2 3 4 5

Do you purchase every volume of your favorite series?

☐ Yes! Gotta have 'em as my own ☐ No. Please explain: ____________________

What kind of manga storylines do you most enjoy? (check all that apply)

☐ Action / Adventure ☐ Science Fiction ☐ Horror
☐ Comedy ☐ Romance (shojo) ☐ Fantasy (shojo)
☐ Fighting ☐ Sports ☐ Historical
☐ Artistic / Alternative ☐ Other ____________________

If you watch the anime or play a video or TCG game from a series, how likely are you to buy the manga? (please circle, with 5 being very likely and 1 being unlikely)

1 2 3 4 5

If unlikely, please explain: ____________________

Who are your favorite authors / artists? ____________________

____

What titles would like you translated and sold in English? ____________________

____

THANK YOU! Please send the completed form to:

NJW Research
42 Catharine Street
Poughkeepsie, NY 12601

Your privacy is very important to us. All information provided will be used for internal purposes only and will not be sold or otherwise divulged.